Writing in the Feminine

Ad Feminam: Women and Literature
Edited by Sandra M. Gilbert

Christina Rosetti
The Poetry of Endurance
By Dolores Rosenblum

Lunacy of Light
Emily Dickinson and the Experience of Metaphor
By Wendy Barker

The Literary Existence of Germaine de Staël
By Charlotte Hogsett

Margaret Atwood
Vision and Forms
Edited by Kathryn VanSpanckeren and Jan Garden Castro

He Knew She Was Right
The Independent Woman in the Novels of Anthony Trollope
By Jane Nardin

The Woman and the Lyre
Women Writers in Classical Greece and Rome
By Jane McIntosh Snyder

Refiguring the Father
New Feminist Readings of Patriarchy
Edited by Patricia Yaeger and Beth Kowaleski-Wallace

Writing in the Feminine

Feminism and Experimental Writing in Quebec

Karen Gould

Southern Illinois University Press
Carbondale and Edwardsville

93 92 91 90   4 3 2 1

Credits for photographs on title page: *Above left,* Nicole Brossard by Denyse Coutu; *right,* Madeleine Gagnon by Kéro; *below left,* Louky Bersianik by Jean Letarte; *right,* France Théoret by Micheline de Jordy

Library of Congress Cataloging-in-Publication Data

Gould, Karen, 1948–
  Writing in the feminine : feminism and experimental writing in
Quebec / Karen Gould.
      p.   cm. — (Ad feminam)
    Bibliography: p.
    Includes index.
    1. French-Canadian literature—20th century—History and
criticism.   2. French-Canadian literature—Women authors—History
and criticism.   3. Literature, Experimental—Québec (Province)—
History and criticism.   4. Feminism and literature—Québec
(Province)   5. Women and literature—Québec (Province)   6. Québec
(Province)—Intellectual life—20th century.   I. Title.
II. Series
PQ3908.G67   1990
840.9'9287—dc20   89-31608
ISBN 0-8093-1582-3   CIP

The paper used in this publication meets the minimum requirements of
American National Standard for Information Sciences—Permanence of Paper for
Printed Library Materials, ANSI z39.48-1984. ∞

For Suzanne, who is deeply missed
And for Rick, "le mâle de mon espèce"

Contents

Ad Feminam: Women and Literature

> Ad Hominem: to the man; appealing to personal interests, prejudices, or emotions rather than to reason; *an argument ad hominem.*
> —*American Heritage Dictionary*

Until quite recently, much literary criticism, like most humanistic studies, has been in some sense constituted out of arguments *ad hominem.* Not only have examinations of literary history tended to address themselves "to the man"—that is, to the identity of what was presumed to be the *man* of letters who created our culture's monuments of unaging intellect—but many aesthetic analyses and evaluations have consciously or unconsciously appealed to the "personal interests, prejudices, or emotions" of male critics and readers. As the title of this series is meant to indicate, the intellectual project called "feminist criticism" has sought to counter the limitations of *ad hominem* thinking about literature by asking a series of questions addressed *ad feminam:* to the woman as both writer and reader of texts.

First, and most crucially, feminist critics ask, what is the relationship between gender and genre, between sexuality and textuality? But in mediating on these issues they raise a number of more specific questions. Does a woman of letters have a literature—a language, a history, a tradition—of her own? Have conventional methods of canon-formation tended to exclude or marginalize female achievements? More generally, do men and women have different modes of literary representation, different definitions of literary production? Do such differences mean that distinctive male- (or female-)

authored images of women (or men), as well as distinctly male and female genres, are part of our intellectual heritage? Perhaps most important, are literary differences between men and women essential or accidental, biologically determined or culturally constructed?

Feminist critics have addressed themselves to these problems with increasing sophistication during the last two decades, as they sought to revise, or at times replace, *ad hominem* arguments with *ad feminam* speculations. Whether explicating individual texts, studying the oeuvre of a single author, examining the permutations of a major theme, or charting the contours of a tradition, these theorists and scholars have consistently sought to define literary manifestations of difference and to understand the dynamics that have shaped the accomplishments of literary women.

As a consequence of such work, feminist critics, often employing new modes of analysis, have begun to uncover a neglected female tradition along with a heretofore hidden history of the literary dialogue between men and women. This series is dedicated to publishing books that will use innovative as well as traditional interpretive methods in order to help readers of both sexes achieve a clearer consciousness of that neglected but powerful tradition and a better understanding of that hidden history. Reason tells us, after all, that if, transcending prejudice and special pleading, we speak to, and focus on, the woman as well as the man—if we think *ad feminam* as well as *ad hominem*—we will have a better chance of understanding what constitutes the human.

Sandra M. Gilbert

Acknowledgments

Since I have been at work on this book in one way or another for over five years, there are many who deserve thanks. I would like to extend an initial thank-you to Paula Gilbert Lewis and to Jonathan Weiss whose encouragement during the early years of my research on Quebec literature was so crucial. I would also like to thank Maïr Verthuy of the Simone de Beauvoir Institute at Concordia University in Montreal, who allowed me to audit her course on Quebec women writers in the fall of 1979 and who introduced me to several of the texts discussed in this study. Since that time, conversations with Mary Jean Green, Jane Moss, Lorna Irvine, Pat Smart, Suzanne Lamy, and a number of other Canadian and American colleagues associated with the activities of the American Council for Québec Studies and the Association for Canadian Studies in the United States have helped make the study of Quebec women writers a rewarding collective effort.

In terms of the book itself, I would especially like to thank my colleagues at Bowling Green State University, Ellen Berry, Vicki Patraka, and Alice Heim, for their willingness to read selected chapters, for their intelligent and useful comments, and for their personal support. Suggestions from Virginia Smith and Mary Jean Green about the introductory chapters have also been most helpful. And throughout the various stages of this study, Nicole Brossard, Madeleine Gagnon, Louky Bersianik, and France Théoret have been kind enough to discuss aspects of their work with me. For their time and interest, I am sincerely grateful.

At a time when increasing teaching, committee, and administrative demands make it difficult for many academics to undertake a

xii   *Acknowledgments*

book-length project, and when the number of grants available in the humanities appear to be diminishing at an alarming rate, funds to support research leaves and travel grants can, as many of us know, make all the difference. I am, therefore, deeply indebted to the Academic Relations Office of the Canadian Embassy for their repeated help in the form of travel and research grants over the years and for the generous financial assistance that the Canadian Studies Senior Fellowship provided me during a critical six-month period. Their active support of scholars like myself, many of whom were not initially trained in Canadian studies, continues to be very important. Both Bowling Green State University and Virginia Polytechnic Institute and State University have also granted me summer stipends to carry out this project.

Finally, I would like to thank my partner, Rick, who, in addition to providing helpful technical assistance all along the way, has given me the emotional support and the mental space needed to explore and to complete this study.

Portions of chapter 3 have appeared in abbreviated form in the following essays: "Madeleine Gagnon's Po(e)litical Vision: Portrait of an Artist and An Era," in *Traditionalism, Feminism, and Nationalism,* edited by Paula Gilbert Lewis, 185–204, and "Unearthing the Female Text: Madeleine Gagnon's *Lueur,*" *L'Esprit Créateur* 23.3 (1983): 86–94. Two sections from chapter 5 have also appeared in "Reclaiming Electra: Disruption and Desire in the Writing of France Théoret," *Modern Language Studies* 7.1 (1987): 17–27 and in "L'Ecrivaine/La putain ou le territoire de l'inscription feminine chez France Théoret," *Voix et images* 14.1 (1988): 31–40.

Introduction

—There has to be somewhere else, I tell myself. And everyone knows that to go somewhere else there are routes, signs, "maps"—for an exploration, a trip.

—That's what books are. Everyone knows that a place exists which is not economically or politically indebted to all the vileness and compromise. That is not obliged to reproduce the system. That is writing. If there is a somewhere else that can escape the infernal repetition, it lies in that direction, where *it* writes itself, where *it* dreams, where *it* invents new worlds.

Hélène Cixous, The Newly Born Woman

To write: I am a woman is full of consequences.

Nicole Brossard, L'Amèr ou le chapitre éffrité

This book is the result of what began as a general interest in Quebec culture and politics well over a decade ago, toward the end of those turbulent years of *indépendance* fever that rocked the political structures of the province of Quebec and for a time the Canadian federation as well. The cultural upheaval that took place in Quebec during the 1960s and early 1970s sparked the interest of a number of American academics like myself and, in my own case, also led rather unexpectedly to an appreciation of the literature of the period. In terms of the focus of this study, the radical questioning of traditional values initiated during the 1960s and the discourse of decolonization that often accompanied it have inspired a number of the directions taken by the women writers discussed here. As numerous critics have already demonstrated, Quebec nationalism exerted a strong and lingering influence on many Quebec writers during the cultural revolution of the 1960s and seriously marked the works of writers as diverse as Hubert Aquin, Paul Chamberland,

André Major, Jacques Godbout, Gaston Miron, and Michèle Lalonde, along with many others. If, however, the political themes
and related social concerns linked to Quebec nationalism can be
said to have impassioned a generation of francophone writers during
the 1960s and early 1970s, Quebec feminism has in turn touched off
an impressive array of creative efforts by women writers, the effects
of which are still being played out in the direction of women's
writing today.

Since 1970, a generation of self-consciously feminist writers has
emerged whose political perspectives and experimental approaches
to the practice of writing have dramatically changed the course of
contemporary Quebec letters. The literary contributions of Nicole
Brossard, Madeleine Gagnon, Louky Bersianik, and France Théoret
have ushered in a new era of textual experimentation and feminist
theorizing on women's writing. Although surprisingly diverse, the
works of these four women writers have added considerable depth
theoretical to the collective efforts of a growing number of Quebec
women writers for whom the political concerns of contemporary
feminism, the experimental forms of literary modernity, and the
question of the specificity or *différence* of women's writing appear
to be inextricably bound. Thus, while the primary focus of this book
is on the literary projects of four important Quebec women writers,
the theoretical assumptions, political issues and cultural perspectives
found in their radical attempts to *inscribe the feminine* have, I believe,
a much broader appeal.

The frames of reference of feminist thought and the experimental
nature of the feminine in writing in Quebec have been internationally as well as regionally inspired. Taken as a whole, the various
and at times conflicting attempts by contemporary Quebec women
writers to voice the difference of women's experience in writing are
firmly grounded in recent feminist analyses of the unequal power
relations in patriarchal cultures; in the related political debates of
the left on racism, imperialism, and nationalism; and in a number
of the important political and philosophical discourses of our time—
Marxism, psychoanalysis, and deconstruction in particular. Indeed,
Quebec feminism and the experimental forms of women's writing
which have developed more or less concurrently since 1970 have

been uniquely situated at the crossroads of radical political thought and recent theoretical discourses on women, language, and the construction of subjectivity. The dynamic evolution and interconnectedness of Quebec feminism and feminist modes of textual inscription can be attributed at least in part to the unusual cross-fertilization of three distinct cultural perspectives—Québécois, French, and American—each of which has provided particular contexts from which to view the dynamics of sexual politics, the social construction of gender, and the conditions under which women live and write in contemporary society. As an American initially trained in the study of French literature and culture and currently an observer of women's experimental writing in Quebec, I also approach the readings of my present study within this particular cultural triangle.

When considered together, the writings of Nicole Brossard, Madeleine Gagnon, Louky Bersianik, and France Théoret constitute some of the most transgressive, politically explosive, and singularly poetic texts to surface anywhere in the last fifteen years. Despite differing responses to the wide range of personal and political issues currently facing contemporary women, the four writers I discuss share a series of common concerns about women, language, and culture that transcend political differences as well as the diversity of tone, style, themes, and structures in their respective works. Whether she is reviewing the past and her relationship to history, exploding traditional myths about how women live and create, reinventing a discourse of female sexuality, or developing different patterns of social relations in her writing, each writer is also reflecting on the "problem" of women in language. Indeed, it is this *re*envisioning of women's relationship to language that has structured their various textual explorations and has ultimately given a collective social meaning to the otherwise unique character of their individual works. This hypersensitivity to language links their writing projects to the overtly nationalist writing of the 1960s as well as to the more experimentally modern texts so prevalent in the 1970s.

The texts of these four writers celebrate women's "new" entry into language by rebelliously exposing the traps and conventions of *phallocentric* discourse and by asserting the significant difference(s) of women's experiences and perspectives in writing. Inspired by contemporary French, American, and Québécois feminisms, Brossard, Gagnon, Bersianik, and Théoret have used their experimental texts to theorize on the nature of women's oppression in patriarchal culture and to delegitimize male authority by undermining the rigid, constricting forms of its discourse. In their efforts to imagine a distinctly feminist poetics, they have explored the multiple sources of female pleasure and have attempted to locate the most fertile sites of their own feminine creativity through approaches to language that, while politically motivated to be sure, are often intensely physical and remarkably intimate.

Focusing on selected texts by Nicole Brossard, Madeleine Gagnon, Louky Bersianik, and France Théoret, this study examines the cultural, political, and theoretical sources of their artistic vision and attempts to follow each writer's evolving approach to the practice of what might be termed a self-consciously *gender-marked writing*. While admittedly drawn to the political content of their exploratory texts, I am not interested merely in promoting a celebration of these writers—although I certainly hope to generate broader excitement about their work—nor am I primarily interested in providing a detached critique of their respective theoretical positions on feminism and writing. What I am interested in pursuing here are the following questions: first, what strategies have been used and what innovations have occurred as a result of their efforts to design women-centered texts?, and second, how do the literary projects of these rather different women writers overlap and diverge with respect to a feminist-inspired aesthetics and to the literary current now commonly referred to in Quebec as *écriture au féminin?*

This study addresses the kinds of gestures made by four women who have elected to write *through a feminist consciousness*. It does not, however, promote a general theory of women's writing that could be applicable to all women writers in all times. Rather, I have attempted to trace some of the ways in which a particular group of women writers in Quebec have discussed and approached the act of writing from the point of view of gender in order to articulate something new about women—about their place in language and in the culture at large. Such forms of writing are almost always situated on the side of subversion or outright opposition (or both) with regard to patriarchal thought. Yet a few of these texts appear to step beyond patriarchal boundaries altogether, to speak of and from a utopian future where the lives, needs, and creative expression of women would be fully integrated. Bolstered by the conceptual force of feminism and deconstruction, these new women's texts stand as conscious attempts "to traverse the limitations erected by phallocentric discourse,"[1] and thereby to move women's writing out of the realm of colonized writing and into a space of multiplicity and affirmative *becoming*.

The political urgency of writing through a feminist consciousness as a way of exploring and ultimately heightening women's consciousness about their oppression as a group is, of course, an important and progressive stance for our time—whether in Quebec or elsewhere. Beyond, however, the indisputable need to critique patriarchal thinking and the institutions that have resulted from it, and the equally pressing need to find ways of conveying the realities of women's lives and the full range of their creative abilities, the notion of *writing in the feminine* as a writing of *difference* (particularly when linked in some way to the physical difference of the female body) is clearly complex and potentially problematic, even for the most sympathetic of feminist readers. Well aware of the thorny theoretical issues associated with it, I have attempted to address the conceptual grounds on which this question of difference has been explored by each of the writers in question. I have also tried to demonstrate the tremendous variety of experimental approaches employed by Brossard, Gagnon, Bersianik, and Théoret to express a sense of difference in their work. This is not to say that all of the texts considered here are equally successful at constructing what might be termed an*other* discourse or even to suggest that the various forms of literary experimentation encountered in these texts are more appropriately feminist than others might be. What is clear, it seems, in the sample of writings I have chosen to explore here is the fluctuation, redirection, and growth in poetic expression and political thought in each writer's project from one text to the next. The unique creative strengths of the four writers discussed in this study are exemplary of the multicentered and multifaceted nature of *writing in the feminine,* a political and literary event in Quebec that has shown signs of considerable breadth. Thus, while I have attempted to emphasize the common ground in their respective views on women's writing today, I have also tried to resist the temptation to reduce their creative efforts to a series of examples that fit a particular theoretical grid.

In addition to Gagnon, Brossard, Bersianik, and Théoret, there are a number of other women writers in Quebec who have contributed in a significant way to what may be regarded as politically motivated gender-marked writing. In order to undertake any serious survey of the field of feminist literary production in Quebec, we would need to consider the works of Yolande Villemaire, Carole Massé, Geneviève Amyot, Michèle Mailhot, and others, not to mention the theatrical innovations of a number of important feminist dramatists such as Jovette Marchessault, Marie Savard, Marie Laberge, and Denise Boucher, none of whose contributions can be properly assessed within the boundaries of this study.[2] Moreover, a new generation of women writers has surfaced in the 1980s—writers such as Louise Bouchard, Louise Dupré, Denise Desautels, Monique LaRue, and Julie Stanton to name but a few, adding other voices and still other forms of feminine inscription to an increasingly diverse body of experimental literature.

My intention in this study is not, however, to summarize or codify the works of so many with the aid of some convenient, overarching formula nor in any way to flatten out the differences in their artistic constructions or to ignore the conflicts in their respective political views. Instead, I have chosen to consider the texts of four women who, in my view, have been among the most influential of Quebec's women writers in recent years. Their influence is due primarily to the innovative nature of their individual writing practices and to the complex ways in which they have woven contemporary feminist thought into the language, thematic considerations, and structure of their texts. In one way or another, each has substantially marked the course of contemporary Quebec literature and of experimental writing in particular. All have received national and, in most cases, international attention. Admittedly, I have also chosen these four writers in lieu of others for reasons of personal taste and because of what—for lack of a better term—I can only call the remarkable originality in their different approaches to feminist literary production.

I offer this book as one reading of selected experimental texts by four important Quebec women writers. It is not meant to be exhaustive in terms of the number of works covered, nor is it intended to be intentionally exclusionary. Although I do explore the common areas of intersection among the four writers under consideration, the organization I have followed allows me to emphasize the originality of each writer's approach as well as the commonality underlying their works as a whole. Rather than force a homogeneity of thought throughout a particular writer's work that might be unjustified, I have also attempted to examine the evolution and changing focus of each writer's literary project as a reflection of her own political and artistic development.

Given the relative lack of familiarity with Quebec culture in the United States, even among professors of French, chapter 1 includes some discussion of the cultural and political climate in Quebec prior to as well as after 1970. This brief overview is intended to provide a basis for understanding the literary project of *writing in the feminine* within the important social contexts of Quebec nationalism and the contemporary feminist movement. The first part of the chapter also draws attention to the particularly acute Québécois sensitivity to language, cultural identity, and collective autonomy, a sensitivity born out of the English Conquest of New France in 1759 and the resulting preoccupation with cultural survival in the context of a predominantly English-speaking North America. I then examine the various ways in which feminist writers in Quebec have come to view language as a positive resource for the creative exploration, redefinition, and collective affirmation of women's lives. Chapter 1 also develops a critical framework through which to link current theories of language, modernity, and women's difference to the evolving practice of writing in the feminine in Quebec.

The remaining four chapters focus on the linguistic experimentations, thematic concerns, innovations in literary form, and theoretical assumptions found in the writings of Nicole Brossard, Madeleine Gagnon, Louky Bersianik, and France Théoret. Chapter 2 is devoted to the highly influential literary contributions of Nicole Brossard. Initially, I explore the ways in which Brossard has moved through and beyond the textual interplay of nationalist themes and formalist concerns to a vision of writing that is radically gender-marked and boldly modern. The discussion of her texts then focuses on the central positioning of the female writer in her work, the extreme degree of self-consciousness brought to the act of writing itself, the physicality of her feminine discourse, and the insistent blurring in her texts of fiction and theory, the imaginary and the real, the erotic and the mundane.

Chapter 3 examines the political perspectives, changing literary forms, and critical theorizing on language and creativity in the writings of Madeleine Gagnon. The major transformations in her literary explorations—from socialism to feminism, from activism to self-reflection—are discussed through both the historical and theoretical intersections of Quebec socialism, post-Lacanian psychoanalysis, and French theories of feminine writing.

Chapter 4 deals with the writing of Louky Bersianik and the persistent recourse in her works to myths and mythologizing about women—whether classical, biblical, or modern. I analyze a number of Bersianik's innovative strategies for deconstructing masculine configurations of "woman" along with her equally inventive attempts to rewrite women and a history of their own making through radically new forms of feminist mythopoesis. In her most recent texts, Bersianik has internalized the myth-making process by initiating a practice of writing that encourages the surfacing of women's unconscious material, which then becomes the source of new myths and other views of the future.

In chapter 5, discussion shifts to the ambiguous position of the female voice in the literary discourse of France Théoret, a discourse which appears to exemplify both modernity's mistrust of language and feminism's passionate pursuit of meaning. In particular, I consider the narrative tensions in Théoret's work between the apparent anxiety of articulation and an uncontrollable flow of words, between serious disruptions of form and the reshaping of syntax. Théoret's thoroughly *modern* artistic sensibility and feminist awareness make the sometimes painful risk of writing an urgent and necessary choice.

Finally, I offer some personal observations about my own experience as a reader of contemporary women writers who directly take issue with the established male canon in their works. While recent feminist criticism has focused considerable attention on the position of the female reader in male-oriented texts, we still have much to learn about the emerging relations between feminist writers and their female readers.

When examining the works of contemporary women writers in Quebec, the questions I raise (either implicitly or explicitly) and the perspectives I bring to bear are derived from a general interest in theory, writing, and the status of women in the dominant culture. I am also interested in the interconnectedness of theory and writing in many of these texts. My own critical approach is eclectic and, I hope, somewhat fluid. As a reader, I am well aware of the difficulties posed by some of the texts discussed in this study. From the standpoint of conventional reading practice, the results of these experimental efforts to inscribe the feminine are sometimes perplexing and the meanings at times so disrupted that one wonders what, in fact, can be said about a particular text with any reasonable amount of assurance or precision. On the other hand, any attempt to be overly categorical or absolute in the interpretive act would, it seems to me, seriously contradict the open-ended quality of the various texts under consideration.

The point I want to make regarding any critical reading of experimental texts such as the ones discussed in this study is that the *coming to writing* of the feminist critic may in some instances be even more problematic than it has been for the woman writer herself. As some feminist critics have already admitted, the much discussed need for an effective feminist practice of criticism necessarily raises a number of questions about the political implications of "mastery" and interpretive power over the text—and in the case of my own study, over the texts of other women who are, for the most part, consciously writing against such forms of critical practice. At issue in this debate over a responsive as well as responsible feminist criticism is, as Caroline Bayard has aptly put it, "how to work *with* rather than *on* a text and how to overturn the old critical relations based on a dynamic of opposition: critic-subject dissecting text-object."[3] Without claiming to have resolved this dilemma for the feminist critic in my own work, I have tried to resist the temptation to close off opportunities for other interpretative readings. At the same time, however, I would agree with Tania Modleski that "the ultimate goal of feminist criticism and theory is female empowerment."[4] For me, the literary explorations of Nicole Brossard, Madeleine Gagnon, Louky Bersianik, and France Théoret have been empowering. It is my hope that the critical readings presented here will stimulate further interest in their work and also convey this sense of feminist discovery.

Since a number of the primary works, critical writings, and interviews quoted in this study are not available in English translation, all translations of French texts are my own unless otherwise indicated. When the plays on words in French are crucial for an appreciation of the plurality of meanings in the writer's own signifying practice, I have separated the major variants with a slash.

Writing in the Feminine

Writing in the Feminine
Social and Theoretical Contexts

One has the imagination of one's century, one's culture, one's generation, one's particular social class, one's decade, and the imagination of what one reads, but above all one has the imagination of one's body and of the sex which inhabits it. What could be more appealing to our imagination than the tenacious forms which haunt memory, mobile female forms which bring into play in us their own pulsating movement.

Nicole Brossard, The Aerial Letter

If we don't invent a language, if we don't find our body's language, it will have too few gestures to accompany our story. We shall tire of the same ones, and leave our desires unexpressed, unrealized. Asleep again, unsatisfied, we shall fall back upon the words of men—who, for their part, have "known" for a long time. But *not our body*. Seduced, attracted, fascinated, ecstatic with our becoming, we shall remain paralyzed. Deprived of *our movements*. Rigid, whereas we are made for endless change. Without leaps or falls, and without repetition.

Luce Irigaray, This Sex Which Is Not One

The force with which the women who write cling to parts of the theoreticians' texts reveals the extent to which the need for theoretical arms is pressing.

Suzanne Lamy, d'elles

One of the most significant developments in contemporary Quebec literature has been the emergence of a group of women writers whose experimental efforts to reshape language and textual production in the feminine have turned conventional writing practice upside down. Since the early 1970s, Nicole Brossard, Madeleine Gagnon, Louky Bersianik, and France Théoret, along with numerous others, have published a variety of radically new, women-centered texts that call attention to the complex relationships between gender and writing, between language, sexual politics, and cultural production. Through their various self-conscious attempts to inscribe the feminine, they have sought to undermine the presumed universality of literature written through male eyes and to shatter patriarchy's pervasive influence over language and thought.

The four writers whose texts provide the primary focus of this book have been influenced in varying degrees by the pressure for social change in Quebec since 1960, by an increasing emphasis on the need for a collective cultural affirmation of the francophone experience in North America, and by the appeal to the "modern" (both modernization and modernity) ushered in during Quebec's dynamic cultural revolution in the early 1960s, a period now commonly referred to in Quebec as *La Révolution Tranquille* or The Quiet Revolution. The initial works of Gagnon and Théoret also reflect the impact of Marxist thought and labor solidarity on a number of Quebec intellectuals in the early 1970s. In addition, the four writers in this study have all been inspired by various American and Québécois feminist perspectives (socialist, cultural, radical), which had gained considerable currency by the mid-1970s. To a greater or lesser extent, the diverse theoretical frameworks and writing practices of Brossard, Gagnon, Bersianik, and Théoret have also been influenced by recent French philosophical reflections on deconstruction, on the psychodynamics of gender and identity, and on what Hélène Cixous has termed *écriture féminine* (feminine writing). Yet despite the significance of French and American feminist influences, the project of writing in the feminine in Quebec has had its own distinct historical roots, cultural life, and theoretical preoccupations as well.

The "newly born"[1] texts of Brossard, Gagnon, Bersianik, and Théoret stand in bold contrast to more traditional literary forms that, in the minds of many Quebec feminists, have served to censor women's words, to devalorize forms of inscription common to women's literature, and to hinder critical appreciation of women's writing in something other than strictly male terms. Acknowledging the subversive character of their respective approaches to textual production, the four writers discussed at length in this study have challenged the making of an in-different text and, in so doing, have worked to unsilence and recover a multitude of female voices, each with its own rhythm, tone, and story to tell.

Although at times unwilling to declare themselves adherents of a specific literary movement per se and often at odds over the same kinds of issues that have frequently separated socialist feminists, radical feminists, and lesbian separatists in Quebec and in the United States as well,[2] Brossard, Gagnon, Bersianik, and Théoret have produced a series of related experimental texts that, despite differences in rhetorical strategies, poetic symbolisms, and sexual politics, do contain certain common aesthetic features and political intentions. The writers themselves are, moreover, acutely aware of the new literary current they and others have put in motion in Quebec. Yet Madeleine Gagnon has remained noticeably wary of confining labels and has resisted characterizing the experimental texts of Quebec feminists as anything resembling a literary school or a distinctly classifiable feminist avant-garde—a term, I should add, much maligned by all of these writers for its militant overtones.[3]

Gagnon's mistrust of sweeping generalizations about Quebec feminist writers and their texts is understandable. For unlike surrealism or existentialism, recent attempts by Quebec women writers to inscribe the feminine do not constitute a cohesive philosophical movement per se and there has been no single organizing manifesto as such. Moreover, as many critics of the proclaimed French *nouveau roman* have also discovered, social perspectives, poetic forms, and narrative designs in the works of Beckett, Sarraute, Simon, and Robbe-Grillet, for example, differ so greatly from one writer to the next that notions of a literary school and a shared literary aesthetic are more than a little misleading for anyone who seriously compares their works. Even so, few critics in Quebec would dispute the fact that the literary efforts of Nicole Brossard, Madeleine Gagnon, Louky Bersianik, and France Théoret to approach writing through a feminist consciousness and in a different voice have signaled a major shift in focus in women's literary production in Quebec. Their works have also generated increased interest on the part of Quebec feminists in more radical forms of textual experimentation. Finally, each of these writers has been an important and influential contributor to the development of a theoretical discourse on feminism, modernity, and experimental writing.

Since the mid-1970s, the project of "writing like a woman,"⁴ that is to say, from a woman's vantage point and experience, from a woman's body, and in a language that could be regarded as primarily woman-made has, in fact, emerged as a new and transgressive literary mode of political intervention in Quebec. And while individual attempts at feminine inscription vary greatly in form and in political outlook from one writer to another, critical debates over the specificity of women's writing and the very possibility of an *écriture au féminin* are clearly rooted in broader cultural questions about the relationships between feminism and artistic expression, ideology and discourse. Indeed, it seems that the very notion of writing in the feminine could not have come into being in Quebec without the various pressures for recognition and change asserted by contemporary feminist politics and thought, both within and outside the francophone province. What follows, then, is a brief survey of the historical, political, and cultural contexts out of which this writing of difference has largely emerged in Quebec.

Quebec Women and *La Révolution Tranquille*

Although the links to French and American feminisms are many, historians, sociologists, and feminist activists in Quebec have also emphasized a number of the underlying cultural differences that have contributed to the rather unique political history and theoretical orientation of feminist thought in the francophone province. It has been persuasively argued, for instance, that relatively swift changes in the institutional structures, economic relations, and cultural life of Quebec during the 1960s and 1970s gave a particular cast to emerging discussions of sexual politics and feminist aesthetics. For a culture that had long considered itself primarily agrarian and Catholic in its orientation and values, the accelerating effects of urbanization after World War II led rather quickly, for example, to increased concern with and over materialism, to a belated but nevertheless determined secularization program, to major educational reforms, to strong nationalist politics, and to various separat-

ist independence projects that called for entirely new ways of thinking about the state and about the cultural survival of the
francophone population as a distinct political entity. The combined
impact of all of these reforms and breaks with the past, coupled
with the new sense of national identity that many younger Québécois were struggling to affirm, would produce a more radical series
of changes in the lives of Quebec women than was generally the
case for either their French or American counterparts. Economist
Caroline Pestieau argued this point in 1976, noting that "in Quebec
there have been so many major changes since 1960 that it has been
difficult to remain unconsciously part of the 'silent majority.' At the
same time, the existence of the Separatist option and the experience
of unequal opportunities for French-Canadians have obliged a large
number of women, who would not otherwise do so, to think about
politics and to be prepared to take a stand of one kind or another."⁵

Like many feminists of her generation, Nicole Brossard is well
aware of the unique set of historical circumstances and the strong
sense of linguistic and cultural differences that have marked the
evolution of Quebec society as a whole and the changing status of
Quebec women in particular during the second half of this century.
Writing in 1975, she underscores the unique set of problems due to
the marginal space Quebec occupies on the economic map of North
America; she also notes the swift and relatively dramatic transformations that have occurred in the lives of many Quebec women during
the past three decades:

My relationship to writing and to knowledge, which is also its support,
seems to be cauterized. Burned as they are, the few (familial and revolutionary) cells inside me are reproduced through a tradition, and by a bourgeoi-
sie, that, although in Europe might have produced new values for its own
use, here has been content with dumping, without batting an eye (and will
never keep an eye open), for it's the multinationals already here, and
that puts the question of bourgeois values and, correspondingly, of the
revolutionary struggle, differently. From serf to consumer. From the revenge of the cradle to feminism. From marriage to homosexuality.⁶

Feminists writing in Quebec during the 1970s and 1980s have
been influenced by many of the same forces for social change that
have brought the predominantly French-speaking province so
quickly and irrevocably out of its isolated, agrarian, and staunchly

Catholic past into an increasingly urbanized, technological, and ideologically contested present. Most had been nurtured on the successes and failures of *La Révolution Tranquille* and then further politicized by the independence fever that swept the province during the late 1960s. Many feminists were also cognizant of the shrinking role of the Catholic Church in the political arena and in the public debate over the question of national identity. The move to secularization in Quebec schools in the 1960s was clearly an important indication of the weakening cultural status of the Church, and it helped speed up the modernization process not only with respect to education, but also with respect to the stereotypical roles assigned women in traditional Catholic teachings. Quebec was moving from a Church-dominated society to an ultramodern secular one almost over night—or so it seemed. As Nadia Fahmy-Eid and Nicole Laurin-Frenette have pointed out, "Since its foundation in 1841 and up to the 'Quiet Revolution,' the Québec school system provided a social domain in which the effective supervision of child and family by the church was equalled by very few Western societies during the same period."[7] In this regard, it is worth noting that for a number of Quebec women writers in the 1950s and 1960s, the convent schools themselves supplied some of the most intolerant and oppressive settings for the subject matter of their fiction and nonfiction. For Claire Martin and Marie-Claire Blais in particular, the atmosphere and ideology that dominated much of convent life in Quebec help explain why childhood and adolescence are so negatively portrayed in their writings.[8]

The diminishing cultural authority of the Church had, in fact, already become evident in the 1950s and 1960s. The erosion of religious authority was particularly noticeable in Quebec's rapidly declining birth rate that tumbled steadily downward after World War II in conjunction with an era of expanding urbanization and a general trend toward the secularization of Quebec society. Nicole Brossard has observed that the Church's loss of control over sexuality—women's sexuality and their attitudes about sexual practice in particular—brought about important modifications and, for some women, radical transformations in the relationships they had previously maintained with fathers, husbands, employers, politicians, and clergymen, figures who had traditionally represented the political, economic, cultural, and sexual power of male authority in Quebec.[9]

Many feminists in Quebec in the late 1960s and early 1970s themselves supported and substantially assisted in the spreading secularization of Quebec society.[10] During this same period, a growing number of women in Quebec were also being politicized by the advent of more aggressive—and sometimes violent—forms of Quebec nationalism and by the evolving political discourse on Quebec independence. Discussions on the economic viability of an independent Quebec, the necessity of cultural autonomy for the francophone community, and the will of the French-speaking majority of the population (80 percent) in determining the direction of the Quebec state would shape the context and set the tone of most of the major political debates in the province until 1980.[11]

Although the year 1960 has little if any meaning in terms of immediate changes in the working conditions and daily lives of the vast majority of Quebec women, the date marked the beginning of a new era of collective examination and national debate (sometimes explosive) over the place and future direction of Québécois culture and the Quebec state in the modern world. With respect to the social and cultural changes that occurred over the course of the decade as well as the political promises made but never kept, the death in 1959 of Maurice Duplessis after twenty years as premier of Quebec (1936–39, 1944–59) was a momentous event. Quebec had lost its devoted conservative patriarch, its "papa" as the *Montréal-Matin* put it.[12]

An autocratic leader, Duplessis had embodied a conservative political ideology that staunchly defended the Catholic Church and rural values—despite increasing urbanization in the province. He had promoted an ideology based on the fear of communism and on a conservative form of nationalism that called for "provincial autonomy" but that, from the liberal point of view of the time, was "a reactionary ideology which favoured cultural and political isolationism, something that seemed inimical to the very notion of progress."[13] Progressive forces within Quebec society welcomed the passing of Duplessis in 1959 and the weakening of the *Union Natio-*

nale party as an opportunity to shake the province loose from the stranglehold of tradition. Many in Quebec were eager to promote a more forward-looking image of their province with modern values that sought to defend and strengthen the urban, aggressively materialist, and increasingly technological era into which Quebec had entered.

From the standpoint of many Quebec feminists today, Duplessis was the "archetypal male and archetypal father,"[14] a political patriarch whose politics of the land (the fertile mother) and the Church repeated "not only a strategic option but, as the positions of Hitler and Mussolini reveal, profoundly patriarchal fantasies."[15] It would take more than a decade of struggle to undo publicly the effects of the antifeminism espoused by the Duplessis regime and to challenge Duplessis' own mystification of woman as perfect wife and "natural" mother whose primary goal in life was to "prove her competence and dynamism at keeping herself beautiful, beautifying her interior surroundings, supporting her husband and giving her children help and an education based on the most recent developments in medicine and psychology."[16]

The early years of Jean Lesage's Liberal government (1960–64) sparked a taste for change in Quebec society in a variety of arenas— education, social services, state government. The Liberals also intensified an ongoing public debate on how to overcome the economic domination of the federal government in Ottawa and at the same time attract and effectively control foreign investment in Quebec.[17] In 1964, a new Ministry of Education was created in Quebec whose progressive reforms included the important move to coeducational public schools, the right of free access to a high school education, and the abolition of the *écoles ménagères* that had traditionally prepared many young Quebec women to become "good" homemakers rather than working professionals. In addition to secondary school reforms, there were changes initiated in higher education as well, including the creation of the *cégeps* (a state-supported junior college system) along with the various campuses of the new Université du Québec, and a much needed modernizing of curricular offerings in university as well as high school programs with new emphases on technology, engineering, administration, marketing, and so on—

areas that had not constituted the traditional "classical" preparation of previous generations of Quebec students. These changes were heralded by many as some of the major accomplishments of The Quiet Revolution and as essential steps toward both the modernization of Quebec society and the institutionalization of a new equality among Quebec's youth.

As the women historians of Le Collectif Clio have noted, however, women as a group did not in fact benefit equally from many of the reforms initiated during the new liberal era. Because of the traditional images of women still conveyed through the media, academic textbooks, and much of the literature of the time, as well as the traditional sex-role stereotyping that continued to influence family life and social relations on virtually every level of Quebec society, most young Québécois women did not fully profit from the tide of structural and curricular changes that were rapidly transforming Quebec's antiquated educational system. Indeed, most women who chose to pursue a university education in Quebec during the 1960s continued to select the "feminine professions"— primary and secondary education, nursing, secretarial work—and for those who stopped short of a university degree, the vast majority would become sales clerks, waitresses, and still more secretaries.[18] No doubt because of her own working-class roots and personal struggle to overcome sex-role stereotyping and subjugation as a woman, France Théoret has, as we shall see, been preoccupied in her writing with the cultural myths, physical and psychological abuse, and real economic barriers that have lowered the professional aspirations, undermined the self-confidence and potential sense of self-worth, and hindered the intellectual development of working-class women in Quebec.

While by 1970 substantially more women were finishing high school, entering the universities, and moving into the workplace, the positions they occupied in Quebec's work force continued to reflect the traditional structures of sexism in the society at large with regard to the low level of women's salaries for the same or comparable work, the relative lack of prestige in employment opportunities for women, and the lack of power women wielded in the institutional structures of Quebec society itself. By the end of the

1960s, it could well be argued that *La Révolution Tranquille* had nudged an ever-increasing number of women into the work force and had seriously undercut the authority of the Church in family matters and in public education. However, the women who found work outside the home remained primarily in traditionally female jobs, and most worked without access to adequate day-care facilities, without maternity leaves, and without help at home. Those who stayed at home lived under another form of unacknowledged exploitation but had lost their status as the privileged guardians of family values and cultural tradition. If the series of accelerated social changes set in motion in the 1960s helped shape a rather distinct political climate in Quebec, the obvious disparities between the lives and opportunities of Quebec women and men were not unlike those found in the United States during the same period of time.

Quebec Nationalism and Its Daughters

Both contemporary Quebec feminism and the ensuing literary experiment of writing in the feminine have developed as a result of an unusually dynamic convergence of social, literary, and intellectual currents in Quebec. Quebec nationalism, for which an important number of Quebec writers became "the privileged articulators" during the 1960s and early 1970s,[19] would offer many feminists a political and theoretical language in which to express their discontent with existing conditions of inequality and oppression. Both the political nature of the discourse of decolonization in Quebec and the extreme seriousness of the language question associated with that discourse underscored for many the crucial ties linking language, oppression, and cultural hegemony. The poetry and fiction of Gaston Miron, Paul Chamberland, Hubert Aquin, Jacques Godbout, Michèle Lalonde, and numerous others, along with the literary reviews, *Liberté* and *Parti pris,* thus provided a social as well as a literary forum for the collective expression of a more general mood of political disaffection and social unrest within the province of Quebec. It is important to note, however, that the desire for radical change explicit in much of the nationalist literary discourse of the 1960s was also frequently an expressed desire for change in the relations of power outside the confines of Quebec society as well.

Politically speaking, the decade that ushered in Quebec's Quiet Revolution also became an important training period for groups of women involved in collective organizing and particularly in the increased activity of labor unions, which by 1972 had become a political force to be reckoned with in Quebec. Some activist women also participated in various moderate and extreme leftist groups and nationalist parties during the same period, each of which critiqued in varying degrees the exploitation (political, economic, cultural) of Quebec within the Canadian federation.[20] Madeleine Gagnon, for example, situates her own early writing within the double context of Quebec's labor movement and the socialist-feminist struggle. Appearing in 1974 and 1975, her political collages bear witness to the serious social unrest in Quebec during the early 1970s and are indicative of the inventive ways in which poetry and political theorizing were being combined in her own writings and in those of numerous others as well. As we shall see in chapter 3, her early texts also reflect an emerging current in feminist politics and feminist theorizing in Quebec that called for organized resistance to the political, economic, and social constraints of class and gender.

For a number of young Quebec feminists who organized women's groups, protests, and political events in 1969 and for several years thereafter, the key women's issues of unequal treatment and economic exploitation in the workplace, as well as women's rights to self-definition, economic independence, and access to juridical and political decision making were all closely tied to the liberation of Quebec itself. Hence the popular feminist slogan launched by the militant leftist *Front de libération des femmes* (FLF) in 1970 and frequently used by the *Centre des femmes* (Women's Center) until 1973: Pas de Québec libre sans libération des femmes! Pas de femmes libres sans libération du Québec! (No free Quebec without the liberation of women! No free women without the liberation of Quebec!).[21] In fact, the politics of the FLF emerged out of the socialist nationalist movement in Quebec during the late 1960s, which identified the "nation" of Quebec as an oppressed people living in a colonial situation with respect to the rest of anglophone

Canada and, economically and culturally speaking, as a colonized people with respect to the foreign investments of the United States and its increasing media penetration of Quebec culture.

Quebec nationalism gave many feminists a political and theoretical language with which to articulate their particular sense of oppression and alienation as women and with which to formulate their desire for collective liberation and radical social change. In terms of Quebec feminism, the decolonization paradigm developed by francophone nationalists also created an international frame of reference for women's political analyses through its identification with Third World liberation struggles. Feminist socialists and nationalists were thus able to link women's oppression under patriarchy with the struggles of developing countries subjected to the dominance of foreign capital. Algeria, Chile, Vietnam, and Argentina were frequently cited at rallies and in the socialist feminist journalism of the time.

Some of the writings of Madeleine Gagnon and France Théoret are good examples of the influence this discourse of decolonization exerted over women's writing throughout the 1970s. Even in "Mon Corps dans l'écriture," an important theoretical text appearing in 1977 in which Madeleine Gagnon explores her own preoccupations with the female body as a generator of new forms of textual production and launches an attack on the psychoanalytic constructs of Freud and Lacan, she continues to stress the connections between feminism and Third World resistance to Western imperialism, between the material bases of class struggle and sexual politics. Thus, the female body in Gagnon's text becomes the site of an erupting force of resistance to sexual repression that is viewed as yet another form of political oppression. As a more detailed discussion of her work suggests (see chapter 3), Gagnon's weapon of revolt is a form of writing that continually moves from the personal (the female writer) to the political (the exploited body politic) and back again:

My body is pain. But from my nocturnal depths, it is a volcano beginning to rumble, it is lights beginning to glimmer: from everywhere, from every country, I come to describe this night. I read myself from one country to the next, I witness my movements of liberation—from America, from China, from Portugal, from France or from Spain, from Cambodia, from

Vietnam and from farther away still—I begin to move and people see me from the inside.[22]

For a number of francophone women on the left who were actively involved in feminist politics during the early 1970s, identification with Third World women sometimes occurred at the expense of potential ties with English Canadian and American women. Such was the case, for instance, when members of the FLF decided they were unable to lend their support to an international conference on women against imperialism that American and anglophone Canadian women were trying to organize in Montreal in 1970. This internalizing of the colonialist-nationalist model within Quebec feminism also made it possible for all but one francophone member of the FLF to justify expelling anglophone feminists from their group on the grounds that the anglophones exerted ideological control over the FLF due to their access to important feminist texts that were coming out of the British and American women's movements at that time.[23]

In an essay on Quebec feminism during the 1970s, Diane Lamoureux argues that Quebec nationalism provided feminists with a view of culture—and especially literature—that was oriented toward a politics of oppression and toward the notion of a territory of "difference" in need of celebration and liberation.[24] For Quebec nationalists, the political body in need of affirmation and liberation was, of course, the province of Quebec and the foreigner was English Canada and, not infrequently, the United States as well. This analogy linking the political to the corporeal can, in fact, be quite useful when examining a number of the works of Madeleine Gagnon and France Théoret. Lamoureux also contends, however, that for many radical feminists in the early 1970s and for some socialist feminists as well, the colonized body was also a woman's body and the source of foreign oppression was, increasingly, men.[25] A number of the feminist historians and sociologists who have reviewed the nationalist politics and related feminist activities of the early 1970s in Quebec concur with Lamoureux's analysis. Yet even though some women on the left were forming separate political groups and meeting centers for women out of frustration with their experiences in male-dominated groups, many of them continued to define themselves primarily in terms of their support for the male revolutionary and independence projects.[26] Again, as we shall see, the early writings of Madeleine Gagnon are an excellent case in point.

The tense and spirited political environment of the early 1970s could not help but influence the character and initial development of Quebec feminism during the same period. The selective terrorist bombings during the late 1960s, the kidnappings and hostage killing of Liberal cabinet minister Pierre Laporte in 1970 by members of the *Front de libération du Québec* (FLQ), and the massive incarcerations of alleged sympathizers that took place in Quebec in October of that year marked the beginning of the end for the radical leftist nationalist project in Quebec. Given the general climate of intensifying political confrontation between militant leftist nationalists on the one hand and Robert Bourassa's new Liberal government and the federal government of Pierre Elliott Trudeau on the other, a politics of moderation among Quebec separatists gained increasing favor. During the early 1970s, most of the supporters of Quebec independence denounced the terrorist tactics of the FLQ and rallied in ever-growing numbers around the emerging Parti Québécois, led by René Lévesque, whose membership worked steadily to distance the new party from political violence and radical social change.

Instead of catering to the socialist agenda of the party's left wing, a majority of Parti Québécois members, including the leadership, sought to legitimize the independence project in the eyes of the general population by looking more and more like a political party the francophone establishment could live with—if not wholeheartedly embrace. Many of the women who had been active in various segments of the women's movement in Quebec since 1969 became members of the Parti Québécois (particularly teachers and other professionals in the service sector) and were promoting it as the only viable political party in Quebec interested in women's issues and serious social reform. Only five years after its founding in 1968, the Parti Québécois became the official opposition party and took over the leadership of the province in 1976. At that time, 55 percent of its members were women and, as Francine Fournier noted two years later, the "dynamism" of women in the party work of the Parti Québécois was already recognized.[27]

For radical and socialist feminists in Quebec in 1976, the rapid rise to power of the Parti Québécois was on the one hand a salutary event, insofar as the independence issue was becoming a part of mainstream politics and therefore would presumably leave greater room for other issues of more direct impact on women's daily lives, both public and private. In its official political program of 1976, the Parti Québécois did present a list of prospective legislative reforms that dealt specifically with the living conditions of many women and that included a proposal for state-supported family allowances based on the number of children in the family unit (a subsidy that some radical feminists deemed too pro-family in its stance). The Parti Québécois also proposed changes in the existing civil code to guarantee the equal rights and autonomous position of the wife under the marriage contract, the establishment of a system of state-supported preschool and day care facilities, new laws to assure equality of treatment for men and women in the work force, and maternity leaves for working women of up to six months.[28]

While women's issues were officially on the agenda of the Parti Québécois, however, it soon became clear to a number of feminists—to radical feminists in particular—that like other political parties in the province, the Parti Québécois remained largely dominated by men.[29] The refusal of the Parti Québécois during the early years of its leadership to support abortion rights for women and free access to abortion, the party's unwillingness to address fully the problem of sexism in educational materials and in other media, and its hard-nosed position against striking women and men in the health and educational services were a few of the crucial issues that demoralized many feminist supporters of the Parti Québécois and eventually led a number of radical feminists, including Nicole Brossard, to criticize the Parti Québécois openly and aggressively. In the eyes of some Quebec women, the party committed to the social transformation and political independence of Quebec had itself come to represent the male political establishment.

At the same time, the surprising ability of the Parti Québécois to mobilize a broad base of popular support in 1976, coupled with the growing strength of male technocrats within the party, were already indications to some feminists that the fundamental mission of the

Parti Québécois was to stay in power in order to become the official party of a progressive (but not too progressive), technologically sophisticated, and future-oriented Quebec state that, it was hoped, would eventually gain the legal status of a country. In the meantime, however, a growing number of Quebec feminists were anxious to focus on how the legal, political, economic, and cultural status of women could be changed for the better.

With the defeat of the Parti Québécois' referendum on "sovereignty-association" in 1980, the ousting of the Parti Québécois itself in 1986, and the death only a year later of René Levesque, supporters of Quebec independence suffered a series of major setbacks from which it will doubtless take many years to recover. On a number of key issues, the political pendulum does, in fact, appear to have swung back with the provincial election victory of the Liberal Party in 1986 and with Robert Bourassa once again serving as prime minister of the province. Yet even Bourassa's remarkable return to the center stage of Quebec politics has been tempered by recent nationalist-leaning protests over a relaxation in Bill 101, the language law legislation enacted while the Parti Québécois was in power to ensure the linguistic and cultural survival of the francophone majority.[30] Francophone feminists in Quebec, and the four writers in this study are no exception, remain sensitive to the national question particularly as it relates to the nefarious consequences of what many in Quebec perceive to be a historic pattern of cultural and linguistic oppression.

Quebec feminists have also become increasingly concerned, as well they should be, with the rise of a more conservative government discourse on the family aimed at promoting pronatalist policies that include allowances for the birth of each child as well as the more welcome extension of day-care facilities. As Sylvain Massé has recently noted, the pronatalist and profamily stance of the current Bourassa government is due in large measure to the intense discussion and general lamenting both in academic circles and in the popular francophone press about the low birth rate (1.38 percent in 1988 and the lowest in North America, the Québécois are repeatedly told) and the prospects for the long-term cultural survival of the francophone majority given this demographic phenomenon.[31]

Feminists in Quebec do not want to be the scapegoats for a conservative ideology of the family that would once again tie women to a biological imperative "for the good of the state." Tensions such as this between what many perceive as "national" concerns in Quebec and the concerns of Quebec women to create lives of dignity and independence are further examples, it seems, of the unique set of cultural circumstances and problems that Quebec feminists have faced and will no doubt continue to face in the years to come.

A Shift in Discourse:
From Nationalism to Modernity

By the late 1960s, while many Quebec writers and critics were continuing their focus on the national question and on the related thematics of country and collective identity, Nicole Brossard, Marcel Saint-Pierre, Jan Stafford, and Roger Soublière had formed what was to become one of the most important reviews devoted to literary modernity in Quebec for well over a decade.[32] Theoretically transgressive in its avowedly modern preference for experimentation over tradition, *La Barre du jour* (*Daybreak*, 1965–77) exemplified the keen interest of a small but increasingly visible portion of Quebec's literary avant-garde in the materiality of language and in the virtually endless possibilities of subversion and play that writing could provide. Nurturing the intense self-consciousness of more formalist writers, *La Barre du jour* gradually became a recognized oasis in Quebec for some of the more subversive literary explorations and for a number of the more theoretically oriented proponents of *une littérature nouvelle*. It was a place where many of the popular political themes of the time lay relatively dormant, where the hierarchical and arbitrary divisions of conventional literary genres and the literary canon itself were openly, even flagrantly contested, and where the practice and pleasure of writing could and would be continually reinvestigated. In a statement issued by the editors of *La Barre du jour* in 1967, their thoroughly modern, forward-looking intentions are made explicit: "In this sense, what matters for *LA BARRE DU JOUR* is literature in the making, but also, and perhaps more importantly, literature that will be made; that is to say, investigation (current). We are wholeheartedly in favor of a new literature; a literature that must come into being (some day soon) and be exploratory (for the moment)."[33]

For Nicole Brossard, the literary posture at *La Barre du jour* in the late 1960s was, in her own words, "resolutely modern." Echoing an increasing weariness on the part of a number of Quebec intellectuals with the nationalist themes and the more overtly realistic forms of political writing that had dominated the Quebec literary scene during the first half of the decade and that were actively advanced in the influential literary and cultural review *Parti pris* (1963–68),[34] Brossard attempted to articulate a set of theoretical positions for *La Barre du jour* that would challenge the conventional semantic system as a whole and, at the same time, resist the internal consumer logic of bourgeois literary production. While she shared with other nationalists the hope of an independent Quebec, Brossard was struggling to move the notion of radicality beyond the transparency of realist writing and into the domain of literary form itself.[35]

Something in the thematics of the country irritated us. Politically speaking, we supported by and large the texts of *Parti pris*. But from a literary point of view, we had the "impression" of a void . . . we wanted to approach and question literature differently. We had a lot of pretension to subversion. We wanted the spirit of protest to enter literature as well. We wanted to approach literature from a formal point of view, from the point of view of writing. We didn't know at that point exactly what this endeavor was going to become but the desire was there to approach writing in its materiality.[36]

For Brossard and later for France Théoret, who also worked for a time at *La Barre du jour,* the emphasis on the materiality of language brought with it an awareness of language as social construction and, in turn, fueled the continuing exploration of writing as an ongoing process of imaginative and transgressive invention. This new, intensely modern sensibility encouraged a heightened self-reflexivity on the part of the writer at the level of enunciation. It also promoted further interest in theorizing on the ways in which words, linguistic structures, and conventional literary forms prescribe cultural codes for organizing reality and fiction. The material substance of literature was thus found to be subject to the same kinds of ideological pressures to conform that were already being challenged and resisted in other areas of the culture.

Considered within a broader sociocultural context, the new forms of literary modernity that gradually began to emerge in Quebec during the late 1960s signaled a pervasive loss of faith in what French theorist Jean-François Lyotard has termed "the metanarratives,"[37] those decisive (European) master discourses of history, philosophy, and religion that, as Alice Jardine has commented in turn, "have determined our sense of legitimacy in the West."[38] As I have already suggested, the master narratives in Quebec society that had traditionally played the most dominant roles in structuring both the institutions and a collective sense of cultural identity were Catholicism, conservative nationalism, and increasingly, North American materialist culture. Brossard's early theoretical positions and poetic practice emphatically broke with both the ideologies and the aesthetics that these various traditions had engendered. In an age of excessive materialistic consumption, argued Brossard, writing was becoming merely another form of blind accumulation, an additional encouragement for the construction of yet another Babel.[39] For Brossard and others publishing at *La Barre du jour,* the crisis of confidence in language was, to a large degree, the result of a historically grounded crisis of confidence in materialist culture itself.

Among Quebec intellectuals influenced by poststructuralist thought and among those at *La Barre du jour* in particular, the loss of confidence in traditional bourgeois values and the pervasive doubt of modernity led to a radical questioning of representational art and of the mimetic abilities of language to reproduce the real. Belief in the transparency of language thus came under increasing attack. Many of the experimental writers publishing in *La Barre du jour* during its early years worked to deprive words of their presumed "essence" and, in so doing, to demonstrate that words in themselves were no longer revered objects of predetermined meaning or signification. As a palpable object, Brossard wanted the word to become familiar, as she put it, "in the bursting, in the rupture. It's a matter of constructing the passkey word which no longer refers uniquely to emotional and intellectual notions, but which primarily creates its own variants: the word-consciousness in oppo-

sition to the word-convention."[40] By exploding conventional meanings, stripping language of anticipated syntax, encouraging the un-
mediated play of new associations, and leaving openings where
meanings were as yet undetermined, Brossard hoped to dismantle
the old logic of writing and, at the same time, to expand dramatically
the semantic system.

By 1970, Brossard's resolutely modern writing projected a certain
Derridian "indeterminacy" and unreadability, characteristics that
many critics of literary modernity now consider the hallmarks of
contemporary experimental writing. Filled with images of the abyss,
the void, the blank space yet to be filled, her texts affirmed the
idea of the now-waiting-to-be-discovered, of a future momentarily
inserting itself into the present where we least expect it. Yet in
the end, both the temporal break with the past and the textual
indeterminacy Brossard sought to explore failed to produce the kind
of experimental neutrality she had initially envisioned, for the very
notion of "neutrality" in the acts of reading and writing denies
the overriding force of determinants that both writer and reader
inevitably bring to any text. This troublesome ruse of neutrality in
the literature of *la modernité* is one with which a number of feminist
writers in Quebec have had to grapple. And it is an issue that
Brossard herself has since acknowledged as having been problematic
in her early works. As Mary Jacobus has also noted with regard to
the act of reading, "Privileging indeterminacy . . . risks ignoring
powerful determinants on the readings which a text may generate,
one of these determinants being the question of sexual difference
(whether signaled by its presence or its absence)."[41]

The heightened "suspicion" and general distancing established
between reader, writer, and the written word in Brossard's early
texts owed more to Blanchot, Barthes, and the French *nouveau
roman* than it did to an emerging feminist critique of patriarchal
thinking and the politics of sexual oppression. Yet despite the experimental anonymity she initially assigned herself as a writer (as an
unnamed and nongendered writing subject), Brossard, like Théoret,
became increasingly disturbed by the apparent erasure of sexual
difference from many avowedly "transgressive" texts. In contrast,
however, to the tenets of modernity that supported her gender-

neutral posture and formalist preoccupations, Brossard's notion of "the pleasure of the text" was already spilling out well beyond the boundaries of the page, creating a strangely intimate complicity between an as yet fractured, sexually "neutral" speaker and a reader whom she continually invited to participate in the seduction of reading ungrammatically and in new ways—of reading differently.

In texts published by Brossard and others in the early issues of *La Barre du jour,* the notion of distinct literary genres gradually withered away, while *textualité* and later *écriture* became the theoretical passwords for a growing number of unconventional writing practices that, among other things, refused the constraints of traditional genre distinctions and privileged the mixing of discourses or *interdiscursivity.* With the languages of poetry, prose, and theory no longer distinct, no longer hierarchized in many experimental texts, the door was thus being opened for the subsequent efforts of Quebec feminists to challenge the traditional marginalization of other forms of *écriture* as well, such as diaries, journals, letters, and autobiographical writing in general.

At the same time, the general orientation of *La Barre du jour* had become increasingly marked by the influence of new theoretical discourses from France: by Barthes' semiological practice and Blanchot's discussions of literary modernity, by the disruptive force of Derridian deconstruction, and finally by Cixous' modernist sensibility and radical philosophy of feminine desire. The keen interest in theory that gave this new writing its distinctive mark would significantly influence the feminist-inspired works of Brossard, Théoret, and numerous other women writing during the latter half of the 1970s. Likewise, the pivotal role Marxist theory had played in the nationalist debate of the 1960s and early 1970s also prepared Quebec women writers like Madeleine Gagnon to engage in feminist theorizing in virtually every kind of literary text. Given the strength of the two theoretical currents of nationalism and modernity, it is not surprising that feminist writers in Quebec have generally been less suspicious of theory than their American counterparts. Moreover, these cultural contexts also help explain why, as in France, the exploration of theory itself has become increasingly visible in the textual experimentation of Quebec women writers. As we shall see, they have been noticeably more inclined than American women writers to explore recent theoretical discussions on textuality and transgression (Blanchot, Barthes), the notion of "woman" as the unnameable other (Irigaray), the *différence* of feminine inscription (Cixous), and the need to displace binary oppositions and defer meaning (Derrida), issues that have been much debated in contemporary French critical thought during the last twenty years.

While the complexities of the transcontinental debates currently taking place over the significance and potential usefulness of terms such as *modernism, modernity,* and *postmodernism* cannot be properly addressed within the scope of this study, certain clarifications are necessary with respect to the use of these particular terms in Quebec. It is essential to note, for instance, that while the French notion of *modernité* is most commonly translated in the United States and even in English-speaking Canada by the term postmodernism, the use of the term *modernité* has had an important and culturally specific life of its own in Quebec, as I have attempted to outline above. Moreover, in Quebec, the term itself has never been entirely disassociated from the accelerated push toward modernization and the accompanying discourse of cultural autonomy that played important roles within the francophone province during the 1960s.

In his poetic reflections on experimental writing since the late 1960s, Quebec critic and poet Philippe Haeck argues that *modernité* has been a political as well as a cultural concept closely tied to a refusal of the conquest mentality. "Modernity is nothing more than this," affirms Haeck, "to be able to master, to take charge of ourselves, to think, to act on our own—a school of freedom."[42] To the extent that modernity's aesthetics in Quebec can be linked to the idea of separation from an oppressive cultural past and to an emerging taste for radical beginnings—as statements by the editors of *La Barre du jour* do in fact suggest—Haeck may be correct to view the roots of Quebec's literary modernity in the driving imperative of cultural affirmation that has marked the history of the province since the English Conquest. The logic of Haeck's position with respect to the unconscious political motivations in Quebec has a certain appeal. Could it be that because of the Conquest and of a conquered mentality in relation to the past, the affirmation of a collective identity in the late 1960s could only be played out for some Quebec writers through the textual creation of a radically new present?

While the word *modernité* has circulated more or less freely among Quebec writers and literary critics since the early 1970s and has been linked at one time or another to the names of very different kinds of experimental writers, including the four writers studied here, modernity's emphatically forward-looking stance has been criticized by some—and eventually by Brossard herself—as essentially ahistorical. At *La Barre du jour* in the early 1970s and in the subsequent efforts of a generation of writers interested in experimenting with the more formal properties of writing, this emphasis on a rupture with tradition and on a positively modern literature is not, in my view, sufficiently rendered by the postmodern label as it is now being used by American critics. For while the prefix *post* has not always conveyed the notion of temporal posteriority in recent discussions of postmodernism,[43] it is nevertheless difficult to rid the word entirely of the suggestion of coming after in time, of occurring in response to modernism. The current use in some Quebec circles of the term *postfeminism* to define a cultural perspective nurtured on and coming after feminism is further proof that the temporal dimension of the prefix can never be altogether eradicated. Indeed, to underscore the relevance of chronology in the use of the term postfeminism, Toril Moi points out that "true post-feminism is impossible without post-patriarchy."[44]

In the case of contemporary Quebec writing, postmodernism thus becomes a somewhat slippery and ambiguous term since the modernist experiment that gained such influence as a prior artistic and intellectual movement in Europe during the early part of the twentieth century did not assume the same shape in Quebec or enjoy the same kind of influence.[45] And although use of the postmodern label is now becoming more visible in Quebec, it is once again a term generated from an external metacritical discourse that tends to gloss over cultural differences and historical contexts in favor of unifying philosophical and artistic currents—a troublesome contradiction, to be sure, when considering the postmodern penchant for valorizing brokenness, marginality, and plurality, as well as its presumed resistance to master codes and metanarratives.[46]

If anything, I would argue that postmodernism in Quebec is a relatively recent development that, at least in terms of contemporary literary production, seeks to expand upon the sphere of the modern in a predominately postreferendum or postindependence era by opening it up even more completely to a proliferation of competing codes, ideological positions, historical moments, and dissonant critical discourses.[47] While Quebec's literature of *modernité* has stressed the disjunctions, the radically other, and the ways in which writing itself may be conceived as a form of transgression as well as a self-consciously affirmative pleasure, *le postmoderne* in Quebec leans toward a reconciliation with the past, toward the incorporation of numerous intertexts and notions of heterogeneity that encourage an eclectic collage of earlier forms of literary expression.

Furthermore, whereas the notion of *modernité* in Quebec cannot escape its own contentious beginnings—an explicit critique of a conservative and constraining past and of the outmoded transparency of realist art, the era of *le postmoderne* appears to be establishing a somewhat different stance with regard to history. As Linda Hutcheon puts it, postmodernism "marks a challenge to received ideas, but it also acknowledges the power of those ideas and is willing to exploit that power in order to effect its own critique."[48] While some have argued that the postmodern aesthetic is, in effect, a trivializing of history and a worrisome form of recuperation, Hutcheon sees it as "the site of internalized change." In a somewhat similar vein, Janet Paterson speaks of "the poetics of transformation" in postmodern fiction in Quebec, emphasizing its "multi-faceted and heterogeneous investigation" of disparate elements.[49] It is probably too soon to determine whether the notion of the postmodern will eventually subsume many of the specific characteristics attributed to Quebec's writing of *la modernité,* but for the moment it seems clear that these two terms are not as interchangeable, historically speaking, as some literary critics would have us believe.[50]

Feminist Misgivings about Modernity

The interest generated in the experimental techniques and transgressive stance of literary modernity and in Brossard's work in particular announced the beginning of the end for many of the forms and thematic concerns of representational art in modern Quebec. It also resulted in an undermining of the assumption that realist texts with overtly political content were the privileged literary sites of revolutionary thought. For Brossard and others writing in *La Barre du jour,* the entire mimetic enterprise of conventional art had, in effect, been called into question, while the new focus of inquiry became for a while the process and pleasure of writing itself. This exploratory approach to the materiality of language had, to be sure, its own politically subversive intent. Moreover, various strands of the sensibility most associated with literary modernity in Quebec, and particularly with modernity's transgressive, exploratory approach to writing, clearly helped prepare the way for the experimental project of writing in the feminine. Eventually, however, a number of feminists, including France Théoret, began to challenge literary modernity's refusal to distinguish between fiction and reality, between the realm of imaginative invention and real historical events.

Initially drawn to the radicality of the new formalist project at *La Barre du jour,* France Théoret feared nevertheless that a possible negative result of modernity's apparent need to "bracket off the referent or real historical world"—to quote Terry Eagleton—might be the bracketing off of political forces capable of promoting progressive social change."[51] The virtual erasure of history in the formalist texts of modernity, like the eclipse of the gendered subject, meant that for Théoret, the speaking subject was becoming "a textual presence abstracted from its history." Furthermore, she argued, "This speaking subject (in formalism) has no social inscription, no individual history and belongs to no nation, generation, or gender/genre. If formalism has brought about the revision of an undeniably gossipy element in literature, it has also tended to make literature aseptic."[52] Even some of the most unsympathetic critics of women's experimental writing in Quebec have recognized the importance of the real social conditions of history that feminist writers such as Brossard and Théoret would eventually bring back to the deconstructive project of *modernité*.[53]

From a woman's point of view, the evacuation of the real and the real speaking subject from many of the more experimentally modern texts in Quebec could only encourage self-denial and self-effacement, a dilemma that ultimately led a number of women writers concerned with feminist issues to rethink the cultural bases of *modernité* for women in general. On a more personal level, France Théoret has candidly acknowledged her own recurrent feelings of failure as a writer during her association with *La Barre du jour:* "We weren't supposed to be a woman. If you were a woman, you introduced something about the order of existence into writing and that was semanticizing writing, returning to representation. In fact, we were supposed to flee representation. It was not allowed to take place in any way."[54]

By the mid-1970s, Brossard herself was publicly admitting the serious risks women engaged in formalist writing practices ran because their texts often effaced any sense of the historical along with the identity of the speaking subject, thereby blurring important distinctions between fiction and the reality of women's daily lives. In addition, a number of Quebec women writers already interested in the writing practices of *la modernité* were becoming increasingly preoccupied with the political concerns of the feminist movements in Quebec, in France, and in the United States. Brossard, Gagnon, Bersianik, Théoret, and others began to experiment with new approaches to writing that could address—both theoretically and poetically—the problematic position and frequent "absence" of women in language, in writing, and in the culture as a whole. Concerned with linking the forward-looking direction of modernity—and in the case of Gagnon in particular, of socialism—to the political agendas of various feminist groups, they also began to reconsider the relationships between political theory (traditionally male) and cultural production (also predominantly male); between language and gender (historically male constructions); between the realms of the symbolic (inaccessible to women, said Lacan), the imaginary, and the concrete realm of women's daily lives; and between a sexuality that had long been repressed in a largely church-dominated culture and the authoritative power of the (male) word.

If Quebec's literature of modernity raised the question of how *one* writes and promoted the "pleasures of the text" in terms that were presumably gender-neutral, by the mid-1970s feminist writers were focusing increasingly on the question of who is writing and on the problem of female identity in a patriarchal culture that denies women's presence. Brossard, Théoret, and others began to rethink the relationship between the subjectivity women aspire to and the language needed to voice that vision. These and other questions issuing out of the encounter between feminism and modernity began to surface in a growing number of their texts. Were the very notions of pleasure, body, urbanity, and even transgression itself—themes so dear to many "resolutely modern" writers in Quebec—actually indifferent notions? Or were such themes (over)determined by an avant-garde discourse that, for all its pretense to subversion, remained locked in struggle and, so far as the question of gender was concerned, in collusion with the dominant patriarchal culture? Was literary modernity yet another (male) model for the "anxiety of literary influence," typifying, as in some ways it did, the rivalry between fathers and sons?[55] Could the mother, the maternal, *la maternité* actually be "modern"?[56] On what grounds did many of the forms of literary modernity commonly exclude the historical—and for whose benefit? Questions such as these could no longer be ignored.

Many feminist writers in Quebec were, of course, quick to acknowledge the extent to which the language women use is also intricately bound up with psychological constructs and socioeconomic systems that have traditionally been designed by men. Thus, like the deconstructive writers of *modernité* who had attempted to sever their ties with bourgeois values through radical experimentations with language and through continuing efforts to underscore the material production of the text, a number of women writers followed suit in a feminist vein and began calling for the disruption and repudiation of conventional male-oriented discourse, often using similar deconstructive strategies for their own political purposes.

But for some, including Brossard, Gagnon, Bersianik, and Théoret, the notion of a writing of transgression was not, in itself, enough. Their need to invent other modes of writing was directly linked to a pressing and doubtless more overriding desire to stress their presence as women in the creative process and in the culture at large.

Louise Dupré has characterized the relationship between the more formal orientation of literary modernity and a feminist-inspired writing of difference in the following way: "The feminist project has made poetry move on from *experimentation* to *experience,* for there has been a real coincidence between research into form and enunciation of a feminine signified."[57] With respect to both the search for different modes of feminine inscription and to the important emphasis placed on the position of the woman writer in her text, France Théoret has further clarified this shift from formal experimentation to experience in many recent texts by insisting that "Language in the feminine has situated its problematic in the area of enunciation. The speaking subject becomes at times the central figure in writing, as does its social and individual inscription."[58] This emphasis on the difficult yet pressing need to insert the female subject into discourse has also meant that the very notion of gender and, more specifically, of what it means to be a woman has had to be addressed in a variety of settings as well.

"The Personal is Political" and the Encounter with American Feminism

While the influence of the left within the Parti Québécois decreased rather quickly during the latter half of the 1970s, the same could also be said of its fading influence among a growing number of Quebec feminists. As Diane Lamoureux notes, by 1976 many of the feminists who had at one time actively participated in socialist feminist groups or in radical feminist groups with strong nationalist sympathies had all but abandoned traditional Marxist analyses and Third World nationalism as their principal frames of reference. Increasingly, women's groups grew dissatisfied with the left's insistence on the institution of the State as the sole focus of struggle, a focus that was maintained at the expense, feminists argued, of the social and the private spheres.[59]

Instead of relying heavily on the male-authored political and social theories of the left as a number of Quebec feminists had initially done in the late 1960s and early 1970s, radical feminists in Quebec were turning increasingly toward one another; toward the tradition of women in Quebec who had preceded them, mothered them, and educated them; toward the collective exchange of views from women of different backgrounds, classes, and cultures; and toward the theoretical contributions of a growing international feminist community in order to build a theoretical framework based directly on women's experience. Radical feminists in Quebec were also encouraging the practice of a more decidedly women-centered politics that would no longer function as a mere appendage to Marxist theories of economic exploitation and class struggle or to the vision of independence of leftist nationalists. In an interview with *Le Devoir* in 1979, Louky Bersianik explains in simple terms the orientation of her own feminist politics and her writing: "I am a radical feminist in the sense that my struggle is based on the specific oppression of women. And the enemy to overthrow is the patriarchy."[60]

One collective example of a growing dissatisfaction with the male-oriented left was the appearance in 1976 of the important radical feminist newspaper, *Les Têtes de Pioche (The Hard Heads)*, founded by France Théoret, Nicole Brossard, Michèle Jean, and three others. In an editorial published in 1978, Quebec historian Michèle Jean cited the theoretical single-mindedness of the male-inspired left in Quebec, its seemingly exclusionary hold on the "truth," and its unwillingness to consider the progressive common ground on which women of different classes might usefully stand as the primary reasons for the incontrovertible schism that was steadily widening between a number of leftist and radical feminist groups.[61]

Yet even among the members of the *Têtes de Pioche* collective, issues of class solidarity, sisterhood, and the politics of sexual preference were problematic at best and the source of much questioning and dissension about the initial political direction of the group.

France Théoret was one of several members who left this writing collective as a result of internal political disputes. As Armande Saint-Jean candidly notes in her discussion of the evolution of the *Têtes de Pioche* collective, "The principal sources of conflict and tension between the successive collective members were based on three types of differences: ideological (the radical feminists versus the feminist Marxists), class (the feminists with working-class backgrounds versus the feminists with bourgeois roots), and sexual (the lesbian feminists as opposed to the heterosexual feminists)."[62]

As far as the newspaper itself was concerned, however, the editorial stance of *Les Têtes de Pioche* was remarkably consistent. On the whole, the radical feminist perspectives articulated from 1976 to 1979 in most of the collective's articles and editorials targeted the patriarchal family and the patriarchal character of existing social policies, political institutions, and cultural myths as the structural foundations of misogyny and male supremacy in Quebec culture. The newspaper called on women to work together to analyze and theorize about the nature of their oppression and to create their own networks of collective resistance and strategies for liberation. Undoubtedly one of the most important contributions of the *Têtes de Pioche* collective to the feminist debates in Quebec was the adaptation and affirmation of the popular American feminist slogan, "The personal is political." For their second issue, which appeared in April of 1976 while France Théoret was still an active member of the collective, Nicole Brossard wrote an important lead article that suggested the large scope intended by the concept of the personal as a political sphere. As we shall see in subsequent chapters, what has motivated much of the thematic focus of writing in the feminine in Quebec is elucidated in Brossard's own reading of the phrase, "La vie privée est politique":

Personal life is the life of a body that eats, sleeps, has orgasms, defecates, sweats, touches, breathes, a body that knows pleasure (*qui jouit*). It's the hidden story of the body suppressed behind the walls of the family home, the clinic, or the reform school. Personal life is when we argue, when we come to blows; when we have been violated, when we beat our kids, when we make love, when we choke from happiness, when we become alcoholics, when we suffer from insomnia; when we marry, when we give birth, when we witness the death of our father or our mother. It's the hidden story of women. It's the story that men suppress. What we call "personal life" (*vie privée*) is essentially the relationship we maintain with our bodies and with those of others. If, for myself, this relationship is political, it's because outside the house this relationship continues, but this time mediated by social values which seem to withdraw the body's right to assert itself. Based on how we conceive of our intimate relationship with our own body, a whole series of behavioral patterns and social attitudes ensue from which subjectivity has presumably been excluded by negating the body when it works, when it projects itself, when it confronts the powers that use it for their own ends.[63]

By the mid-1970s, then, the socialist feminist politics of activist women in Quebec were being influenced substantially by the radical feminist current in the American women's movement. In particular, there was growing interest in the new theorizing in the United States and France on the sources of women's oppression in the dominant male culture. An activist in union politics at the Université du Québec in Montreal for a number of years, Madeleine Gagnon has expressed some of the reasons for this change in the direction of Quebec feminism in terms of her own personal experience within the university setting. For her, the work site of students, professors, and supporting staff reflected both the structure and institutional dynamics of sexual politics at all levels of patriarchal culture.

It's in her place of work, her place of everyday activity, that woman can act. Concretely. We, as university women, live in a privileged setting but we are not any less cornered, any less a minority. 98% of the bosses are men, 90% subordinate employees, women who suffer the effects of sexism in a more refined fashioned—violated with words, beaten with concepts—but how devastating nevertheless. The role of women in the university—secretaries, women students, professors at every level—is to speak, to change the direction of things, to put mechanisms in place. To react to this subtle power, this power of SEDUCTION to which women students and secretaries answer out of VENERATION. Look out for those who don't participate in this game of SEDUCTION, who reject it. . . .[64]

Quebec feminist historians and writers alike generally agree that American feminism played a considerable role during the latter half of the 1970s in prompting the gradual shift for many Quebec feminists on the left from predominantly nationalist and materialist approaches to women's issues to a more emphatically woman-centered view of gender politics in patriarchal cultures. Already in the early 1970s, Quebec feminism in its various forms had been marked by the initial militancy of some radical feminists in the United States as well as by the more pragmatic orientation of many "mainstream" American feminists interested in creating a more equitable place for women within existing institutions and within the established system of government. Shortly thereafter, many Quebec feminists all along the political spectrum were reading the landmark works of Kate Millett, Shulamith Firestone, Adrienne Rich, and the Australian-born Germaine Greer. At a time when Quebec was, itself, looking outward and when aspiring *indépendantistes* within the Parti Québécois were attempting to carve out a place for Quebec in the international community as a future nation state, Quebec feminists were also expanding their frames of reference to include the political activism and theoretical analyses of feminists from other countries.

The influence of American feminism in Quebec was widespread for a variety of reasons. The proximity of the United States, the extensive media coverage in Quebec of American political issues and events—including the growing women's movement, the visits of Germaine Greer in 1971 and Kate Millett in 1973, the teach-ins on women in Quebec universities modeled on the American approach of politicizing the academy—all worked to link Quebec feminists to an English-speaking women's movement in the United States from which most of them had remained relatively cutoff during the late 1960s and early 1970s. By 1976, there was also a growing perception among a number of Quebec feminists that American and Quebec women on the left had gone through similarly radicalizing experiences and that they may also have received similar treatment in male-dominated groups during the anti-war movement in the United States and during the height of socialist nationalist organizing in Quebec in the late 1960s.

The initial radical feminist current in Quebec grew out of a desire to "feminize" the political ideals and the more pragmatic organizational politics of socialist nationalism in the early 1970s. However, the kinds of issues with which Quebec radical feminists identified in the latter half of the decade were much more closely tied to the radical feminist perspectives developing in the United States and, to a lesser extent perhaps, in France as well. Abortion, rape, violence toward women, lesbianism and lesbian rights, and sexism in the media, in the schools, and in the practices of the male medical establishment became the central issues of radical feminism in Quebec, echoing the preoccupations of several currents in American feminism during approximately the same period of time. Feminist consciousness-raising groups in the United States, with their emphasis on collective support and the sharing of personal experience and repressed material, also became a dynamic model for radical feminists in Quebec in the mid-1970s. The number of women's collectives, women's centers, and general women's resources in Quebec grew dramatically during the same period. The interest of Brossard and Bersianik in American feminist thought is well known. In addition to her frequent references to Anglo-American feminist thought, Nicole Brossard also made a film with Luce Guilbeault during 1975 and 1976 entitled *Some American Feminists,* a project that appears to have been motivated by their mutual desire to turn the attention of Quebec women to the development and contributions of radical feminist thought in the United States.

The frequently acknowledged debt to feminist thought in the United States is especially strong with respect to the writings of Adrienne Rich and Mary Daly—the former for the physicality of her feminist poetics, the latter for her bold efforts to tear through the fabric of patriarchal mythologies and to refashion language to celebrate women's "converging power."[65] Further parallels could also be drawn between the experimental writing of Quebec feminists and the radical poetic theorizing of Audre Lorde, especially in the welding of poetry and political praxis through what Lorde herself has termed "a revelatory distillation of experience." And in a much cited phrase whose political perspective reverberates throughout the writings of Brossard, Gagnon, Bersianik, and Théoret, Lorde adds that for women, "poetry is not a luxury."[66] Likewise, for the writers discussed here, writing is an indispensable facet of feminist thinking and feminist practice.

As the decade drew to a close, the collective political agenda of various radical feminist groups in Quebec—although not without their own internal and external conflicts—paralleled many of the positions taken by radical feminists in the United States as well. In a relatively short period of time and despite the notable differences of national histories and cultural traditions, the bond between American and Quebec radical feminists had become remarkably strong. For the four Quebec writers in question, the historical complexities of Quebec culture and even the most influential aspects of French theorizing on the feminine have thus been traversed by political issues and theoretical perspectives grounded in the realities of contemporary North American life and persuasively addressed by leading American feminist thinkers.

In an essay from a volume published in 1987, France Théoret reflects on the literary consequences of the American feminist connection, noting among other things the importance of a creative feminine space grounded in the politics of the real world. The language of Kate Millett and Mary Daly, Théoret argues, oscillates between classical analysis and poetic invention. For a number of feminists writing in Quebec since the mid-1970s, this mixing of tone and discursive strategies has been crucial for the development of their own theoretical fiction and poetic theory. Most important, Théoret finds that "the American nature of this writing [*écriture au féminin*] can be seen in statements that offer a direct and spontaneous mixture of the intimate and the social, the everyday and the learned. When reading it, we have the impression of a utopia which already exists, a utopia which promises nothing more than that the imaginary realm become visible in language."[67]

French Theory and Inscriptions of Difference

Intellectual debates in France have exerted considerable influence on feminist thought in Quebec, particularly among feminist writers, academics, and intellectuals. French philosophical disputes over the configuration of "woman" in contemporary psychoanalytic thought, as well as related discussions concerning women's position in language and in the realm of the symbolic, have been followed by a small but articulate number of Quebec feminists with considerable interest. There is, moreover, a particular way in which the French call for an *écriture féminine* appears to bridge radical feminist theories of women's difference with a more uniquely Québécois malaise about speaking and writing that stems from their own sense of cultural marginality and otherness. In Quebec, however, writing in the feminine has not been viewed as a writing practice in which all or even many women writers engage. On the contrary, there is a cultural specificity to this concept that must be emphasized. For a number of feminists writing in Quebec, the notion of an *écriture au féminin* has developed as a political project, that is to say, as a potentially useful strategy for subverting conventional literary forms, deconstructing patriarchal thought, and asserting the central-ity of women's experience in writing. Indeed, for the writers exam-ined in this study, the project of writing as a woman and from a woman's place has invited the inscription of what announces itself as "the *very possibility of change,* the space that can serve as a spring-board for subversive thought, the precursory movement of a trans-formation of social and cultural structures."[68]

Hélène Cixous' much-discussed invitation to women to "write themselves" in another language captures the new point of departure and the new spirit of women's experimental writing in Quebec after 1975: "Woman must write her self: must write about women and bring women to writing, from which they have been driven away as violently as from their bodies—for the same reasons, by the same law, with the same fatal goal," affirms Cixous. "Woman must put herself into the text—as into the world and into history—by her own movement."[69] Although on the whole, the work of Luce Irigaray has probably been more influential than the writing of Hélène Cixous, the four writers discussed in this study appear to have read Cixous' works as well as the works of other theoreticians of women's differ-ence such as Annie Leclerc and Claire Lejeune with genuine interest. The writings of Julia Kristeva, on the other hand, have until recently generated considerably less enthusiasm.

Certainly, the 1972–73 seminars that Cixous gave in Montreal furthered the discussion of her thought and work among Quebec intellectuals and students alike. While too abstract and elitist for some, recent French theoretical discussions of women's identity, language, and access to the symbolic have sparked numerous women writers in Quebec to view their own "coming to writing" as a serious site of feminist inquiry. And in so doing, many have approached the writing process as a textual investigation of the relationships between writing, repression, and male authority, between gender and the imaginary.

Along with other feminist writers in Quebec who are troubled by the inherent complicity under patriarchy between discourse and power, between the father's word and institutional authority, Brossard, Gagnon, Bersianik, and Théoret have conceived the project of writing "otherwise"—against and possibly even outside paternal reason, truth, and phallic desire—as a radical attempt to destablize and ultimately dislocate the phallocentric hierarchy, both real and symbolic. On the level of textuality, the project of writing in the feminine in Quebec has also prompted continuing efforts to derange patriarchal discourse by overthrowing its syntax, "by suspending its eternally teleological order," as French theorist Luce Irigaray would have it, "by snipping the wires, cutting the current, breaking the circuits, switching the connections, by modifying continuity, alternation, frequency, intensity."[70]

The regions opened up by this new territory of feminist theorizing and feminine inscription appear to be boundless, the terrain constantly fluctuating. Experimental efforts by Brossard, Gagnon, Bersianik, and Théoret have unveiled a vast, ever-shifting field of linguistic discovery not unlike what Luce Irigaray refers to in her own work as the "flowing," "fluctuating," "excess" of women's discourse,[71] and not unlike the haunting depths of Hélène Cixous' oceanic expanses or the liberating "flight" (*vol*) she attributes to women who dare to "steal" (*vole*) the words of men and make them their own.[72] The notion of theft—of a willful and joyous thieving—is, in fact, at the very center of many of these texts. Yet surely this emphasis on feminist thieving and retrieving is not surprising since language has traditionally been the property of men, rendered property through a politics of unequal distribution and hoarding that, as we know, spans much of western history.

In addition to their more general call to women to speak and to write "otherwise," Cixous and Irigaray have proposed a number of theoretical constructs that have significantly influenced women's experimental writing in Quebec during the last twenty years. Several of the positions developed by Cixous as part of her radical critiques of Freud and Lacan have been crucial. In particular, her privileging

of the imaginary over the symbolic, of excess and desire over censorship and repression, have helped map the direction of feminist
inquiry in many of the texts to be discussed in this study.[73] Cixous'
notion of a writing practice in which sexuality and textuality continuously intertwine has also been at the center of feminist literary
explorations in Quebec for well over a decade. Likewise, Irigaray's
feminist critiques of the "blind spots" of western metaphysics have
been timely and empowering. Her contention, moreover, that phallocentric discourse constructs an erroneous image of man as a unified, centered, and clearly defined subject while projecting an image
of woman as a pale reflection (at best) of that same identity, has
been particularly important for the writers in question.

While the extent of the influence of Irigaray and Cixous—certainly the most well-known French theoreticians of feminine difference—may be difficult to assess summarily, it does appear that many
of their deconstructive moves against phallocentrism along with a
number of more affirmative efforts to valorize the feminine have
resurfaced under various guises in the feminist-inspired texts of
Brossard, Gagnon, Bersianik, and Théoret. The process of rethink-
ing the functions and transformational power of language from the
point of view of women has prompted these four writers and others
in Quebec to develop textual strategies that work to displace hierarchical thinking by dismantling conventional writing practices. At
the same time, each of the writers examined in this study has sought
to reposition the discussion of women's identity around the more
fluid and expansive concepts of movement, fluctuation, contradiction, and plurality—concepts clearly identifiable with the somewhat
different, but nevertheless contiguous projects of Cixous and Irigaray.

Faced with an oppressive and often overtly hostile environment
for women, Brossard considers the notion of an *écriture au féminin*—or what she has sometimes termed *écriture féminine*—both as
an imaginative site on which to construct new identities for women
and as an indication of the emerging desire of contemporary women
to transform themselves, both individually and collectively, into
autonomous agents in the process of signification. During the last
decade, Brossard and Bersianik have used the terms *écriture au*

féminin and *écriture féminine* to speak of feminine modes of writing. Yet although the latter is an obvious borrowing from Hélène Cixous, Brossard, Bersianik, and Théoret have—unlike Cixous—consistently understood their own approach to writing in the feminine as a gender-marked experimental writing practice in which women alone are engaged, rather than as an anti-logocentric or anti-phallocentric approach to writing that male and female writers alike might pursue. "To write in the feminine," affirms Brossard, "means that women must work at making their own hope and history, in the one place where these can take shape, where there is *textual matter*."[74] Cixous, on the other hand, has gone to considerable length to clarify her notion of *écriture féminine* as a writing practice that hinges on a libidinal economy that is "genital," without necessitating that a writer be either male or female.[75]

For each of the writers in this study, however, writing in the feminine has entailed the inventive mapping of women's resistance to patriarchal thinking as well as the continuing expansion of female subjectivity through the fusing of feminist theory, poetry, and fiction. Brossard argues that for women, recent gender-marked approaches to writing are beginning to provide a space of radical opening or *ouverture* in the world where the woman writer's personal and political aspirations may finally join in the thoroughly dangerous expression of her own desirous being: "Desire slowly emanates from what is inadmissible in her project: transformation of the self, and the collectivity. Inadmissible will to change life, to change her life."[76]

While Brossard's writing stretches toward the utopian future and toward the invention of new forms of seeing and being-in-the-world, the works of Bersianik continually question and reassess women's relations to the past and to the language and symbolic constructs of the fathers. "To transform darkness into light, to give new energy to the imagination's symbolizing function, to convert existing symbols, to manipulate them according to a new symbolic logic so that they emerge with new resonances, new interpretations, this is the task of creative feminists," wrote Bersianik in 1986.[77] Ever cognizant of the biased readings of male critics, she also cautions women writers against thinking that literary expressions of the male imaginary are somehow more universal than their own. Moreover, for women who have never been encouraged to know themselves or to establish a concept of their own female subjectivity in writing, even explorations into the most intimate and creative realms of the imagination cannot be undertaken apolitically—without regard to the material en-gendering of consciousness itself.

Writing with Women Present

For the writers in this study, creating a significant space in which the voices of other women can be heard involves more than merely inserting a cast of female characters and a myriad of "women's issues" into their texts. In the case of Louky Bersianik, writing in the feminine appears to result in continuing gestures of women-identification throughout her work in an effort to reclaim the text as a site of women's political strength, collective affirmation, and artistic nourishment. This activist stance evolves out of resistance, confrontation, and rupture with male-oriented history and leads, in turn, to the unearthing and rediscovery of other women—past and present. Bersianik refuses, however, to view the displacements and creative reconstructions she initiates as a simple reversal of the male-female dichotomy. Indeed, she argues that when viewed in its broadest conceptual framework, feminism requires not only rigorous analyses of sexual politics and accompanying proposals to correct the unequal relations of the sexes, but also "the capacity to 'think from the outside' in order to create another world . . . where new relations of reciprocity and new values would come into being, the will to create an imaginary space in this world as well via language because it is language that conveys reality and transports fiction."[78]

Rescuing the silenced voices of forgotten women in their own texts as well, Madeleine Gagnon and France Théoret have invoked the reappropriative powers extended to women through the act of writing as a way of contesting the political marginalization and general disconnectedness women have experienced in patriarchal culture. Both Gagnon and Théoret have been highly conscious of the evolving political awareness they and other feminist writers want to inspire in their readers, and both have demonstrated over

the years varying degrees of kinship with Marxist readings of literature, recognizing that writing is never politically neutral, never
entirely indifferent to the dominant ideological forces already in
place during the period in which it is produced. The social implications of the act of writing have thus been given considerable attention in their own creative theories as well as in their actual writing
practice. As Brossard, Gagnon, Bersianik, and Théoret have in their
different ways envisioned it, writing in the feminine is an effort to
move beyond the realm of the "purely literary" (in any restricted
sense of the term) toward a broader view of cultural production
and to embrace the various forms of linguistic disruption, poetic
reappropriation, and overtly political critique designed to subvert
male authority and to protest the silencing of women throughout
much of our history. It is primarily in this regard that each of the
four writers discussed here may be said to view her own experimental writing practice as a real mode of political intervention and
resistance rather than merely as an abstract and culturally disengaged
intellectual project.

For Brossard, Gagnon, Bersianik, and Théoret, writing in the
feminine has meant contemplating women's differences in all their
conceivable forms of expression—philosophical, psychological, intellectual, biological, sociological, political, and aesthetic. From a
political standpoint, the project of writing in the feminine has
resulted in a new feminist-inspired poetics that valorizes other ways
of writing, of relating, and of reimagining the world that are unmistakably marked by the presence of women. In a text written in 1975,
Brossard records both the personal and the collective realignment
taking place in women's writing at that time when she describes the
dramatic shift in her own stance vis-à-vis her readers and her work:
"I wrote in a common-law relationship with and while men were
reading me. But, deep down, I write only under a woman's gaze,
feverishly received. Between us, the descent."[79]

In retrospect, Brossard's comments capture exceptionally well an
important current of feminist literary production during the mid-
1970s. Indeed, the notion of writing to, through, and for other
women quickly becomes a central theme of this newly emerging

feminist poetics. For many of these writers, however, writing for other women is more than merely a political stance of feminist solidarity and, as in the case of Brossard, an equally important affirmation of lesbian identity; it also serves as a route to creative discovery, as a way of inviting and responding to the presence of women readers and as a way of investing the text with the sustenance and the complicitous presence of a female angle of vision.

Recognizing the collective nature of their efforts to approach writing differently and acknowledging their historical ties to other women writers as well, Brossard, Gagnon, Bersianik, and Théoret have made frequent and effective use of a variety of literary techniques to underscore the plurality of women's voices that traverse their own literary explorations. Bersianik has consciously sought to incorporate the many sources of her own literary and political inspiration through the voices of other women. References in her writing to Mary Daly, Phyllis Chesler, Adrienne Rich, Margaret Mead, Luce Irigaray, Awa Thiam, and others are central to Bersianik's notion of the necessity of developing an international vantage point for feminist creation. And while Brossard has often cited writers such as Mary Daly, Adrienne Rich, Ti-Grace Atkinson, Monique Wittig, Virginia Woolf, Djuna Barnes, and Gertrude Stein in her work, France Théoret has conjured up the presence of Marie-Claire Blais, Virginia Woolf, Colette, and a silent aunt whose potentially dangerous words were carefully kept under wraps.

Madeleine Gagnon, on the other hand, has looked to Annie Leclerc, Eva Forest, Marguerite Duras, her own grandmother, and to women collectively for inspiration, literary companionship, and solidarity. In a preface to Denise Boucher's *Cyprine,* Gagnon celebrates the intentional references to other women writers in many of these new and increasingly unclassifiable approaches to writing in the feminine. She also extends the concept of women addressing women in feminist-inspired texts by suggesting that women readers are themselves writers of the text since they harbor the writer's own words within them. In so doing, Gagnon debunks the old myth of the privileged poetic voice that, by virtue of being elevated and alone, could enlighten others.

We're going to tell them what resemblances we share. How we repeat ourselves, plagiarize one another; how our writings become collective. How we will never again be wretched and clandestine little poets. Separated in their anthologies, their analyses, their libraries, their dissecting tables, their literary prizes, their competitions that divide. Their competition. Their little individual genius not like anyone else. We speak your words to all [women]: me too, me too; I could have written it; I'll write it for you; you'll write it for me. Others and others still.[80]

For Bersianik, conjuring up the voices and contributions of women writers over the centuries is a necessary political act of recollection and recognition. Integrated into women's texts in a variety of ways, *la parole des femmes* or what Bersianik herself has ironically christened "*la Parole sans Histoire*" (the Word without History),[81] has exploded the concept of a single, neutral poetic voice and forced history back into the text. Thus, while particular historical stances vary considerably (Brossard addresses the women of tomorrow, Bersianik looks to the women of our mythologized past, Gagnon speaks to her contemporaries in struggle, and Théoret speaks to women of all ages entrapped in cultural myths), the notion of writing to other women as a form of acknowledgment, encouragement, and political identification is clearly at the core of the literary experiment of writing in the feminine. This stance of solidarity can be noted in the public sphere as well. Indeed, it is not coincidental that the number of collective women's writing projects and poetry readings in Quebec began to mount swiftly after 1975. Because of the plurality of voices speaking in many of these experimental texts, writing in the feminine in Quebec has often meant writing in the feminine plural, invoking the voices of others in order to encourage and nourish the woman writer's indefatigable impulse to name herself and, in so doing, rename her relations with others.

Our Bodies in Writing

The year 1977 marked a decisive turning point for women's writing in Quebec as the centrality of the female body became increasingly apparent in numerous experimental works. The series of short texts appearing in *La Barre du jour* in the summer of 1977 conveyed both the new physicality of women's writing and the extent to which the expression of this physicality was becoming multifaceted, poetically distinctive, and increasingly political. The title of this special issue draws attention to feminist theorizing on the physicality of women's language and to the emerging poetics of the female body as text:

le corps	(body)
les mots	(words)
l'imaginaire	(imaginary)

Along with the words themselves, the iconography of the issue's title is particularly revealing. When read from top to bottom, the vertical, nonlinear distribution of three key concepts in Quebec's *écriture au féminin* exemplifies a new mode of conceptualizing the female body as a generator of women's words and of the feminine imaginary as well. When read from bottom to top, the body is the inscribed result of the feminine imaginary put into words. In both cases, the interconnection and necessary interplay of body, words, and the imaginary inform us that for the group of women contributing to this special volume (which included Brossard, Gagnon, Bersianik, and Théoret), creativity and language continually flow out of and back through the female body. Since the female body has, until recently, rarely been seen or read from a woman's vantage point, this writing from and toward women's bodies must therefore be viewed as an important effort to recontextualize and reshape the substance (the physical matter) of women's writing in Quebec.

Historically speaking, it is worth reiterating that the repression of the female body in writing and in real life has often been more overt and more fiercely maintained in Quebec than in either France or the United States, due to the pervasive cultural and political influence of a conservative Catholic Church. During the 1950s, 1960s, and early 1970s, a number of Quebec's critically acclaimed women writers such as Claire Martin, Marie-Claire Blais, and Anne Hébert began to expose a number of the social, political, and familial attitudes reinforced by Church dogma that have traditionally defined, molded, and restricted the female body in Quebec. Yet despite the gravity of their critiques, it is important to emphasize that, with respect to the female body, a crucial conceptual change has occurred in the more recent experimental writings of Brossard, Gagnon, Bersianik, Théoret and others. This discursive transformation involves not only an important shift from thematics to textuality, but also a striking change of focus from victimization to self-affirmation, from the forces acting upon women's bodies to the power women possess to reposition their bodies as active agents in the political, social, and artistic spheres. Hence the female body previously defined and contained by existing cultural norms has become a body actively engaged in the transformation of those same norms and of culture itself. The significance of this evolving view of women's bodies in writing should not be underestimated, even by those most critical of the "essentialist problem."

Many critics have already noted the pronounced presence of the female body in the writings of Quebec feminists by the mid-1970s. Highlighting the extreme physicality of their literary explorations, Marcelle Brisson has defined the recent advent of "feminist writing" in Quebec as a writing of the body (*"écriture du corps"*) in which the female writer puts her body into words in order to discover and recover herself. Brisson views this dramatic move toward corporeal inscription in the works of Quebec feminists as a politically motivated search for identity—personal and collective—and as a reappropriation of the right to speak of and about the female body from a woman's point of view. Brisson also portrays this new writing of the body as a more general affirmation of women's physical difference: "Woman's writing says to us: This is my body. It starts from there and returns there. It is a constant in this writing, regardless of whether or not we situate it before or after the avant-garde philosophical movements of its time. Woman writes from her own hills and caverns and mountains. . . . If there is no reference to the body, there is no feminist writing."[82]

Although undoubtedly overstating the case in her attempt to categorize various forms of feminist-inspired writing in Quebec, Brisson's analysis does underscore the central placement of the female body in many experimental texts and, by extension, resituates the physicality of women's discourse that works to displace phallocentric thinking and thereby to alter the relationship between the center and the periphery in patriarchal culture. For despite the remarkably wide range of formal structures, themes, and generating symbolisms that Quebec women writers have employed to write against patriarchal politics and to write for other women, it is from, to, and through the female body as a site of political and textual empowerment and as a focus of creative inspiration that some of the most radical forms of feminine inscription have, in fact, taken place. Indeed, this most recent putting into discourse of women's bodies is both a central theoretical construct used to underscore the links between the corporeal, the intellectual, and the creative as well as a more literal thematics designed to expose the very real political repression and mutilation of women's bodies even today. As I note in chapter 4, Bersianik makes these connections repeatedly with respect to clitoridectomy, which she evokes as a real practice of intentional sexual maiming as well as a metaphor for the acceptable excision of women in numerous aspects of patriarchal culture. Brossard echoes Bersianik's desire to inscribe the historic pain of the female body as well: "My body's plural memory also tells me that 'women's memory is torrential when it has to do with torture.' "[83]

Given the particularly strong taboos concerning the female body in traditional Quebec culture, however, this move by Quebec feminists to foreground the female body also constitutes a strategic form of resistance to a specific cultural history. Thus as a literary project, writing in the feminine has encouraged the exploration of the female body in at least two fundamental directions: first, as a personal gesture of self-recognition and self-affirmation and second, as a theoretical point of departure for the articulation of women's differences in a discourse that addresses the political, aesthetic, and material issues of the female form.

In 1977, three texts appeared that emphasized the new corporeal grounding of feminine inscription in Quebec. While strikingly dissimilar in many ways, Gagnon's poetic essay, "Mon Corps dans l'écriture," ("My Body in Writing"), Brossard's radical theoretical fiction in *L'Amèr* (*The Sea/Mother/Sour*), and France Théoret's first major text, *Bloody Mary,* all bear the insistent markings of a new physicality in women's discourse and attest to the tremendous vitality it began to infuse into Quebec letters. By strategically linking the exploration and celebration of women's bodies—previously repressed in writing as in life—with a theoretical discourse on language and the differences of women's experience, Gagnon, Brossard, and Théoret were able to combine modernity's tendency toward transgression and rupture with a more overtly political feminist stance. Important social issues such as abortion, rape and other forms of violence toward women, traditional male medical practice, institutional sexism, and heterosexuality as a political institution have since found their way into women's texts in Quebec in large part as a result of this new *body writing*.

Released from centuries of statuesque silence like the caryatid of the Acropolis whom Bersianik delightfully brought to life and to language two years later in *Le Pique-nique sur l'Acropole,* the desiring female bodies in "Mon Corps dans l'écriture," *L'Amèr,* and *Bloody Mary* yearn, cry out, even "bleed" for a language of their own making, a language capable of subverting and breaking up both the fictional (discursive) and the real (institutional) order of things. Each text also develops the compelling analogy between the silenced female body and women's historical absence in the political and cultural spheres. As we shall see in more detail in the chapters that follow, various attempts undertaken since 1977 to write in the feminine (and from the female body) have brought forth new forms of corporeal imagery, increasingly transgressive thematics centering on the insurgent libidinal desires and creative power of women's bodies, and fluctuating poetic structures suggestive of the body's alternating rhythms and of the fluidity of language itself.

Yet if women's bodies function as important generators of poetic movement and political reflection, they are not universalized in these texts. Above all, we are struck by their differences and, perhaps, by an abundance of skin—especially in the later works of Brossard and Bersianik, for as Bersianik notes in *Axes et eau* (1984), "The deep voice that we hear right here is the skin."[84] Still, the only thing that can really be said with any certainty about the texts of the four writers in this study is that women's bodies are excessively present. Canadian critic Shirley Neuman appears to agree with this view when she notes that "there is no particular body inscribed in these feminist writers' texts, but rather many bodies: mothering bodies, erotic bodies. The mothering body appears in many rhetorical shapes. What those shapes have in common . . . is an unremitting emphasis on 'real' bodies at the expense of the symbolic: on the exhaustion and the exhilaration of labor, on bleeding and crowning and suckling and washing as positive, sensuous experience mediated by a female relation to language."[85]

It does seem that despite undeniable differences in their thematic material, stylistic devices, and political approach, Brossard, Gagnon, Bersianik, and Théoret appear to support Irigaray's contention that female sexuality "has always been conceptualized on the basis of masculine parameters," and that in reality it has a rather different economy since *"woman has sex organs more or less everywhere."*[86] In a number of the texts examined in this study, we are able to locate the traces of women's pleasures and pain all over their bodies, inside and out. The ruptured, rearranged syntax, the use of female intertexts, the recourse to feminist mythopoesis, and the reconstituted literary forms encountered in many of these works thus signal not only a radical break with conventional forms of discourse and the emergence of the female form, but also a continuing collective effort to disassociate women's writing from the unifying authority of the phallus in all its possible modes of expression.

It has, of course, been noted that this move to inscribe the body's surfaces and pulsations, the female unconscious, and for that matter all that challenges male logocentrism in the West is not unique to contemporary women's writing as it has been practiced either in France or in Quebec. In the context of the modern French literary tradition, there are surely earlier attempts to *de-center* male hegemony through a discourse of rupture in the writing of Artaud, Breton, Leiris, Bataille, and others. Yet as Christiane Makward points out: "Never before has this been claimed so insistently, so consciously, and never before by women. Rather, these [pulsations, the body, the unconscious, the anti-Logos] were traditionally the qualities attributed to women as intrinsic defects of their nature, not as a conscious poetics and aesthetic."[87]

At first glance then, the specificity of an *écriture au féminin* in Quebec may appear to be located primarily in biological difference itself. Yet a closer look suggests that the theoretical considerations underlying these inscriptions of the female body are as firmly rooted in political analyses of the various forms of women's oppression as they are in some of the more essentialist paradigms of biological difference which have sometimes been targeted by the critics as still other versions of (over)determined categories and dualistic thinking.[88] In "Mon Corps dans l'écriture," for example, Gagnon argues for an approach to women's writing that would displace patriarchy's phallic "conceit" by putting female sexuality and women's desires back at the very center of discourse. For Gagnon, the historic repression of women's sexuality and desire for life in phallocentric discourse has resulted in the continued cultural repression of the female form and, likewise, in the suppression of women's creativity at all levels of society.

Echoing American feminist Adrienne Rich, who has also urged women to "touch the unity and resonance of our physicality, our bond with the natural order, the corporeal ground of our intelligence,"[89] Gagnon considers the link between textuality and corporeality a fundamental one in the struggle to revolutionize women's consciousness. As women write their bodies, so will they write the changing contours of the female form and thus begin to reconceptualize their infinite possibilities—a notion central to Cixous' position in *La Venue à l'écriture* (*The Coming to Writing*) as well. By writing with and through a desiring female body—a body awakened to the multiplicity and fullness of life in all its forms, Gagnon hopes to destroy the false binary opposition of mind (reason) and body (sexuality) that has long dominated phallocentric discourse in the West. From the vantage point she articulates in "Mon Corps dans l'écriture," the knowledge that has (mis)guided western thinking for centuries is "structured by a discourse without sexuality: without drives or fantasies. It is a knowledge without desire" (83).

Like Brossard, Bersianik, and Théoret, Gagnon's commitment to write through her body and thereby to establish a direct relationship between her own physicality and the unfolding text rests with the belief that the scriptorial, the corporeal, and the political are essentially one. To give voice to the female body's story in this way is not to abandon the domain of the intellect and succumb to the patriarchal dichotomy of Man-Culture/Woman-Nature as American feminists have sometimes charged, but to supplement and extend the very meaning of knowledge. Thus for Théoret, the feminization of language does not so much involve the invention of new idioms or the relating of a particular physical sensation as it does the displacement of the male symbolic system. "By abolishing the boundary between nature and culture," Théoret argues, "by revising the relations between nature and culture, women writers are engaged in a rehabilitative cultural rereading, reinvigorating women's literature, and producing their own readings of all literature."[90] It is with this goal of boundary breaking in mind that both Gagnon and Théoret have positioned women's bodies at the center of many of their texts. In so doing, they have underlined the concrete, material realities of women's oppression in a culture that seeks, on the one hand, to harness and ignore women and, on the other, to render the female body the forever dangerous site of taboo and transgression, of wickedness and punishment—a site always imagined, of course, from a male point of view.

In a similar vein, Brossard and Bersianik have consciously tempered their own intellectual training and their respective interests in the theoretical foundations of western thinking with the sensorial as well as the sexual. In so doing, they write to emphasize the inherent deficiency of a metaphysical orientation that has repeatedly privileged a removed rationality over the body's lived experience. While intellectual theorizing is rigorous in the works of Brossard, Gagnon, Bersianik, and Théoret, the rigor itself is of a different nature. Their theorizing does not forget the body but moves outward from it, always citing it as the origin of narrative movement and poetic invention, returning to it for creative inspiration, analyzing and theorizing its power, its resources.

For the writers in this study, *writing in the feminine* is their response to a historic moment of radical cultural re-assessment, signaling the first steps in a period of transition from a patriarchal to a more egalitarian society, from a notion of sexuality based on reproduction and commodification to an understanding of sexuality that incorporates the polyvalent, fluctuating, and regenerative aspects of the female body, its passions and its knowledge. Women who write as women, from their bodies and in utter defiance of patriarchal structures and paternal law, break the censure of silence, reconceive women's trajectory of thought about themselves, and replace traditional approaches to writing with a writing of approximation and an orientation toward the future: "To write is always to make the inadmissible emerge; to produce, from the collective imaginary territory we occupy, other cues, other vehicles for thought. It is to conceive of a link between mental space, body, and reality: in sum, through the very practice of language to conceive of what is inconceivable outside language. It is to know how *to be synchronized* there."[91]

This synchrony of which Brossard speaks is a potentially useful concept when discussing a number of the characteristics of writing in the feminine in Quebec since the notion of the synchronic forces us to acknowledge the ways in which the intellectual, the corporeal, and the political constantly traverse one another at any given textual moment in these experimental works—whether or not the woman writer is fully aware of it and whether or not the text allows us to witness this process in full view. As we shall see, Gagnon, Bersianik, and Théoret are, like Brossard, fully cognizant of and intent on highlighting the powerful linkages between the space of the mind, the body, and historical reality in their own literary production. At the same time, their efforts to explore what it means to write *as a woman* have also led them to inscribe the feminine, in the words of France Théoret, "wherever it has been erased."[92]

Although differences in style, theme, and political perspectives remain critical, the combined works of the four women writers discussed in the following chapters exemplify the continually affirming movements from women's bodies to writing and from theorizing to being-in-the-world that have characterized many of the efforts to write in the feminine in Quebec during the 1970s and 1980s. At various times, however, each of these writers has also acknowledged that the act of writing is but one site of resistance in the struggle to liberate women from the institutional structures, cultural myths, and philosophical discourses that continue to subjugate us as a group and that contribute to our historic sense of dispossession and exile.

In terms of the theoretical reflections on difference that are currently circulating in the United States, France, and Canada, the writings of Brossard, Gagnon, Bersianik, and Théoret offer inspiring models for women's entry into language and into the various processes of signification that writing allows. While it may be argued that their linguistic explorations are never entirely free from the oppressive forms of discourse they have sought to overthrow nor from the binary logic of sexual difference that patriarchal thinking has for so long encouraged, their writings nevertheless move beyond resistance and rupture to the more open spaces of reflection, desire, and rebirth, where women's bodies, minds, and voices no longer tremble uncontrollably under the male gaze. More often than not, their efforts at literary subversion lead us beyond particular instances of linguistic "awkwardness" and beyond rebellious battles with conventional discourse as well to some of the most dynamic and innovative examples of gender-marked writing witnessed anywhere. Along with renewed efforts to undo and remake the text, the continuing originality of their poetic visions and the plurality of their tongues suggest that women's writing today—particularly in Quebec—may well provide one of the most provocative social forums for exploring differences and for imagining another kind of future.

2 Nicole Brossard

Beyond Modernity or Writing in the Third Dimension

To imagine a language means to imagine a form of life.

Wittgenstein, *Philosophical Investigations*

Political liberation of sexuality: this is a double transgression, of politics by the sexual, and conversely. But this is nothing at all: let us now imagine reintroducing into the politico-sexual field thus discovered, recognized, traversed, and liberated . . . *a touch of sentimentality:* would that not be the *ultimate* transgression? For, after all, that would be *love:* which would return: *but in another place.*

Roland Barthes, *Roland Barthes by Roland Barthes*

Women whirling in be-ing shift the center of gravity.

Mary Daly, *Gyn/Ecology*

The writing of Nicole Brossard lies at a unique historical and cultural juncture between a literature of modernity that has consciously broken with the past and an experimental women's writing that has added a gender specificity and an unavoidably political dimension to some of the more radical practices of textual modernity in Quebec. The link between Brossard's work and modernity has been the subject of much recent critical commentary. Among Quebec intellectuals (whether feminists or not), Brossard and *modernité*—that "radical impulse"[1] to sever with tradition and become *résolument moderne*—have often been uttered in the same breath. Brossard herself has distinguished between Rimbaud's etiquette, "Il faut être absolument moderne" ("One must be absolutely modern"), which she reads as the urgent modernist necessity to risk all, includ-

ing sanity, and the more contemporary version, "Il faut être résolument moderne" (resolutely modern), which shifts the writer's focus
away from the exploration of intensely personal experience and
toward the vigorous pursuit of new avenues in textual production.[2]
For Brossard, this resolve to be modern was initially conceived as
a political and literary stance of defiance, an open challenge to the
ideological forces that had helped shape and perpetuate social norms
and conventional literary forms in Quebec.

Although currently regarded as one of the leading theoreticians
of *écriture au féminin*, Nicole Brossard was one of the emerging
voices of modernity in Quebec literature during the late 1960s, as I
have already indicated in the previous chapter. Her early works
(1964–73) clearly exemplified modernity's ostensibly gender-neutral
preoccupations with rupture, deconstruction, and transgression,
notions that have forged much of the direction of literary experimentation in Quebec since the late 1960s. However, with the move
toward a self-consciously gender-marked writing in the mid-1970s,
Brossard's forward-looking gaze has lost all vestiges of neutrality,
having entered the realms of the forbidden and the repressed with
the particular knowledge, force, and pleasure of her own experience
as a woman.

More so than any other writer in Quebec, Brossard has attentively
mapped the crucial points of intersection and divergence between
literary modernity and contemporary feminist practices of writing
and reading. Indeed, the theoretical aspects of her work provide the
pivotal link between the projects of *modernité* and radical feminism
in the francophone province. Brossard's early poetry and theoretical
efforts to chart the direction of Quebec's avant-garde during the
late 1960s had already given her a solid literary reputation long
before her move toward the experimental forms of gender-marked
writing that began to surface in 1974. Moreover, it is likely that at
least some of the critical attention accorded her more recent feminist-inspired texts is due in part to her prior work and association
with the project of literary modernity in Quebec. Brossard's ability
to theorize on the connections and distinctions between a writing
of modernity and a more emphatically women-centered writing as
well as her own success in spanning these two cultural currents in

Quebec are impressive indicators of the centrality of her work in contemporary Quebec literature and are also of considerable consequence for the project of feminist writing elsewhere and for recent American discussions of feminism and postmodernism in particular.

With the publication in 1970 of two volumes of poetry, *Suite logique* (*Logical Consequences/Succession*) and *Le Centre blanc*, (*The White Center*), along with a first novel bearing the insistently auto-referential title of *Un livre* (*A Book*), Nicole Brossard confirmed her compelling presence on the modern stage of Quebec letters. In these relatively early writings, Brossard formulated as well as conveyed the new mood of experimental writing in Quebec—what has been described by many contemporary critics and writers alike as an emerging "crisis" of confidence in the representational powers of language and a mounting mistrust regarding the organic wholeness, the ostensibly unified sign system, and the presumed signification or predetermined meaning of the literary text. Quebec critic and poet Philippe Haeck, whose own poetry has been influenced by both Brossard's early formalism and subsequent *body writing*, credits her with circulating two key ideas in the work of her initial formalist period, "the death of the author and the death of meaning."[3]

The texts Brossard published in 1970 also echoed an increasing weariness on the part of a number of Quebec intellectuals with the nationalist themes and overtly political forms of nationalist writings that had dominated the literary scene in Quebec during the early 1960s. The appearance of important experimental works by Brossard and others at *La Barre du jour* called attention to the gap between the revolutionary themes of Quebec's nationalistic literature of the 1960s and the revolutionary nature of experimentations in form that were beginning to take place in some of the formal constructions of the avant-garde. Determinedly modern in her outlook, Brossard challenged the prevailing belief in representational literature, in the ability of words to name effectively the sociopolitical reality of Quebec or, for that matter, any other social reality.

Brossard's writing practice in *Un livre* called into question the very notion of the "real" in a way that both delighted and shocked her reading public. As Quebec critic and writer Claude Beausoleil has noted, the appearance of *Un livre* was a major literary event and a sign that the Quebec novel had lost its endearing innocence and had finally "come of age."⁴ Brossard's first novel is marked with all of the textual self-consciousness, implied narrative distance, and heightened incredulity regarding language that this new age seemed to elicit. For Brossard and her contemporaries, Nathalie Sarraute's "age of suspicion" was perhaps dawning a little later in Quebec, but it was dawning nevertheless.⁵ By 1970, there seemed little chance of turning back.

Even prior to the appearance of *Un livre* and *Le Centre blanc,* Nicole Brossard had already asserted substantial influence on the development of the notion of *modernité* in Quebec through her editorial work and writing for the avant-garde review, *La Barre du jour* (1965–77). As already noted in chapter 1 and as will be noted again in chapter 5 on the writing of France Théoret, Brossard's emphasis at *La Barre du jour* on the materiality of language brought with it a new sense of how words, linguistic structures, and literary forms may be viewed as sociocultural constructions rather than as fixed objects of predetermined meaning. As was the case for a number of intellectuals in her generation, Brossard's theoretical positions during her formative years with *La Barre du jour* were nurtured by the formal experimentation of new novelists such as Sarraute, Robbe-Grillet, Butor, and Duras in France and by Aquin and others in Quebec as well as by the new criticism in France of Barthes, Ricardou, and the Marxist formalist review *Tel Quel.* The structuralist and formalist preoccupations of many of these writers called attention to the act of writing as process rather than as mimetic enterprise moving inevitably toward closure. By exposing the complex interplay of syntax, grammar, and formal structures that provide the actual matter for the text's own genesis, their writings underscored the auto-referential and internal generating properties of the text.

The impact of Brossard's initial concerns with the nature of textual production and with language as a forever new space of ecstatic, if nevertheless solitary invention, can in fact still be traced in even her most radically women-centered writing. In *Picture Theory* for example, which she published in 1982, we find repeated evidence of Brossard's earlier transgressive efforts to reverse the linear logic of mastery, undermine anticipated structures of meaning, confront the void or dense "whiteness," as she initially termed it, of unnarratability, and demonstrate how the text works—how it proceeds, falters, is condensed, and overflows the recognizable semantic field. From formalism to radical feminism, Brossard's extreme literary self-consciousness and fundamental questioning of virtually every aspect of the writing process have never really ceased, even though the act of writing itself has also become a way of exploring feminist consciousness, as well as a way of articulating her own desire for other women and for other ways of organizing reality. "What form can a contemporary thought best take that would give words another cast of mind, for the body has its reasons," writes Brossard in *Picture Theory*. "How does she keep her distance with words without by the same token relinquishing her place, without reaching the point of neutralizing herself in the text, without losing sight of an image of self liberated at last from negativity, without neglecting what reflects it (women and the sense of honor, as Adrienne Rich would put it) and also what always transforms it and reveals its meaning."[6]

With its emphases on undermining traditional writing conventions and on dismantling the authority of the author and the word, literary modernity in Quebec gave Brossard a crucial theoretical basis from which to explore and develop a new theory and practice of women's writing.

Le Centre blanc or Writing from the Zero Point

In an interview with some of the writers and editors working at *La Nouvelle Barre du jour* in the 1980s, Hugues Corriveau cites the 1972–73 Montreal seminars of Hélène Cixous as the birthplace of modernity in Quebec. He also notes two other works of major significance for Quebec's literary modernity: Brossard's *Le Centre blanc* and *Un livre*.[7] *Le Centre blanc* was certainly a key text for Brossard in her own development as a poet, and as the title suggests, its publication immediately placed her work in the resolutely modern camp of Blanchot's "writing without writing," what he describes in the works of Mallarmé, Beckett, and others as the movement of writing away from literature as convention and ideological practice, toward the point of its absence, the point as it were where literature observes its own dissolution or erasure and ultimately "disappears."[8] Brossard has explained her incorporation of Blanchot's neutral literary space in the following manner:

Blanchot was very important for me. What was involved in the question of neutrality was the white space, which was linked to the question of ecstasy, to the present, the place where the "I" is dispersed to make room for the science of being, its contemplation. Neutrality also meant putting a halt to lyricism and to romanticism, to inspiration, in the ways in which I of course understood these words. Needless to say, neutrality was undoubtedly a fine displacement allowing me to forget that I was a woman, that is to say that I belonged to that category of non-thinkers. Feminist consciousness would de-neutralize me, by that I mean it would allow for an integrative formal presence rather than a formalist presence, so to speak.[9]

Brossard's notion of a *centre blanc* as a space of absolute nakedness, ecstasy, and concentrated meanings functions as a unifying concept in much of her early poetry. Already in 1968 in *L'Echo bouge beau* (*The Echo Moves Beautiful*), there is constant visual attention to whiteness, blackness, nudity, emptiness, and shadows. While the exterior world is characterized as a space of solitude and contradiction, "nu désolé et aspire quand même"[10] ("naked desolate yet still aspiring"), Brossard's poetic eye moves nostalgically inward in the hopes of regeneration, intoxication, and some kind of elevation. Her voice draws us toward the mysterious center of ourselves, to words seemingly still in formation, tremulous words that reach for the obscure origins of desire and indulgence: "sans mémoire deviner au zéro dans le blanc / faire le chiffre le mot extrême" (109) ("without memory imagine the zero in white / figure the extreme word").

In *Suite logique* and *Le Centre blanc,* the exploration of a language of neutrality and excess is intensified. Brossard conveys an increased bareness of vision here as she strips away the last traces of realistic description and empties her poems of conventional punctuation and syntax. The key verb in both texts is, in fact, *dénuder* with its sense of stripping, of laying bare, and, of course, of uncovering: "dénuder le sens sa non-évidence" (194) ("strip/uncover meaning its unclearness"). While commonly anticipated meanings are neutralized, formal structures are repeatedly fractured or erased altogether. In place of continuity, solidity, and certainty, we confront a discourse of instability and rebellious doubt in which "l'exil s'impose radical / la certitude n'est que vérifiable / en ce moment la démesure renverse" (155) ("exile is radically imposed / certainty is only verifiable / at this time excess overthrows"). For Brossard, these calculated efforts to destabilize meaning and identity are both destructive and fascinating; indeed, she marvels at the ruins:

> rien ne se confirme
> c'est
> ce qui ruine
> ruine et merveille
> du pareil au même
> l'éclosion se fait mal
> laissant croire qu'un jour
> elle se fera divine
> éclosion de rien pourtant   (150)

> nothing is confirmed
> that is
> what ruins
> ruins and marvels
> all the same
> the opening hurts
> letting us believe that one day
> it will make itself divine
> the opening of nothing however

Brossard's approach to language at this point is not only to strip it bare but to split it open as well, to hollow it out and thereby create a space of entry into meanings that are as yet uncharted, undetermined. She beckons us to press inside these spatial openings without conventional preconceptions, to move and become excited by them: "les ouvertures font bondir et trembler" ("the openings make us leap and tremble"). Quebec critic Pierre Nepveu has argued that for Brossard and for those affiliated with *La Barre du jour* during the late 1960s, to be modern meant to "look lucidly into the hole" and to refuse to fill it with anything in particular. In so doing, he argues, they sought to reject the lure of myth, ideology, and nostalgia.[11]

In *Le Centre blanc,* however, this hole in the writing of modernity is not entirely empty. On the one hand, Brossard describes it as an interior magnet, a space where everything converges: "choses devinées lentement éprouvées de l'intérieur qui convergent" (185) ("conjectured things experienced from the inside which converge"). It is a space of extreme contradiction as well where desire and lack of desire, pleasure and pain, ecstasy and death, movement and calm coexist and intermingle in the color white—the only color to contain all the visible rays of the spectrum. *Le centre blanc* is the place in which Brossard's poetic voice maintains its "pure vigilance," an internal space of concentrated attention to the infinite and contradictory possibilities of language itself.

Prior to 1970 Brossard's literary inspiration appears to be uniformly grounded in the internal, in the depths of her own interior consciousness, a direction that in many ways seems to contradict the more outward-looking and politically motivated perspectives of her more recent women-centered texts. Yet the inward movement of her early poetry also reflects a refusal of imposed values from the outside, a literary posture central to the project of a thoroughly modern writing in Quebec, but not without a certain influence on feminists searching for other ways to write self-consciously as women. *Le Centre blanc* reads as an affirmatively modern quest for those inner sources of contemplation and energy that bring words into writing *autrement*—a key word that both French and Quebec feminists have invested with new meaning in recent years: "Je écrire (autrement) fissure renouveau aboli refaire or ce mutisme comblé verbal autrement"[12] ("I write [otherwise] fissure renewal abolished recommence now this silence overwhelmed verbal otherwise").

Although physicality is evoked only in the most abstract of terms rather than particularized in any way as female, Brossard already understands in *Le Centre blanc* that writing is both a form of seduction and a powerful release of desire. Thus she revels in her interior descent into whiteness, which she characterizes as the primary source of her own physical and intellectual vitality. The orgasm her writing unleashes during this insistently modern descent is autoerotic in nature, even though also portrayed at a careful distance:

rien   le moment venu se fondre à la source de sa propre vitalité s'isoler
l'impression l'action d'être hors de soi figée paisible un aboutissement
immobile à l'accueil des forces inaccessible de toute part blanche seule la
croissance interne s'accomplissant ou l'irradiation la joie diffusant hors
d'atteinte si intensément là cet état et d'abriter pendant un temps d'arrêt
extase ou sourire   (203)

nothing   at the right moment melt into the source of one's own vitality
isolate oneself the impression the action of being outside oneself stiff
peaceful a result unmoved by the greeting of forces inaccessible from all
sides white alone the internal growth taking place or the irradiation the joy
becoming diffuse out of reach so intensely there this state and to screen
during an interim ecstasy or a smile

With *Le Centre blanc* and *Suite logique,* Brossard brings our attention to the functioning of language, to its initial formlessness, to
the "doubt" of modernity that results in a displacement of words
and meanings outside the realm of the expected, and to a discourse
of desire that remains excessively abstract yet undeniably subversive.
The notion of the unrepresentable is perceptible throughout this
early poetry and its increasingly experimental form refuses to allow
us the accustomed conventional pleasures of reading. Brossard has
said that her move from poetry to prose in the early 1970s was the
result of a need to "intervene more directly in everyday scenes" and
the result also of a desire to look at herself from a greater distance.[13]
As we shall see in *Un livre, French Kiss,* and *L'Amèr ou le chapitre
effrité,* this new interest in prose is also indicative of a growing
fascination with the problematic place of language in society, with
the relationships Brossard was beginning to discern between fiction,
theory, and everyday life, between gender and urbanity, between
politics and writing.

Thus, while not without contradictions for the subsequent project
of writing through a feminist consciousness, the move to inscribe
modernity in Quebec, as Brossard herself had originally promoted
it, would bring language to the foreground without attaching it to
a specific political agenda per se the way nationalist writers had
frequently done. Rather, Brossard viewed language as a site of
rupture and continually new beginnings and as a source of abstract
pleasure in the infinite possibilities of creativity itself—even if the
traces of gender were to a large extent obfuscated and even if the
text did not appear to be historically grounded. The demandingly

modern ethic to "inaugurate" rather than to "repeat," which Quebec critic Suzanne Lamy aptly associated with the most innovative examples of *écriture au féminin,* certainly has its roots in the deconstructive moves and radically experimental positions that Brossard and others wanted modernity to assume in Quebec.[14] From the outset, then, Brossard's emphasis on theorizing about her own personal writing practice prepared the way in Quebec for the subsequent integration of various theoretical discourses within feminism into women's writing. Ultimately, the literary project of *modernité* provided Brossard with much of the theoretical grounding for her subsequent experimentation with *écriture au féminin* and, perhaps more importantly, strengthened her affinity for the unexpected, the unexplored, and the vitally new.

Filling in the Gaps: Reading *Un livre*

Although *Un livre* reads in many ways like a prototype for the Quebec *nouveau roman,* the issues of modernity that Brossard underscores so vigorously in this text have left their unmistakable traces on her subsequent and more markedly feminist work as well. In *Amantes* (1980) and *Picture Theory* (1982), for example, we still find the rejection of realism and traditional notions of characterization, an emphasis on exploring the nature and limits of textuality and its relationship to the real, and numerous reflections on the process of writing. Moreover, opposition to the laws of tradition (especially patriarchal tradition) continues to be expressed through the dislocation of conventional language and through efforts to suspend meaning as a way of bringing attention to the gaps or fissures in the narrative construction. All of these textual strategies are already dynamically at work in *Un livre* although they have not yet been incorporated into Brossard's rigorous feminist designs for a writing of difference. While decidedly modern in its discourse on the text and the invention of its own internal codes, many of the raw materials of *Un livre* thus reveal themselves to be the rudiments for a writing of the future as well.

Brossard's perspectives on the positions the Quebec woman writer occupies in language and in society differ significantly over the decade and more that separates *Un livre* from *Amantes* and *Picture Theory*. In more recent years, and particularly since the appearance of *Amantes* in 1980, her own relationships to language and to the act of writing itself have undergone dramatic, if not altogether unanticipated changes. In line with an ever-increasing commitment to feminist politics and a lesbian identity, Brossard's language has become emphatically gender-marked, intensely physical, and more radically expectant. By 1980, the space between fiction and reality, between the female writer and her words, is no longer the seemingly immeasurable gulf found in *Un livre*. Instead, we find a "marée spirale amoureuse"[15] ("loving spiral tide"), a passionate and integrative space in which fiction and everyday life, sexuality and discourse, literary theory and literary practice continually converge in a whirling spiral, through what Quebec writer and critic Louise Dupré has appropriately termed "a practice of excess."[16]

From the very beginning, *Un livre* demands multiple readings. On the level of what we might loosely refer to as plot, the text offers a discontinuous series of poses, gestures, and events from the lives of two female characters, O.R. and Dominique C., and three males, Dominique, Henri, and Mathieu. We learn little about these characters individually, with the exception of O.R. and Henri. Their respective activities as writer and political activist, however nominally described, are directly linked to the book's major themes. The five characters come together as lovers and friends in various configurations and with varying degrees of freedom and initiative. But Brossard's narrator is quick to relegate them to a secondary role in the unfolding narrative process:

Des personnages dans le texte, mais qui passent en second lieu. Qui sont là à titre de prétexte pour que le texte puisse continuer sans autre but que celui de raconter sa génèse au fur et à mesure que la vie apparaît. Etrange narration mais plausible.[17]

Characters who are in the text, but who remain backstage. Who are there as a pretext for the text to continue with no other goal than to keep telling of its own genesis as life gradually takes form. Strange but plausible narration.[18]

On the level of form, Brossard's first attempt at fiction produces a discourse that is both self-reflexive and self-directing. Using a remarkably restrained number of words, images, and themes, the novel progresses from one page to the next and from one word to the next through the active, almost self-indulgent contemplation of its own formal genesis. This narrative movement, however, is not necessarily linear or chronological. Scenes, phrases, words, are continually repeated, reviewed, and redistributed throughout the text. Indeed, the text appears to fetishize itself with the continual marking of its own progression or lack thereof. We find no noticeable movement toward epiphany or resolution in *Un livre* since, as one character puts it, "words and days look alike" (6). In an exemplary modern fashion, Brossard demystifies not only the characters in *Un livre* but, in a broader context, both her literary predecessors and her own fictional project as well:

L'exécution d'un texte.
   Très peu différent de ceux qui précèdent mais unique, sans pareil. Le texte d'une seule page, inscrit dans la continuité d'un mode de composition qui en rappelle d'autres, qui en prépare d'autres.
   La mise à mort d'une chose au profit d'une autre. Le texte devant l'insolite du texte. Des mots qui s'expliquent les uns par rapport aux autres aux dépens des personnages, ébauches d'hommes et de femmes faites pour demeurer telles.   (31)

The production of a text.
   Not much different from existing ones, but unique, unmatched. A single page of text. Written in the continuity of a mode of composition resembling others in the past, suggesting others to come.
   The cancellation of one thing for the benefit of another. The text confronting the text's precipitousness. Words which take their meaning from other words at the expense of the characters, sketches of men and women made to remain as such.   (31)

Brossard's writing here is terse, even dry. Sentences frequently lack verbs, and there is extensive use of the present participle. Such syntactic strategies result in a necessarily immediate temporal mode and heighten our sense of simultaneous impressions and occurrences:

O.R. et Dominique à cinq heures. Vers le métro. Sous la pluie. La foule compacte. Envahissante. L'odeur des vêtements humides. Le regard inquiet (seulement inquiet) de Dominique.
   La foule.   (62)

O.R. and Dominique at five o'clock. Towards the métro. In the rain. The
crowd compact. Crushing. The smell of wet clothes. Dominique looking
uneasy (only uneasy).
The crowd.   (62)

Clearly, *Un livre* reads like a prototype for a new novel, a text
whose primary subject is itself. A book about a book in the process
of being written as we read it. This is, of course, a fictionalized
genesis, since the entire book is already written before we actually
begin to turn its pages—a fact the narrator rather cleverly notes
when she acknowledges that the act of reading is the only "real"
event of the novel. But this too has been fictionalized since the act
of reading itself also functions as a thematic generator for the text's
own internal development: "Le seul [événement] qui soit actuel est
cette lecture en train de se faire, la seule chose réelle, qui fasse bouger
imperceptiblement quelques muscles et qui rende conscient de sa
respiration" (15) ("All that is happening is this reading being done,
the only real thing, causing a few muscles to move imperceptibly
and making one conscious of his [or her] own breathing" [15]).

Like the daily reality outside the text, words themselves are problematic in *Un livre,* rendering the writer's role in society more
contradictory and at the same time, Brossard suggests, more honest.
Yet *Un livre* does call attention to certain politically charged circumstances and culturally specific themes in the narrative. This is accomplished, however, through opaque references and ellipses rather
than through direct elaboration. In fact, Brossard's narrator repeatedly speaks to us (*vous*) while drawing our eyes to what is being left
out:

Le texte et les espaces. Car les mots ne peuvent tout combler pour vous:
   O.R., Dominique, Mathieu, Dominique C., Henri, vous, les autres.
                                                                  (97)

The text and the spaces. For the words cannot sum up everything for you:
   O.R., Dominique, Mathieu, Dominique C., Henri, you, the
   others.   (97)

Between the words and the lines, we are told, the blank spaces
reveal more of the essential text than the words themselves could
ever do. This narrative clue appears worth pursuing. For the gaps
in Brossard's text constitute an invisible subtext of considerable, if

undetermined, significance. As investigative readers, we want to know what is being left out here and, more importantly, why these narrative holes remain. Brossard's enigmatic tone provokes us to ask questions such as these and to formulate our own readings in response. The implied subtext of *Un livre* evokes at least three fundamental concerns that emerge in various shapes in Brossard's later theoretical fiction and poetry as well: the frustrated aspirations of the body politic, the liberating power of the female body, and the essential identification of the woman writer with a female character who also writes. Over the twelve years that separate *Un livre* from *Amantes* and *Picture Theory,* these particular preoccupations will become more visibly present.

Although schematic at best, references to the political climate in Quebec in 1970 are not infrequent in this novel. A bomb goes off at midnight, for instance, and Mathieu smiles. Is this complicity or merely a nod of approval? Numerous other bombings are also mentioned. The summer heat is oppressive. People fill the streets at night, and eventually, a discernible crowd assembles. In fact, the crowd becomes a kind of sixth character in *Un livre* from which the five fictional characters originally emerge and to which they also presumably return beyond the space of the text. Moreover, this crowd has a definite political character. It forms along la rue Saint-Hubert, an area known for its firm support of the Parti Québécois in the early 1970s. The formation of the crowd is therefore indicative of some alternate vision of society. And in fact, the five characters wait for and mingle with the crowd much the way they wait for and arrange to meet with one other. This insistence on waiting and meeting becomes the textual evidence of a political collectivity that calls for change well beyond the boundaries of the text. Moreover, these comings and goings in Brossard's narrative suggest that her characters are themselves interchangeable with others—part of the larger crowd.

A change in the order of things is also alluded to within the confines of the text as the five characters anxiously watch election results that will not satisfy their hopes. But the political present "outside the text" is once again relegated to silence until we read of Henri's arrest and provisional release in September. His political incarceration operates as a form of textual prelude to the mass arrests of writers and activists that we know took place in Montreal under the War Measures Act of October 1970. This attempt by Trudeau's federal government to intimidate the nationalist left in Quebec occurred in response to prior political bombings, to the kidnappings of James Cross and Pierre Laporte in particular, and to the general social unrest of the period. As a gesture of support for the hundreds of activists and intellectuals who were arbitrarily rounded up and incarcerated without bail or legal representation for as long as three months, Brossard and Roger Soublière organized a conference to protest the reactionary nature of these arrests. While none of this autobiographical information nor the specific political events lead-ing up to and during the enactment of the War Measures Act are evoked in anyway, the explosive and repressive climate of the period is clearly established. Brossard's highlighting of the date reminds us of the reality behind the reality of fiction.

As a novel about its own genesis, *Un livre* may well be as ordinary as any other, a point the narrator reiterates on several occasions. There is, however, nothing ordinary about the political subtext of this narrative: the real battle over Quebec identity in 1970 that is taking place outside on the streets. And Henri is, in many ways, the key to this political subtext. His words are not given in the text itself, we are told, because they speak directly to the political turbulence of the real world outside and carry with them the full weight of political commitment. Yet despite their intentional omission, the political nature of Henri's words is described, and we are left to imagine them carrying more force than those encountered anywhere else in the text.

Les mots d'Henri.
    Peu nombreux, mais lourds de conséquences. Parce que politiques. Des mots à la portée de tous. Clairs et précis. Qui révèlent l'escroquerie, qui font réagir le meilleur et le pire. Henri au-delà des mots problématiques. En ce sens, engagé dans l'histoire, dans la trajectoire des gestes démesurés.
    Des mots qui n'ont rien à voir avec ce texte: des mots nécessaires, des prérequis qui demandent à être continuellement répétés.   (34)

Henri's words.
    Few, but full of consequence. Because political. Words within everyone's reach. Clear and precise. Exposing corruption, provoking reactions for

better or worse. Henri beyond problematical words. In this sense, engaged in history, in the trajectory of inordinate actions.

Words which have nothing to do with this text: necessary words, prerequisites which need continually to be repeated.   (34)

Henri's words are anything but poetic, anything but the stuff of fiction. Yet in their textual absence, his words are even more strangely present—an ironic political twist for Brossard's feminist readers, given the insignificance and virtual disappearance of male words in her later works. The apparent contradiction in *Un livre* between the language of fiction and the language of politics is itself a strikingly modern consideration. Henri's discourse of violent political action and radical social change is both indispensable to and necessarily outside of the realm of the describable in Brossard's fictional construction. Yet while Henri's discourse speaks about revolution and radical change *in* society and *outside* the text, the exploratory nature of Brossard's own words in *Un livre* is no doubt more subversive and revolutionary in terms of the construction of an alternate discourse than the words of the activist himself. It is worth mentioning that the lines drawn here between the revolutionary in literature and the revolutionary in politics are notably more restrictive than the relationships Brossard establishes between politics and literature in her more recent feminist-inspired writing.

The coming of age of women's sexual independence and explicit desire for pleasure is another thematic component in Brossard's political subtext that leaves its occasional traces throughout the narrative. Primarily associated with O.R., women's sexuality in *Un livre* is beautiful, "scandalous," and continually in search of new modes of expression. And, like Henri's subversive discourse and political acts, O.R.'s naked body is both provocative and unnarratable:

O.R., à cinq heures de l'après-midi, devant une tasse de café. Les mains autour. Présente. Nue. La chaleur écrasante. Décrire: peut-être, mais O.R. n'en sortirait pas vivante. Plutôt morte (pareille à autre chose).   (7)

O.R., at five o'clock in the afternoon, with a cup of tea. Her hands around it. Attentive. Naked. Crushing heat. Description: perhaps, but O.R. would not emerge from it alive. Dead rather (like something else).   (7)

Ironically, her glimpsed nudity on the balcony on a hot summer day provokes numerous words of approval or condemnation from passersby, "trop belle, laide, vulgaire, putain" ("too pretty, ugly, vulgar, whorish"), but the words themselves only accumulate—they signify nothing. O.R.'s nakedness, which the narrator later associates with "le scandale de la liberté" ("the scandal of freedom"), is in effect assigned both meaning and power as a result of its untranslatable force in reality. It also becomes clear that, although brief in its description, the open-ended, unrestricted nature of sexuality in *Un livre* can be read as another legitimate form of revolt, another effort to formulate a future of radical difference and euphoric freedom.

O.R.'s body in the act of love is the symbolic key to a sexual polyvalence that erupts with considerable force amid an otherwise relatively neutral narration. She is alternately viewed in the intimate company of Dominique, Dominique and Mathieu, her female friend Dominique C., or Henri and Dominique C. As such, she becomes the pivotal sexual presence, the only sexualized body whose physicality inspires all of the other characters and both sexes. Moreover, in these few short passages of explicit sexual intimacy, Brossard's text comes closest to evoking the kind of language of desire so prevalent in a text such as *Amantes*.

Finally, Brossard's novel presents us with a narrative persona who is visibly engaged in the act of writing and in the contemplation of herself in the process of writing the book that *Un livre* will ostensibly become. Indeed, the woman writer in Brossard's text is a subject-in-process, searching for herself in and through writing. And while avoiding any use of the first person pronoun, Brossard continually reminds us of her own creative presence as the writer of the text by situating her search for words and for herself in the present tense:

Ecrire le passage présent. Un passage qui s'ouvre sur nulle autre chose qu'une attitude de la main et de l'oeil vis-à-vis du papier. Le passage des mots désirés aux mots écrits. Un geste qui attire l'attention et qui la concentre à l'intérieur de quelques phrases, espérant par là, quelques dimensions inédites pour le regard.   (28)

To write the present passage. A passage which opens on nothing but the relative positions of a hand and eye and some paper. The passage from desired words to written words. A gesture which draws attention and concentrates it within a few sentences, hoping thus to attain various new dimensions in seeing.   (28)

This emphasis on the woman writer's presence is also reinforced by the figure of O.R. herself who appears to duplicate many of the poses, reflections, and applied understanding of the writer of *Un livre*. Although all of the characters appear excessively attentive to language—whether personal, political, or literary, O.R. is nevertheless the only character who writes. O.R. writes words on a page late at night, searches for words in the dictionary, writes an open letter whose subject is open letters for the newspapers and, likewise, an anonymous letter whose subject is anonymous letters. O.R.'s writing is clearly self-referential as well as undecipherable according to the conventional rules of grammar. More fascinating still in terms of its thematic duplication, a crucial discursive transformation takes place when, for a moment, O.R. imaginatively becomes a reader of the text rather than a character in it. Like Brossard's own narrative voice, O.R.-as-reader brings pleasure and knowledge to the text of her own making through the intensity of her reader's gaze:

A supposer ainsi, O.R. devient lectrice et ne se cache plus sous l'apparence d'un personnage. O.R. face aux mots, appliquée devant la page comme si elle tenait elle-même le stylo qui prolonge indéfiniment les phrases et qui les enligne sur des perspectives différentes à chaque fois que la chair pense son plaisir et le formule ainsi, de manière à ce que, tout autour, les choses restent en suspens.   (73)

Supposing that O.R. also becomes a reader and is no longer hidden in the guise of a character. O.R. with the page before her, diligently confronting the words as if she herself held the pen that indefinitely lengthens the sentences and arranges them in different perspectives each time the flesh conceives of its pleasure and thus formulates it, with the result that, all around, things remain suspended.   (73)

As well as any in her work, the passage above highlights Brossard's thoroughly modern attention to the internal dynamics of writing. At the same time, it establishes a visionary fusion of the woman writer-reader-character, for O.R. is precisely the kind of reader Brossard has become and wants for her texts, particularly the more recent ones: a reader who actively writes the text through what can only be called an intense physical involvement, "lire comme s'il s'agissait d'écrire au fur et à mesure que les mots dessinés par un autre avancent sous le regard" (11) ("reading as though you were writing another's words as they appear and move through your vision" [11]). Brossard's ideal reader in *Un livre* is one who takes pleasure in the text at that moment when, as Barthes poetically characterized it, the body "pursues its own ideas."[19] Yet like Brossard, O.R. continues to acknowledge the inescapable distance between the words and her reader's gaze, between O.R. as reader and the fictional character of her own text. Her initials have become the enigmatic code for that distance: "O.R.: la distance qui sépare ses initiales de son personnage, son personnage d'elle-même. O.R. lectrice" (74) ("O.R.: the distance separating her initials from her character, her character from herself. O.R. the reader" [74]).

Thus, at the center of *Un livre* and of Brossard's entire literary project lies the woman writer—at work in fiction and reality—whether as narrator or as fictional character or both. What Louise Forsyth has noted as Brossard's splitting or *dédoublement* of the woman writer into both artist and the artist observed in the 1976 production of *La Nef des sorcières*[20] can, as we have seen, be traced back to *Un livre*. Admittedly, this *dédoublement* is even more striking in recent texts such as *Amantes, Le Sens apparent* and *Picture Theory,* due to the heightened erotic quality and lesbian positioning of these works. While Brossard's exploration in *Un livre* does not insist upon gender specificity as such, however, the initial elements are already in place for further contemplation of the woman-writer-as-she-writes—a woman who will eventually explore her difference through the words she writes for other women.

Sexuality, Textuality, and Desire: The Body Text

In an interview appearing in 1977, Brossard characterized her own relationship to writing and desire in the following manner: "I am a being of desire, therefore a being of words, a being who looks for her body and looks for the body of the other: for me, this is the whole story [also the 'history'] of writing."[21] The influence of Barthes, Bataille, and Cixous is self-evident here. Hence, the privileging in her work since 1973 of such notions as the desiring body, *le cortext* (the body text), the pleasure of writing, and *jouissance* (bliss) or *extase* (ecstasy). Yet the discourses of Barthes and Cixous in the early 1970s speak of a body in writing whose gender is secondary at best, even if *le féminin* is the term of preference to describe that body's libidinal economy, as in the case of Cixous.[22] By 1974, however, Brossard's emerging feminist consciousness and political activism cause her to give that "neutral" body (and text) a distinctly female sex and to *feminize* as well both the desire to write and the inscription of her own desire.

With the appearance of *French Kiss* in 1974 and a volume of poetry in 1975, *La Partie pour le tout* (*Part for the Whole*), Brossard moves her writing beyond the generalized and seemingly anonymous sexuality of her early texts and into the realm of women's *différence*— emotional, psychological, intellectual, and sexual. Thus Brossard's text gains a sex, and the female body begins to inspire and generate new approaches to various formal and political aspects of the text: narrative development, internal codes, syntactic structures, and theoretical perspectives. As we will also note in the works of Bersianik and Gagnon during this same period (1974–80), Brossard comes to recognize in the female body a powerful creative force, capable of engendering new linguistic sites and liberating symbolisms that are uniquely feminine and female in their insights and execution.

In *French Kiss,* Brossard locates and inscribes the female body and the feminine text in the spatial arena of Montreal, the metropolitan center of contemporary Quebec culture and the privileged site of the writings of modernity. For Brossard and others of her generation, Montreal has become a crucial symbol of the modern and of modern patriarchal culture in particular. Through it, she evokes both fascination and revolt for the power (money) and the legitimacy (institutions, law) the urban center confers. Thus, Brossard opens *French Kiss* with a strategic positioning of the female narrator in the grammar of her body, a grammar of woman's desire mirrored in the cityscape:

Chevauche la grammaire. Je m'étale, ardent, dérisoire et désir.
Jusqu'au déplacement le plus total et réversible de la conscience. A la ville et dans la poitrine: des irrigations lentes et progressives.[23]

Ride astride grammar. I spread myself, eager, inconsequential and desire.
Destination the point of furthest (though reversible) displacement of my conscious state. Slow progressive irrigations in the city and in my breast.[24]

Brossard projects the female body in *French Kiss* onto virtually every section of the city's surface, which becomes a veritable topography of bodily excitement and sexual energy. Streets, lights, traffic, and pedestrian movement serve as important narrative generators and as analogies for the female body's arteries, breasts, pulsations, and constantly changing rhythms. Brossard's political strategy here is to carry women's bodies (both fictional and real) into the urban sphere and, in so doing, to radically alter our own conceptions of urbanity and modernity as well—the space of the city, says Brossard, *"habitée autrement"* (*"lived otherwise"*). The unusual approach in *French Kiss* to the city-body correlative involves superimposing various narrative movements by mapping the internal terrain of female organs and arteries as well as the body's exterior surfaces onto continuously changing scenes of urban geography. Here the nature of textual production is visibly underscored as the text emerges out of the subtle and continual interplay of external and internal geography, of analogy and metaphor. Brossard's renderings of physical desire in this body-text are executed with a vibrant immediacy rarely found in fiction and much closer to the expressive intimacy of poetry:

FRENCH KISS
Poursuite du baiser, de la densité qui étrangle les articulations; le plaisir gémit. Pleurer parler rire le plaisir étouffe et fait monter les larmes jusqu'aux yeux, redescendre en douce le long, le rond des joues.   (87)

FRENCH KISS
On with the kiss, so dense it strangulates articulation; pleasure moans. Weep talk laugh pleasure suffocates and makes tears well up in eyes and trickle back down over rounded cheeks.   (66)

By constructing numerous analogies that break down the distance between women and the urban city, between the female body in motion and the male-dominated metropole, Brossard turns an impressive symbol of male power (Montreal) into a physical site of female self-discovery and an exciting point of entry for *l'écriture au féminin.*[25] Moreover, the exploratory nature of Brossard's language in *French Kiss* demonstrates how the structures of patriarchal language must themselves be disassembled and reassembled so that discourses on the city and on modernity in general are no longer constructed within the restrictive frameworks of linear, quantitative, and scientific modes of expression:

> D'abord, *la décomposition* des rues, des images familières au bord des trottoirs, la destruction du pouvoir linguistique qui contrôle l'agglomération. Sectionnée, pourcentagrammée en quadrilatères saisissants—dont il est difficile de sortir une fois qu'on a pénétré à l'intérieur. Grammaire vaseuse d'immitation. (54–55)

> First, *decomposition* of the streets, those familiar images beside the sidewalks; destruction of the language-power which controls the agglomeration. Segmented, percentiled in arresting quadrilaterals—hard to get out of once you're inside. The grammatical silt of imitation. (44)

The textual link between the female body and the feminization of urban space lies in the extended moment of a "French kiss," an erotic gesture that prompts the fictional voyage through city streets. This "kissing of tongues" also becomes Brossard's provocative metaphor for the passionate *lingual* journey of the text itself. The sexual ebullience witnessed here is unmistakably modern, free-spirited, and women-centered:

> le mord, la mord, elle grimace et ses yeux la détaillent comme un kaléidoscope la recompose, détail par détail, pétale une à une, ou forme contre forme, texte de surprise en surprise; ville de ruelles en rues. Elle de concentration, animée de toutes pulsions, variant les espaces, le jeu à inventer. Animatrice pour elle-même et lignes de force—perspective dans le décalque des bouches. Le calque.

> Introduire sa langue dans la bouche de l'autre. Son désir dans la ville et la géographie. La maison/le sentier de l'autre. (83)

> bullet bitten, bit in teeth, she squints and her eyes itemize, recompose like a kaleidoscope, detail by detail, one shape and then another, a text of successive surprises; a city where lanes become streets. Elle in a nutshell, animated by all possible pulsations, varying the spaces, invention at play. Emcee for herself and for lines of force—prospects in mouths duplicated—a tracing.

> Now to put her tongue in the other's mouth. Her desire in the city and geography. The other's house/garden path. (63)

Brossard's repeated emphasis on the word *langue* is paradoxically playful, sensual, and insistently theoretical since *langue* in French, like the word *tongue* in English, can signify both the vital physical organ and the language we speak. *La langue* in this text is thus the initial source of sexual contact and physical pleasure for the narrator and her characters as well as the essential element of fictional exploration, inciting a unique kind of fervor into the analogous acts of loving and writing. In this way, the narrative of *French Kiss* intentionally disconcerts and fascinates the reader by fusing and confusing kissing and writing, the female body and the metropolitan center, in much the same way that Brossard fuses and confuses sexuality and textuality, creativity and politics in many of her works. The result is a veritable spatial and textual explosion during which the territory of the female body, the topography of the urban landscape, and the process of textual production offer endlessly new paths of discovery. Brossard thus turns the act of writing into a geographical and corporeal site of stimulation and contact. It is "l'écriture mangeuse de zigzags, de détours" (54) ("writing that feeds on zigs and zags and detours" [43]), reflecting the circulatory movements of bodies in contact and of active city streets.

French Kiss prepared Brossard's readers for a marked evolution in her writing from a discourse of rupture and self-conscious formalism to one of reappropriation and intense female desire, as she moved toward an increasingly affirmative inscription of the feminine. Only a year after its publication, Brossard would address a landmark conference in Quebec on "Woman and Writing" to underscore the new feminist vantage point she and others were adopting in their writing. "What is important at the present time," Brossard remarked, "is that women write, aware that their difference must be explored in the knowledge of themselves who have become subjects, and further, subjects involved in a struggle. To explore this difference is necessarily to inscribe it in a language which questions the sexism of the tongues we speak and write."[26] Once the site of rupture with tradition and exploratory pleasure, language had become the site of personal struggle and solidarity with other women, an *engendered* space of inquiry.

In the major work that follows *French Kiss*, entitled *L'Amèr ou le chapitre effrité* (1977),[27] Brossard's creative resistance to patriarchal power manifests itself in the form of a dramatized break with the language of the father through a practice of what she terms a *déconditionnement*. Like Irigaray's prescription for a "disconcerting of language,"[28] Brossard's call for a deconditioning with regard to language involves a radical process of linguistic and social unlearning, a setting fire to previous discursive constraints. *L'Amèr* provides an entry into a world of proliferating maternal words and discursive spaces where the lost warmth, regenerative power, and repressed desire of the mother are uncovered and linguistically reconstituted.[29] In the depaternalized writing of *L'Amèr,* severence with the father's words must take place in order to avoid what Brossard's narrative voice remembers as the initial paternal theft of her own youthful female identity:

> Entre lui(sa chair son pouvoir) et moi donc une distance: les mots. Y avoir accès. Mouvoir un autre corps, que le mien, autre fonction que femelle, m'émouvoir de la différence qui agit en moi, comme les mots, espacée, lapsus agité. Je suis entrée fixe vive dans le livre, par ce premier combat, de ma main repoussant le corps de ma mère, de ma bouche écartée à m'organiser comme lui, pour parler *vrai.* Sous ses yeux. Puis pour me ranger à ses côtés. Mais *de fait,* étrangère comme un autre sexe.[30]

> So between him (his flesh his power) and me a distance: words. To have access to them. To move a body different from mine, a function different from the female, to be moved by the difference which works in me, like the words, spaced out, agitated lapsus. I have entered the book pinned down alive by this first struggle, my hand pushing back my mother's body, my mouth parted to organize myself like him, to speak *the truth,* to lay down the law. Under his eyes. Then to align myself at his side. But actually/acted upon, stranger like a different sex.[31]

This passage poetically renders the discursive alienation and the conflict of gender identity that the female child experiences when she chooses to align herself with the father's authority and his law. The daughter then gravitates toward the language of the father at the expense of maternal ties. This sense of loss or defection from the mother constitutes a difference that cannot express itself. And along with this silenced difference, Brossard's text suggests a secret awareness of otherness that constantly undermines the female child's apparent bid for subjectivity. This uneasy shift in alliances and the repression of difference it necessarily entails are conditions Brossard clearly wishes to overthrow in her positive break with the real and symbolic power of *man-made* language. Brossard calls her exploration of the mother figure in *L'Amèr* a history of *le non-dit* (the un-spoken), a linguistic reappropriation of the lost physicality of maternal warmth and sexual intimacy:

J'ouvre sa bouche avec mon pouce et mon index. La lutte s'engage dans le silence. La fouille. J'écarte ses lèvres: 'gueule du monstre' ou 'lèvres d'ange'. Il me faut voir pour arriver à mes fins. Elle me laisse faire, je ne menace rien encore de sa véritable identité. C'est ma m're, elle le sait et je suis censée le savoir tout autant. Sa bouche comme un oeuf essentiel et vital, ambiguë. A l'origine. AAAAA. Mon pouce maîtrise la mâchoire inférieure. J'ai son souffle dans les yeux. Connaître ce qu'il en est de son souffle. Des aliments dont elle se nourrit.   (17)

I open her mouth with my thumb and index finger. The struggle begins in silence. I part her lips: 'monster's chops' or 'angel's lips.' I have to see for my own ends. She lets me do it, I don't threaten any part of her true identity yet. She's my m ther, she knows it and I am supposed to know it just as well. Her mouth like an essential and vital egg, ambiguous. In the beginning. AAAAA. My thumb masters the lower jaw. Her breath is in my eyes. To know all about her breath. About the foods she feeds herself.[32]   (19)

Brossard's writing in *L'Amèr* is first and foremost an act of reparation that invests the mother in her fiction with a newly fashioned physical freedom and discursive force previously denied her throughout patriarchal history. Situating herself in the middle of life, between two generations of women—between mother and daughter, Brossard undertakes an imaginative rewriting of the mother figure by reappropriating both the physically productive attributes of the mother's body (brain, uterus, vagina, mouth) and the symbolic domain of the maternal archetype (the giving of life, nurturance, love, fidelity): "J'ai tué le ventre et fait éclater la mer. . . . Grande fiction vorace" (12) ("I have killed the womb and exploded the sea/our/sour mother. . . . Great voracious fiction" [14]).

This urgent need to liberate the female body from the traditional burden of sexual reproduction forms the textual imperative of *L'Amèr*. Brossard wants, in essence, to construct a discourse capable of transmitting the maternal body and the maternal voice to a new generation of daughters who will resist any impregnation— physical, intellectual or artistic—that might enslave them. In *L'Amèr,* we see how woman's submission to the male father, husband, lover, or brother, has invariably led to her own painful illegitimacy. Brossard's attempt here to rewrite the physicality of the traditional mother figure, who has remained the historic symbol of reproduction and sacrifice, is therefore explicitly lesbian in both theory and practice:

Et *de fait*, pourtant, si elle veut survivre, une femme doit s'affirmer en réalité se faire reconnaître comme mère symbolique: incestueuse en puissance mais inaccessible sexuellement pour la reproduction. Elle occupe alors entièrement l'espace du désir et peut ainsi s'approprier le travail de l'autre. Inversion stratégique: cette femme-mère symbolique a perdu son ventre. Mais conserver la couleur de son sexe. Seconde mère, elle ne peut être que marâtre. Forte mais retranchée dans un patriarcat. (15)

And actually/acted upon however, if she wants to survive, a woman must assert herself in reality and become recognized as symbolic mother: incestuous in power but inaccessible sexually for reproduction. She then completely fills the space of desire and so can appropriate for herself the work of the other. Strategic inversion: this symbolic woman-mother has lost her womb. But preserves the hues and stripes of her sex. Second mother, she can only be the cruel stepmother. Strong but entrenched within a patriarchy. (17)

While the practical politics of this complete reversal of the mother's reproductive potential are problematic at the very least, particularly given Brossard's closeness with her own daughter, the deconstructive strategies Brossard employs to rethink women's identity outside the traditional biological sphere have been both courageous and influential. Brossard's poetic success at stripping the mother figure of her domesticated breasts and womb, and thereby transforming her into a powerful and effective symbol of resistance to male domination and man-made language, is yet another persuasive example of the defiant character of her writing: "On ne tue pas la mère biologique sans que n'éclatent tout à la fois la fiction, l'idéologie, le propos" (21) ("The biological mother isn't killed without a simultaneous explosion of fiction, ideology, utterance" [23]). This striking reappraisal of the maternal figure is also indicative of the increasingly important role feminist theory plays in Brossard's recent textual production. In *L'Amèr*, she formulates a concept of writing that risks all through its effort to "kill" the old maternal imperative "pour faire vomir la muse endormie" (82) ("to make the sleeping muse vomit" [84]). Brossard writes on the side of the daughter looking for another image, another way.

Symbolically and politically, Brossard's rewriting of the mother figure is one of radical reappropriation—an attempt to retrieve on the one hand the maternal body and, at the same time, to assign new possibilities for meaning to the ideological space of the daughter's desire. More so than in *French Kiss,* the writing in *L'Amèr* is theoretical, highly analytical, and pointedly autobiographical:

Analyse: pour que les lèvres se représentent à moi comme une motivation à suivre les bouches pleines d'affinités. En cela, je travaille à ce que se perde la convulsive habitude d'initier les filles au mâle comme une pratique courante de lobotomie. Je veux *en effet* voir s'organiser la forme des femmes dans la trajectoire de l'espèce.   (99)

Analysis: so that for me lips are represented as a motivation to follow mouths replete with affinities. In that way, I am working so that the convulsive habit of initiating girls to the male as in a contemporary practice of lobotomy will be lost. I want to see *in fact* the form of women organizing in the trajectory of the species.   (101)

In her search for the mother who has been idealized and then silenced, Brossard finds her own form and discovers the mouths and bodies of other women as well. The mother thus becomes a beacon for a new female-centered vision of language, textual production, and social organization. Above all, *L'Amèr* reads as a positive lesbian utterance as well as an invitation to reflection, an intellectual yet poetic attempt to engage the reader in a dialogue on women as mothers, daughters, and lovers of other women. The open-ended nature of Brossard's invited dialogue accounts at least in part for the abundance of blank spaces in her text. Here and in more recent works as well, she gives her reader ample space in which to become actively involved with the body of the text. And just as the blank spaces in her earlier poetry brought attention to the unrepresentable, prompting us to consider the holes between the words themselves, Brossard's recent feminist writing solicits our involvement in those female spaces and frames her own explorations with the female reader's intervention in mind.

The Spiral and Women's Difference: *Amantes* and *Le Sens apparent*

In 1980, Nicole Brossard published two texts, *Amantes (Female Lovers)* and *Le Sens apparent (The Apparent Sense)*, which her editors have since categorized as poetry in the case of the former and prose in the case of the latter. But such perfunctory distinctions are hardly adequate classifications of these particular texts and actually work against her own writing strategies, which include the intentional blurring of distinctions between poetry and prose, between theory, fiction, and lived experience. In *Amantes*, a text which fuses poetry, fiction, and theory with what Brossard terms *le quotidien* (the everyday), the presence of the female writer engaged in the process of writing becomes the text's central organizing principle. As I have already mentioned, this preoccupation with the female writer observed and at work can be traced back to her earlier writing as well.

More so than in *Un livre*, however, the fact that Brossard, the writer of *Amantes*, is also openly a lover of women has altered her relationship to the text she writes as if the acts of loving and writing were somehow inextricably bound to one another. This merging of the intimately personal, the literary, and the political has clearly become a crucial aspect of Brossard's work. Thus, the poetic project that she enunciates so boldly in the opening lines of *Amantes* carries with it a distinctly political stance as well. Brossard's use here of an unconventional syntax with its absent verbs, highlighted adjectives, and unusual images, along with her general disregard for conventional punctuation, break up heterosexual, patrilinear logic on the level of enunciation itself:

> quelque part toujours un énoncé, la peau concentrée
> à l'inverse du système
> attentive aux circonstances amoureuses, ce texte
> à l'oeil: juin suscité par l'audace
> lèvres précises ou cet attrait du clitoris
> sa pensée inédite qui rend au corps son intelligence   (10)
>
> somewhere always a statement, skin concentrated
> system inverted
> attentive to the phases of love, this text
> under the eye: June aroused by audacity
> precise lips or this allurement of the clitoris
> its unrecorded thought giving the body back intelligence[33]

Because writing and desire are now fully enmeshed, the beloved other, who plays so prominent a role in the two initial sections of

Amantes, becomes a source of creative inspiration as well as an effective mediator between the real and the imaginary, the erotic and the intellectual, for the beloved in *Amantes* is also a writer whose works mirror Brossard's own writings in both spirit and intent, with their emphasis on abstraction, female creativity, and daily life:

> je ne sais pas pourquoi, mais plutôt que de lire ce que tu as écrit, je voudrais l'imaginer. je t'imagine d'une manière obsessive en train d'écrire d'une manière excessive comme si rien ne pouvait t'arrêter . . . en lisant le texte de ton projet, je me rends compte à quel point nos fictions se recoupent: cherchant dans nos lieux respectifs l'énoncé de la théorie et la théorie du jeu qui met en mouvement l'émotion même du mouvement.   (17)

> i don't know why, but rather than reading what you have written, i'd like to imagine it. i picture you obsessively in the midst of writing excessively as if nothing could stop you . . . reading the text of your project, i become aware of the extent to which our fictions intersect: looking in our respective circles for the statement of the theory and the theory play which will put into motion the very emotion of motion.   (25–26)

Through the acts of reading and writing, Brossard quickly establishes an intimate dialogue with the absent lover who is hauntingly present nevertheless in the words she has written. In fact, the lover's text provides Brossard's narrative voice with a kind of emotional and intellectual refuge from which to survey new angles of vision. The lover's words invite and mirror her own desire:

> je cherche en te lisant à me déplacer constamment dans tes mots, pour les voir sous tous leurs angles, pour trouver des zones d'accueil: m'y lover, my love.   (18)

> in reading you i am constantly seeking to displace myself in your words, to see them from all of their angles, to find areas of welcome there: *m'y lover, my love.*   (26)

The result of this remarkable scriptorial coupling in *Amantes* is an intensely intellectual and erotic feminine space in which the woman writer reads her lover's literary project, probes the various codes therein, and eagerly anticipates the possible variants of meaning in her text as if she were discovering the writer of the text as well. The poetic "action," if there is any in this text, is the internal development of lesbian desire itself. Upon encountering in her lover's writing project those feminist quotations and allusions that the two writers share, the narrator's physical and mental excitement mounts. These are common references for a shared passion.

As in the act of love, Brossard's "reading" of the lover's text, which functions both as a pretext and a *pre*-text for her own writing, becomes, of necessity, a reading of the lover as well. This most private of readings begins as an intellectual provocation, then extends into an exploration of those hidden tensions behind each word, and ultimately ends in the secret complicity the two women share as female writers who love and write about women:

je te dis ma passion de la lecture de toi cachée derrière tes citations. les faits sont tels que le projet du texte et le texte de projet s'accomplissent au goût des mots, au goût du baiser. je sais que tu m'es réelle / alors   (21)

i am telling you about my passion for reading you hidden behind these quotations. the facts are such that your project of the text and the text of the project are completed in the taste of the words, in the taste of the kiss. i know that you are real to me / therefore   (29–30)

Words and kisses, sexual intimacy and writing are no longer separable. For Brossard, the personal, the political, and the aesthetic have indeed converged—without apology—in the form of another woman. *Amantes* is both a love story about women's writing and a lesbian love story about women writing to one another. The urgency that marks Brossard's passion for writing in this text stems from an avid desire to unite the female body at work in language with the image of female bodies in love. And yet, although explicitly lesbian in its inspiration and intent, Brossard's poetic depiction of female loving is, I find, remarkably inviting for the heterosexual reader as well. Indeed, there is a generosity of tone in many of Brossard's lesbian texts that undoubtedly accounts for the broad interest in her work.

For Brossard, writing her love of women is both an affirmation of lesbian identity and an attempt to inscribe women's most daring possibilities—to push what it means to be a woman beyond the boundaries of patriarchal law and conventional morality in search of another dimension. Thus, she expands the range of the term *amante* (female lover or "lovher," says translator Barbara Godard) beyond its more restricted use in order to encompass the full radical potential of its poetic power and to imagine the expression of female ardor as a site of *rapprochement* with other women.

In *Amantes,* Brossard creates an integrated theory and practice of writing in which women's sexuality and discourse are no longer dicotomized or split off from one another. Instead, we explore a radical lesbian space in which the poetic, the everyday, and the analytical interlace to capture the totality of women's experience. Moreover, the notion of tradition remains static and politically reactionary in this text. Hence, the women who write in *Amantes* are uncompromisingly modern and intensely experimental, inventing words and amorous gestures to insure their own survival as poets and lovers. As a result, the tone of Brossard's refashioned *invitation au voyage* is tremulous, private, and feverish with expectation:

> alors transforme-moi, dit-elle
> en aquarelle dans le lit
> comme orbite récente
> les rideaux, l'émotion
> ce soir nous irons au *Sahara*   (61)

> so transform me, she said
> into a water-colour in the bed
> like a recent orbit
> the curtains, the emotion
> tonight we are going to the *Sahara*   (72)

If the image of *le centre blanc* exemplified Brossard's spatial con-figuration of modernity in her early work, the figure of the spiral becomes the primary poetic symbol and structural principle of Bros-sard's evolving concept of an *écriture au féminin*. In *Amantes* as well as in *Le Sens apparent* (1980), the progressive ascension and continually widening movement of the spiral evoke the expansive exuberance of the radical feminist text. Through her use of the spiral, Brossard indicates her rejection of both the linear form of more traditionally representational fiction and the circular, "no exit" construction of many modernist works—which, incidentally, would include her own *Un livre*. Instead, she favors a spiraling literary structure in which each of the text's parts naturally builds on the others in a flowing continuum of repetitions, analogies, and modulated rhythms. The act of writing thus becomes *la forme ardente* (the ardent form), a fluid coil of real and imaginary images that evoke rather than name the texture of a woman's skin, the shades of feminine exuberance, the silence of reflection, and the nature of lesbian ecstasy:

> J'imaginais ce jour-là ma pensée: attentive aux mouvements qui se déroulent en spirale dans les livres écrits par des femmes. J'étais comme saisie par la logique interne qui appelle sans cesse des femmes à se fondre/à s'expulser de la forme première du coquillage, emportant avec elles le rythme et le bruit des vagues, se répétant, se modulant, s'arrachant des eaux; fertiles et assidues dans le cycle des naissances et de la renaissance. Cherchant loin des eaux la bonne fréquence.
>
> Le motif de la spirale s'ouvre sur de l'inédit. Et l'inédit circule, circule, produisant des émanations comme il en est aux portes d'une voie initiatique.[34]

I imagined my thought that day: attentive to movements that spread out in a spiral in books written by women. I was virtually struck by the internal logic which constantly beckons women to merge/to expel themselves from the initial form of the shell, bringing with them the rhythm and the noise of the waves, repeating one another, modulating one another, breaking away from the sea; fertile and diligent in the cycle of births and of rebirth. Searching far from the sea for the right frequency.

The design of the spiral opens onto the new. And the new circulates, circulates, producing emanations such as those at the gates of an initiatory path.

Readers already familiar with Mary Daly's work will no doubt recognize the influence here. For Brossard's spiraling construction clearly and quite intentionally echoes Daly's radical feminist "Spinsters" and their "spiraling columns of air."[35] Indeed, toward the end of *Amantes,* Brossard celebrates her affinities with Daly as well as with Djuna Barnes, Gertrude Stein, Adrienne Rich, Jane Rule, and still others who have inscribed their love of women as an expression of difference (108). Because, for both Brossard and Daly, the spiral is always in movement as are all its contiguous parts, meanings are multiple and in a state of perpetual transformation. This radically new textual space opens out on the world and toward the woman reader with a multiplicity of significations and senses. Through the spiral, Brossard stresses her notion of writing in the feminine as a discourse of *ouverture,* an ever-expanding and unending ascension of a language always in process. Like Daly, she too wants women to push language "out of this world"—a world of patriarchal restrictions and endless repetitions. At the same time, the spiral in *Amantes* functions as a powerfully erotic lesbian symbol, evoking both the corporeal opening up and ecstatic whirling movements of female bodies in love.

In her provocative discussion of the "Uses of the Erotic" in *Sister Outsider,* Audre Lorde has emphasized the replenishing force of the erotic in women's writing. Both Lorde and Brossard have, in fact, developed an expansive notion of the erotic, which is no longer limited to the purely sexual or physical and which has everything to do with women's entry into language and with a women-centered vision of the future. For Lorde, the power of the erotic touches all her endeavors "as an assertion of the lifeforce of women; of that creative energy empowered, the knowledge and use of which we are now reclaiming in our language, our history, our dancing, our loving, our work, our lives."[36] In *Amantes,* the notion of the erotic is equally integrative since Brossard continually associates it with the transformative, whirling power to be found in the fusion of women's love and women's words.

Brossard's poetic exploration of a new erotic knowledge in *Amantes* invites us to discover a new land and a new political space— a feminine continent where the lesbian body and the lesbian body of writing form the fundamental bases for artistic exploration and social consciousness. *Ma continent femme* (my woman continent) thus becomes the concluding leitmotif, metaphorically capturing the expansive vigor of Brossard's lesbian *cortext*. With the litany of *ma continent femme,* Brossard also creates a historical bond with other women writers—both in and outside of Quebec, all those who have dared to write their bodies alive in the defiant tradition of the radical feminine:

> *ma continent femme* de tous les espaces
> cortex et flot: un sens de la gravité
> qui *me met au monde*
> ma différente matière à existence qui
> comble et évacue cette tension *unique*
> qui ressemble à l'ultime vitalité et

sagesse où intelligence et seins, cuisses
successivement dormantes et d'agitation
les poitrines ont la raison du souffle
que nous y trouvons/écriture   (106)

my continent woman of all the spaces
cortext and flood: a sense of gravity
bringing me into the world
my different matter into existence which
fills and drains this *singular* tension
like the ultimate vitality and
wisdom where intelligence and breasts, thighs
one after the other sleeping and agitation
breasts get the better of breath
we find there/writing   (106)

Theory/Fiction/Utopia: *Picture Theory*

"To write: I am a woman is heavy with consequences," affirms
Nicole Brossard in *L'Amèr* in 1977,[37] but it is not until the appearance
of *Picture Theory* in 1982 that we appreciate the full and irrevocable
weight of this assertion. It is, in fact, in *Picture Theory* that Brossard
has explored most thoroughly what it means to place the word
woman at the center of the text and as the primary source of textual
production. Moreover, it is here that she attempts the most ambitious synthesis of her work thus far. In an interview given shortly
after its publication, Brossard raises the fundamental question behind the project of *Picture Theory,* one that lies at the heart of all
her textual explorations since *L'Amèr:* "How can we insure that the
word *woman* will be the source and will also generate particular and
general meaning, that it will propel a reading of all realities and, at
the same time, be plausible?"[38]

This more recent example of Brossard's theoretical fiction, or
fiction théorique as she later began to call it, is about the failure of
patriarchy's conceptual models; about the deadening effects for
women of masculine time, urban monuments, leftist and humanistic
ideologies; and about the drowning of those female voices that dare
to speak *otherwise*. On the one hand, Brossard's text offers a warning
against the machinelike nature of the patrilinear model. And to

that end, the striking use of English in the following passage is particularly effective since the words *dismissed* and *machine gun* convey both the force and the exclusionary politics of macho culture:

Sans une vision globale, nous serons noyées dans la foule des fils cherchant leur père en ligne droite, pères abstraits dans le désert. La soif. Pères et fils dismissed, fantômes errants et orgueilleux qu'ils ont générés. Machines à tout faire, machine gun, machisme pensant.   (96)

Without a global vision, we will be drowned in the crowd of sons searching for their fathers in a straight line, abstract fathers in the desert. The thirst. Fathers and sons dismissed, arrogant and wandering phantoms which they have generated. Machines that do everything, machine gun, thinking machismo.

More importantly, however, *Picture Theory* is a probing meditation on the invisibility of women's desire made visible through fiction, on the unrepresentable *extase* of a lesbian love scene rendered emotionally "real" through abstraction. While Brossard's prior preoccupations with *textualité,* textual production, and the problematic opposition of truth and fiction are still very much in evidence here, *Picture Theory* also encourages a radical feminist contemplation of the origins, pleasure, and utopian potential of women's writing for the future. As the following passage suggests, the temporal and political emphases of this work are on the future over the past, on lesbian utopia over patriarchy. Brossard's language verges here on the mythical, even mystical:

L'utopie luit dans mes yeux. La langue fièvreuse comme un recours polysémique. Le point de non-retour de toute affirmation amoureuse est atteint. Je suis là où commence "l'apparence magique," la cohérence des mondes, trouée par d'invisibles spirales qui l'activent. Je glisse hors-lieu-dit emportée par la pensée d'une femme convergente. Tranche anatomique de l'imaginaire: être coupée des villes linéaires pour entreprendre mon rêve dans la durée, casquée, virtuelle comme celle qui rassemble un jour ses connaissances pour un livre.   (170)

Utopia glistens in my eyes. The tongue feverish like a polysemic space. The point of no return of all affirmations of love is reached. I am there where "the magical appearance" begins, the coherence of worlds, opened up by invisible spirals which stir it up. I glide beyond-the-known-place carried off by the thought of a convergent woman. Anatomical section of the imaginary: to be cut off from linear cities in order to attempt my dream in duration, helmeted, virtual like she who one day gathers her knowledge for a book.

The underlying enigma in Brossard's narrative construction is, in fact, of mythic proportions. Toward the end of *Picture Theory*, the narrator (usually referred to as "M.V.") evokes the ancient mythic encounter of a stranger, whom we all know to be Oedipus, with the Sphinx, whose female head, bust, and lion's body cannot be ignored since the feminine identity of the Sphinx is clearly at the heart of the issue here. Brossard's narrator wants to debunk the more traditional reading of this mythic encounter, which insists upon the defeat of a femalelike creature by a man who neatly "solves" her riddle with the word *Man*. Yet as Jane Gallop reminds us when considering Freud's Oedipal need to assert his intellectual prowess and interpretive authority over women: "A 'solved' riddle is the reduction of heterogeneous material to logic, to the homogeneity of logical thought, which produces a blind spot, the inability to see the otherness that gets lost in the reduction. Only the unsolved riddle, the process of riddle-work before its final completion, is a confrontation with otherness."[39]

Defeated and with no further sense of purpose, the Sphinx of antiquity in the Oedipal plot of "patriarchal memory" was forced to choose death. Amid a flow of poetic associations and insistent alliterations, M.V. *re*reads this death as the mental space that women occupy as readers of patriarchal myths and as the real-life victims of those same myths in a male-oriented culture. With real deconstructive flair, Brossard's narrator exposes the reductive logic of the riddle's single-minded solution, as well as the deadliness of its exclusionary sexual politics, in an effort to undermine the power of the patriarchal mythmaking machine. The story of the Sphinx is, of course, only the tip of the iceberg, for throughout the narrative of *Picture Theory*, M.V. is clearly preoccupied with her own enigma, with the puzzling difficulty of writing and reading "woman" in the extreme fullness of her possibilities—without reducing her to any riddle that might be too easily solved at the expense, perhaps, of her life. But the idea of woman in *Picture Theory* continually defies reductionism and limitations of any kind. Indeed, for M.V., she will remain "celle par qui tout peut arriver" (165) ("she through whom everything can occur").

In the novel's first chapter, entitled "L'Ordinaire" ("The Ordinary"), M.V. (or Michèle Valley as she is sometimes called) writes four successive sections on *la scène blanche* (the white scene), the name she gives to a previous morning of passionate discovery spent with a woman she identifies as Claire Dérive. M.V. wants to write a book about *la scène blanche* and its effects on her, but repeatedly finds that *le blanc de la scène* (the white of the scene) is unnarratable, at least in any known grammar. Existentially as well as sexually speaking, the profoundly revelatory nature of this prior encounter has made it impossible to transpose it into any ordinary language.

In choosing to refer to this crucial event as *la scène blanche,* Brossard is, of course, creating an intertextual link with her own earlier poetic volume, *Le Centre blanc.* The unnarratability of the lesbian love scene in *Picture Theory* thus functions both as a reminder of Brossard's literary beginnings and of the space that still exists between signifier and signified, between language and lived experience in her texts. However, the woman writer in *Picture Theory* is no longer satisfied with the impossibility of writing, nor with modernity's marked preference for anonymity and neutral abstraction. Indeed, M.V.'s artistic struggle with *la scène blanche* corresponds closely to the kinds of theoretical issues Brossard herself has raised in *The Aerial Letter.* Reflecting on the limits of expressivity and the importance of the real, Brossard characterizes the direction of her more recent literary practice as an *écriture de dérive* (a writing that is both *derived from* and *adrift*) somewhere "at the border between what's real and what's fictive, between what it seems possible to say, to write, but which proves to be, at the moment of writing, unthinkable, and that which seems obvious but appears, at the last second, inexpressible. . . ."[40]

There are numerous echoes in *Picture Theory* of Brossard's prior emphasis on the necessary rupture with realism and representational art, such as the repeated phrase, "j'essaie de ne rien reconstituer, de mémoire, j'entame" ("I try not to reconstruct anything, from memory, I begin"). Yet if a realistic reconstruction is incapable of transmitting the intensity of excitement, pleasure, and ecstasy experienced in real life during her matinal encounter with Claire Dérive, the narrator's obsessive return to this site of *amour/clair* or clear/love nevertheless suggests the generative (fiction-producing) power of the ardent white light associated with this scene. All of the women in this text are, in fact, linked with the sun, with daybreak, with celestial trajectories of light, and with a sunny island retreat. These attributive elements function in poetic counterpoint to the blackness of the masculine cities they inhabit. And as we shall see, these visual and spatial thematics reappear in a slightly different form in *Le Désert mauve* (1987).

M.V.'s inability to narrate to her satisfaction the inaugural textual moment of *la scène blanche* is due in large part to the transformational energy that this initiatory lesbian scene has unleashed:

> inéluctable Claire Dérive m'approchait
> sur toute la surface la peau pellicule
> le plaisir d'audace sur mon sexe
> sa main me touchait comme une raison
> écrire allait devenir un souci permanent
> dès lors que sa main était justement là
> saisie dans le matin clair par la clairvoyance
> des peaux prêtes à reproduire l'infini   (57)

> irresistible Claire Dérive was approaching me
> over the entire surface the thin skin
> the pleasure of audacity on my vulva
> her hand was touching me like an understanding
> writing was going to become a continual worry
> from the moment her hand was precisely there
> struck in the clear morning by clear-sightedness
> skin ready to reproduce infinity

Thus, as her name suggests, Claire Dérive is the woman who destablizes the narrator's field of vision. She is also the woman who displaces and disperses the narrator's own sexual identity—the woman who follows the unconventional lesbian path. Throughout M.V.'s preparations for writing, Claire Dérive serves as the invisible narrative source of eros and emotion, memory and freedom, rendered visible and hence readable through the power of abstraction which she conveys:

J'étais l'énergie sans fin, la sensation de l'idée, j'étais dans l'expression de l'utopie une femme touchée par l'apparence d'une rose. J'étais ce matin du 16 mai, avec Claire Dérive, exposée à l'abstraction vitale.   (72)

I was never ending energy, the sensation of the idea, I was in the expression of utopia a woman moved by the appearance of a rose. I was that morning of May 16, with Claire Dérive, exposed to the vital abstraction.

La scène blanche introduces a mysterious sense of awareness (not to be confused with patriarchal "knowledge") into Brossard's text, an awareness that hinges on the privileged relationships in her thought between emotion, abstraction, utopia, and writing. Emotion, which has jarred M.V. out of her static subjectivity, is also the central topic of discussion in the novel's third section. As the narrative scene changes, the temporal modes oscillate between present and imperfect past, as poetry yields to prose, and M.V. remembers (or perhaps imagines?) Claire Dérive, three other women, and herself on a holiday on an island off Cape Cod. This island retreat becomes a privileged space of contemplation and clarity of insight for the women who gather there. Symbolically cut off from the urban sphere, the unique setting of this feminine domain facilitates a serious intellectual and communal search for a vision of woman that is somehow essential.

Claire Dérive reflects one of the underlying concepts of *Picture Theory* when she proposes that emotion, and particularly the emotion women experience together, is a kind of prerequisite for abstract thinking and creative invention. In the case of M.V., the intensity of her emotion with Claire Dérive leads to further contemplation of their encounter, which, in turn, fuels her ardent desire to write about Claire Dérive as an abstraction. Within the theoretical framework of *Picture Theory,* emotion and abstraction are moments of extreme exuberance and concentration, respectively. Both are necessary for women in search of themselves and of what they can become. Thus it is that the emotion experienced with another woman ultimately releases the figure of woman from her historical bondage through an enigmatic, yet forceful inscription of woman as abstraction:

A la source de chaque *émotion,* il y a une *abstraction* dont l'effet est l'émotion mais dont les conséquences *dérivent* la fixité du *regard* et des *idées.* Chaque abstraction est une forme potentielle dans *l'espace* mental. Et quand l'abstraction prend forme, elle *s'inscrit radicalement* comme *énigme* et *affirmation.*
                                                              (89, my emphasis)

At the source of each *emotion,* there is an *abstraction* whose result is emotion but whose consequences *divert* stability from the *gaze* and from *ideas.* Each abstraction is a potential form in mental *space.* And when the abstraction takes a form, it is *radically inscribed* as *enigma* and *affirmation.*

Although somewhat unnerving in its didactic tone, the mystical formula presented here by Claire Dérive does help to *clair*ify some of the more private codes and occasional poetic obscurity of *Picture Theory*. It is worth emphasizing as well that the words *emotion, space, enigma,* and *abstraction* are charged with unusual power in Brossard's writing, so much so, in fact, that they appear to develop a context all their own that has very little to do with their common usage beyond the boundaries of the text.

It is no doubt ironic that in a work that demands so much intellectual concentration—as do most of Brossard's writings, the most privileged term is, unequivocally, *emotion*. But Brossard's use of the word appears to be closely tied not only to the realm of women's feelings and profound longings, but also to modernity's more general critique of western knowledge and to the debilitating split it has fostered between the body and the intellect. Brossard, in effect, views emotion as an aspect of what has been marginalized and ignored in patriarchal discourse but what nevertheless remains as a feared undercurrent. Likewise, Alice Jardine has characterized this repression of the emotional realm as "the master narrative's own nonknowledge, what has eluded them, what has engulfed them."[41] The valorization of emotion in *Picture Theory* thus points to what has been left out in more conventional modes of thinking and writing. This space of intense emotion (*la scène blanche*) is coded as inevitably feminine and lesbian in Brossard's text and leads to a new and more vital form of knowledge about the world and women's place. Indeed, Brossard argues that lesbian desire synchronizes women's energy, motivation, and positioning with regard to other women in a uniquely concentrated creative moment, producing a rare instant when the image and the presence of "woman" coalesce.[42]

For M.V., the emotion first experienced in the presence of Claire Dérive unharnesses an imaginative energy that insinuates itself throughout Brossard's text and eventually engenders the abstraction of woman in the narrator's own writing. This abstraction, however, is neither static nor objectifying since it emanates from a spatial realm that is everchanging and virtually without boundaries. Brossard's recurrent use of the words *spiral* and *aerial* underscore the openness and out-of-this-worldliness of women's space—in fiction and in reality.

Emotion in *Picture Theory* is also associated with the pleasure behind the novel's recurrent screen, which conceals a feminine opening or *fente* (slit) that is both sexual and textual, a space where women's ink and lips meet. At the same time, this feminine slit into which the text repeatedly draws us may also be read as a rip or tear in the fabric of conventional (male-oriented) discourse. For Brossard, this opening of emotion and feminine pleasure constitutes a unique space of textual-sexual discovery, which will become a site of transformation and radical difference.

In the shimmering white light of Brossard's new poetic territory behind the screen, reality is condensed into a subversive spatial abstraction as M.V. joins in a vital trajectory of female bodies, "une succession d'images visiblement de femmes (sans ordre chronologique) tri-dimensionnelles" (130) ("a succession of images visibly of women [without chronological order] three-dimensional"). Reminiscent of the spiraling images of *Amantes* and *Le Sens apparent,* the collective aerial positioning of female identity toward the end of *Picture Theory* signals the potential of mystical transcendence for the radical urbanites of Brossard's theoretical fiction.

In the end, as if the act of imagining "woman" in language were too restrictive, Brossard returns in the final chapter to her title, *Picture Theory*—a term borrowed from Wittgenstein[43]—and proposes a new pictorial representation of woman in the form of a hologram. A fascinating product of high technology and an ultramodern sensibility in art, the hologram uses laser light or white light, a mirror, and lensless photographic methods to produce three-dimensional images that appear to move in space with the movement and angle of the viewer. With this process in mind, M.V.'s curious fascination with the alignment of the oval mirror and with her own angle of vision during *la scène blanche* takes on new meaning as an analogous source of image displacement and reconstitution beyond the plane of the mirror itself. The text does, in fact, reflect M.V.'s radical discovery of Claire Dérive well beyond the narrative plane of the scene in question: "Je la vois venir les femmes synchrones au matin chaque fois plus nombreuse, élan vital" (189) ("I see her coming in the morning the synchronous women each time more numerous, vital impulse").

In *Picture Theory,* the hologram becomes a visual model for Brossard's tentative response to the enigma of woman, for like the hologram, which is constructed to be viewed or read from an infinite number of physical positions and under conditions that are always changing, the abstraction of woman in Brossard's text extends well beyond the page to the eye of the beholder and to the enigma each woman carries within:

la forme humaine venait vers elle visible dans toute sa morphologie occupant sa pensée comme un territoire allant de soi elle en était venue en pleine fiction d'abondance à se dire parfaitement lisible   (206–7)

the human form was coming toward her visible in all its morphology occupying her thoughts like a territory quite naturally she had come in the midst of abundant fiction to the point of considering herself perfectly readable

In the tradition of Brossard's previous texts of modernity, particularly *Un livre* and *French Kiss, Picture Theory* is once again a novel about its own genesis, about how writing in the feminine proceeds. More importantly for our discussion, however, *Picture Theory* is also a fictional exploration of the genesis of the woman writer and of woman herself. In the end, it is by virtue of the formal abstraction of woman projected from the hologram that M.V. will write not only her text but her own life and name as well. Indeed, as Brossard's strategic plays in English and French with the capital letters *M* and *V* suggest, the writer-narrator known as M.V. is looking for *Ma Vie* (My Life), a feminist quest that the following passage works to affirm:

Ma Vie privée est une carte sphérique d'influences de points de rencontre, elle tourne autour de la langue comme hypothèse et filtre du quotidien fictif et théorique.   (107)

My personal Life is a spherical map of influences of points of discovery, it turns around language as a hypothesis and filters out of the everyday fictional and theoretical.

In an address given in 1982, Brossard explains her personal preoccupation with the hologram as follows: "I thus come to imagine myself hologram, actual, virtual, three-dimensional in the imperative of coherent light. Yet, I imagine more and more, times being what they are, that fiction brings us closer and closer to what resembles the energy bodies we are."[44] In *Picture Theory,* Brossard offers us a seductive, utopian look at how a particular woman's emotional awakening and ecstatic sexual discovery become, of necessity, the generative sources for her own literary exploration, the seeds of a new sexual-textual identity, and the basis for the undeniable pleasure of writing woman herself. Like Brossard, M.V. is the writer who has glimpsed the shape of a culture yet to come and found that its contours are unmistakably and resolutely feminine.

A Horizon in Mauve

The space of women's creativity and spatial configurations have assumed important poetic and theoretical functions in Brossard's writing from *le centre blanc* of her early poetry to the whirling spirals in *Amantes* and *Le Sens apparent* and finally to the wonder of the hologram in *Picture Theory.*[45] The setting of Brossard's seventh novel is the desert expanse of Arizona and New Mexico, a vaste and heterogenous space where poetry and reality collide, where the dramatic beauty of nature and the anxious vitality and passions of youth meet with hedonistic tourists, intrusive televisions, guns, and pornographic magazines, all of which are apparent signs in Brossard's text of a North American culture whose values no longer appear to nurture or sustain life. Excessively preoccupied with materialism, violence, and power, it is a culture in which fear and escapism deaden women's creativity on a daily basis, hindering efforts to rechart the future.

The American Southwest of *Le Désert mauve* becomes a haunting space of contrasts and contradictions, a place of refuge, vulnerability, deception, and inextinguishable hope. On the one hand, Brossard has poetically captured the rich colors and geographical expansiveness that constitute the desert's fascination for the modern sensibility. The physicality of the desert's appeal, its seemingly endless terrain, and the complex ways in which it functions as an altogether different space from the brutal concrete cityscapes that dominate contemporary life help explain its magnetism for Brossard, who has become increasingly ambivalent about the potential for radical feminist inscription in the urban sphere. Yet Brossard's desert is also a space visibly marked by the trappings of modern culture—its roads, motels, pools, and bars. Its purity has, in a sense, already been violated. More important in terms of her overall project, the southwestern desert explored in *Le Désert mauve* is a historicized site, serving as a troubling reminder of the birthplace of the bomb and the real-life terror it continues to foster.

The desert Brossard has chosen to depict through the eyes of a narrator (Mélanie), a fictionalized writer (Laure Angstelle), and a reader-turned-translator (Maude Laures) thus embodies the very concept of heterogeneity. It is a space in which the boundaries of the perennial, the historical, and the imaginary are continually blurred, as are the textual distinctions between continuity and rupture, fiction and reality, creativity and destruction. At the same time, the desert explored in *Le Désert mauve* is a site from which we witness the forces of nature and culture as they clash, merge, complement, and continually defy one another. Like most of the formal structures and signs in this text, however, the desert resists definitions and descriptive containment; it is uninscribable: "Le désert est indescriptible"[46] ("The desert is indescribable").

More so perhaps than any of Brossard's previous works, *Le Désert mauve* stands at the crossroads of modernist, postmodernist, and feminist thinking and literary experimentation in Quebec. In this regard *Le Désert mauve* appears to be a work of synthesis as well as innovation. Disenchantedly modern in its caustic observance of a civilization on the brink of self-destruction and in its critique of North America's obsessive belief in technological progress, Brossard's text is at the same time characteristically postmodern in its emphasis on ambiguity and polyvalent structures of signification; it is postmodern as well in the attention paid to *textualité*—to the process of textual construction—in its collagelike presentation of disparate objects, voices, and gestures, and in its "impurity."[47] But *Le Désert mauve* is also grounded in feminism, as we note in Brossard's focus on reading women's writing as a creative act, in her examination of the fragility and strength of lesbian love, and in her analysis of a politics of community entirely at odds with the dominant patriarchal ideology. In its commitment to a feminine-inspired horizon where the forces of life ultimately overshadow the forces of death, *Le Désert mauve* maps the topology of women's passions, alienation, and self-discovery with exceptional power and in a setting that, for Brossard, is entirely new. More accessible than most of Brossard's recent works in style and syntax, its appeal will likely be considerably broader.

Despite its originality, however, *Le Désert mauve* continues a politically motivated approach already initiated in *Amantes* and further expanded in *Picture Theory,* wherein lesbian desire becomes the crucial mobile for writing. The principal female characters in *Le Désert mauve* respond to the desert's excessive beauty and heat, as well as to their own sense of dislocation and need for reconnection, through the intensity of their emotional ties to other women, through a heightened sense of physical desire, and through writing. Desire, it seems, occupies this desert expanse in all directions. However fragmented, however indeterminate the text at times becomes, it is nevertheless traversed by a need to overcome our modern legacy of violence and affirm the simple right to love and to be loved.

As is the case with much of Brossard's theoretical fiction, *Le Désert mauve* is not easily summarized. On the one hand, it presents us with a series of disparate cultural scenes and images: the color mauve at sunrise, the excessive light and heat of midday; tourists around a motel pool; a television; two women whom the desert has drawn together, intensely; a teenage daughter alienated from her mother who drives "so fast" in search of herself, in search of love, in search of a future in the twilight years of our century; the bomb that is never forgotten, despite the secrecy surrounding it; fear and death in the air, painted on the horizon.

Yet in keeping with her long-standing fascination with the creative process *au féminin,* in *Le Désert mauve* Brossard has written a novel about a woman's novel, about a woman reader's responses to it, and about its translation or rewriting in another voice. Indeed, within the pages of Brossard's fictional work, the text bearing the title of *Le Désert mauve* takes on a rather complicated identity. Initially, *Le Désert mauve* is presented as a brief and overlooked novel written by Laure Angstelle, a woman whose only work of fiction has been rescued from literary oblivion by a Québécoise reader, Maude Laures. The book written by Laure Angstelle thus constitutes the first section of Brossard's novel, which also carries the same title. In Angstelle's brief text, we encounter the essential themes, tensions, and narrative moments that will be contemplated and repeated in the remainder of Brossard's novel.

The second section of Brossard's text presents the various elements (objects, locale, characters, scenes, thematics, the reader's self-portrait) that Maude Laures wants to explore further during her prolonged reading of *Le Désert mauve*. It is, first and foremost, a meditative space in which a fictionalized reader becomes increasingly invested in both the interpretive and creative aspects of reading as a vital form of self-awareness and self-discovery. At the same time, however, Maude Laures refers to these expanded textual moments that constitute her reader's journal as "un *temps de restauration*" (66) ("a *moment of restoration*"). During this extended textual moment she will not only consider the possible meanings and intentions behind another woman's words but will also attempt to rearrange, under slightly different conditions, the scenes and signs in a text whose power over her emotions remains strong, despite her dissatisfaction with some of the incidents and perspectives Laure Angstelle has developed.

It is only after engaging in this crucial process of contemplation, resistance, and creative expansion that Maude Laures can actually embark on a translation of *Le Désert mauve,* a project that will be profoundly marked by her own temperament. To her own translated version of Angstelle's book, Maude Laures will give the title, *Mauve, l'horizon*. Her work of translation thereby becomes the final literary segment in Brossard's intriguing feminist triptych.

With this tripartite construction, Brossard thus establishes three distinct, yet interrelated centers of textual concentration: the initial and significantly uncanonized story by Laure Angstelle; a journal filled with the reader's reactions, interpretations, and autobiographical commentary; and Maude Laures' work of translation that becomes yet another form of creative production. The unusual nature of this three-part presentation generates a series of probing reflections on the projects of reading, interpreting, and translating the text of another woman. What is remarkable in this triple focus is the fact that Brossard writes the entire novel in French, while still daring to deal with the problematics of interpretation and translation from one novel to another, from one "language" to another, and of course, from one woman to another. Throughout her text, however, the continual appearance of words and phrases in Spanish and English will draw attention to the "problem" of language, to the foreignness of other languages, and to the potential nontransferability of meanings from one language to another.

Nicole Brossard has always brought a sense of intense concentration to the act of writing in her texts. In *Le Désert mauve* by Laure Angstelle, writing is at times portrayed as a form of emotional and intellectual refuge. For the adolescent Mélanie, whose physical and emotional needs are just beginning to assert themselves and whose refusal to heed her mother's cautions about the dangers of living is a continual source of generational conflict, writing becomes a way of anchoring her desire in the domain of the real and of shielding herself from the violence of our collective past. For this reason Mélanie struggles to relate words to the tangible, the concrete, rather than to a given abstraction or theory. Alerted to the mistakes of history, her unswerving vigilance will, she believes, make a difference. The essential "optimism" and self-protectionism of this position is to some extent reminiscent of the younger Brossard in *Le Centre blanc:*

> Tout l'avant-midi, j'écrirais. Le climatiseur serait bruyant. Tout autour de moi, la réalité: le rideau transparent, la couleur des murs, une aquarelle superflue, un téléviseur, mon corps immobile devant le miroir. J'aurais l'impression d'une ultime compréhension de la nuit, du désert et des hasards intimes qui se succèdent en nous comme une loi de la réalité. Ma main serait lente. L'humanité ne pourrait pas se répéter. J'existerais alerte dans le questionnement.   (42)

> The entire afternoon, I would write. The air conditioner would be noisy. All around me, reality: the sheer draperies, the color of the walls, a superfluous watercolor painting, a television set, my immobile body in front of the mirror. I would have the sense of a profound understanding of the night, the desert, and the intimate dangers that occur successively within us like one of reality's laws. My hand would be slow. Humanity could not repeat itself. I would be alert in a state of questioning.

The desert landscape in *Le Désert mauve* functions as a rich and colorful metaphor for the vaste possibilities of women's creative life.

Yet if the modern desert becomes a place of affirmation for Mélanie's nascent desire and inner artistic drive as well as a place of refuge for the love her mother shares with another woman, it also carries with it a far darker history as the original test site for the ultimate weapons of human destruction. Angstelle's novel introduces this menacing other side of the desert through the shadowy presence of an un-named male scientist—a troubled, secretive man whose physical appearance and educational background suggest, even if only in the sketchiest manner, the real-life figure of Robert Oppenheimer, director of the original atomic bomb project at Los Alamos, New Mexico (1942–45).

In a series of fragments devoted to the description of *l'homme long* (the long man), a woman-identified narrator emphasizes the cold scientific brillance of the physicist's dream, his detachment from life, and the horror of his achievement. The choppiness, repetitive syntax, and enumeration of only the barest details in each descrip-tion of this enigmatic male figure all work to accentuate the marked distance between the female writer—Laure Angstelle—and her male character—one of the very few in Brossard's writing since the mid-1970s. This distance is further accentuated by the evocation of the first atomic explosion ("Now we are all sons of bitches") and by the reference to Oppenheimer's apocalyptic vision borrowed from the *Bhagavad-Gita* ("Now I am become Death, the destroyer of worlds"). These historic comments expose the sterility and deadly sense of fraternity that characterize man-as-symbol in her text.[48] For despite the direct references to Oppenheimer's well-documented habits and trademarks—the cigarette and the felt hat in particular—the anonymity of this lone male character in an otherwise emphati-cally women-centered text clearly reinforces his function as a primar-ily symbolic presence:

Il allume une cigarette. Il joue avec le rebord de son chapeau en feutre qu'il ne quitte presque jamais. Il pense à l'explosion. Il récite pour le plaisir des sons quelques phrases en sanscrit, les mêmes qui tantôt ont ravi son entourage. Il marche de long en large dans la chambre. La fumée de sa cigarette le suit comme une présence spectrale. L'homme long connaît la valeur magique des formules. Il pense à l'explosion. La moindre erreur pouvait avoir des conséquences catastrophiques. L'homme long s'allonge avec des visions blanches puis orange puis le sol sous ses pieds se transforme en jade—*I/am/become/Death*—maintenant nous sommes tous des fils de chiennes. L'homme long appuie sa tête sur l'équation.   (17)

He lights a cigarette. He plays with the brim of his felt hat which he hardly ever parts with. He thinks about the explosion. He recites some phrases in Sanskrit for the pleasure of the sounds, the same ones that delighted his listeners a little while ago. He walks back and forth in the room. The smoke from his cigarette follows him like a phantom. The long man knows the magical value of formulas. He thinks about the explosion. The slightest error could have catastrophic consequences. The long man lies down with white visions then orange then the ground beneath his feet is transformed into jade—*I/am/become/Death*—now we are all sons of bitches. The long man rests his head against the equation.

The potential for violence and devastation in Angstelle's narrative surfaces not only through the constant references to nuclear explosions, but also in the fears of women for their personal safety, in their need to carry guns for protection, and most dramatically, in the brutally cold murder of Angela Parkins, a mathematician working with a group of male scientists on a top secret project that presumably involves explosive weaponry. The murder occurs suddenly and unexplainably as the young Mélanie and the mature Angela dance together in fluid, sensual abandon late at night in the rowdy bar of the Red Arrow Motel. No one has seen the weapon; the cold stare of the anonymous scientist is the reader's only clue. The event itself "kills" all further narrative development in Angstelle's text.

For Mélanie, there has been no clear warning or signal before the disaster, before the moment when Angela Parkin's body falls limp in her arms. For the reader, however, who has followed the juxtaposing scenes and reflections of Mélanie and *l'homme long* throughout Laure Angstelle's narrative, the source of such unprovoked violence is perhaps more decipherable. Structurally and thematically, the male scientist's obsessive preoccupation with explosions and with his own graceless body repeatedly prepare us for this final scene as does Mélanie's own thirst for emotional contact. Has the male death wish thus culminated in yet another form of carnage? While as readers we can never be absolutely certain, we are left to contemplate the motivation behind this murder of a woman of learning and insight who, only moments before her death, had urged Mélanie to hold on to her belief in the horizon (50).

After witnessing this controlled act of madness, Mélanie the "night teen"⁴⁹ extends her view to the mauve of daybreak and the desert road colored with blood. In the end, she remains alone, deprived of the intimacy she longed for and without the insight she had hoped to gain. Brossard's desert is, then, a polysemic space, a site of extreme beauty, desire, violence, and calculated death—the unexplainable death of a woman and death on a massive scale. It is also the site of both a historic and an individual loss of innocence that, although long considered a male trope in modern fiction, has clearly taken on an altogether different configuration in Brossard's text.

In Maude Laures' *Mauve, l'horizon,* we find much that echoes the original text by Laure Angstelle, including many key phrases that reappear verbatim. As their interrelated names suggest, the text of Laure A . . . can be found in the text of M . . . Laures—two Laures, two texts with moments of clear intersection and duplication. But, as one would expect with any translation, there are also subtle and not so subtle changes and alterations in the text of Maude Laures. Words, expressions, and phrases are occasionally left out or given a slightly different emphasis. Imagery is at times less complex or reworked to give another effect. For the very notion of translation precludes the exact duplication of a writer's work since no two languages have identical lexicons, syntax, or structures. By the same token, each writer relates to language in a unique way—a point Brossard makes rather clear by using French in both the text of Laure Angstelle and that of Maude Laures.

Like every translation, then, the rewritten work by Maude Laures builds upon, takes away from, and alters the original text. The same kinds of deletions and creative substitutions that can be noted in translation work as a rule and that typically signal the transformational aspect of any exercise in rewriting are, in fact, what gives the novel of Maude Laures its originality, its difference. And although the transformations brought about by the act of translation are sometimes minimal or occasionally nonexistent, this subtle shift in point of view begins nevertheless to have significant consequences for our own reading of the text.

The transposition of meanings from one version to the other is

perhaps most apparent in the final pages of Maude Laures' translation and especially in Mélanie's account of the encounter-turned-
death-scene of Angela Parkins. Whereas Laure Angstelle prepares
us for the meeting of Mélanie and Angela with lengthy phrases, a
self-questioning stance, and words that emphasize Mélanie's adolescent indecisiveness, the translated version of the same encounter is
quick, pulsating, and filled with aggressive anticipation. Maude
Laures' version also appears to be more explicitly sexual.

The impact of Angela Parkins' death in both the original text and
its translation further develop this sense of difference in Mélanie's
response. For Laure Angstelle, Mélanie's final view of the desert
has been markedly altered by "un profil sanglant" (41) ("a bloody
profile") that dominates our own vision of the horizon as readers.
However, in Maude Laures' concluding passage, Mélanie's eyes
move from the disaster to the horizon, an important shift in the
young female gaze: "Puis ce fut le profil menaçant de toute chose.
Puis l'aube, le désert et mauve, l'horizon" (220) ("Then there was
the menacing profile of everything. Then daybreak, the desert and
mauve, the horizon"). Is Maude Laures suggesting that Mélanie's
strength may lie in her ability to face and live beyond the tragedy
of the real, to suffer the loss of Angela Parkins at night and still be
drawn toward the dramatic beauty of daybreak? As Angela Parkins
herself had noted, a few "concise words" can change the course of
death, which is precisely the relationship to language that Maude
Laures struggles to produce in her own version of Laure Angstelle's
book.

The seeds of Maude Laures' self-styled adaptation and reviewing
can be found in the central and most lengthy section of Brossard's
text. During her continuing efforts to read, interpret, and comment
on *Le Désert mauve,* Maude Laures begins to bring another dimension to the novel with which she has become so consumed:

Le monde de Laure Angstelle prenait place en elle et cela bien différemment
de ce qu'elle avait ressenti au tout début alors que durant ses premières
lectures, elle avait éprouvé le sentiment diffus d'une réciprocité. Maintenant
le monde de Laure Angstelle avait en elle la portée d'une musique toute en
durée qui la laissait devant sa table de travail comme un *bloc de
concentration . . .*   (64–65)

The world of Laure Angstelle took hold in her very differently from the way in which she had first felt it during her initial readings, when she had felt a sense of spreading reciprocity. Now the world of Laure Angstelle had taken on the significance of enduring music which left her in front of her desk like a *block of concentration* . . .

As a reader-soon-to-become-translator, Maude Laures enters into an imaginary dialogue with the woman writer, a dialogue in which she will ask Laure Angstelle to respond to questions about her choice of narrative direction, about the harsh death sentence she imposes on Angela Parkins, and about the relationship between writing and the real. In her reader's notebook, Maude Laures constructs additional dialogues as well between a number of the characters in Angstelle's novel in an attempt to fill in the gaps and clarify certain textual ambiguities. She will also expand upon the psychological portraits of each character, imagining in particular the tall man's dependency on the presence of the loaded revolver as he reads. Here, as elsewhere, Maude Laures' efforts to expand the original text often tell us as much, if not more, about her own preoccupations as they do about those of Laure Angstelle herself.

The feminist reading paradigm that Brossard constructs in the novel's second section closely parallels a number of recent American models for a feminist reading posture, particularly the "intersubjective encounter" of female writer and female reader proposed by Patrocinio Schweickart in her discussion of a dialectical feminist approach to reading women writers.[50] As Schwickart suggests, a feminist reading of another woman's text involves moments of intense identification, resistance, and respectful difference. Moreover, the interpretations that result from this kind of woman-to-woman encounter are necessarily influenced by the reader's own passions and personal needs. For Brossard, translation work appears to demand a similarly intimate stance or as Mélanie puts it, a "corps à corps avec le livre" (177) ("body to body with the book").

In *Le Désert mauve,* a female reader becomes fervently involved with the text of another woman, with the emotions it produces, and with the meanings it holds for her own life. Maude Laures' creative involvement is so keen that we are forced to read her own translation with a heightened sensitivity, even as we attempt to recall or go back to compare the text of Laure Angstelle in its original form. And what forms of interpretive rendering do our own readings effect on Angstelle's narrative construction, on Laures' translation, and on Brossard's text as a whole? The *mise en abîme* or continuous mirroring effect is dizzying, to say the least. There is, then, no possible narrative closure since Maude Laures' translation invariably prompts us to move back to Laure Angstelle's initial work. Yet Brossard's text defies the very circularity it appears to set up. Ultimately, the textual movement is multidirectional rather than circular since the reader of Brossard's text is also continually drawn into the role of sympathetic interpreter. *Le Désert mauve* thus affirms the importance of women's interpretive role in reading and in life itself. In an era when the concept of unity is being continually contested in experimental writing and in other art forms, when the distinctions between artifice and reality no longer appear fixed, and when the desiring voices of women are particularized as well as interconnected, no single reading is sufficient or even possible here. What is striking, however, is that Maude Laures' rendering of Laure Angstelle's text moves beyond destruction toward daybreak and, despite all else, embraces life.

Le Désert mauve is very much in keeping with the attention Brossard has long devoted to the *matter* (in both senses of the word) of the text and to processes of writing that have underscored the density of language and the slippages in meaning that allow the text to resist any definitive interpretation. At the same time, however, there is an increased emphasis on an exchange of words in this novel, which is grounded in the notion of female empowerment through the speech act. Indeed, the words women speak to one another in *Le Désert mauve* appear to function as a form of creative resistance. The strong and defiant words that Angela Parkins addresses to Mélanie only moments before her death can thus be read as Angela's attempt at an alternative utterance. Likewise, there are words to convey women's love of one another, the intimate words Lorna speaks only in the arms of Mélanie's mother, for example. We also note the intimacy Mélanie herself shares with her friend Grazie when they talk—"Il y a des phrases entre nous" (33) ("There are phrases between us"). What remains unsaid is often a source of uneasiness in this text. The unspoken words between mother and daughter trouble the reader, Maude Laures, who seeks to unite them in her own notes through an imagined dialogue. It is, in fact, through her mediating efforts that mother and daughter eventually confront the differences that divide them while finally recognizing one another's strengths.

In addition to Brossard's focus on the interpretation, translation, and thematics of words, it is difficult to ignore the phonic value clearly assigned them in this text. Moreover, Brossard's emphasis on the phonic would appear to be strategic in *Le Désert mauve*. When combined with certain key words, for instance, the sounds of her characters' names form a series of interwoven auditory patterns and linguistic motifs that create a veritable symphony of poetic assonance and alliteration. These sonorous effects are not accomplished for aesthetic purposes alone, however, since they also create important linkages between words, symbols, and literary projects from one page to the next and from the text of Laure Angstelle to the text of Maude Laures. In the instance of the latter, a transformation has certainly occurred, but the textual echo that can still be noted in the translator's version of the original work is also played out linguistically through the poetic resonance in the translator's own name—an imperfect doubling, to be sure, of authorial inscription.

Another example of the attention Brossard gives to the phonic component in her text can be noted in the sensual fascination of the *m,* which Mélanie herself admires when Lorna and her mother pronounce the letter (12), and which is further underscored in the repetitive references to *Mélanie, Meteor, Maude,* and *mauve.* Likewise, there is a persistent return to the letters *ang* in *Angela, Angstelle,* and *angle,* which reminds us on the one hand of a woman writer's *angst* (Angst/elle) in recounting the violent story of *Le Désert mauve* and, on the other hand, of how the text necessarily shifts its *angle* of view in the hands of another reader. The phonic insistence on the letter *l* is yet another unmistakable element in this poetic network of sounds and images; hence, *Lorna, Laure Angstelle,* Maude *Laures, l'homme long* and *l'hom'oblong, lumière, l'horizon.*[51] Suzanne Lamy argued that in the experimental forms of contemporary women's writing we find reminders of the female voice,[52] traces of a female presence that move subversively beyond the scriptorial. Attempts to inscribe the feminine voice are also found in the writings of Hélène Cixous and Marguerite Duras, as a number of feminist critics have already noted. This attention to language as it is uttered and physically experienced has become a significant element in the kind of feminist poetics Brossard wants to construct.

While Brossard is clearly exploring new subject matter and a unique poetic site in *Le Désert mauve,* there is much here that echoes and enhances earlier texts. For despite a noticeably sharper focus on the politics of violence and the climate of disaster that hang over contemporary culture, she has not abandoned her vision of a strong and intimate women's community, nor has she been swayed in her commitment to a utopian feminist poetics, both of which have by now become familiar elements in her writing practice. What Brossard has added in *Le Désert mauve* is a historical grounding for the contemporary malaise women experience in their struggle to live and create in what remains an aggressively patriarchal and blindly modern culture. At the same time, this new emphasis on the historical undoubtedly reflects a renewed interest on her part in situating the real need for a feminist consciousness in political action and in writing. "It is through a feminist consciousness," Brossard affirms, "that *moral* suffering enters our lives like an initiatory torment. It terrifies us, it exhausts us. But it is also because of a feminist consciousness that the creative dimension of our lives begins, the meaning and dignity of our lives, for when breaking the patriarchal sound barrier, feminist consciousness constantly finds itself on the side of creation."[53] For Nicole Brossard, who believes that language engenders as much as it reveals, writing on the side of creativity means writing toward the future with the lessons of the past still well within view.

Although considerably more intimate in her writing over the last decade, Nicole Brossard continues to explore the complex relationships between reading and writing, gender and meaning, between the fictional and the real, the imaginary and the mundane, all of which she first raised in *Un livre* alongside more formal concerns.

The urgent vitality that has marked her particular passion for writing since 1970 has found its most original expression in an avid desire to reunite the female body at work in language with the female body in love. Yet even the most audacious intimacy found in more recent works has necessarily led Brossard beyond individual experience to a reevaluation of contemporary culture and of what it means for women to be "modern."

The contributions of Nicole Brossard to contemporary literature and literary theory and their inevitable intersection through feminist thought have been visionary. Her continuing efforts to articulate a feminist writing practice that is both women-centered and future-oriented constitute a dynamic, forward-looking project linking poetry and radical feminist politics with the subliminal, the corporeal, and the reflectively conscious. It is a vision of the future necessarily in process. Already, however, it has nurtured an entire generation of readers and writers in Quebec, all those who read and write to discover Brossard's "ultime intime ailleurs,"[54] that ultimate intimate elsewhere among the words on a woman's page.

3   *Madeleine Gagnon*
The Solidarity and Solitude of Women's Words

The shape of a cave, this emptiness we seek out like water. The void that we are. That we wash into as sleep washes over us, and we are blanketed in darkness. We see nothing. We are in the center of our ignorance. Nothingness spreads around us. But in this nothing we find what we did not know existed. With our hands, we begin to trace faint images etched into the walls. And now, beneath these images we can see the gleam of older images. And these peel back to reveal the older still. The past, the dead, once breathing, the forgotten, the secret, the buried, the once blood and bone, the vanished, shimmering now like an answer from these walls, bright and red. Drawn by the one who came before. And before her. And before. Back to the beginning. To the one who first swam from the mouth of this cave. And now we know all she knew, see the newness of her vision. What we did not know existed but saw as children, our whole lives drawn here, image over image, past time, beyond space.

Susan Griffin, *Woman and Nature: The Roaring Inside Her*

The flesh is writing and writing is never read: it is always still to be read, to be studied, to be discovered, to be invented.

Hélène Cixous, "La Venue à l'écriture"

Madeleine Gagnon has been at the forefront of artistic experimentation in Quebec letters since the early 1970s. Spanning nearly two decades with considerable scope and power, her writings have helped formulate and have responded to many of the central preoccupations of feminist literary production in Quebec. Because of the political sophistication and underlying contradictions that have formed the essential character of her literary project, Gagnon's writings have reproduced many of the inner struggles of Quebec's feminist movement from 1970 onward. Frequently torn between issues of gender and class, between a strong sense of collective allegiance and the real necessity for personal exploration and self-reflection, Gagnon has been chastised by some feminists for her public critique of radical feminist separatism and political dogmatism, occasionally dismissed by male critics as an all too difficult and meandering voice lost in her own solipsistic labyrinth, and heralded by others still as one of Quebec's leading practitioners and theoreticians of a self-consciously gender-marked approach to women's writing.[1]

A former student of philosophy, professor of literature, and committed political activist, Gagnon initially sought to combine socialist politics with poetry in her early works in an effort to undermine what she considered the conventional, bourgeois separation of the political and the poetic. By 1977, however, she had largely abandoned traditional Marxist analyses in her writing along with the rhetoric of Quebec independence for a more subjective expression of women's experience in writing. Texts such as *Retailles* and "Mon Corps dans l'écriture" would offer a more probing critique of patriarchy and its attendant institutions. The collective socialist revolution espoused in *Poélitique* (1975) and *Pour les femmes et tous les autres* (1974) had become a revolution of the female body inscribing sexual difference with words and rhythms uncovered in the farthest corners of the feminine unconscious. As was the case for a number of women writers on the left during the early 1970s, Gagnon's Marxist analyses of class conflict and the dialectics of alienation would yield center stage in the latter half of the decade to a discourse of female solidarity and to questions concerning the relationships between patriarchal institutions, women's writing, and women's private lives.

With the publications of *Antre* (1978), *Lueur* (1979), *Au coeur de la lettre* (1982), and *La Lettre infinie* (1984), Madeleine Gagnon moved the focus of her textual explorations increasingly inward, mining her personal and linguistic depths in a slow, arduous, almost groping manner. Although less overtly political, these works continue to probe what Gabrielle Frémont has referred to as the "mysterious alchemy" of language,[2] the origins of women's words and of life itself. With a multiplicity of discursive tones and poetic forms

so characteristic of many of the works discussed in this study,
Gagnon's writings have fluctuated between reality and fantasy, between the conscious and the unconscious, between the private and
the collective, and between fiction and autobiography, poetry, and
theory. Exceptionally moving in their pursuit of the hidden, the
unexpressed, her more recent texts are intensely intimate explorations of a woman writer's secrets about the sources of writing's
pleasures and the obstacles to her desire to create.

Like Brossard, Madeleine Gagnon is well known to many feminist
critics in France and the United States, due no doubt in Gagnon's
case to the appearance of her essay "Mon Corps dans l'écriture"
alongside essays by Hélène Cixous and Annie Leclerc in *La Venue
à l'écriture* (1977). This text is already considered by many to be an
indispensable introduction to the theoretical argumentation for the
concept of writing the female body.[3] Although Gagnon has not
enjoyed the same kind of resounding critical acclaim in Quebec as
Brossard nor the artistic notoriety of her *collaboratrice* on *Retailles,*
Denise Boucher,[4] she is the only writer from Quebec to be included
in the ground-breaking anthology on *New French Feminisms* edited
by Marks and Courtivron.[5] Like Théoret and Brossard, Gagnon is
a "difficult" writer whose most ambitious texts demand unusual
concentration and multiple readings. However, her work is not as
indecipherable as some critics would have us believe. Considered
collectively, Gagnon's texts offer a dynamic and compelling mixture
of socialist politics, feminist psychoanalysis, autobiographical detail,
and critical theorizing on language and feminine creativity—creating the kind of multifocused perception Irigaray is fond of inciting
women to acknowledge in themselves and in their writing. Ultimately, however, Gagnon's most significant contribution to writing
in the feminine may well lie in her powerfully personal reflections
on the physical, emotional, and intellectual connections between
the woman writer and her words.

Socialism, Feminism, and the Militant Text

Throughout her literary career, Madeleine Gagnon has been an
iconoclast, continually working to sabotage traditional ap-

proaches—be they "male" or "bourgeois"—to the acts of reading and writing. From her earliest works onward, she has invoked the need for radically new forms of discourse capable of disrupting the dominant symbolic and political order. Whether focusing on relations between the classes or between the sexes, the issue of creating a new language and a new position from which to speak has thus been at the center of Gagnon's textual experimentation virturally since the beginning.

Two of Gagnon's early texts, *Pour les femmes et tous les autres* (*For Women and for Everyone Else*) and *Poélitique* (*Poelitical*), have received considerably less critical attention than later works, no doubt due to their militant political stance and excessive deference to Marxist thought. Yet these works are already experimental in terms of their formal construction, particularly in the ways in which they violate conventional distinctions of genre and notions of acceptable poetic tone. Although still closely tied to the polemics of the ideological debate between Marxism and capitalism, Gagnon is struggling even in these early years with textuality, discourse, and the cultural production of gender. In *Pour les femmes et tous les autres* in particular, the notion of women's *différence* is clearly linked to the cultural production of what Michèle Barrett has referred to as the "division, oppression, inequality, [and] internalized inferiority for women" living in contemporary capitalist society.[6]

In *Poélitique*, Gagnon offers a radical collage of poems, quotations, and political analyses, written and assembled from June 1972 to May 1974. In addition to her own poetic reflections on literature, class consciousness, and progressive social change, Gagnon's text includes snatches of Brecht, Mao, and Mayakovsky on Marxist aesthetics and the role of literature in society. She juxtaposes these privileged political voices with excerpts from the first issue of *Le Québec littéraire* (1974),[7] a newly formed literary magazine in which the editors naively claim the right of literature to remain outside the realms of the social, the political, the ideological. Interspersed amid the debate over the relationship of art to politics are Gagnon's own poems and political reflections on a decade and a half (1960–74) of progressive struggle in Quebec. In their most inspiring form, her poems act on the reader with the force and conviction of a

political conjuration. This occurs, for instance, when Gagnon invokes the names, historical events, and mass demonstrations that so
profoundly marked the people of Quebec from 1960 onward, from
the various forms of social unrest manifested during The Quiet
Revolution to the dreams of independence of the early 1970s:

> dans les chantiers de construction
> grève des employés d'hôpitaux
> grève du rail grève de la faim
> pour la reconnaissance du crime
> politique grève à Air-Canada
> à la Dominion Ayers Wood
> et grève à la Manic
> juillet 66 chaleur au Québec
> quarante-cinq-mille grévistes
> des intellectuels se prennent pour
> une classe à part 1962: grève
> des étudiants de l'U. de M. au nom
> de la solidarité syndicale appelons
> les choses par leur nom la poésie
> c'est l'histoire en souffrance[8]

> in the construction yards
> strike of hospital employees
> railroad strike hunger strike
> for the recognition of political
> crimes strike at Air Canada
> at the Dominion Ayers Wood
> and strike at the Manic
> July 66 heat in Quebec
> forty-five thousand strikers
> intellectuals see themselves as
> a class apart 1962: strike
> of students at the U. of Montreal in the name
> of union solidarity let's call
> things by their names poetry
> is history in suspense / in pain

The mission of poetry in *Poélitique* is double in nature. It is first
and foremost a call to participate in the making of tomorrow's
history, which is already silhouetted in the literary visions of socialist
writers and political philosophers. Secondly and no less importantly,
the task of poetry is to transmit the historical suffering of the

common people—both past and present. If, as Gagnon would have us believe, history is the inquisitorial subject that inscribes itself in both the events and the delirium of human experience, the activist-poet is the writer whose literary project seeks to obliterate all barriers between language and action, between ideology and desire:

> le DÉSIR inscrit non plus aux creux de nos cervelles
> mais de nos actes inscrits dans les mémorables
> j'écris c'est ce qu'on m'a appris à l'école
> j'écris pour déchirer la poésie tordre les alphabets
> rompre les codes jusqu'aux formes sonores de la carte
> c'est derrière un discours que se noue le désir oui

> DESIRE no longer inscribed in the hollow of our brains
> but in our actions inscribed in the memorable
> I write it's what they taught me at school
> I write to tear up poetry to bend the alphabets
> break down the codes to the sonorous forms of the map
> it's behind a discourse that desire is formed yes

There are no page numbers in *Poélitique,* which immediately subverts the notion of linear progression in this text and undermines conventional reader expectations as well. In fact, *Poélitique* does not need to be read chronologically or even from left to right or top to bottom as would an ordinary text since Gagnon places comments and quotations lengthwise in the margins and at the bottom of the page. She uses numerous varieties of typescript as well to highlight her intentional mixing of discursive modes. Visually then, *Poélitique* appears every bit the "cut and paste" collage that Gagnon surely intended, with entries spilling into the more traditionally blank spaces of her pages and disrupting even our most basic notions of linearity and spatial boundaries during the act of reading. The effect of this de-centered, nonlinear composition looks rather like the graffitti encountered in public places. And like graffitti, the text's material appearance valorizes the "quick read," the many and diverse sources of inspiration, and the more spontaneous outbursts of social commentary and popularized political thought.

Heavily influenced by Marxist theories of cultural production during the early 1970s, Gagnon views language in *Poélitique* not only as a tool of bourgeois oppression but also, and more importantly for her later work, as a key to the radical transformation of reality through praxis: "Lutter jusque dans les mines profondes et obscures du code grammatical" ("Struggle down into the profound and obscure mines of the grammatical code"). For Gagnon, subverting the dominant lexical, grammatical, and syntactic order entails an uncompromising militancy in her text that is both sweeping in its rebellion and creative in its outlook. As a result, the act of writing becomes a revolutionary activity of some privilege, since it too engages in the struggle to construct a more liberating collective identity. This necessary bonding of the word and the collective social body is precisely the kind of relationship Gagnon establishes in the final lines of *Poélitique:*

> une longue trace descendait rue Papineau
> une lettre pour l'inscrire à l'Histoire
> 20,000 bouches des millions de paroles
> tapageuses et signifiantes
> 1er mai 1974
>
> a long trail was coming down Papineau Street
> one letter to inscribe it in History
> 20,000 mouths millions of words
> noisy and significant
> the first of May 1974

Although Gagnon constructs the theoretical framework of *Poélitique* with considerable clarity and with the force of conviction, she relies far too heavily on external voices of authority—in this case Marxist, to ensure the philosophical rigor she demands of her text. In fact, the frequent intrusions of her extratextual and empowered sources unwittingly widen the gap between intellectualism and the popular culture she so self-consciously works to combine in most of her own poems. In the final analysis, *Poélitique* is more a literary manifesto and less of a poetic exploration of politics and aesthetics than even Gagnon herself might have wished. This troubling imbalance between Gagnon's own poetic voice and the male voices of political theory begins to correct itself, however, in the much more complex textual development of *Pour les femmes et tous les autres.*

As in *Poélitique, Pour les femmes et tous les autres* is a vibrantly modern, interdiscursive collage that mixes theory and poetry, fiction and reality, literature and journalism, while still endeavoring to ground the work of poetry more concretely in the daily lives and aspirations of Quebec's common people. It presents us with a disquieting people's portfolio, filled with working-class portraits of struggle and despair among French-speaking Québécois. The characters in Gagnon's poems speak in *joual*, a working-class dialect of Montreal's east side. Because of its mark of the common people, *le joual* was elevated to a kind of alternate national language by some Quebec separatists on the left during the late 1960s and early 1970s. And as was the case in much of Quebec's nationalist literature during this period, the turn to *joual* in *Pour les femmes et tous les autres* focuses the reader's attention on the politics and economics of language use. It also serves, of course, as a source of linguistic solidarity (or alienation) between the reader and Gagnon's poetic voice. Certainly, the privileged position of *joual* in this text politicizes language in a uniquely Québécois fashion and, at the same time, invalidates the theoretical usefulness of traditional differentiations between spoken language and literary discourse, between the language of high culture and the everyday language of the working class. Moreover, the fragmentary and nonlinear composition of Gagnon's text evokes the abrupt changes in direction and incomplete nature of spoken language in general, even as it is traversed by more academic political theorizing and by direct quotations from other sources.

The family concerns and work-related problems of the characters Gagnon depicts in her poetic sketches reflect both the social burden and the psychological damage of economic hard times and class exploitation in capitalist society. Her family portraits and theatrical monologues are poignant depictions of human tragedy in materialist culture. Although brief and fragmentary in construction, they create a particularly human context for understanding the insidious effects of economic misery on the stability of the family unit, on a working man's pride, and on the confused mental state of an abandoned young mother. These poetic accounts also reveal the ways in which the legacy of economic oppression and dependency invariably repeats itself from one generation to the next, crushing all prospects for an exit out of poverty, humiliation, and subjugation:

Pi là a sait pus trop
c'qui s'est passé dans l'temps
Pourquoi Raoul pi elle
y en sont arrivés là
c'est comme si y s'retrouvaient
pareils comme leux parents
les fois qu'y parlent c'est pour chiâler
on dirait qu'à c't'heure
y peuvent même pus se r'garder
la chicane est pognée
y peuvent pus l'arrêter
a' souvient pus pantoutte
comment tout ça ça commencer[9]

An' so she don't know no more
what happened back there
Why Raoul an' her
got to that thar point
it's like they found 'emselves
jus' like thar parents
the times they talk is fer cryin'
seems like these days
can't even look at each other no more
the squabble gets goin'
can't stop it no more
she don't member neither
how it all got started

Gagnon does propose a political way out of this vicious circle of rising expectations and inevitable deceptions through her socialist vision of a more egalitarian society. As a writer, her vehicle toward that political end is a language of resistance and revolt. The accessibility of poetic language thus becomes of primary importance to Gagnon in her struggle to reach ordinary people and to encourage them to write. In the second in a series of three poems entitled "POÈMES TRÈS LISIBLES" ("VERY READABLE POEMS"), she urges a collective outpouring of the people's voices to drown the official discourses of Capital, the State, and those poets who have failed to speak with and through the masses: "MAIS LES POÈTES EUX-MÊMES VOUS ASSOMMENT ET LEURS VAINES RECHERCHES D'ÉCRITURES INSONORES SONT ÉCRANS ENTRE VOS PAROLES ET LA MIENNE

PARLEZ PLUS FORT ENCORE" (45) ("BUT THE POETS
THEMSELVES BEAT YOU TO DEATH AND THEIR VAIN
SEARCHES FOR SOUND-PROOF WRITING ARE
SCREENS BETWEEN YOUR WORDS AND MINE SPEAK
EVEN LOUDER").

As a revolutionary poet in the early 1970s, Madeleine Gagnon
refused to envision the act of writing as a romantic calling or as the
golden fruit of an educated elite that has privatized artistic expression for its own pleasure. Thus, one of her female characters demands an end to "leurs beaux poèmes polis" (16) ("their pretty
polished poems") in favor of poems that address human experience
in concrete terms. Hence, the poet's task is to bear sober witness to
the collective plight of the working class and to reject the cultural
and economic domination of intellectual elites. Underscoring the
tie that binds her own artistic production to the realities of people's
daily lives, Gagnon addresses her readers directly and concludes,
"NOUS NE POUVONS PLUS RIEN SI VOUS NE PARLEZ
PAS" (45) ("WE CAN'T DO ANYTHING ANYMORE IF YOU
DON'T SPEAK OUT"). No longer the sacred realm of an individual imagination or a privileged class, poetry is first and foremost
the realm of the people, the realm of the real.

Yet if *Pour les femmes et tous les autres* is one level an attempt to
fuse the voices of working people with the words of the poet, it is
also a text about women and dedicated to women, as the title
indicates. Although fragmentary at best, Gagnon's reflections on
the experiences that bind women together clearly bear the early seeds
of her subsequent feminist politics and gender-marked approach to
writing. Already Gagnon notes, for example, that female friendship
can assuage women's sense of loneliness and provide the only authentic communication in an otherwise mute and alien environment. Gagnon also makes ironic use of the advertising of feminine
apparel in *La Presse,* Quebec's most widely read newspaper, in order
to emphasize the injurious effects of bourgeois recipes for feminine
beauty on the self-perceptions of working-class women:

> Quand j'regarde des revues
> j'me trouve ben laide
> j'me r'connais pus chus toute perdue

ça s'peut pas comme y sont belles les
    femmes par là
La mode on dirait c'est pour eux autres
    qu'est faite   (34)

When I look at magazines
I feel real ugly
I don't see myself an' I feel terrible lost
can't get over how perty those
    women thar are
the styles I reckon it's for them thar
    they make 'em

The alienation depicted here is no less real, Gagnon suggests, and
no less pernicious than the specific forms of alienation experienced
by workers in the division of labor under capitalism and in the
capitalist mode of production in general. Gagnon makes the crucial
link here between the public and the private spheres, a link that
traditional Marxist theory has neglected to emphasize, as contemporary feminist thinkers have been quick to point out.

In the concluding pages of *Pour les femmes et tous les autres,*
Gagnon joins theories of class conflict and gender politics in a rare
blending of sexual pleasure and terrorism, revolutionary love and
social justice:

vagin fleuri fleurdelysé sexe et médecine nos sexes
débouchent dans le ventre amour et terrorisme
contradictoires vérités de nos jouissances leur sexe
n'a rien à voir avec un ventre ouvert   (42)

Cela n'empêche pas le désir et la fête multiple
cela ne refoule plus le délire enfin qui rompt les
amarres coule libre et puis trace nous sommes amants
camarades nous sommes nombreux cela n'est pas facile
et pour le dire il faut creuser des mots de tous les
jours   (46)

flowery vagina fleur-de-lised sex and medicine our
    sex organs
emerge in the womb love and terrorism
contradictory truths and our pleasures their sex
has nothing to do with an open belly

That doesn't hinder desire and the multiple cele-
    bration
that no longer represses the ecstasy which breaks
adrift flows free and then traces we are lovers
comrades we are numerous that's not easy
and in order to say so we must dig for everyday words

What Gagnon posits here is a new kind of loving: the unrepressed, unashamed sexual love of male and female equals that literally becomes a subversive act, uniting male and female bodies in a manner wholly at odds with the social codes established by the dominant economic order. Ultimately, she assures us, the all too familiar rhythms and outworn images of the bourgeois ballad—despite its popular appeal, will, of necessity, yield to the visionary love poetry of a revolutionary era.

Pour les femmes et tous les autres is, above all, an early attempt by Gagnon to chart the possible directions of a poetic writing of the future capable of breaking up the existing symbolic order of materialist culture. As Philippe Haeck notes in his review of Gagnon's textual collage, "Instead of the beautiful, smooth and cold writing to which Anne Hébert and Nicole Brossard have accustomed us, here we are presented with a writing full of ruptures, warm, combative."[10] Although the challenge of Gagnon's literary project is a formidable one and less accessible to the common people than she perhaps imagined at the time, the prospect for change in her early writing is a thing of beauty: "Pour nos enfants comment devenir en armes nos caresses en combats nos amours" (14) ("For our children how to become in arms our caresses in combat our loves").

Writing, Repression, and Sisterhood: *Retailles*

"I always knew that history was writing me. But that I am written with others and through others has become self-evident at this meeting."[11] So began Gagnon in a series of opening remarks at the international conference on "La Femme et l'écriture," held in Montreal in 1975. Midway through an explosive decade for women in Quebec, Gagnon's prophetic comments marked a personal as well as a collective turning point—both in the development of women's writing in the French-speaking province and in Quebec's feminist movement as well. Among those who attended this important conference on women and writing, a number of female participants were drawn together because of common political concerns. Many also shared their increasing dissatisfaction over the fact that women's issues continued to be marginalized in most of Quebec's political groups on the left.

During the year that followed this conference, some of the women writers began forming a series of consciousness-raising groups, comprised of five or six women who met regularly to share their thoughts and feelings about the myths and realities of women's lives. Gagnon and Denise Boucher participated in one such group with three other women and subsequently recorded the aspirations and failures associated with their collective experience in a thoroughly unique, albeit controversial text entitled: *Retailles: complaintes politiques* (*Shreds: Political Laments*), which appeared in 1977. Divergent views on the politics of sexual preference appear to have been the central point of contention that ultimately split the group apart and led to the publication of *Retailles*. Some radical feminists, like Jovette Marchessault, immediately denounced *Retailles* as an irreverent attack against female solidarity, while others saw in it further evidence of the widening political schism between heterosexual and lesbian feminists active in the women's movement.

Yet despite the political debate it unleashed in feminist circles in Quebec, or perhaps in some measure because of it, *Retailles* brought a number of painful realities about women working together out in the open for all to consider. In an important sense, *Retailles* remains a crucial historical and literary document for contemporary feminist thought, for in addition to its inside view of some aspects of feminist politics in Quebec, it also highlights the kind of factionalism, divisiveness, and deep-seated insecurities that were plaguing many of the women's groups in France and in the United States during approximately the same time. But *Retailles* also offers a more affirmative vision of women's future together in a series of poetic and political reflections that call on women to form a new collective identity through a language of their own making.

The collaborative effort of Boucher and Gagnon clearly adds an important dimension to the text's bold frankness of spirit and intent. Yet the most important function for its authors may well have been the extent to which *Retailles* served as a liberating confession of disillusionment that freed each writer from her own internal censorship. This, in turn, encouraged an opening up of repressed thoughts and words about sexual identity and women's love. For Gagnon, this outpouring of personal pain and anger, in combination with her theoretical reflections on women, initiated a change of tone and direction in her writing the fruits of which we continue to see throughout the decade that follows. Gagnon herself admits that without the sharing of such honesty, she would have been unable to continue writing:

Il n'y a plus de mots taboos. Cette confusion qui à la fois me hante et me séduit. Toute ma vie passée et mon histoire récente avec nous cinq m'aura appris que parfois la plus profonde vérité du fond de soi, lorsque proférée, peut être reçue par l'autre comme violence, comme aggression. De là les nombreuses censures pour tous ces textes—littéraires ou politiques—qui dans le cours des siècles n'étaient pourtant que des cris isolés de vérité.[12]

There are no longer any taboo words. This confusion which haunts me and seduces me at the same time. All my past life and my recent history with the five of us will have taught me that sometimes the most profound truth from our inner depths can, when uttered, be understood by the other as violence, as aggression. Hence the numerous censures which over the course of centuries were but the isolated cries of truth.

This uneasy confrontation with previously unspoken truths about women speaking to one another is what gives *Retailles* a rare sense of urgency and a persuasive strength. Ironically perhaps for Boucher and Gagnon, their detection of some of the unsettling fissures that hinder women's solidarity centers around issues of sexual preference—whether heterosexual, bisexual, or lesbian—and feminine desire, subjects whose explorations link *Retailles* to many of the feminist and radical lesbian texts that have appeared in Quebec since 1975. Both Gagnon and Boucher artfully weave considerations of the politics of sexual repression and the obliteration of women's desire into their poetry and prose fragments in order to expose the dangers and abuses of power, whether in the hands of men or other women. In so doing, their dialogue of deception reveals the risks women of commitment continually run of duplicating the most destructive aspects of men's history and male-oriented culture. In Gagnon's view, history and culture have in fact been dominated by Thanatos rather than Eros, a path she does not encourage women to follow:

Je les ai vues vouloir vous tuer une à une comme on tue trop d'amour quand on souffre du manque. Si au moins j'avais vu leur souffrance se dire.
(44)

I saw them wanting to kill you one by one like killing too much love when one suffers from its absence. If only I had seen their suffering express itself.

Refusing all pacts with power, Gagnon denounces the growing cleavage between heterosexual and lesbian feminists as a deplorable schism that will shatter all hope for a collective and supportive dialogue among women and a tolerant love of one another. "Etouffer la parole n'a jamais été et ne sera jamais un geste de tendresse" (67), says Gagnon. ("Stifling the word has never been and will never be a gesture of tenderness.") For Gagnon, to write is to refuse death and repression in all its forms, a position that clearly echoes the work of Hélène Cixous during this same period. In a special dossier assembled by Cixous on women and writing, which appeared in France prior to the publication of *Retailles,* Gagnon argues that women's writing must resist the inscription of violence and ward off the deadening control of textual-sexual manipulation. Instead, she envisions an *écriture au féminin* that tends toward explorations of the previously unrepresented and, in her own words, "records those fluctuating spaces that have escaped the stratified codifications of power."[13]

The imagery Gagnon develops in *Retailles* reflects her deepening preoccupation with the need to undo the history of women's repression through the invention of new forms of feminine discourse, a political and artistic concern that motivates her writing throughout the latter half of the 1970s. Images of knotting and unknotting, knitting and unknitting or unraveling previous depictions of women's lives permeate *Retailles* from beginning to end: "Eux à nouer les stratégies dont je suis. Moi à découdre les fils de l'intrigue où ils se trouvent" (42) ("For them to knot the strategies from whence I am. For me to unstitch the threads of the intrigue in which they find themselves"). Gagnon's extensive use of the infinitive and present participle in both *Retailles* and "Mon Corps dans l'écriture" explodes the temporal boundaries while also creating a striking textual immediacy by drawing the reader into a verb that is seemingly subject-free:

> Essayer de presser si fort l'orange
> du désir qu'il en sortira de la tendresse.
> Presser si fort l'orange, faire le défi qu'à
> la limite du désir, dans l'absolu du
> sexe, jusqu'à la lie: c'est là que
> le jus de la tendresse peut le mieux
> sortir. Entrer sur le terrain du pouvoir
> et du désir pour me défaire de l'intérieur.
> Pour le découdre jusque dans ses
> doublures les plus cachées. C'est
> pénétrer jusqu'à la moelle là où le
> désir dit mieux la puissance d'être.
> C'est vouloir détruire le pouvoir sur
> le terrain même de la puissance de
> vivre.   (112)

> Try to press so strongly the orange
> of desire that tenderness will come out of it.
> Press the orange so firmly, challenge it to
> the limit of desire, in the absoluteness of
> sex, to the last drop: it's there that
> the juice of tenderness can most easily
> come out. Enter onto the field of power
> and desire so as to undo me from the inside.
> So as to unsew it even in its
> most hidden linings. This is
> penetrating to the very marrow there where
> desire speaks the force of being more clearly.
> This is wanting to destroy power over
> the very basis of the strength
> to live.

The mixture of literary tones (ironic, accusatory, intimate, detached, intellectual) and formal structures (poetry, dialogue, political analysis, autobiographical account) in *Retailles* is so complete as to obliterate the notion of genre altogether. Indeed, the collaborative effort of Boucher and Gagnon highlights the differences as well as the common ground in their respective writing practices, as the text alternates between poetry and prose, political contexts and personal musings, between Gagnon's own distinctly intellectual approach to writing and Boucher's more satiric humor. This intentional move to bring down the walls of literary convention that have separated the political, the poetic, and the personal is indicative of Gagnon's desire to seriously rethink the new forms literary discourse might assume. It also mirrors some of the kinds of theoretical concerns being raised by Brossard, Théoret, and others about the politics of textual construction. That Gagnon slips so easily into the first person plural (*nous*) throughout much of the text suggests that she herself was well aware of the extent to which the unconventional, interdiscursive construction of *Retailles* reflected not only the joint vision of the two authors, but also the general direction of women's experimental writing in the late 1970s:

Que l'on nomme fiction ou poésie, ou encore philosophie ces venues de nous dans l'écriture, importe peu. Seule nous emporte, avec les formes qu'elle génère, cette libre course qui doit plonger dans la pénombre des symbolismes introjectés pour enfin remonter aux vérités étrangères que, seules, nous pouvons divulguer. Nous savons qu'un jour, grâce à tous ces risques passionnés d'actions, de paroles et d'écritures, nous aurons transformé, non seulement le poétique, en apportant au texte son corps à corps censuré, mais aussi le politique en nous plaçant, non plus comme objet dans la phallocratie mais comme sujet d'une nouvelle histoire de partage entre les femmes et les hommes.   (8–9)

Whether one calls it fiction or poetry, or even philosophy, these advents of ours in writing, matter very little. Ultimately, what transports us, along with the forms it generates, is the unhampered course that plunges introjected symbolisms into semidarkness in order to reach far back to the strange truths that only we can divulge. We know that one day, thanks to all these passionate risks of actions, words, and writing, we will have transformed not only the poetic realm by bringing to the text its censored body, but also the political realm by no longer placing ourselves as objects in the phallocratic system but rather as subjects in a new history of sharing between women and men.

Despite the severity of the criticism Gagnon and Boucher direct against lesbian separatist politics in the women's movement, *Retailles* offers a powerful challenge to the nature of male-dominated politics and aesthetics as well. Although not altogether the kind of "feminine dialogue" that Suzanne Lamy described in *d'elles*, particularly since Boucher and Gagnon's text is not based on verbal conversations per se (except in a reconstituted and fragmentary form), *Retailles* is nevertheless an example of how a collaborative women's writing project can also produce a plural feminine voice in which "the most intimate and unprecedented admissions" can be quite naturally articulated.[14] And despite its critique of separatist politics within Quebec feminism, it nevertheless exemplifies a number of the qualities contemporary feminist critics have attributed to feminist thinking and writing.

While they remain skeptical regarding a feminist political stance that might incite women to wage indiscriminate war on their male compatriots, Gagnon and Boucher look to the progressive future for political inspiration, to further efforts to unsilence the voices of preceding generations of women, and to the growing number of feminist mothers offering new models for their children. Both writers express the hope that one day men and women will no longer shape their respective identities through a politics of opposition that is always played out at the other's expense. This position appears to be entirely consistent with Hélène Cixous' view of sexual politics during this same period, for as Verena Andermatt Conley notes in her comprehensive study of Cixous' work, "The martial female . . . is nothing but 'a woman who has killed the woman in her,' coming into femininity only by death and still more sexual opposition."[15] It is this perceived movement toward separation and death that Gagnon seeks to counter in both her concluding "birth poem" and in her writing as a whole:

> La nuit suivante, il me fut donné
> de vivre un si grand bonheur. Calme,
> allongée sur un plateau gazeux de
> lumineuse obscurité, je donnai la vie
> comme indéfiniment. Des dizaines de
> bébés sortirent de mon ventre.
> Aucun effort, aucune douleur; ILS
> venaient, de moi, prendre leur
> place dans l'histoire.   (147)

> The following night, I was given the chance
> to live such a great happiness. Calm,

stretched out on a gaseous plateau of
luminous obscurity, I gave life
almost indefinitely. Dozens of
babies emerged from my womb.
No effort, no pain: THEY
came, from inside me, to take their
place in history.

Toward a Theory of the Female Body in Writing

If *Retailles* invokes the need for new forms of feminine discourse
that would push back the forces of repression and death, it is
Gagnon's ground-breaking essay, "Mon Corps dans l'écriture" that
presents us with the theoretical argumentation for the fashioning
of a new approach to writing in which women and the life-giving
resources of women's bodies in particular become the sources of
scriptorial inspiration and linguistic invention. Published in France
in 1977, "Mon Corps dans l'écriture" immediately gave Gagnon the
kind of international recognition that many Quebec women writers
of her generation would lack for some time, with the notable exception of Brossard.[16]

At ease in the rigorously intellectual company of Hélène Cixous
and Annie Leclerc—the two other contributors to the series of
essays in *La Venue à l'écriture,* Gagnon is impressive and at her
combative best in her theoretical critiques of such issues as women's
place in patriarchal philosophy and in theories of "human" knowledge, capitalism's economic exploitation of women, the brutality of
male-dominated medical practice for women in the West, Freud's
obsession with the Oedipal complex, and Lacan's erasure of
"woman" altogether from the realm of the Symbolic. Thoroughly
at odds with Freud's theorizing on female castration, Gagnon argues
that the castration young women experience has nothing to do with
"penis envy;" rather, it is based on the continued exclusion of
womankind from symbolic and abstract discourse.

Gagnon's particular quarrel with Lacan's insistence on the privileged signifying function of the phallus in contemporary Freudian
theory is both feminist and socialist in its inspiration.[17] But the basis
of her argumentation is, at the same time, uniquely Québécois in

its targeted attack, since France is the "cocky" and judgmental Father with regard to Quebec. For Gagnon, the symbolic seduction of Lacan's signifying phallus is but one more tragic example of man's inability to achieve self-understanding and acceptance without the aid of his own reinforcing double; this is the phallic "conceit."[18] Gagnon reads Lacan's need to assign a special signifying status to the phallus as exemplary of man's need to mirror his own erect image that, she claims, is nothing more than a phantasm of his own making:

Le phallus est pour moi en ce moment capitaux contraignants, bourgeois exploiteurs, haut-savoir à franchir, France érigée qui regarde, analyse et sanctionne. Tout ce qui s'érige en miroir. Tout ce qui bande perfection. Tout ce qui veut ordonnance et représentation. Ce qui n'efface pas et convoite. Ce qui aligne dans les musées de l'histoire. Ce qui se mesure constamment au pouvoir de l'immoralité. Pourtant, je saisis cette langue qui m'est étrangère et la retourne à ma façon. J'enfile des vérités qui seront reproduites. Mais sur l'ardoise, il y avait la craie souveraine. Elle disait de moi la partie qui domine. Je me suis étrangère en ma langue et me traduis moi-même en citant tous les autres.   (70–71)

The phallus is for me at this time compulsive capital, bourgeois exploiters, authoritative knowledge to be surpassed, an erect France who gazes upon, analyzes, and sanctions. Everything that is erected as mirror. Everything that ejaculates perfection. Everything that wants regulation and representation. What doesn't erase and covets. What is aligned in the museums of history. What constantly measures itself in terms of immoral power. However, I seize this language which is foreign to me and turn it around in my own way. I thread truths that will be reproduced. But on the slate, there was the sovereign chalk. She told me of the adversary who dominates. I am a foreigner myself in my own language and translate myself by quoting all the others.

Although far less satiric and insolent than Bersianik in her critique of the comic horrors of western phallocentric thought (exemplified here in the discourses of Freud and Lacan), Gagnon is every bit as committed to deconstructing phallocentrism within the context of her own politically inspired approach to writing. And like her French counterparts in *La Venue à l'écriture*, Gagnon views the contemporary woman's "coming to writing" as an act of self-repossession and survival, as well as a radical indictment of phallocentric history as we have known it: "Je revendique ma place de sujet dans l'histoire. Je revendique mon pouvoir de représentation et de nomination" (64) ("I reclaim my place as subject in history. I reclaim my power of representation and of naming"). Moreover, as she indicates elsewhere, Gagnon is also reclaiming her rights of access to theory in this essay and expressing her need to enter the realm of the symbolic on women's terms. Thus, with the problem of language, which Gagnon originally placed in a materialist context, she has shifted ground to reflect her increasing preoccupations with phallocentrism, with the immense power of "naming," and with a number of the issues most commonly associated with feminist theories of women's difference.

In this pivotal essay, Gagnon calls for the birth of a "body writing" that is insistently gender-marked, intimately personal, and politically astute. The body from which Gagnon herself wishes to speak in this text is a maternal body marked by the physical travail and creative joy she experienced in the act of giving birth. She does not fetishize the maternal body, however, since motherhood is clearly not, in her mind, the only route to women-centered literary production. But it has been an important dimension in her own life, and she does urge women to use their maternal tongue to explore the strategic links between *maternité* and writing.

Along with Adrienne Rich, Hélène Cixous, and Annie Leclerc, Gagnon views language corporeally in this essay. For her, language is not only a skin with which to touch and feel the other—an image offered by Roland Barthes who has greatly influenced the work of Brossard and Bersianik as well[19]—but also a body capable of receiving, nurturing, and procreating. Thus, Gagnon enters into the rarely mapped territory of mothers who write about maternity and about their own maternity in writing. American critic Susan Suleiman has, in fact, pointed out that in general "we know very little about the inner discourse of a mother; and as long as our own emphasis, encouraged by psychoanalytic theory and by the looming presence of (mostly male) mother-fixated writers, continues to be on the-mother-as-she-is-written rather than on the-mother-as-she-writes, we shall continue in our ignorance."[20]

In order to explore this correspondence between writing and motherhood, Gagnon shares with her readers several grotesque scenes from her own experiences with childbirth. She recounts these intense personal moments in order to underscore both the phallocentric institutionization of childbirth in the West and the severe repression of her pleasure as a mother, situations she will then link to the analogous repression of women's writing:

C'était dans un petit hôpital de Provence où le gynécologue ressemblait à s'y méprendre au boucher de mon ancien village. Tablier blanc rempli de sang,manches de chemises retroussées pour la besogne, cigarette à la main. Il ne manquait que le couteau. Assis à l'autre bout de la salle, juste en face de moi, les yeux centrés sur mon vagin béant, c'est tout ce qu'il voyait de moi. Moi, allongée, tête en arrière, les pieds attachés aux étriers, mes mains bloquées par la sage-femme, essayant de reprendre mon souffle, pendant qu'il criait "poussez" "poussez" et que la sage-femme exécutait ses ordres. Montée sur moi comme un cavalier, ses genoux sur mes épaules et les deux mains qui pressaient sur le ventre pour que ça descende enfin. Ils étaient fatigués d'attendre. Cette scène grotesque m'a semblé durer des heures . . . j'eus assez d'énergies pour arracher dessus mon corps la sage-femme, la projeter par terre ou bien dans les nuages, j'ai oublié, en hurlant que je voulais mon enfant à ma façon, que j'avais besoin de l'écouter lentement descendre et suivre ses mouvements, que je n'avais rien à prouver à personne . . . Acceptant ni ma lenteur (qui était aussi celle de l'enfant) ni ma révolte, l'énorme boucher se précipita sur moi pour m'endormir au chloroforme. Ce fut une nouvelle lutte à mort pour rester en éveil, aux écoutes de mon ventre, et dans la lutte je vis soudain sortir cette terre ronde entre mes deux cuisses, celle que j'avais senti tourner juste avant, suivie d'un immense cri de victoire dans le mouvement des fleuves et des océans rouges qui coulaient avec elle. Je m'endormis les astres et toutes les planètes sur mon ventre pendant que la sage-femme essuyait le sang par terre et que le gynécologue se rallumait une cigarette en criant: "Au moins, c'est un garçon."

(73–74)

It was in a little hospital in Provence where the gynecologist could have been taken for the butcher from my old village. White jacket covered with blood, shirt sleeves rolled up for the job, cigarette in hand. Only the knife was missing. Seated at the other end of the room, right across from me, eyes centered on my open vagina, that's all he saw of me. Stretched out, head back, feet attached to the stirrups, my hands pinned down by the midwife, trying to catch my breath, while he yelled "push" "push" and the midwife executed his orders. Climbed up on me like a horseman, her knees on my shoulders and two hands that pressed on my abdomen so that it would finally move downward. They were tired of waiting. This grotesque scene seemed to last for hours . . . I had enough energy to pull the midwife off my body, throw her on the ground or else in the clouds, I've forgotten, yelling that I wanted my child in my own way, that I needed to listen to it slowly descend and follow its movements, that I had nothing to prove to anyone . . . Accepting neither my slowness (which was also that of the child) nor my revolt, the enormous butcher hurled himself at me in order to anaesthetize me with chloroform. It was a new deadly struggle to remain conscious, listening to my abdomen, and in the struggle I suddenly saw this round earth come out between my two thighs, what I had just felt turn a moment ago, followed by an immense cry of victory in the movement of rivers and red oceans which flowed with it. I fell asleep with the stars and all the planets on my belly while the midwife wiped up the blood on the floor and the gynecologist was lighting a cigarette exclaiming: "At least it's a boy."

The analogy Gagnon constructs between the struggling woman writer and the young mother in labor is painfully clear. Increasingly, men in western societies control the birth process in much the same way that they have controlled women's language, women's discourse, women's lives. For the feminist writer and reader, this expanding analogy has a stirring if nonetheless distressing effect since it skillfully points to the tremendous power women may exert when they resist male intervention and domination in order to give birth and write in the full and naked intensity of their own corporeal experience and their own desires.

In "Mon Corps dans l'écriture," Gagnon wants, in effect, to put her own body into language and thus create an immediate and compelling relationship between the body she lives and the progression of her own unfolding text. Although indisputably personal, this commitment to "write" her own maternal body becomes a political act by virtue of the parallels she establishes between the historic censoring of virtually all aspects of the female body and of women's words, women's texts. While the collective socialist revolution called for in Gagnon's earlier works has not disappeared altogether, it has taken a back seat to a revolution of women struggling to reach beyond their social isolation, class differences, and physical distance in patriarchal-heterosexual society toward a political union with other women. Since no viable female models for such a revolutionary endeavor exist in the dominant culture, Gagnon urges women to recapture the power and inherent multiplicity of lost female forms through an exploratory language that traces the inscription of an infinite number of differences on women's flesh, in their varied fantasies and their words, and in the farthest recesses of what may be a collective feminine unconscious:

Nos révolutions vont sourdre de toutes parts. Visqueses, défilées, emmêlées, nouées ou tendues. Mon cerveau n'est pas linéaire; mon sexe est circulaire, il se plie, se délie et décrit des circonvolutions; mes yeux sont ronds, mes oreilles compliquées à déjouer toute description; ma langue tordue, mes langues d'écritures étranges et semblables; mes langues de paroles plus que contradictoires.   (115–16)

Our revolutions are going to gush from all sides. Viscous, filing past, entangled, tied together or strained. My brain is not linear; my sex is circular, it bends, unties itself and depicts circumvolutions; my eyes are round, my ears intricate enough to elude all description; my tongue twisted, my languages of writing strange and similar; my languages of speech more than contradictory.

The vision of a feminine approach to writing grounded in the uniqueness of women's physical being thus becomes not only an individual act of self-possession but an act of collective reappropriation as well. It is important to stress, however, that what keeps Gagnon's emphasis on the corporeal grounding of women's writing from appearing to return too easily to the old reductive masculinist categories of Woman = Body + Nature (versus Man = Mind + Culture) is the extent to which the female body in Gagnon's writing touches and relates to every aspect of human experience, including the most intellectual and abstract of human activities. Gagnon's efforts both in this essay and in subsequent texts to weld together intellectual theory with remarkably intimate narrative descriptions and with poetic reflections on her own life is, as we shall see, an indication of her ability to resist categorizing and limiting women's experience in writing and in the world.

Archaeological Writing: *Lueur*

In the works that follow "Mon Corps dans l'écriture," Gagnon has focused increasingly on the female body as a primary generator of textual production. At the same time, this desire to inscribe the female body becomes the catalyst for a crucial psychoanalytic journey backward through her earliest memories to the lost warmth of the maternal womb, the period of her own birth, and the initial beginnings of language itself—events that constitute Gagnon's primal visions of love, nurturance, and a language still connected to the sensate and sexual world of the female body. Both *Antre* (*Den*) and *Lueur* (*Glimmer*) are *auto*-biographical to the extent that they write the self and *"bio*-graphical"—to borrow from Christiane Mak-ward—to the extent that they write the life of the body as well.[21]

The *archaeological writing* Gagnon develops in texts such as *Antre* (1978) and *Lueur* (1979) presents us with an unusual and challenging mixture of feminist psychoanalysis, autobiographical detail, poetic fantasies, and critical theorizing on the creative process. In tying her own approach to a writing of difference to an exploration of early memories and repressed desires, Gagnon has of course politicized both the search for and content of what might be termed a collective feminine unconscious. At the same time, she has pro-vided an important theoretical framework for understanding the move to inscribe the female body and the need to articulate the nature of women's original longings, sense of loss, and desire for a language that loves life. The result of Gagnon's textual explorations in *Antre* and *Lueur* is the emergence of a language that appears in many ways to resemble an unconscious writing from the female body. It is a language in which grammatical and syntactic construc-tions have been devised to evoke the backward and inward move-ments of a female consciousness in active pursuit of the traces of her own corporeal, psychological, and linguistic development on the "body" of the feminine text.

In many respects her most ambitious work to date, *Lueur* carries the subtitle of *roman archéologique* (archaeological novel), evoking the long, slow, internal excavation of the woman writer's own depths. Gagnon's subtitle also comments on the laborious and painstaking nature of the process of writing itself. In particular, the text's archaeological motif draws our attention to the acts of unearthing and stripping language bare, of emptying words of commonly anticipated meanings, and finally, of exposing what has long remained hidden from the woman writer and from history. In an interview with Gagnon, Quebec critic Jean Royer writes: *"Lueur* is a novel that bathes 'in the water of words,' in this great white night where the traces of birth, life, and death are inscribed, where inscriptions from before the law of the father are revealed, but where 'the veritable enigma' of this 'waterwriting of absence' still reigns."[22]

We can read *Lueur* on a number of levels, as a personal search for origins, as a collective recuperative act that binds generations of women together in a common history, and most important, as an original inquiry into the re-viewing and re-formulation of women's language. The textual exploration in *Lueur* begins by carrying us back in time to fleeting images of the writer's birth and to inaugural scenes of her own linguistic beginnings. Gagnon probes for her body and for the bodies of other women amid the shadowy landscapes and warm recesses of the maternal womb, the symbolic den of female births, or in the darkest corners of ancient caves, the physical sites of life's earliest beginnings. In this primordial landscape, the writer rediscovers the faint contours of her own female shape emerging from a fluid world of rivers, lakes, and amniotic waters that constitute her earliest liquid memories. There she begins to hear the muffled sounds of a far away, primeval language that has been buried within her:

Dans la longue nuit qui nous entoure, nous entendons des paroles d'eau. Nous avions si longtemps renoncé au fluide. Sa venue nous effraie. Nés de cela pourtant, nous imaginons, de son retour, la catastrophe.[23]

In the long night that surrounds us, we hear watery words.
We had renounced fluid for so long. Its arrival frightens us. Born of it, we still imagine catastrophe with its return.

Likewise in *Antre,* Gagnon describes a dark and protected world where both the infant's body and the mouth's initial sounds are still in a state of flux, neither solid nor articulate, and where she discovers traces of "des morphèmes, des sèmes, sans paroles. Un corps qui coule, une écriture qui suit, s'écoulant avec lui, s'insinuant partout où celui-ci le porte" ("morphemes, semes, without words. A body that flows, a writing that follows, flowing with it, creeping everywhere the latter takes it").[24] Gagnon's fascination with formlessness in both *Antre* and *Lueur* is the result of her conviction that women must rediscover their bodies in order to reformulate a language that speaks of and to their own corporeal existence. "Laisser parler le corps," she enjoins, "juste le corps, tout le corps sans fragments, sans morcellements" (*Lueur,* 59) ("Let the body speak, just the body, the whole body without fragments, without cutting it up").
    The narrative in *Lueur* originates in the deepest recesses of inner life as an *écriture de nuit* (night writing) in which the woman writer

struggles to decipher the obscured outlines of "la première page de ma première nuit" (13) ("the first page of my first night"). Archaic liquids seem to ebb and swell, as the eye moves slowly inward, in half-darkness, catching no more than brief glimpses from an ancient past and a personal past that speak to one another outside of time. Gagnon's psychoanalytic journey back to the birth and prebirth scenes focuses on the pre-Oedipal phase of feminine development and on the close ties between mother and daughter. Her search for origins, and for a language in which to convey them, also links personal sensations and desires for the maternal to a collective female past that has been shrouded in cheerless secrecy for centuries. Only the syntax of dreams, it would seem, can recall those immemorial sites, linguistically rendered through a mysterious and yet strangely familiar topology of origins.

Gagnon's linguistic odyssey soon takes on a more visceral quality as she moves us through the dreamlike, watery darkness of the maternal womb to confront the mute and eclipsed mother whose language has been lost to women for generations. The prevalence of the labial sounds and alliterations produced with the letter *m* are striking here:

Se remémorant leur mère muette à chacun, la même et différente, celle qui n'avait pas su donner de sens à ses signes qui les lui reliaient; celle qui n'avait rien su dire du si grand carnage humain tout autour; celle qui s'était éclipsée avant même que ses pauvres enfants ne puissent figurer son destin de morte muette.   (62)

Remembering their mother each one mute, the same and different, the one who hadn't known how to make sense out of the signs that linked them to her; the one who hadn't known what to say about the great human carnage all around; the one who had vanished long before her poor children were able to understand her destiny of a dead mute.

As the preceding passage suggests, Gagnon views silence as the fundamental psychological space of motherhood throughout patriarchal history. The muffled maternal voice becomes the focal point for a series of poetic reflections on the silencing of women's words and creative impulses. But restoration of the mother's mute discourse can only occur, Gagnon tells us, by relocating the maternal body and, like the archaeologist, by carefully inspecting the linguistic traces that have been solemnly inscribed on her surfaces over the centuries. Like Brossard's *L'Amèr* (1977), *Lueur* attempts to explore the hidden power of the silenced mother figure and the subversive, secret knowledge that mothers transmit to their daughters through the fleshy terrain of *la chair linguistique* (the linguistic body).[25]

Already in "Mon Corps dans l'écriture," the mother figure functioned as a radical point of departure for a new linguistic site from which to affirm the female subject and women's collective body politic. In *Lueur*, Gagnon dares to descend to the depths of the maternal body in order to unearth a feminine discourse that speaks of *le corps féminin* from the inside. The groping style of her nocturnal search moves the reader along the interior walls of women's bodies on which liquid words have inscribed the blood of their menses, the amniotic waters of maternity, and the milk of lactation—leaving indelible traces of the joys, suffering, and physical intensity of women's lives:

Les mots couleraient d'elle sans phonèmes, sans bruit, si non, de loin, le clapotis de ses eaux caressant des sables d'or. Des sables d'os, d'hécatombes, de sangs larvaires de sueurs mnémésiques de ses lointaines enfantemailles orgiaques. Des sables de poudres d'amniose et de lactose. Des sables rives qui la ramènent à son centre et la retiennent de mourir. Des sables de plages où ils viendront s'étendre, se reposer, les mains sur le ventre brûlant, les seins contre la bouche sucrée, se remémorant ces temps anciens où ils étaient dedans. (61–62)

The words would flow from her without phonemes, without noise, except for the distant rippling of her waters caressing golden sands. Sands of bone, hecatombs, larval blood from the mnemonic labour of her distant orgiastic infant stitches. Sands of amniotic powder and lactose. Shoreline sands that bring her back to her center and prevent her from dying. Sands from beaches where they will come to stretch out, rest, hands on the hot belly, breasts against the sweet mouth, remembering that former time when they were inside.

Gagnon's description of the internal female landscape creates a pulsating corporeal litany that gently bathes the reader in its fluid visions. This view from "the inside" also evokes the generative and consolatory powers of the feminine form. Echoing Bersianik, who considers the maternal womb to be the privileged site of our earliest memories,[26] Gagnon seeks poetic inspiration amid the nurturing spaces of uterine walls, for it is there, she suggests, that women's creativity is most freely and most generously expressed. In *Lueur,* the womb is also the place from which, to use Susan Gubar's powerful image, the feminine text is first "bled into print."[27] For Gagnon, Bersianik, and a number of their Quebec contemporaries, the womb has indeed become the acknowledged *lieu de fécondité* (fertile space), one of the most inventive and productive spaces for the literary exploration of feminine difference.

If, however, the womb is the privileged space for the engendering of Gagnon's feminine text, it is also the corporeal site that registers physical loss most acutely. In *Lueur* as well as in *Au coeur de la lettre* (*At the Heart of the Letter,* 1981), Gagnon describes the act of writing as a painful but necessary inscription of death as well as birth. It is therefore from deep within the maternal womb that the melancholy memories of dead children surge forth and are then articulated. The significance of the womb-tomb analogy in Gagnon's recent texts helps explain why the image of her dying grandmother plays such a pivotal role in *Lueur.* The grandmother's efforts to recall her lost children do, in fact, dominate the latter half of "Fiction," the text's longest section. And as in Jovette Marchessault's *La Mère des herbes* (*Mother of the Grass*), which also explores the intimate relationship between grandmother and granddaughter,[28] Gagnon has chosen to focus on the dynamic force of the grandmother figure in *Lueur* no doubt because she functions as a crucial bridge between generations of women and as an active disseminator of feminine power. The grandmother is also linked to the image of the matriarch, more commonly associated with agrarian life in rural Quebec prior to the 1940s.

The grandmother's approaching death in *Lueur* liberates her from fears of recrimination and allows her body the freedom to express itself without censorship. As her grown children gather around the deathbed urging her to offer words that would constitute some kind of final testament, the grandmother instinctively bares her body, her own lifelong "text," and attempts to convey all the knowledge she has of them inscribed on her flesh. She realizes, however, that she is unable to give them the succor they need. In the end, her body serves instead as a primary textual generator for forgotten images of her dead offspring. The children she has borne and lost are remembered through the body that knew them first.

This initial conjuration of the dead is followed by the grandmother's more active attempt to reconstruct those long ago maternal memories of joyous discovery and despair. Receding into an inner world of kaleidoscopic visions and fleeting memories, the grandmother in *Lueur* struggles to retrieve and record the meaningful events and sensations of her life one final time: "Cette tâche du dedans qui consistait à classer tous ces minimes souvenirs jusqu'ici tassés sous les labeurs, à les laisser se réanimer d'eux-mêmes et prendre sens, dans ce fouillis de la mémoire, pêle-mêle avec tous les blancs" (85) ("This task from within which consisted of classifying all those scanty memories piled under work up until now, of letting them recharge themselves and take on meaning, in this jumble of memory, pell-mell with all the blanks"). Although her search for lost time among the subterranean strata of the feminine unconscious is less satisfying than Proust's fictional journey because the results are noticeably more fragmentary, it is precisely the unevenness of the dying woman's recollections, replete with all the holes and faded visions such memory work often entails, that adds considerable poignancy and a sense of immediacy to the grandmother's physical and mental efforts to read from her maternal past.

The grandmother's internal fiction is, of course, an extended metaphor for writing in the feminine. Paradoxically, the grandmother's aged womb has once again become a symbolic source of feminine creativity and rebirth even as she lies on her deathbed. Once her silence is finally broken, the dying women bequeaths a legacy of shadowy words and aching secrets to her granddaughter, the writer, whose task it will be to transcribe an authentic written testament based on the surfacing fragments of pleasure and pain from her grandmother's life. This literary undertaking becomes in effect the basis for further narrative probings in the section entitled "Archéologie." Increasingly self-conscious and introspective, Gagnon suggests that death and maternal suffering over the loss of a loved one are made bearable only through writing. After the death of a child, the maternal body loves and speaks differently:

Les mots sonores, les mots musiques, les mots écrits. Les mots pour dire que mon corps aime autrement quand la mort passe. Si j'étais philosophe, ancien ou nouveau, j'écrirais un chapitre exactement ici, sur cette dernière

phrase. Je parlerais du corps-objet. Ou si j'étais psychanalyste, je parlerais
de l'objet, de la lettre et de la castration. Mais je suis écrivante, mon métier
c'est d'écrire. Comme les balais, les mots conjurent les sorts. Ne les changent
pas. Les sorts économiques, politiques, sexuels. L'écriture est une conjuration. Un phare allumé pour les signes des sorts. A lire dans les replis des
ombres tracées, dans les indices, l'interstice, le flou, l'à peu près, l'humble
objet, et non dans l'éclatement lumière aveuglante, évidences coercitives,
phallophores. A lire dans ce qui ne s'abstrait ni ne se formalise. Dans sa
singularité fluctuante fluide.   (133–34)

The sonorous words, musical words, written words. The words to say that
my body loves otherwise when death passes. If I were a philosopher, ancient
or modern, I would write a chapter right here, on this previous sentence.
I would speak about the body-object. Or if I were a psychoanalyst, I would
speak about the object, the letter and castration. But I am a "womanwriter,"
my job is to write. Like broomsticks, words conjure up conditions. Don't
change them. Economic, political, sexual conditions. Writing is a conjuration. A lighted beacon for indications of fortune. Read it in the folds
of sketched shadows, in the markings, the crevices, the indistinct, the
approximate, the humble object, and not in the explosion blinding light,
coercive, phallophoric evidence. Read it in what isn't abstract or formal. In
its fluid fluctuating singularity.

The blinding light that Gagnon rejects in the preceding passage
from *Lueur* is the light of reason, certainty, and plenitude, the
cerebral brightness of the traditional masculine text. In contrast,
however, the text of *Lueur* itself spins a mysterious web of distant
figures, buried voices, and implied silences out of the corporeal
memories of the feminine form. Gagnon's sentences are the fluid
fragments of a discourse still in reconstruction. Her writing emanates out of the pregnant void and develops in a darkened world
where a woman's words seek to illuminate the forgotten strata
of hidden personal and collective memories. *Lueur* records those
glimmering flashes from an archaic past, and they, in turn, produce
a dreamlike syntax, a new visceral imagery, and a vision of textual
space that is expressly female. Yet, as the grandmother cautions,
the accessibility of her granddaughter's text will be limited—an
observation Gagnon has publicly made about her more recent writing as well. But those who choose to avoid the obscure pathways of
Gagnon's archaeological descent will also fail to sound the sonorous
depths of a woman's anguish and desire:

Ne pense pas que je m'égare. C'est ici que je suis au plus proche, au si
proche de nous que j'échapperai à toute approximation, j'en suis certaine,

puisqu'ils ne pourront même plus voir et comprendre ce que tu écris, collée de trop près à nos corps cette écriture adhérante qu'ils ne pourront prendre pour rien au monde. Trop lisse et à peine audible, ils ne la verront ni ne l'entendront. Ils ne comprendront pas. Ils continueront de croire qu'il s'agit d'une plainte innocente, ou d'une branche d'arbre, ou d'une rose aquarelle, ou de n'importe quoi, Moi je dis que c'était une femme.   (97)

Don't think that I am rambling. It's here that I am closest, so close to us that I will escape all approximation, I am certain of it, since they won't even see or understand what you write, stuck so close to our bodies this adhering writing that they won't be able to take it for all the world. Too smooth and barely audible, they won't see it nor hear it. They won't understand. They'll continue to believe that it's about an innocent complaint, or a tree branch, or a watercolor rose, or any old thing, I say it was about a woman.

In *Lueur,* Gagnon insists on the fluidlike coalescence of body and text, a fusion that has dramatic consequences for the pace and direction of her textual explorations. Disregarding more traditional approaches to linear development, Gagnon has replaced them with a meandering and, at times, halting narrative that allows the body's pulsations to function as catalysts for the production of poetic images and crucial thematic concerns. Indeed, the frequent changes here in narrative direction are designed, it would appear, to bring a sense of constant discovery to her nascent body-text. Like Brossard, she too appears to be motivated by the demanding ethic to inaugurate rather than to repeat. And as in her earlier political texts, Gagnon continues to undermine the structures of conventional grammar in *Lueur* in order to encourage the generation of new phrase groupings. The net result of these stylistic innovations and the general narrative fluidity is a highly personalized grammar and syntax that appear to chart the body's rhythms from the inside. In the end, Gagnon's attempt to write the female body becomes both a creative celebration of what Cécile Cloutier has termed "the liturgy of the body" and an act of solidarity among women.[29]

The written text of *Lueur* is beautifully illustrated with photographs of ancient Algonquin petroglyphs inscribed on early cave dwellings. These distant markings suggest the prelinguistic symbols of Gagnon's "new-ancient" language, the grandmother's unwritten language, that can only be transcribed in some hidden field far removed from our modern institutions, where words themselves no longer adhere to any known set of written conventions or rules of grammar. In an idyllic fantasy that functions as a recurrent and pivotal motif in *Lueur,* a woman writer (the granddaughter's significant double) is awakened to the ambiguous power of hieroglyphic inscriptions while reclining on an ancient slate. Because of her dreamlike openness and physical attentiveness to these unrecognizable, mysterious inscriptions, Gagnon's female writer is unusually susceptible to their power and at the same time able to set them free to form new meanings, explore new terrain, and translate desires that are truly different. Only in this state of openness to new meanings and through her willingness to embrace a vantage point of creative difference can the woman in the field and the granddaughter who will write the text uncover words no longer spoken and as yet unimagined:

Un pré de blé. En plein milieu de la forêt touffue, un pré de blé. Immense. Je ne l'aurais pas cru possible. Elle est allongée de tout son long dedans, une femme, comme endormie, la tête sur une ardoise plate où c'est écrit, hiéroglyphes. Des lettres sont gravées dont elle ne comprend ni la disposition ni le sens. Elle se repose et ne semble pas vouloir chercher; de son index, elle balaie la poussière de blé sur hiéroglyphes. Elle souffle sur l'ardoise. Emergent des mots signifiants jamais appris nulle part. Et comment, si ces mots ne furent pas appris, peut-elle prétendre au sens? Justement, elle n'a aucun préjugé, elle tend à tout sens, dans ce pré. Elle ne sait plus rien de ce qui l'attend ici, elle ne se demande pas ce qui suivra cette halte, elle n'est pas inquiète, dans les blés, elle ne veut que déchiffrer les inscriptions qui l'ont éveillée. Se laisser tendre par ce qui surgira, demeurer en pleine lumière, attentive, vibrant au moindre son, au moindre signe, coulant se demander en même temps d'où ça vient et pourquoi ça vient jusqu'à elle.

(58)

A field of wheat. Right in the middle of a thick forest, a field of wheat. Immense. I wouldn't have thought it possible. She is fully stretched out in it, a woman, as if asleep, her head on a flat slate on which there is writing, hieroglyphics. Letters are engraved whose placement and meaning she fails to understand. She rests and doesn't seem to want to search further; with her index finger, she brushes away the wheat dust on the hieroglyphics. She breathes on the slate. Meaningful words emerge never before learned anywhere. And how, if these words were never learned, can she lay claim to their meaning? Indeed, she has no prejudices, she leans toward all meanings in this field. She no longer knows anything about what awaits her here, she doesn't wonder about what will follow this resting place, she isn't worried, in the wheat, she only wants to decipher the inscriptions that have roused her. To let herself be oriented by what will arise, to remain in the full sunlight, attentive, vibrating at the smallest sound, at the smallest sign, wanting to ask herself at the same time where it comes from and why it's coming toward her.

The archaeological writing explored in *Lueur* transcribes the intensity of the maternal body and the layers of secrets left by generations of women into a language that is both skillfully subversive and highly original in form. The various textual strategies Gagnon employs to reposition the maternal figure as a subject of her own discourse not only valorize the maternal as a crucial life-giving element of the feminine, but contribute to the radical otherness of Gagnon's text as well. More extensive and ambitious in its scope than her previous works,[30] *Lueur* suggests that an alternative approach to writing is possible, an approach that whispers the gift of life into every word. "*Lueur*," remarked Gagnon in an interview shortly after its publication, "is not a feminist book. It is a feminine book: traversed by the feminine, by women's struggle against oppression. It is not a militant book nor a book of propaganda. There are no longer any poem-collages as in my earlier writings which had not taken their distance with regard to the political. *Lueur* is not a writing based on power."[31]

The Journey Inward: Recent Writings

While *Lueur* beckons us to follow in Gagnon's nocturnal tracks during a psychoanalytic journey back to the sources of feminine creativity and to her own repressed memories, fantasies, and drives, *Au coeur de la lettre* (*At the Heart of the Letter*) moves into the realm of words themselves and their beginnings. Published in 1982, *Au coeur de la lettre* offers a series of intimate reflections on the physical, emotional, and intellectual relationships Gagnon has acknowledged more recently between herself and her words, between the worldly events that occur beyond the poetic space of the text and her increasingly inward and self-reflective literary stance. Despite or perhaps because of Gagnon's maturing skills as a writer, her tone in *Au coeur de la lettre* is noticeably more uncertain and more tentative than in previous works. Moreover, Gagnon's efforts to assert her own subjectivity in this text through an imaginative reshaping of conventional language appear considerably more problematic as well:

Jamais ne m'arrivera ce que je veux raconter. Je ne suis ni eux ni morte. De connivence, affublés. Toujours l'énigme le plus important. Quelle est cette eau perdue? Elle ne se trouve plus, redescendue.

"Que reste-t-il de nos silences. Sinon ce que nous sommes?"
(Jean Royer, Nuit de la poésie, inédite)

Inconnue, de l'intime, celle qui ne sera jamais publique, malgré le slogan, on n'en parlera pas, elle s'insinuera partout.[32]

What I want to write about will never happen to me. I am neither them nor dead. In complicity, made-up. Always the most important enigma. What is this lost water? It can no longer find itself, submerged again.

"What remains of our silences. Except what we are?"
(Jean Royer, Nuit de la poésie, unpublished)

Unknown, in intimacy, she who will never be public, despite the slogan, we won't talk about it, she will insinuate herself everywhere.

The preceding passage is indicative of the particular attention Gagnon pays to her own positioning in this text. While the focus in *Lueur* was on retrieving the past—both personal and collective— as well as on the creative force of the woman writer during the psychoanalytic odyssey itself, in *Au coeur de la lettre,* Gagnon considers the enigmatic figure of the woman writer in search of her own words. The issue of silence, of the unrevealed, is more painful than ever before in this work, perhaps because it has lost much of the staunchly political overtones found in earlier texts. Gagnon's incorporation of Quebec writer Jean Royer's poetic query, "What remains of our silences. Except what we are?," is equally characteristic of the text as a whole since she makes frequent use of quotations from Blanchot, René Char, Marguerite Duras, Claude Gauvreau, and others. Although far less intrusive than the plethora of political quotations in *Poélitique,* these intertextual elements add a kind of collective legitimacy to the otherwise highly personal probings in *Au coeur de la lettre.* Given the text's contemplative tone, it is also likely that Gagnon finds some comfort in the words of other writers whose works are, for the most part and with the notable exception of Duras, as much linked to the kinds of textual experimentation and thematic concerns of literary modernity as they are to the more radically gendered-marked writing practices of Brossard or Bersianik, for example.

While the more recent introspective direction of Gagnon's writing has certainly been underscored with the publication of *Au coeur de la lettre,* her political conscience continues to remind us of repressive geopolitical sites such as Zaire, Iran, Afganistan, Chile, and Vietnam, while the female speaker in her text persists in her struggle against the omnipresence of the male voice. Yet despite repeated allusions to conditions of social and political injustice around the globe, Gagnon plunges ever more inward in *Au coeur de la lettre* in an effort to disengage herself to some extent from the external world and thereby to move toward what she considers the essential in herself and in her writing. She regards this deepening sense of withdrawal in her recent work as a kind of social and artistic *dégagement,* a tendency toward the inscription of doubt, loss, and the unknown, a tendency sometimes noted in the work of Théoret as well that leads on occasion to what Théoret has described as the "unnarratability" of things, a certain linguistic paralysis vis-à-vis the external world.

The dramatic tensions that unify the prosaic poems and poetic reflections found in *Au coeur de la lettre* hinge on the subtle interplay of absence and plenitude, language and silence, love, death, and feminine desire. In an almost mystical fashion, the process of writing appears to have a mediating function in Gagnon's text, transforming memories of personal loss into heightened moments of artistic discovery. Through writing all suffering is made bearable, as she herself emphasizes with a revealing quote from Marguerite Duras: "Mais il y a un moyen de faire que cette souffrance soit supportable, c'est d'en être l'auteur" (69) ("But there is a way to assure that this suffering is bearable, by being its author").

Whether contemplating forgotten Northern landscapes from her childhood, her ancestral Indian heritage, her mother, the female child who would never be born, or the male lover whose absence she so forcefully describes in the text's final section, "La crise du coeur," Gagnon continues to bring a unique psychoanalytic perspective to the process of writing: "Fouiller l'écrit comme on cherche la mère, redevenir l'infante des songes creux. Faire un lieu-dit de cette absence" (42) ("Probe the written like we search for the mother, become the female child of cavernous dreams again. Give the space of this absence a name"). For Gagnon, writing has indeed become the privileged realm of self-analysis and immersion in absence appears to be a requisite for the woman writer's rebirth. In the process of probing for a language of difference, Madeleine Gagnon is both a witness to loss and the inspired creator of her own further promise of life.

Following the publication of *Au coeur de la lettre,* Gagnon commented that for her, the writing experience is "an experience of infinite solitude, which is desertlike and at times hopeless."[33] Triggered by the archaeological soundings of *Antre* and *Lueur,* this recent and more resolutely inward phase of artistic self-disclosure gives evidence of some of the possible fruits of de-centering the privileged male vision and signals in Gagnon's work an increasing candor about the personal nature and silent sources of her own coming to writing. This recent phase of heightened personal exploration stands in marked contrast not only to the more politically motivated and polemical tone of texts such as *Poélitique* and *Pour les femmes et tous les autres,* but also to the collective orientation, theoretical explorations, and collaborative efforts that characterized "Mon Corps dans l'écriture" and especially *Retailles.* More so than ever in recent years, the challenge of Gagnon's literary journey lies in the unmarked path, *l'inédit* (the new, the unpublished), and in a vigilant pursuit of the essential. In *Au coeur de la lettre,* the "heart of things" surfaces in the hidden and the inexpressed of the concluding letter in which Gagnon writes of love and disaster in words that follow their own natural, urgent imperative:

Comment te dire, maintenant, dans le non-pouvoir qui est su, éprouvé, peut-on dire encore le bonheur, oui, le bonheur et le désastre, dire leur conjugaison parce que vivre qu'ils ne s'excluent pas, tenir à cette certitude et pourquoi pas l'écrire, à cette foi, à cette "foi jurée," quand, sous la secousse tellurique ont été ébranlées toutes les certitudes extérieures et les solitudes territoriales, et l'affirmer simplement dans le souffle du poème, défiant toutes lois y compris celles de la forme, refusant ces phrases qui se tiendraient toutes seules, dit-on, ne pas terminer à la ligne où c'est dû, à la limite ne pas commencer, chapitre ou livre, graver la lettre, ni pur signifiant ni trace pulsionnelle, graver la lettre d'amour, comment te dire alors cette brûlure?   (93)

How to tell you, now, in the nonpower that is understood, felt, can we still say happiness, yes, happiness and disaster, speak their conjugation because of living so that they don't exclude one another, hold to this certainty and why not write it, to this faith, to this "sworn faith," when all the exterior certainties and territorial solitudes have been shaken under the telluric blow, and affirm it simply in the inspiration of a poem, defying all laws including those of form, refusing those phrases that would be self-contained, as they say, to not finish the sentence where one should, in the extreme instance not begin chapter or book, inscribe the letter, neither pure signifier nor libidinal trace, inscribe the letter of love, how then to tell you of this burning feeling?

Gagnon develops the epistolary genre of the love letter more skillfully and more extensively in *La Lettre infinie* (The Endless Letter), published in 1984. But what could be more tradition-bound than a woman's (heterosexual) love letter, we might ask, and consequently a more unlikely genre for both the political and experimental nature of *l'écriture au féminin?* At the same time, what could be more personal, more decidedly intimate, and, women have been told, less universal? Like the diary, the letter has been an important, if traditional avenue for women to "organize the satisfaction of creating in a private way."[34] And as in the case of the diary, the love letter has been commonly associated with the realm of women's private emotions and secret longings. But Jane Gallop's scintillating reading of Annie Leclerc's "Lettre d'amour" also reminds us that love letters "have always been written from the body, in connection with love." Gallop argues that Leclerc wants all writing to develop out of this fundamental connection with the body in love. Leclerc's decision to publish her lesbian love letter in *La Venue à l'écriture* thus constitutes an act of public transgression—as all writing should be in her view—when she "brings the love letter out of the closet and into the public domain."[35] Gagnon's letter of love offers a subversion of another sort based on an incestuous transgressive content that privileges the son over the absent father and the maternal body over the lover's body as the locus of this infinite love.

Well aware of the traditional characteristics and implications of the epistolary genre for women, Gagnon has, like Annie Leclerc, radically feminized the nature of the love letter, marking it with a language, vision, and form that inscribe the feminine at every turn. As her title suggests, *La Lettre infinie* has been conceived as a letter of "infinite" directions and "nomadic" distractions that defy closure or easy incasement—yet another example of what Cixous has referred to as the "overflowing" of feminine writing. Annie Leclerc also speaks of the love letter as a "new and perhaps *interminable* text of birth love."[36]

Gagnon initially addresses the various written fragments of her own infinite love letter to the absent lover-father in a free-flowing form reminiscent of that of *Antre* and *Lueur*. Brief autobiographical accounts of their previous life together melt into fictional scenes and precipitate further theoretical reflections on the writing process without any visible transitions, as in many of Gagnon's preceding works. The complete intertwining of the real, the theoretical, and the imaginary in this text underscores the problematic nature of traditional distinctions between fiction and real life, memory and fantasy—issues that, as we have seen, lie at the heart of Brossard's literary explorations of women's difference as well:

> Tout aussi fictive et tout aussi réelle. Ce que J'écris précédemment est véridique. Ce qui suit. La véracité n'est pas l'authenticité. Je me méfie des écrits authentiques. L'écriture est apocryphe.[37]

> Just as ficticious and just as real. What I write in the preceding passages is truthful. What follows. Truthfulness is not authenticity. I distrust authentic writings. Writing is apocryphal.

Gagnon's intentional blurring of real and fictional elements is, in fact, closely tied to the particular thematics of her text. For *La Lettre infinie* is on the one hand an attempt to name the love Gagnon once shared with another and at the same time a vehicle through which to speak of her loss. Writing thus becomes the mediating object between "the presence of love and its absence."[38] But during this struggle to name the truth of her love, Gagnon also acknowledges in *La Lettre infinie* the insufficiencies of particular memories and objects to articulate her previous passion: "Tout ce que je n'écris pas est beaucoup plus important mais échappe à ma responsabilité, m'échappe, je n'y peux RIEN" (65) ("Everything that I don't write is much more important but escapes my responsibility, gets away from me, I can do NOTHING"). Drawing attention to her own opaque poetic style, Gagnon contrasts her efforts to write from within with the kind of clear, intelligent logic and need of veracity preferred by her former lover. With languages so different, there never really was any clear "text" between them. In the end, Gagnon offers no singular resolution, no illusory happy book or tragic tale of their love, only a series of recollected gestures toward the (male) other as well as her own reflections on the (female) self in love—all of this written without apparent nostalgia or romanticism.

Gagnon runs a substantial risk, however, when reentering that prior world of devoted passion for the father of her sons, particularly since the emotional territory that accompanies it is clearly filled with pain and confusion as well as with tenderness. At times, she allows herself to slip momentarily into the previous captivity of this oppressive love from the past and once again becomes the "imprecise object," lacking any real center or sense of her own subjectivity while "in love." But these occasional slippages or leanings toward an overpowering male figure from her past only serve to heighten our awareness of the transformation that has taken place in the writer of this love letter. The strength we trace in *La Lettre infinie* is the strength Gagnon has harnessed over the years in order to see herself and to approach writing through her own eyes rather than those of a male lover:

Je suis celle qui ne voit plus l'homme aimé me contemplant, ivre-vivante, celle qui ne se sait plus devenir encore le corps de sa passion.   (71)

I am she who no longer sees the beloved contemplating me, alive-drunk, she who no longer knows how to become the body of his passion again.

The final section of *La Lettre infinie* breaks with the more prosaic form and analytical tone of preceding letters and offers a series of poetic entries addressed to a lover-son who is no longer irretrievably linked to the father Gagnon once loved. For the absent father in *La Lettre infinie* is he who names and assigns meaning over all and who, like Abraham the initial biblical patriarch, is even willing to sacrifice his own son in the name of the Law. The intended recipient of Gagnon's infinite letter of love has broken the pact with Abraham and resembles the male of a new age—perhaps Bersianik's "mâle de mon espèce,"[39] the man who has left the paternal house and returned to the mother as the prodigal son of Gagnon's revisionary fable. And while she notes in an earlier section that letters to sons are often impossible to write since sons are as absent from their mothers' words as mothers are from those of their sons, Gagnon chooses nevertheless to write beyond the silent, absent father to the lover-son in an expression of continuing hope and unending desire:

Il t'a fallu quitter la maison du père, c'est ce que maintenant j'entends, tu m'enlaces à nouveau et j'attends qu'avec moi tu te fasses toute nuit, quand, dans l'illumination du dedans le corps se meut, sous la voûte courbée, chaude du sang des noces, bouge par la seule pulsion des particules; un fleuve dénouant nous délie, les méduses là sont endormies, les serpents, les requins, les monstres marins devenus innocents, les chaînes nos "outils nuptiaux" pour les chairs nouées dans leurs dentelles. Sur un vaste lit doux de pierres de lune irradiant cette nuit-là.   (94)

You needed to leave the father's house, that's what I now understand, you embrace me again and I expect that with me you will make yourself complete night, when, in the illumination from within the body stirs, under the curved canopy, warm with nuptial blood, moves by the mere drive of particles; a loosening river releases us, the medusas are asleep there, the serpents, the sharks, the marine monsters turned innocent, the chains our "nuptial tools" for the bodies tied in their lace. On a vast, soft bed of radiating moon stones that night.

Gagnon's letter of love makes a conceptual leap of faith toward a writing and loving that will shed patriarchal constraints and open themselves up to receive the maternal body's infinite love—a love that, like the letter itself, can never be "wrapped up" or concluded since such an action would be contrary to its very nature. Any initial suggestion in *La Lettre infinie* of the tragic dimension of love lost has all but disappeared in the final pages of this letter from a woman who views herself above all else perhaps as a survivor. While it may be true that the male whom Gagnon ultimately addresses exists only within the confines of her own fictional constructions, her extended love letter stands between herself and the lover-father in the uncharted interval as a form of communication that, while acknowledging distance, still points toward the desirability of an eventual reconciliation.[40] Awaiting a worthy and tender correspondent for her infinite letter of love, Gagnon continues her pursuit of a *birth love writing* with the same visionary intensity that has marked her work virtually from the beginning.

Since the appearance of *Poélitique* and throughout the various modifications in her political stance and general approach to writing, Madeleine Gagnon has viewed the act of writing first and foremost as a mode of resistance to established forms of power within the dominant culture. This perspective remains valid even today in her most introspective texts. While the disruption of traditional discourse has provided a substantial and continued focus to her literary project, Gagnon's inventive linguistic journeys continue to pursue a radically other center from which to affirm the self and the collective body politic. Although Gagnon's earlier efforts to address the political nature and function of literature have more recently yielded ground to a series of internal self-explorations, her gradual move toward the intimate and away from an insistently social and political content is to some degree characteristic of the later writings of Bersianik and Théoret as well, as we shall see in the subsequent chapters on their respective work. On the whole, Gagnon's current interest in surveying her own innermost secrets and repressed material is indicative of the general direction taken in the most recent phase, if we can call it that, of Quebec feminist thought since 1980 with its increasing emphasis on exploring the intimately personal in women's experience and in problematizing women's relationships to language in terms of the variety of individual experiences among women without, however, abandoning the collective common ground of gender itself.

Given the breadth and considerable evolution in Gagnon's work since the early 1970s, it would seem that her most enduring contributions thus far lie in her political theorizing on a writing that valorizes the female body—and the maternal body in particular—as well as in the more painful and poetic introspection of her own psychoanalytic literary project, two somewhat divergent tendencies that are nevertheless fundamentally linked in her work. In Gagnon's recent writings, the woman writer has indeed become an archaeologist of her own body-thought as she retraces the shadowy clues and hidden cracks in her own internal development. Her texts furnish the blueprints for a writing of the future borne out of the mysteries of the past, a writing capable of transmitting "the traces of archaic flashes shooting forth new meaning" (*Lueur,* 25). Written in solidarity and solitude, the words of Madeleine Gagnon have engaged the social conscience of a number of writers and intellectuals in her generation and have mined the inner depths and bases of a woman's love and anguish with an unusual sense of personal and political purpose.

4 *Louky Bersianik*
Language, Myth, and the Remapping of Herstory

I saw you once, Medusa; we were alone.
I looked you straight in the cold eye, cold.
I was not punished, was not turned into stone—
How to believe the legends I am told?
May Sarton, "The Muse as Medusa"

In order to create an alternative an oppressed group must at once shatter the self-reflecting world which encircles it and, at the same time, project its own image into history. In order to discover its own identity as distinct from that of the oppressor it has to become visible to itself.
Sheila Rowbotham, *Woman's Consciousness, Man's World*

M.D.—Lots and lots of women are horrified by their name. Even women who don't write.
X.G.—Can a woman write while keeping the name of her father?
Marguerite Duras and Xavière Gauthier, *Les Parleuses*

"From the beginning," affirms Elizabeth Meese, "women have been trespassers in the world's literary communities."[1] Louky Bersianik is well aware of the transgressive cultural roles women writers have assumed throughout much of recorded history. She is also equally aware of the extent to which feminist writers in Quebec continue to be viewed as presumptuous intruders whose distinctive contributions to the field of Quebec contemporary letters remain intellectually and politically suspect in the minds of some. Along with a growing number of contemporary women writers, Bersianik believes that the western European and North American literary traditions in particular, with their regulative authority, elitist aesthetics, and the implicit value accorded to male-oriented thematics, have repeatedly betrayed women writers by allowing them only infrequent representation, by dismissing their contributions as minor accomplishments, and by denying their existence with a troubling regularity. Time and again in her own writing, Bersianik has noted how the dominant literary traditions, which women have commonly adopted as their own, have worked to remove all traces of the female signature and to cover up the significance of this act.

More theatrical than most in her defiant stance toward western European thought and the literary canons it has engendered, Bersianik has embraced, even flaunted her role as a literary violator. Moreover, she has done so with unusual toughness and with her own unique brand of outrageously disobedient wit. Yet even as she writes against it, Bersianik never loses sight of the past, of the lies tradition has repeatedly told women about themselves and of the secrets they have privately whispered back to one another in restless discontent. Bersianik's training and degrees in French, the classical literatures, music, and linguistics have clearly contributed to her keen sense of the past and to her awareness of the continuing power of ancient cultural representations in contemporary culture. In her fiction, poetry, and theoretical discussions, she is both a virulent desecrator of the old patriarchal world she has inherited and a jubilant visionary of an emerging *culture au féminin*.[2]

While perhaps less well known outside Canada than either Brossard or Gagnon, Bersianik has been widely recognized since the mid-1970s as one of the leading proponents of writing in the feminine in Quebec. She has also participated widely in feminist readings, plays, conferences, and special speaking engagements both in and outside Quebec. And like Brossard, Gagnon, and Théoret, she has fashioned her literary project as a far-reaching political critique of patriarchal thought and of the modes of discourse in which it has been disseminated. In so doing, Bersianik challenges both the status of women in the discourse of the dominant culture and the primacy of the patriarchal word. In conjunction with this effort, she has consciously addressed the issue of women's position in language and in patriarchal culture within the framework of *his*tory—a disturbing and problematic notion for Bersianik and one that continually takes on an insurgent double meaning in her texts.

History, insofar as women have traditionally been permitted to learn about it, has been characterized as the systematic recording and analysis of significant human events. For Bersianik, however, who subscribes to a decidedly feminist view of the discipline and of narration about the past in general, what we have come to know as history is, in fact, a fictional reconstruction of the past narrated almost exclusively in the masculine for the benefit and pleasure of certain privileged classes and races of men. Like fiction, history is a discourse whose purpose is to create patterns of signification that order and explain the human story from a particular—if unacknowledged—point of view. History is, therefore, a cultural product invested with the socioeconomic, ethnic, and gender biases of its authors and with one or more of the specific ideological currents of the period in which it is shaped. As a product of patriarchal thought, history in particular provides a given collectivity with a preestablished reading of prior events, social structures, and intellectual as well as popular ideas from a privileged, male-oriented point of view.

In the writings of Louky Bersianik, history as "his story"—one that systematically deflects attention away from the stories of women—is repeatedly undermined and ultimately exposed as a fraudulent story that women must rewrite. Indeed, despite the severity of her critique of traditional historiography, Bersianik regards history as an essential area of intellectual investigation and analysis. And, she argues, it is one that feminists must take seriously since the study of human events, cultural institutions, and ideological currents from the past necessarily provides a more thorough context for understanding the various patterns of political injustice and oppression that exist today, patterns that, for women and other exploited groups, have been recurrent and very real.

Bersianik's work draws attention to the inescapable effects of patriarchal socialization that, over time, have left their traces on virtually every aspect of female identity, including the kinds of images women have presumably constructed of themselves. Because of the nature of women's oppression in patriarchal cultures, however, images of mute, quietly domesticated, and absent women have usually been authored and authorized by men. It is these images from the past in particular that Bersianik urges women to seize upon, expose, and reconstruct in order to reflect more closely their lived experience—past and present—if history is to mean anything to them today. Insisting that the very existence of women's collective future is at stake in the current feminist moves to repossess history, she contends that "it is only through the optic of history rectified through the aid of our rediscovered memory, however partial, however fragmentary, that the elaboration of this famous memory of the future will be possible. . . ."[3] Thus conceived, writing in the feminine becomes an imaginative way of remembering and reconnecting with the historical breadth and complexities of women's lives, a way of reenvisioning the categories, issues, and social realities about which "history" speaks.

While these two notions of history (viewed simultaneously as fictitious construction and as unarticulated reality) can surely be posed in opposition to one another, they are manifestations of two crucial and not incompatible impulses in Bersianik's writing as a whole—the need on the one hand to delegitimize male-centered views of and from the past as self-serving, totalizing fabrications, and the equally pressing need to re-view the past from the perspectives of real women in order to gain an understanding, however incomplete, of women's place in and contributions to the historical process. Hence, the very notion of history-as-contested-story in Bersianik's writing creates a site of severe narrative dislocation and lost authority. Yet in so doing, it also provides an important textual opening for critical reinvestigations of the past, for the pursuit of a collective female memory, and for an increasingly staunch affirmation of difference. For Bersianik, thinking and writing about history means, in effect, engaging in an ongoing process of radical critique and reinvention. Such a process parallels in more than a few ways the kinds of self-consciously gender-marked reassessments of the past that American feminists in the fields of literature and history have also been pursuing since the early 1970s.

Like some of the more ambitious feminist critics today, Bersianik has organized her literary efforts around the project of reconsidering and rewriting the history, structures, and "sex" of western European knowledge from the vantage point of women and of contemporary feminist thought. Her attempts to view women as significant historical subjects have not, however, been as ideologically bound to a materialist reading of history as were similar efforts by Gagnon in her early texts. Yet both of these writers assume that questions of gender, subjectivity, and creative production are inseparable from the broader field of social-sexual relations and from the historical development of those relations in western European and North American cultures in particular.

To speak of history in Bersianik's texts is to speak of language. For when considering history as a series of privileged narrative accounts written by and for men, Bersianik must also assess the pivotal role of language in the invention and consecration of the historical account. Her efforts to link, confuse, and intentionally conflate history and fiction—strategies so thoroughly in keeping with the forcefully modern perspective of Brossard and her continuous overlapping of *le fictif* and *le réel,* highlight the extent to which the types of discourse men have traditionally used to construct their own versions of history no longer appear adequate, no longer correspond to our current "sense" of the past. There are too many holes, contradictions, deletions, and biased judgments in existing historical accounts for women to go on believing men's stories about the past.

Language, insists Bersianik, has long been the complicitous partner of western European philosophy in the patriarchal lie of women's inferiority. Both the forms and the scope of language have been shaped largely by men to convey their authoritative status as the privileged gender group. Concurring with a number of contemporary feminist linguists, Bersianik argues that men have commonly been the esteemed "proprietors of language"[4] and have continually defined, ordered, and classified language for their own purposes and with their own interests as a group in mind. In much of Bersianik's writing, language, like history, thus becomes a key site of narrative inquiry, while the centuries long repression of women's words has emerged as one of her central themes.

It is readily apparent to anyone who studies her texts that Bersianik, like Brossard, Gagnon, and Théoret, has been heavily influenced by the literary theories of *modernité* in Quebec and by the French poststructualist discourses of deconstruction and Lacanian psychoanalysis. For the dramatic destablizing of language, meaning, and authority that prompted much of the initial textual experimentation at *La Barre du jour* (already noted in chapters 1 and 2) and that lies at the very core of Bersianik's deconstructive intentions also appears to be one of the primary bases for the crises of representation, knowledge, and continuity in contemporary western European thought, as Derrida, Deleuze, Lyotard and others have pointed out from their various philosophical positions.[5] However, the particular forms of dislocation, disinheritance, and "ex-centrism"[6] that Bersianik has encountered when confronting the canonized, male-centered texts of the past are more feminist than they are postmodern.

For Bersianik, the move to delegitimize male metanarratives from and about the past constitutes a conscious act of revolt against structures of oppression that have been designed to keep women out of the human story. As a result, there is no room in her texts for nostalgia about the lost authority of the western philosophical tradition and the resultant unreliability of paternal authorship, a nostalgia so often noted in male postmodern writing. Nor is there any sign in her work of amused relief at the thought that all value systems may henceforward be suspect. To call tradition into question and oppose history's masters when both the tradition and the masters have been proud advocates of the male experience cannot be a matter of sexual indifference. Martha Noel Evans makes a similar point when she compares contemporary women's writing in France with male postmodern texts, concluding that the "asymmetry of men's and women's representation in tradition means that their reaction to tradition not only will be qualitatively different, it also will determine a recursive structural redefinition of that tradition from the point of view of the misrepresented (women)."[7]

Bersianik's attempts to expose the contradictions and the "blind spots"[8] in canonical texts, to undermine previous concepts of closure, and finally to strip bare the buried motives of the father's discourse (from the Greeks to the present day) must therefore be understood as initial steps in her determined move to reinsert women into history and to valorize their continuous presence in the historical process. However central to her writing posture, deconstruction is therefore a preliminary gesture in the inscription of difference, since re-vision and re-invention must necessarily follow. The historicized feminist stance Bersianik adopts in order to look backward to a patriarchal past and forward to a feminist future thus gives her deconstructive efforts a decidedly female cast.

Undoing the Father's Text: *L'Euguélionne*

Bersianik's "disloyalty to civilization"[8] has been flagrant and devastatingly thorough. Her disillusionment with the venerated texts of our western cultural tradition along with her blistering critique of women's historical invisibility in those texts account for much of the force and originality of her first two major fictional works, *L'Euguélionne* (1976) and *Le Pique-nique sur l'Acropole* (1979). Both are ambitious attempts to undo the roles history has assigned women by unraveling the language in which those roles have been originally fashioned and then endlessly represented. Indeed, since her earliest writings Bersianik has emphasized the numerous ways in which language functions as social convention, as a reflection of historical patterns of social and sexual injustice, and as one of the most important legitimating tools of concept formation about the past, present, and future in contemporary culture. Bersianik writes, in effect, to undo a linguistic system and a western philosophical tradition in which women have been continually subdued and silenced by patriarchal law and by a male-oriented grammar and lexicon that have alienated them from their own history, from meaningful patterns of self-expression, and ultimately, from one other. If *herstories* are to be written, they must be conveyed in a language capable of articulating different views of the past and of privileging, when necessary, different ways of approaching social relations, personal autonomy, sexual identity, and human knowledge—much more broadly defined.

At a time when feminist literary production was just beginning to capture the attention of a few critics and readers in Quebec, and at a time also when the initial, feminist-inspired texts of Brossard and Gagnon were appealing to a small group of educated readers, the appearance of *L'Euguélionne* quickly catapulted Bersianik out of relative obscurity and into a surprisingly bright, albeit somewhat controversial literary limelight.[10] In terms of the breadth of issues raised in this text, the scope of its indictment of patriarchal culture, and the remarkable popularity of the book in Quebec, the publication of *L'Euguélionne* undoubtedly was the most significant feminist literary event of 1976—along with, perhaps, the theatrical event of the year, the collectively written and produced *La Nef des sorcières* (*Ship of Witches*).[11] Both the novel and the play explore the imposed silences in women's lives, while also disclosing the patterns of oppression and repression to which women have been consciously and unconsciously subjected. On a more formal level, each of these works introduces a collective tableau of female experiences in order to emphasize the sharing of women's stories and the necessity for dialogue. Moreover, both works offer a variety of perspectives that, while highlighting certain differences among women, tend nevertheless to underscore the common concerns that unite them.

Although not written specifically for dramatic presentation, *L'Euguélionne* is strikingly theatrical due to the constant scene changes, the continual movement of its characters, and the importance placed on dialogue and monologue that add immediacy and a certain concreteness to the underlying theoretical issues Bersianik wants to address. In 1976, the feminist subject matter raised in *L'Euguélionne* reflected many of the political and socioeconomic concerns of the women's movement in Quebec and in the United States as well, a fact that helps explain the surprising and almost immediate success of Bersianik's first major literary effort. It is also the case that many readers found (and still find) *L'Euguélionne* to be a more accessible text than some of the more experimental feminist writing produced by Brossard, Gagnon, and others at that time.

Altogether unique in its rare blending of biblical forms, philosophical discussions, feminist theorizing, and science fiction elements, *L'Euguélionne* nevertheless epitomizes a tendency in Quebec toward deconstruction, revision, and reaffirmation that could already be noted in other feminist-inspired texts of the same period. It is in *L'Euguélionne*, however, that Bersianik articulates most clearly and relatively early on the crucial theoretical connections between language and cultural authority, between a discourse of constructed signification in which women have been continually marginalized and a historic tradition of institutionalized exclusion that has left women dangling on the fringes, well outside the political arenas of power, and often without a broader sense of female community through which to view their own experience.

In a tone mixed with indignation, passion, and satirical humor, Bersianik considers the major sociopolitical and symbolic functions of language in light of the historically unequal relations of the sexes and the more blatantly unjust manifestations of those relations in contemporary life. She conducts her feminist investigation through the incredulous eyes and detailed observations of the Euguélionne, an extraterrestrial female being who has left a planet ruled by tyrannical and misogynist "Legislators" to search elsewhere for "a positive planet" on which to find "the male of her species." Bersianik has underscored the link between this extraterrestrial being and women generally in a subsequent interview, noting in particular that neither the Euguélionne nor her female counterparts on earth have as yet located a territory of their own dimensions. "We [women] are all extraterrestrials," insists Bersianik, but we are also preparing to land.[12]

So that readers of *L'Euguélionne* will not miss the point, Bersianik names one of her principal female characters "Exil," a woman writer who, like the Euguélionne, is also looking for a homeland. This notion of walking on alien ground has, in fact, become one of the themes of preference in much of Bersianik's writing since 1976. Moreover, like a number of Bersianik's characters, Exil returns in another text to remind us of the importance of her namesake. In the more recent *Axes et eau,* for instance, she is reinvoked in an effort to render her territorial dispossession more poetic and even more urgent. In a series of attempts to describe the dimensions of her exclusion and to name her status as outcast, we find a vocabulary and a political perspective that consciously echo both the language and the thematics of *L'Euguélionne*. Exil is once again an "extraterritorial" as well as an errant "pilgrim," inhabiting "a no woman's land" in which she continues to be "unimaginable" in the minds of men who have settled there.[13] The political point of this extended analogy, which spans nearly a decade of writing, is, of course, that the feminine subject in exile must not remain so indefinitely.

In *L'Euguélionne,* one existing set of cultural values (patriarchal) is examined in the light of another (feminist). Reminiscent of Montesquieu's ironic social critique of French society by Persian visitors in *Les Lettres persanes* and reminiscent as well of Voltaire's satirical efforts in *Micromégas* and *Candide* to expose the irrationality, greed, and hypocrisy of his own culture through the reflections of "foreigners," Bersianik's choice of an alien refugee is likewise a strategic one for it allows enormous latitude in the focus of her feminist exposé. As a result, the Euguélionne raises questions and expresses continual dismay about virtually everything she sees, from the most grievous institutional injustices to the most humdrum occurrences. And as in the philosophical fiction of her Enlightenment predecessors, the destablizing effects that irony, paradox, and well-placed ridicule produce in her text are central to her re-visionary purpose.

The satirical nature of the more than two hundred parables that compose Bersianik's ambitious fresco of misogyny and sexual oppression is fierce, setting the tone for a veritable human comedy of negativity viewed through feminist eyes. In terms of the novel's formal construction and politicizing intent, the parables themselves are more than merely amusing subversions of biblical format or satirical denunciations of male notions of the divine. The compilation and numbering of so many episodes (1,386 in all) create a sense of the inescapable and accumulative weight of patriarchal thinking throughout history. At the same time, the relentless listing of incident after incident, insult after insult, serves as a massive feminist inventory of abuses suffered by the female inhabitants of this planet. Like the Bible and other voluminous philosophical treatises in which discussions of spiritual matters, the issue of our origins, human psychology, human relations, and the codification of the law go on at great length, the sheer size of Bersianik's book is impressive and adds to the material gravity of the feminist case against western misogyny. Intent on undermining the sacred authority of the biblical text, with its archaic views and heavily didactic modes, Bersianik mockingly parodies the Bible's triple emphasis on parable, gospel, and sermon, discursive forms that Jennifer Waelti-Walters has aptly linked to the three distinct divisions of the novel.[14]

The triptych construction of *L'Euguélionne* also functions as a historical and religious referent, evoking the medieval three-paneled carvings and paintings used as altar pieces to tell the sacred story of the male Trinity through a visual medium. The story Bersianik tells in her own tri-partite narrative is, of course, anything but sacred and the lessons taught by the Euguélionne pointedly reject the insistently phallic religiosity of the Judeo-Christian tradition whose ethical models have encouraged women to remain meek, self-sacrificing, and always obedient to the Father. In her disdain for the phallocratic structures, symbolisms, and teachings of the Church, Bersianik echoes the radical theological critique undertaken by Mary Daly a few years prior to the publication of *L'Euguélionne*. Unfamiliar with Daly's work while writing *L'Euguélionne* (1972–74), Bersianik nevertheless gives literary voice to a number of Daly's theoretical positions.[15]

Although clearly modeled as a feminist counterpoint to the male Messiah complex of western Judeo-Christian tradition, the Euguélionne is more akin to a wise elder sister, the "sister from another planet" whom Bersianik wants us to adopt rather than to worship. Indeed, despite her advanced awareness—or perhaps because of it, the Euguélionne refuses to become the sole spiritual "master" of her flock of admirers, disbelievers, and traitors, for there is no one God the Father in whom we must trust, no one truth, no single organizing principle. Instead, the Euguélionne places her faith in the infinite possibilities of women. As our alien ally, she enjoins us to take a more attentive look around and finally come to our senses— all of them. The Euguélionne herself does just that when she surveys our male-oriented culture in many different locales and from various angles, traveling from home to home and from one disappointing event to another, in search of a place where females can live productive lives with the respect and the support of their male counterparts. While her general assessment of "La Planète des hommes" ("Planet of Men") is clearly negative, she does find small pockets of positive and creative resistance that need to be nurtured.

Toward the end of the novel, at the height of her disillusionment with earth dwellers and even as she is assailed by the planet's authori-

ties and sentenced to die, the Euguélionne's spirit remains un-
daunted. Like the biblical Christ figure, her only apparent crime is
the words she has uttered, the pervasive hypocrisy and injustices
enunuciated and laid bare for all to see. Yet these words are enough
to bring down the wrath of the authorities. In addition to the
severity of her observations, however, the Euguélionne's words also
bring hope to the women who are endeavoring to resist patriarchal
oppression in its myriad forms. As Bersianik has acknowledged, her
protagonist's name takes its origin from the Greek word *euaggeion*,
which means "good tidings." The Euguélionne's very name thus
evokes parallels with the New Testament teachings of Jesus of
Nazareth—*l'évangile*, the gospel.

Bersianik's intended analogy to the Christian Savior is not, however, as systematically sustained as some critics have implied. Indeed,
in her radical departure from biblical accounts, Bersianik does not
depict the Euguélionne's death as an agonizing test of filial devotion
to a supreme Father such as we find in the Christian story nor will
her resurrection occur as a gift from God and a sign of spiritual
salvation. In the instant after her body is literally blown to bits by
rifle fire, the glowing remains of the Euguélionne's dispersed female
form hang momentarily suspended in space, "traçant de longues
traînées blanchâtres et comme hors foyer"[16] ("tracing long, whitish,
almost unfocussed trails"[17]). This is a powerful image of spatial
expansion, indeterminacy, and free-floating movement in which any
male notion of the divine is entirely absent. Moreover, shortly
thereafter the Euguélionne reappears intact, on her own power and
of her own volition, in order to reaffirm her dedication to a feminist
quest still in its initial stage of investigation. This final return to
earth before continuing her search among the stars further underscores both the sadness and the hope she holds out for this strange
and backward place we call earth.

1350. —Je vous ai dit que je ne mourrais pas, dit l'Euguélionne. Trop de
choses à faire. Programme trop chargé. Pas le temps de crever. Je m'en vais.
Je quitte votre planète de mon plein gré. Votre planète négative . . .
1351. Et, disant cela, et avant de disparaître, elle regardait la foule avec un
oeil triste et l'autre gai, tout comme le jour de son arrivée.
Toute la tristesse amassée dans le premier oeil resta en suspens dans l'air

au moment de la disparition définitive de l'Euguélionne. Elle resta, cette tristesse, sous forme d'une outre pleine de larmes.

Et toute la gaieté amassée dans le deuxième oeil resta en suspens dans l'air sous une forme indescriptible qui rappelait l'Euguélionne, ce qu'elle était, ce qu'elle avait été tout le temps de son séjour parmi nous. (390)

1350. —I told you I would not die, said the Euguélionne. Too much to do. No time to croak. I'm going. I leave your planet of my own free will. Your negative planet. . . .
1351. And so saying, and before disappearing, she looked at the crowd with one sad eye, the other gay, as she had on the day of her arrival.

All the sadness amassed in the first eye remained suspended in mid-air at the time of the Euguélionne's final disappearance. This sadness remained in the form of a goatskin full of tears.

And all the gaiety amassed in the other eye remained suspended in mid-air in an indescribable shape which called to mind the Euguélionne, what she was, what she had been all during her stay among us.   (338)

Bersianik's lengthy and fantastic feminist tale is global in its attacks and its scope. Although references and allusions to Quebec culture are consciously made from time to time, the places visited and the names of most of the characters have a curiously ancient and/or futuristic ring: Omicronne, Alyssonirik, Ancyl, Kappa, Lambda, the Aegean sea, and so on. We are dealing in *L'Euguélionne* with white western elite culture, with its daily preoccupations, political institutions, philosophical traditions, and aesthetics. Disappointed with what she finds during her interviews and travels, the Euguélionne concludes that women on the planet earth need to be stirred out of their resignation and reeducated. They must refuse to accept their role as secondary members of the species. Instead, she urges them to carve out new sites of meaningful activity and to invent other forms of self-expressivity in which to do this.

Throughout her travels, the Euguélionne's focus on the power of enunciation in the symbolic process and her interest in language as a general tool of cultural transformation support Bersianik's own belief that women need to create modes of discourse capable of countering traditional male-centered views of history, of challenging existing patriarchal structures, and of envisioning more equitable patterns of relating for women and men. With the aid of her advanced female creature, Bersianik seeks to transform the ways in which women conceptualize their historical contributions, contemporary aspirations, and future potential by transforming language itself. Through the use of feminist parables, she examines both the role of language in the legitimation of western, male-oriented thought and its conservative institutional use by the dominant culture. And what better place to scrutinize this paradigm of linguistic misogyny than in the home of a pompous and myopic male academic?[18]

244. A quelque temps de là, dit L'Euguélionne, Omiconne nous invita chez elle, Exil et moi, pour un dîner entre amis.

Ce jour-là, j'ai eu l'honneur de faire la connaissance de Monsieur Alfred Oméga en personne.

Monsieur Alfred Oméga est un professeur d'université, relativement jeune. Monsieur Oméga dirige même une revue spécialisée qu'il considère très importante. Monsieur Oméga est très actif.

Il a, nous le savons déjà, une femme à la maison qui s'appelle Omicronne. Il a aussi deux ou trois enfants.

Monsieur Oméga a donné son nom respectable à la petite Omicronne. Monsieur Oméga a même donné son nom respecté à deux ou trois enfants. Monsieur Oméga est très généreux.

245. Pendant le repas, Monsieur Oméga parle des cours qu'il donne généreusement à l'Université.

—Les cours magistraux, c'est fini, c'est dépassé, on n'en fait plus, dit-il sur un ton très très magistral.

Ça y est, me suis-je dit. Voilà bien le mot. Monsieur Oméga a un langage magistral. Lui-même est un Maître. Monsieur Oméga parle en maître. Il sait ce qu'il dit. (81)

244. Sometime later, said the Euguélionne, Omicronne invited Exil and me over to her place for an intimate dinner among friends.

That day I had the honour of meeting Mr. Alfred Omega in person.

Mr. Alfred Omega is a relatively young university professor. He also has his moments as a literary critic. Mr. Omega even directs a specialized journal that he considers very important. Mr. Omega is very active.

As we know already, he has a wife at home named Omicronne. He also has two or three children.

Mr. Omega has given his respectable name to little Omicronne. Mr. Omega has even given his respected name to two or three children. Mr. Omega is very generous.

245. During the meal, Mr. Omega talks about the courses he is generously giving at the university.

—Professorial lectures are finished, out of date, no one gives them anymore, he says in a *very* professorial tone.

That's it, I say to myself. That's the word. Mr. Omega uses professorial language. He, himself, is a Master. He knows what he is saying.

(76–77)

In the two preceding parables, Bersianik raises a series of concerns regarding the motivations, delivery, and anticipated effects of patriarchal discourse, particularly when it falls on female ears. The first and most fundamental issue is that of naming itself. For as feminist linguists have pointed out, naming is a way of both contributing to and constraining concept formation. Indeed, in its most powerful form, naming can become a persuasive mode of shaping social reality. In parable 244, the ludicrous pride Omega takes in his literary work and academic post serves as a prefatory remark to an even more unsettling pride in the name he so "generously" confers on his spouse and children. Bersianik invites us to read Omega's self-congratulatory manner as symptomatic of the masculine hubris men still demonstrate in their inflated role as name giver, a role they have historically assigned themselves in marriage, in the family, in the dominant cultural institutions, and in writing.

Following with an equally derisive description, parable 245 alerts us to the imperious weight Omega, the professor and literary critic, gives to his own masterful words. The professor justifies his arrogance quite naturally by underscoring the importance of his scholarly work. But his far-reaching article on the essence of the contemporary novel will undoubtedly limit itself to the works of a handful of white, male authors already canonized by the (male) literary establishment. Women writers, we can be sure, will not be acknowledged in his most important critical assessment. It seems that Omega is quite blind to other ways of seeing and to the disruptive force of feminine creativity that meets his gaze daily in his own home. For when the Euguélionne asks about the artist responsible for a remarkable painting of revolt that hangs in their kitchen, Omega summarily dismisses both the painting and the frenzied talent of his wife, Omicronne, whose violent canvas appears to challenge the very domesticity that sequesters her artistic voice. In terms of a gender-marked spatial poetics, the kitchen functions paradoxically here as both the site of Omicronne's confinement and of her revolt. Thus, it evokes the social servitude to which women have been required to submit and the subversive traces they have also been known to leave on the walls of their domestic cells.

In symbolic submission, Omicronne's response to the humiliating dismissal of her artistic vision is to bite her lip in silence. Omega's worth is thus established solely through the privileging of his own words and at the inevitable expense of Omicronne's artistic voice. The Euguélionne's denunciation of Omega's verbal cockiness in this family scene is, of course, also leveled at the dominant role men's words play generally in familial relations and in the culture at large. Shortly after this episode, the ill-treated Omicronne will leave her husband in search of her "real" name and, we presume, a more authentic mode of existence. In a far humbler manner, she will thereby join in the feminist quest already initiated by the Euguélionne upon her arrival. For Omicronne, this search for a female name, freed from patrilinear tradition, does in fact constitute a positive first step toward the creation of a new woman-centered identity. Bersianik (formerly Lucile Durand) has spoken of the importance of this search in her own personal life and of how, as a result, she decided to give herself a new name and a unique identity.[19]

The penetrating sarcasm with which Bersianik mocks the intellectual pretentions and linguistic smugness of "primitive beings" such as Omega is encountered throughout her text. It is, in fact, an important comic vehicle through which the writer controls and clearly enjoys her attacks. There is no pretense of "objectivity" here, no ruse of impartiality or playful distance. The arrogance and abusive disrespect for women that the Euguélionne encounters during her exhaustive expedition are cleverly denounced through varied and often extreme forms of ridicule. Indignant witticisms, burlesque caricatures, derisive mimicry, irreverent language, and scandalous reversals abound in this text all of which serve to strengthen the rhetorical strategy of the ironic mode. Outrageously entertaining, Bersianik's blasphemous humor attacks patriarchal authority with deadly serious aim from every conceivable angle.

One of the most significant and impertinent mockeries in Bersianik's subversive anti-Bible is her portrait of the buffoonlike prophet of psychoanalysis, Saint Siegfried. The Euguélionne describes him as a bombastic religious fanatic who preaches about the transcendental value of the Phallus from a mountaintop. Among his band of fervent disciples is Saint Jacques Linquant (Lacan in disguise) whom we will again encounter in Bersianik's second novel. A larger than life foil for the revisionary focus of feminist psychologizing that Bersianik clearly wants to promote, Freud's leading role in *L'Euguélionne* is that of master architect for the erection and eternal preservation of the male monolith. In his preposterous litany to the "All-Powerful-Phallus," St. Siegfried proposes a new divinity for modern worship, the always erect, transcendental Obelisk that must be recognized as "la Valeur Fondamentale" ("the Fundamental Value"), "la Norme Essentielle" ("the Essential Norm").

After assaulting us with the hyperbolic discourse of psychiatry's patriarchal master, Bersianik calls upon a young, subway-schooled Zazie to deflate his pompous assertions with the spontaneous and devilish retorts that only a child can provide. When Saint Siegfried begins to lecture Exil on her unacknowledged penis envy, Zazie blurts into the fray with the kind of transgressive humor that Queneau, her creator, would no doubt be proud of, and with a feminist wit more than equal to the task. In the snappy character of Zazie, Bersianik has in fact feminized the iconoclastic moves of Queneau (decanonization, fragmentation, carnivalesque parody) with a few broad and marvelously funny strokes:[20]

641. —Envie du pénis mon cul, cria une petite voix effrontée.
—Qui a parlé, s'enquit St Siegfried sans se troubler?
—C'est moi, dit une fillette à l'air déluré, assise à califourchon sur une branche.
—Comment t'appelles-tu, dit le Maître?
—Moi? J'm'appelle Zazie, et vous?
—Ne parlons pas de moi. Dis-moi, Zazie, où as-tu fait tes classes?
—Dans l'métro, quoi, comme tout l'monde! Et vous?
—Ne parlons pas de moi, dit St. Siegfried. Ainsi, ma petite Zazie, tu n'as pas envie d'une petite chose que ton petit frère possède et que toi, hélas, tu ne possèdes pas?
—De quoi vous voulez parlez au juste, dit Zazie? Ça serait-y du zizi à Jojo? Ça alors, vous êtes un rien marrant, vous. Mais j'veux bien vous l'dire en confidence: j'aimerais mieux avoir des nichons comme manman qu'un zizi. Ça serait plus pratique pour attraper les jules.
—Mais, tu ne trouves pas ça pratique le petit robinet de Jojo?
642. —Robinet mon cul, dit Zazie, j'peux faire pipi sans ça, alors, j'vois pas pourquoi j'aurais en plus de la tuyauterie. A quoi ce me servirait? Et puis, msieu, toujours entre nous, moi aussi j'ai des choses qu'il a pas le frangin. Croyez-le ou non, quand i's'fourre les doigts dans l'nez, c'est pas moi qui lui envierais son p'tit robinet, comme vous dites, parce que moi, meussieu, j'mets bien mes doigts quelque part mais c'est pas dans mon nez, ça, j'vous

l'garantis sur mesure! Même que c'est dans ce "quelque part" que je cache mes billes! Toujours entre nous, c'pas? Des fois que vous auriez envie vous aussi d'avoir une cachette dans ce genre-là, tout ce que j'peux vous dire, céxé vachement bath! (217)

641. —Penis envy, my ass, shouted a cheeky little voice.
—Who said that? inquired St. Siegfried, untroubled.
—Me, said a sharp-looking little girl, sitting astride a branch.
—What's your name? said the Master.
—I'm Zazie, an'you?
—Let's not talk about me. Tell me, Zazie, where do you go to school?
—In the subway, like everybody else! An'you?
—Let's not talk about me, said St. Siegfried. So my little Zazie, you don't want a little thing your little brother has that you, alas, don't have?
—What exactly do you wanna talk about? said Zazie. Could it be Jojo's dink? Gee, you're a real riot. Still, I'll tell you in confidence: I'd much rather have boobs like mummy than a dink. They'd be more useful for catchin' guys.
—But don't you think Jojo's little tap is useful?
642. —Tap, my ass, said Zazie, I can pee without that so I don't see why I should have extra plumbing. What would I do with it? And then, Mister, still between you an'me, I've got things my little brother hasn't got. Believe it or not, when he puts his fingers up his nose, I'm not wishin' I had his little tap, like you call it, Mister, because I can put my fingers somewhere but it isn't up my nose, that I can guarantee for sure. I even hide my marbles in that "somewhere"! Still between us, right? If y'ever wanna hidin' place like that too, all I can tell you is that it's really neat! (191–92)

Paralleling Luce Irigaray's ground-breaking argumentation in *Speculum of the Other Woman,* Bersianik demonstrates her interest in discrediting the *oculocentrism* of Freudian theory that places an excessive emphasis on what men can see, on their visual evaluation of male and female genitalia from a male viewpoint. In short, as Irigaray puts it, *"the* [male] *gaze is at stake from the outset."*[21] This is certainly the case when Bersianik's St. Siegfried construes what he can't see in female sexual anatomy as a lack, a flaw, an atrophied member. Woman is man with something missing, he concludes. Irigaray explains the implications of this kind of assessment in simple, yet pointed terms: *"Nothing to be seen is equivalent to having no thing. No being* and *no truth."*[22] But as Zazie's sense of touch tells her in the passage cited above, there is more than meets the eye here—and "it's really neat." Bersianik will, in fact, expand upon the centrality of touching in her subsequent text, *Le Pique-nique sur l'Acropole,* and in the works that follow.

Like Freud's Dora, Zazie rejects the very grounds on which the male analyst has built his case. As a result, she refuses to take his analysis seriously. With Zazie's help, Bersianik wants to expose Freud's reductive, male-centered views of femininity that have proved so damaging for the construction of female subjectivity generally and for more specific efforts to represent female sexual desire and the feminine unconscious in nonphallocentric terms. As Bersianik suggests and as Irigaray concurs, Freud's relations to women appear to have been grounded in artificial projections of an imaginary other who was little more than his own reflection. Woman was never really encountered at all.[23]

Intent on demystifying male mastery over the conceptualization and discourse of female subjectivity, Bersianik makes sure that in her own text Freud's immoderate claims are gleefully countered and then dismissed in fits of laughter. In so doing, she manages to use the paternalistic personas and phallocentric discourse of Freud and Lacan to her own political advantage, invoking their authority merely in order to attack it, poke fun at it, and ultimately delegitimize it. While the immediate effects of her many hit-and-run attacks on Freudian thought are indeed hilarious, the political intent of this decanonization process is anything but comical.

Canadian critic Shirley Neuman has already examined the central role of Freudian and Lacanian theory in *L'Euguélionne,* arguing that psychoanalytic discourse is patriarchal in its constructs, contexts, and codes. Like the discourse of the Judeo-Christian tradition, it privileges male power—genital, social, symbolic—while rendering female experience invisible and thus of no consequence. And as Neuman emphasizes, psychoanalytic discourse "is culturally determined and determining, articulating experience from the point of view of those with the power to construct it."[24] If Bersianik takes such obvious pleasure in her parodies of our psychoanalytic fathers, it is because their discourse has been responsible for legitimizing men's continual blindness to the differences of women's experience and for repressing any notion of desire or subjectivity that falls outside the phallic function.

The concern Bersianik expresses in *L'Euguélionne* over the arbitrary power of men to assign selective meaning to surrounding phenomena through the act of naming, to continually appropriate what is named for themselves, and to shamelessly model it after their own likeness can be noted throughout her work. Indeed, the political, material, and symbolic implications of men's efforts to base authority on naming are parodied with a bit of clever Cartesian irony in another brief, but much cited poetic text that appeared in *La Barre du jour* in 1977. Here, Bersianik illuminates the unconscious law of the male verb over women and things that has led to the historical appropriation of female subjectivity and to the denial of difference altogether, except insofar as the notion of difference has added to the centrality of male theoretical models (those of Lacan and Derrida, for example):

> —J'ai fait un rêve, dit le Verbe-Mâle
> Le rêve de nommer les êtres et les choses
> Car je suis le *Nomen-Patri*
> Ce que je nomme je le possède
> Et ce que je possède je le suis.[25]

> —I had a dream, says the Male Verb
> The dream of naming living beings and things
> For I am the *Nomen-Patri*
> What I name I possess
> And what I possess I am.

The ideological imperative behind men's safely guarded control of the social functions and symbolic codes of discourse shows up in the grammar and syntax of language practice as well. For the categories and established rules of language send important cultural messages to speakers and listeners, writers and readers alike—whether or not they are consciously acknowledged. Like Brossard, Bersianik contends that the links between the form of an enunciation and its symbolic content are so crucial that their social impact cannot be ignored. Hence she argues that the patriarchal exploitation and repression of women will not be overcome solely through progressive legislation and the establishment of more equitable forms of social relations, however worthy they are of our support. The very structures of discourse must also be overhauled. "For, even if mentalities are changing," argues Bersianik, "the symbolic code remains, stronger than ever. And even if they begin to admit that woman is an equal, 'les hommes continuent à exiger qu'elle demeure l'inessentiel' ('men continue to insist that she remain inessential'), as Simone de Beauvoir wrote thirty-five years ago."[26]

In terms of French grammar, the Euguélionne discovers what every female speaker of French already knows but usually chooses to ignore. She learns, for example, that when a male is present in the French language, the female subject (or subjects) is not recognized grammatically, and hence her symbolic value is indeed impoverished in the eyes of men. Moreover, masculine and feminine forms of the same noun or adjective often carry different cultural values (*maître/ maîtresse, viril/féminin, entraîneur/entraîneuse* [trainer or coach/bar entertainer]). For Bersianik's advanced female creature, the inherent sexism of a language in which masculine nouns, pronouns, and adjectives always dominate their feminine counterparts is more than a little disconcerting. In the end, she concludes that this lack of linguistic recognition and parity is directly tied to the female subject's sense of inadequacy in the symbolic realm.

In the third and final section of Bersianik's feminist triptych, there is much discussion between the female alien and a group of feminist protesters about the effects of linguistic alienation for women and about what positive measures can be taken. When the Euguélionne hears of the women's plan to present their petition, grievances, and corrective demands to the Académie Française—hallmark of the cultural institutionalization of patriarchal authority—she mocks their political naïveté and encourages creative initiative instead:

> N'attendez plus de permission pour agir, parler et écrire comme vous l'entendez.
> Faites des fautes volontairement pour rétablir l'équilibre des sexes. Inventez la forme neutre, assouplissez la grammaire, détournez l'orthographe, retournez la situation à votre avantage, implantez un nouveau style, de nouvelles tournures de phrases, contournez les difficultés, dérogez aux genres littéraires, faites-les sauter tout bonnement.   (230)

> Don't wait any longer for permission to act, speak, and write as you see fit.
> Make mistakes intentionally to re-establish the balance between the sexes. Invent neuter forms, bend the rules of grammar, rearrange the spelling, turn the situation to your advantage, establish a new style and new patterns

of speech, overcome the difficulties, leave behind the standard literary forms, in short, simply overturn the whole show. (203)

In her search for other ways of articulating the specificity of women's experiences and of representing women's cultural presence in language, the Euguélionne also scrutinizes the etymology of selected words having only masculine forms (*un auteur, un écrivain, un peintre, un sculpteur, un médecin, un témoin* [witness]) and encourages women in their efforts to create new nouns and adjectives that render visible the complex and multiple roles women exercise in both the private and public spheres. In this regard, Bersianik is no doubt delighted with the radical redefining of words, symbols, and mythical figures undertaken by French writers such as Monique Wittig and Sande Zeig and with the subsequent efforts of Cheris Kramarae and Paula Treichler in the United States to write a feminist dictionary that speaks directly to the important relationships between women and language.[27] In her call for a radical "unmaking" of those inherited words, syntax, poetic symbolisms, and narrative forms that demean, constrain, and ignore women, the Euguélionne initiates a program of revolt against the most common structures of linguistic sexism in everyday speech, in literature, and in the discourse of western philosophical thought generally. Through the rousing words of her alien visitor, Bersianik has, in fact, proposed strategies of linguistic revolt that have since helped chart much of the direction of feminist literary experimentation in Quebec.

As Bersianik sees it, the language issue is at the very heart of women's feminist awakening, which is why her own Euguélionne refuses to give the women of earth yet another sacred book—even in feminist form—that would once again excuse them from finding their own way in and through language. Rather, the Euguélionne urges women to consider her extraordinary visit as a critical point of departure in herstory, a zero point in women's struggle to assume subjectivity through the spoken and the written word. Advancing a belief also articulated by Daly that the transformation of patriarchal language will necessarily lead to transformations in the politics, social relations, and creative projects of culture itself,[28] the Euguélionne offers herself as the blank page on which women must begin to write their collective future in a different voice: "I am the unwritten book which I leave to you to compose" (196).

Addressed to the women of the earth, this general call to writing is an invitation to begin a new historical era. Indeed, the Euguélionne judges that women are still in a period of prehistory, served only by a prehistoric language that continues to disregard their existence. Women's time in Bersianik's fiction is, therefore, the historical moment when women take charge of language and begin to inscribe their place in it. This final debunking of the paternal authority of authorship, suggested by the very notion of women's prehistoric status in language, is an enabling move for many feminist writers today who, like Bersianik, are attempting to counter centuries of male authorial privilege and conceit through various experimental practices that reclaim the past and reenvision the future. Just as women must surely secure a room and a name of their own, Bersianik argues, so too must they invent words, phrases, syntax, and styles of their own making in order to reinvent not only the silenced history of their female ancestry, but also the liberating images that may nurture the descendants of tomorrow. Like Brossard, Bersianik believes that these scriptorial efforts to reclaim women's powers of authorship—an authorship based on experimentation and exploration rather than on the assertion of any particular set of truths—will significantly alter both our sense of the future and its actual direction.

Picnicking and Historical Heresy

A number of our best and most influential feminist critics (Rich, Kolodny, Miller, Schor, Showalter) have already said much about feminist reading as a revisionary project—a project of reinterpretation and reappropriation. Indeed, it would seem that Nancy Miller speaks for numerous feminist critics today when she affirms that "one of the tasks of feminist criticism in the age of poststructuralism is to read over the familiar texts of the library for the ideological support a culture supplies to its own self-representation."[29] Miller's observation prompts questions of considerable concern for many feminist readers, in particular, the question of what to read (texts by women and/or texts by men) as well as the closely related question of how to read (with gender and/or race and/or class in mind). While Louky Bersianik is first and foremost a feminist writer, she is also—as are many of her contemporaries—a feminist reader of texts, and an avid one at that. Like Millett, Showalter, Fetterley and others who have worked to redress the persistent male bias in Western literature through their own resistant and radical forms of rereading, Bersianik is also out to "disrupt the canonical economy," as Christine Froula has put it,[30] by challenging the universality of the male-canonized text and by questioning the very grounds on which male-oriented poetics and philosophies of value have developed and been allowed to flourish. In so doing, she too hopes to disrupt a system of power relations in place since Aristotle that has privileged the cultural authority of men—white, western men, that is—in our great halls of learning and, at the same time, has relegated most of the works of women to the basement, if they were lucky enough to be published and put on the shelves at all.

In *Le Pique-nique sur l'Acropole*, Bersianik demonstrates just how powerful a conjoining of the acts of rereading and writing can be when used to reconsider the philosophical foundations on which patriarchal thought has been built and when, moreover, the process prompts us to review the systems of dominance that have sustained the authority of male elites over the centuries. Appearing three years after *L'Euguélionne*, *Le Pique-nique sur l'Acropole* (*Picnic at the Acropolis*) calls attention, by its very title, to one of the most venerated architectural sites of Western civilization. This famous location will perform a dual function in Bersianik's text, embodying on the one hand the historical period and the particular cultural values of ancient Athens and, on the other, the mythopoetic power for the modern psyche of a place that has been so ennobled in western literature. But the implicit humor in this title also contests the triumphant stature of the high art form Bersianik has chosen to evoke by associating the esteemed Athenian locale with the banal and decidedly less "classy" idea of a picnic. This is a curiously amusing pairing, to be sure, and one that alerts us to the kind of irreverent and transgressive encoding continually encountered in her text.

Whereas the Bible provided Bersianik with much of the structural and thematic material for *L'Euguélionne*—material that she would borrow and then turn on its head—the historical context and many of the key issues addressed in *Le Pique-nique* are developed in response to her rereading of another canonized text, Plato's *Banquet* or *Symposium* (depending upon the translation), a dialogue on love based on the recounting of speeches delivered at a banquet given by the Greek poet Agathon.[31] For Bersianik's purposes, the image of a decadent, self-indulgent male feast will be central to her deconstructive project. Indicative of the satirical mode that shapes this text, the menu of Plato's banquet is described in startling misogynist terms as Bersianik's characters learn that this (in)famous meal was composed entirely of female animals cooked in elaborate femininized sauces and herbs for the male guests. Bersianik will underscore this issue of female victimization for the sake of male pleasure further still through repeated references to the plethora of raped and abducted women in Greek mythology.

Addressed exclusively to men, women's place in Plato's celebrated dialogue is ancillary, to say the least (*ancillary* coming from the Latin *ancilla* or *maidservant*). Intent on making this point in a variety of ways, Bersianik engages among other things in political wordplay with the sonority and etymology of the word *ancillaire* by naming one of the principal characters in her text *Ancyl*.[32] More recently, Luce Irigaray has echoed Bersianik's critique of the ancillary status of women in this same master text by noting that the only female perspective encountered in Plato's *Banquet* is that of the wise Diotima and even her words are mediated through the voice of Socrates since Diotima, herself, has not been invited.[33] In terms of the status of the male reader in her own text, Bersianik will counter Plato by means of a sarcastic prefatory warning to male readers that they should not expect to find themselves represented at her picnic because their own lengthy banquet is still going on. Targeting psychoanalytic thought as well, she consoles the potential male reader by adding that any offensive parts of her text are merely intended as "une blessure symbolique" ("a symbolic wound") and will not harm him—unless, she mockingly concedes, he is one of the "innombrables et négligeables exceptions" ("innumerable and negligible exceptions")![34]

Le Pique-nique sur l'Acropole is arranged as a symphonic response to Lacan and to the absent presence of the feminine in his writing—despite Lacan's own acknowledgment of woman's status as pure complementarity to man in Freudian thought. Bersianik appears particularly troubled by the notion that female sexuality can never really be represented except as an excess to the masculine,[35] for in essence, female sexuality remains a mystery to Lacan. To mark the parodic intentions of her orchestrated composition, Bersianik proposes a "prélude en la mineure sur l'écriture" ("prelude in the feminine minor on writing"), follows with two concertos that give form to most of her text, and ends with a "fugue en la majeure" ("fugue in the feminine major"). Although extremely varied in its focus and rhythms, the feminized musical scheme in *Le Pique-nique* thus moves from minor to major key, giving us a "progressive" musical movement. This post-Lacanian arrangement allows Bersianik to undermine yet another example of philosophical phallocentrism while also highlighting the complex interweaving of themes and counterthemes that deal with the historical suppression and subordination of women and women's words. Like the structure of the fugue itself, Bersianik's text is written in counterpoint and its primary theme and successive variations move off in separate directions and reconnect around the notion of an affirmative female presence.

Le Pique-nique is feminist parody at its best—repetition with a difference. Through parody, Bersianik confronts the canonical text for what it refuses to tell us about the social and sexual realities of women's lives in ancient Greece. At the same time, her parodic stance aims at the present by contesting patriarchal attitudes about women and judgments regarding literary value all of which continue to circulate. Her parody is thus multiple—invoking a specific work, an unacknowledged historical space, a philosophical tradition, and her own contemporary culture. Bersianik restages literary history by transforming Plato's account of the raucous banquet and ensuing conversations of Socrates, Aristophanes, and five other male companions into a modest picnic attended by five modern women, a young African girl soon to be sexually excised, and Socrates' little known wife, Xanthippe. Nocturnal trespassers on the guarded grounds of the Acropolis, these six women and the endangered child gather together after dark and in secret to exchange stories of exclusion, neglect, and mutilation in the age of Socrates and in modern times. Clearly, their very presence at the ancient devotional site of the Acropolis is a form of unlawful provocation. It is also a befitting occasion on which to rethink the bases of a philosophical tradition that has consciously performed an excision of the female for the purpose of assuring fidelity to the concept of male dominance. According to Bersianik, this politically inspired removal and historical silencing of all that evokes and pertains to women and their lives has been carried out at every level of patriarchal culture.

In the realm of female sexuality and sexual abuse, Bersianik will take the position that clitoridectomy and, along with it, other forms of physical mutilation and mistreatment have been a literal fact for females of all ages, affecting their physical responsiveness, their ability to experience pleasure, and their symbolic function in the patriarchal equation of unequal gender relations.[36] Indeed, it appears as if the entire network of meanings in Bersianik's narrative is organized around a preliminary theoretical inscription presented in large bold type that outlines the political vision examined in this text: "PATRIARCHAL POWER RESTS ON THE PROHIBITION OF THE MATERNAL BODY AND ON CLITORIDECTOMY REAL OR PSYCHOLOGICAL." This view correlates closely with arguments made by Mary Daly and Adrienne Rich on female mutilation and on the myths of motherhood in writings that appeared not long before the publication of *Le Pique-nique*.[37]

In both *L'Euguélionne* and *Le Pique-nique sur l'Acropole*, Bersianik's radical inversions of the canonical—canonized text, site, and philosophical tradition—are deconstructive, polemical, and remarkably inventive. In terms of its attack on the western philosophical tradition, however, *Le Pique-nique* appears to be even more virulent than *L'Euguélionne* and, for the most part, its critique of contemporary forms of phallocentrism is even harsher. Whereas the honored guests at Plato's banquet primarily concerned themselves with the exposition and competitive evaluation of their respective theories on male love and with their own amorous rivalries, Bersianik's picnickers share their diverse thoughts on the nature of women's sexual pleasure and on the meaning of love in a spirit of mutual support and understanding. During their exchange of personal experiences, a process that in many ways ressembles the feminist consciousness raising sessions of the early to mid-1970s, Bersianik's female intruders also analyze the politics of sexual objectification and abuse to which they have been subjected in their intimate private lives. As we shall see, Bersianik's position on the politics of female sexuality is clearly indebted to the "personal is political" focus which Brossard and other Quebec feminists were beginning to articulate by 1975 (see chapter 1).

Bersianik's theoretical frame of reference in *Le Pique-nique sur l'Acropole* moves considerably beyond the borders of Quebec as well. This larger feminist focus is established by incorporating the voices of numerous other women writers, scholars, and professionals into her text. Among others, she cites Phyllis Chesler, Margaret Mead, Betty Dodson, Edith Hamilton, Shere Hite, Luce Irigaray, and the African writer Awa Thiam—all of whom have addressed issues whose impact extends well beyond the realm of the purely literary. Inserted into hand-drawn window boxes and circular glass panes, quotations from their works serve as emphatic reminders that women's literature cannot afford to be dissociated from the political, economic, psychological, and social realities of women's lives. Bersianik clearly wants these direct references to female specialists in the areas of psychology, anthropology, sociology, philosophy, and myth in her text to lend credibility to her own poetic meditations on the place women have historically occupied in patriarchal culture and thought. But like a number of her feminist contemporaries, she also wants to "explode the limits of individuality" in order to create a new and expanded sense of female subjectivity.[38] At the same time, this borrowing of female voices serves as a crucial counterpoint to the more traditional male views of Plato, Aristotle, Henry Miller, and her character St. Jacques Linquant, whom Bersianik also invokes in order to debunk. Thus, she enacts her feminist exorcism on two intertextual fronts by repeatedly calling our attention to the suppression, mutilation, and silencing of women in the discourse, history, mythologies, and literary classics of men and by allowing women's self-expression to reemerge through the words of feminist thinkers who have already broken the silence.

Providing both the theoretical points of departure and the narrative inspiration for *Le Pique-nique,* this recourse to intertextuality enables Bersianik to situate herself within an emerging current of feminist thought that, in various ways, has wreaked havoc on male-oriented culture and on its on gender-biased versions of history. The names, words, and texts of other women underscore Bersianik's belief in the power of feminist creativity and further promote her vision of a collective feminist enterprise. It is, therefore, clearly a mistake to view the numerous examples of intertextuality in *Le Pique-nique* as simply further manifestations of the kinds of carnivalesque play and *bricolage* that have exploded the boundaries of textuality in so much of postmodern writing today. Likewise, the same observation could be made regarding Carole Massé's extreme use of intertextuality in *Dieu,* another ambitious gender-marked approach to experimental writing in Quebec that also appeared in 1979.[39] For Massé and for Bersianik, the privileged "citationist aesthetic" has an overtly feminist design that cannot be adequately apprehended when stripped of its political intent and classified as merely another principle of postmodern aesthetics.[40]

Intent on mocking and rewriting phallocentric thought by exposing and then reversing the negative intertexts of Plato, Lacan, and others, Bersianik engages in both a negative and positive intertextuality[41] in *Le Pique-nique* by underscoring the politics behind the silenced woman in the male intertext and, at the same time, by incorporating the words of feminist thinkers from a variety of cultures and professional fields to back her up. In so doing, she emphasizes the deepening international reservoir of feminist voices that are challenging the philosophical assumptions of patriarchal thought and the canonical tradition it continues to sanction and even to glorify. Bearing Plato's influential "master" narrative in mind, the discussion that takes place in *Le Pique-nique* among Bersianik's female characters marks an undeniable shift from male-centered to female-centered frames of reference. But the change in point of view from Plato to Bersianik, from men to women, is not merely one of gender. It is one of ideology as well. And the politics of reading occupies a central place in this shift. Intent on problematizing the status of the female reader in Plato's masterpiece, Bersianik initiates the kind of revisionary reading practice in her own text that Judith Fetterley had argued for so persuasively only a year before:

> To expose and question that complex of ideas and mythologies about women and men which exist in our society and are confirmed in our literature is to make the system of power embodied in the literature open not only to discussion but even to change. Such questioning and exposure can, of course, be carried on only by a consciousness radically different from the one that informs the literature. Such a closed system cannot be opened up from within but only from without. It must be entered into from a point of view which questions its values and assumptions and which has its investment in making available to consciousness precisely that which the literature wishes to keep hidden.[42]

The radicality of Bersianik's deconstructive agenda does more than merely substitute one gender-partial perspective for another or one implied woman reader for her male counterpart. Not satisfied with simple reversals, Bersianik asks us to consider why, for centuries, women have been taught to read the male-oriented texts of the philosophical canon—from the Greeks to Lacan—for the "universality" of their message. Like Catherine MacKinnon and a growing number of feminist thinkers today, Bersianik subscribes to the view that feminism—and feminist approaches to reading and writing— "not only challenges masculine partiality but questions the universality imperative itself. Aperspectivity is revealed as a strategy of male hegemony."[43] In the realm of literature, Bersianik argues that the male writer's claim to universality denies that gender matters and acts as a screen to mask what he is up to in a given text; it is a claim rooted in naïveté or deception (or both). In either case, women are usually its targets as well as its victims.

To underscore the point that her own subversive dialogue is transgressive rather than recuperative in its intent,[44] Bersianik places it at the base rather than at the top of the Acropolis, a point from which the seven female characters can observe the physical dominance of the masculine monument over the city's inhabitants.

It is also the place from which Bersianik invites her characters and her readers to contemplate the sacred temple of the Erechtheum whose southernmost support columns are the six sculptured caryatids, nameless female figures who have been forced to strike a phallic pose (i.e., erect and rigid) and who continue to bear the weight of the male structure on their weary heads.[45] Through a highly original blending of political and architectural reflections, these rigid, armless statues will become the central symbol in Bersianik's text for the suppressed voices and curtailed, utilitarian function of women in Athenian culture. However, the Grecian caryatid also epitomizes the restricted movement and secondary status of women in all patriarchal cultures, a point made repeatedly throughout *Le Pique-nique:*

On veut redresser le vétuste patriarcat semble-t-il, dit Xanthippe, relever le primat de l'Erection, dit Ancyl, restaurer les Caryatides, pour qu'elles continuent à supporter l'insupportable, dit Aphélie en plaquant des accords dissonants sur son instrument de bal musette. Elles n'en ont pas assez de ce destin de colonnes colonisées, soutiens d'un système qui leur est étranger et hostile? On comprend les Atlantes de continuer à porter le monde sur leurs épaules puisque le monde leur appartient, mais elles! Qu'est-ce qu'elles attendent pour se tailler en douce, le moment pourtant est propice.   (85)

They want to reerect the antiquated patriarchate it seems, says Xanthippe, raise again the primacy of the Erection, says Ancyl, restore the Caryatids so that they can continue to bear the unbearable, says Aphélie as she strikes some dissonant chords on her dancing-hall accordion. Haven't they had enough of this fate of colonized columns, supports for a system they know to be alien and hostile? It's understandable that the Atlases continue to carry the world on their shoulders since the world belongs to them, but the caryatids! What are they waiting for to slip away, the time is certainly right.

It is almost impossible to ignore the parallels in Bersianik's poetic reappropriation of the caryatids with the imagery of Luce Irigaray who also uses the figure of the statue to speak of women's immobility in patriarchal discourse: "Their 'truth' immobilizes us, turns us into statues, if we can't loose its hold on us. If we can't defuse its power by trying to say, right here and now, how we are moved."[46] Both Bersianik and Irigaray link women's statuesque passivity in patriarchal thought to creative paralysis, silence, and death. Dedicated to Luce Irigaray and Françoise d'Eaubonne, *Le Pique-nique sur l'Acropole* is clearly traversed on the one hand by Irigaray's assertion in *Speculum* that the phallocentrism illustrated in the discourses of Freud and Lacan can be traced back to the philosophies of Plato and Aristotle, and, on the other, by her subsequent contention in *This Sex Which Is Not One* that in order for women to turn their "organless body" into a place of sexual pleasure, they will need to construct "a relation to language and to sex—to the organs— that women have never had."[47]

Even before we are introduced to Bersianik's female picnickers, each of whom has her own distinct personality and point of view, the signifying power of the caryatid has already been well established. In fact, the notion that since the ancient Greeks, men have sought to bridle women's creative impulses and arrest them in stone orients our reading from the very first page of *Le Pique-nique*. Serving as Bersianik's own projected self-image, the woman writer in this opening section emphasizes the corporeal production of her own words: "Corps producteur de mots, de salive muette, de mue, de linge propre, de mucus, de faillites, de jouissance. Souillures déla-vées" (15) ("Body producer of words, of muted saliva, of a breaking voice, of clean linen, of mucus, of failure, of pleasure. Stains washed out"). In contrast, her writing also allows us to contemplate the muted discourse of ancient, inert statues:

> Maintenant je génère du marbre à travers le bois du papier. Main tenant mordue le stylo. Froids vêtements en marbre pentélique, pieds et carotides en sommeil. Onirique? Langage laconique. Support pour d'autres. Tout dans la corniche. Expression décorporée.   (15)

> Now I generate out of marble through the wooded paper. Nibbled hand holding pen. Cold clothing in pentelic marble, feet and carotids asleep. Dreamlike? Laconic language. Support for others. Everything in the cornice. Disembodied expression.

The desire to bring the caryatids to life in this text is Bersianik's way of signaling her intention to retrieve the lives of women buried under centuries of silence and thus to chisel out of the voiceless stone of antiquity a dynamic historical dialogue of female figures speaking to one another and to contemporary readers from across the ages. Even more importantly, however, this restorative act is also a revealing metaphor for Bersianik's own conception of writing in the feminine. For the awakening of the statue's cold, colorless marble body and the genesis of Bersianik's woman-centered text are both marked by the woman writer's inscription of her own physical gestures, bodily rhythms, and sexual desire. "Writing is a corporeal expression," affirms the writer in this text (16). This statement highlights the importance she will place on the physicality of writing and on the text within her. A crucial, if frequently misunderstood concept, this focus on the woman's body-as-it-writes is closely linked to key structures, themes, symbolisms, and to the overall political stance of *Le Pique-nique*.

The extreme self-consciousness of the woman writer in Bersianik's text is, moreover, reminiscent of Brossard's recurrent preoccupation with the image of the woman writer writing, which I have already discussed at some length in chapter 2. Like Brossard, Bersianik has been especially influenced by structuralism's attention to how the text comes into being and by more recent poststructuralist interests in the construction of the subject as it is constituted in language. But as is the case in many of the feminist-inspired texts of Brossard, Gagnon, and Théoret, the very notion of textual production in Bersianik's text, as well as the codes and symbolic structures generated through the act of writing, are unmistakably gender-marked. In *Le Pique-nique*, Bersianik presents a mise en scène of the woman writer's body that is textually and politically significant. A female writer is visibly and physically present in the writing process, and her sensory responses flow through the written word. There is nothing rigid (phallic) or inert about the rhythms, syntax, or formal structures of *Le Pique-nique* precisely because Bersianik wants the text to create the sense of a living female presence and to affirm a certain difference that cannot be overlooked.[48] Shortly after its publication, Bersianik emphasized the corporeal aspect of her text: "Writing really is corporeal. It's flesh and blood. It's my respiration. And we need to emerge in order to breathe. I don't want to ghettoize women's writing. I want writing to be human writing. But we can't ignore that there is a difference."[49]

If *L'Euguélionne* exhorted women to write and provided them with a manifesto asserting their need and right to do so, *Le Pique-nique* addresses the issue of how women might begin to write themselves into existence—individually as well as collectively—by speaking from the bodies and the experiences they know to be especially their own. In the opening pages of *Le Pique-nique,* we are immediately alerted to the existence of a hand, arm, and shoulder that move irregularly and with some tension so that a woman's words may be inscribed on the space of an empty page. More than anything else, however, the woman writer's initial presence in this text is conveyed through the sense of touch: her hand touches the paper, touches the sources of her own physical pleasure, introduces the theme of the untouched women (the caryatids), and seeks the arousal of these ancient Greek statues from their patriarchal sleep through the aid of another woman's touch.

This theme of touching is, in fact, of primary importance in the experiences recounted by Bersianik's picnickers. For Xanthippe whom Socrates would not touch, for Aphélie whose body bleeds whenever it is touched by a man, and for the young Adizetu whose imminent clitoridectomy will deprive her of the pleasures of a certain touch, the issue of physical contact is real, it is painful—psychologically and sometimes physically, and it is political. Echoing Brossard's rallying call of the mid-1970s, "Touchez-moi, la vie privée est politique" ("Touch me, the personal is political"), a phrase that reconnected the private and the social spheres and also politicized lesbian love as an affirmation of women-for-women identification, Xanthippe expresses a similar desire to be touched by the female friends who have joined her at the Acropolis. Xanthippe's intense longing is rooted in her need to rediscover the world of the senses and her love of self. As a result, the collective touching initiated at her request is more sensual than sexual, more self-affirming than ecstatic. In the end, it is this moment of shared intimacy that allows the unknown wife of Socrates to be reborn as a woman, without shame and confident in her own potential:

Ce que je perçois par le toucher c'est ce qu'il y a de meilleur au monde, dit Xanthippe. Touchez-moi! Vous me ferez exister. Touchez-moi et je saurai mes limites spatiales, je saurai que je suis vivante et même *terriblement vivante.* Touchez-moi et vous me mettrez au monde, vous me rendrez à terme, je serai celle qui naît. Je serai celle qui peut tout.   (51)

What I feel through touching is the best there is, says Xanthippe. Touch me! You will make me exist. Touch me and I'll know my own spatial limitations, I'll know that I am alive and even *terribly alive*. Touch me and you will bring me to life, you will deliver me full term, I'll be the one who is born. I'll be the one who can do everything.

From the start, then, *Le Pique-nique* is grounded in the senses and in a woman's bodily rhythms. We are also reminded of the extent to which writing is a question of breath, a physical activity dependent on the intake and exhalation of air. For that reason, the flow of the woman writer's words will be punctuated by the pauses, panting, and normal respiration characteristic of all living beings. Her breathing will also, however, give life and movement to the upper torso and to her female breasts. But rather than consider this embodiment of difference an impediment or an irrelevancy to writing, or yet another site for the male gaze, the woman writer at work in the opening pages of Bersianik's text will acknowledge the existence of her breasts as she writes and will accept the autoerotic pleasures they may bring. As Hélène Cixous had done in *Souffles,*[50] Bersianik thus alerts us to the woman writer's breathing body in order to underscore, in yet another fashion, the new and transgressive physicality of her discourse. But Bersianik also links this motif of respiration to the image of the "statuefied woman" (one of the central images in this text) to stress the political reasoning behind her desire to explore the physicality of writing as a woman. Women must learn to breathe as they write, Bersianik suggests, in order to affirm their subjectivity through a voice that emanates from within. Otherwise, they risk being silenced by the universalizing truths of an externally imposed discourse that, while enlisting women's support, removes all traces of their experience.[51] It is worth noting that Bersianik's efforts to valorize the interior female voice through the body's pulsations are quite compatible with Gagnon's vision in *Lueur,* which also appeared in 1979.

This imperative to break the silence imposed by the deadening weight of patriarchal thought, which is so carefully tied to the image of the caryatid, provides the central focus of Bersianik's text. The major portion of *Le Pique-nique* is, in fact, devoted to the sayings (*les dits*) of each of her seven female characters regarding their most intimate fears, their own accounts of mistreatment, and their desiring sexualities (hetero, homo, plural). For each woman, the act of relating to other women her most silenced thoughts prompts a disclosure of abuses suffered, a personal indictment of phallocentric thought, and the positive expression of yet another facet of female sexuality. Through the various case herstories and allegations presented by her female characters, Bersianik insists upon the diversity of women's experience. The strength of this testimonial approach lies in Bersianik's ability to record the differing intensities and timbres in their voices and to emphasize the notable differences in their perspectives on the possibilities and the realities of women's love.

In juxtaposing the vital physicality of writing in the feminine with the frozen female discourse of ancient Athenian statues, Bersianik manages to place a remote past alongside a more immediate present, thereby assuring that the woman writer inscribed in her text and the silenced statues of the Acropolis will be equally present in the reader's mind. Bersianik will hearken back to this study in contrasts towards the end of her text as well when another young writer, Avertine, confronts a sleeping caryatid and invites her to shake off more than two thousand years of silent patriarchal service and begin to speak. Describing herself as the "inconsolable daughter" in search of a mother whose identity and whereabouts remain unknown, Avertine is associated with the tragic separation and seasonal reunification of Demeter and Persephone. Reappropriating this well-known Greek myth about the origin of the seasons much the way many American feminists have done over the last few decades, Bersianik's version stresses the unchanging strength of the mother-daughter bond and, at the same time, offers a harsh indictment of the discontinuity fostered between mothers and daughters in patriarchal cultures.

A daughter who writes with admitted difficulty, Avertine searches relentlessly for her mother the way Demeter looked for her daughter, Persephone. Avertine presents her story of a daughter's bereavement and describes her slow death in the exclusive company of men to the other female picknickers at the Acropolis. Her writing has never been well received, we are told; and her body has been repeatedly violated; she is dying of "pernicious anemia" and "of fragmentation" (211). As in the Greek myth to which her search is consciously linked—another form of classical intertext, Avertine knows that her mother must be found and that a reunion must be celebrated if she is to experience a creative rebirth that can save her and her writing from a lifeless existence. Hence it is no accident that in the final pages of *Le Pique-nique,* Avertine appears at the base of one of the giant caryatids and then beckons her with loving imperatives to come down from the patriarchal monument and embrace the daughter-writer who can infuse her marble body with life. Avertine's long, intimate, and increasingly accelerated invocation is surely one of the most poetic passages in Bersianik's text. And as the following excerpt demonstrates, the marked physicality noted in both the caryatid's nascent transformation and in the source of Avertine's words is exceptionally powerful:

La chaleur circule, le marbre se fait chair, les veines s'étirent et se gorgent de sang, prends mon sang j'en ai pour deux. Ton coeur glacé comme un balancier hésite à s'élancer je te donne mon coeur. Tes paupières cristallisées ont du mal à se déplier après tant de siècles immobiles, je te donne mes larmes. Tes oreilles desséchées s'attendrissent sous les vagues de ta coiffure, tes cheveux font leur bulbe sur ton crâne frémissant, ton nez s'invente des narines nouvelles, ta bouche veut s'ouvrir et ta langue givrée sort du froid avec des picotements de monosyllabes, prends ma salive. Tes lèvres gélives fendues par le gel te font souffrir, prends mes lèvres et guéris-toi. Tes dents s'entrechoquent pour broyer des mots, prends mes mots dans ma bouche, prends ma langue, prends mon verbe, prends mon délire, accroche-toi à mon désir, prends mon désir de naître et NAIS, prends mon désir de vivre et VIS.   (226)

Warmth circulates, marble becomes flesh, the veins stretch and swell with blood, take my blood I have enough for two. Frozen like a pendulum your heart hesitates to move I give you my heart. Your cristallized eyelids struggle to open after so many centuries of immobility, I give you my tears. Your dried-out ears soften under the waves of your hairdo, your hair make its roots on your quivering skull, new nostrils are created for your nose, your mouth wants to open and your frost-covered tongue shakes off the cold with tingling monosyllables, take my saliva. Your cracked lips split by the frost are painful, take my lips and heal yourself. Your teeth knock against one another grinding out words, take my words in my mouth, take my tongue, take my verb, take my exuberance, grab on to my desire, take my desire to be born and COME INTO THE WORLD, take my desire to be alive and LIVE.

There is a certain musicality here and perhaps even an air of reverence in the form of Avertine's delivery as well as in the insistent repetition of possessive adjectives and the recurrence of the verb *prends* (take) that emphasizes the gift of a voice longing to recreate the mother by imbuing her with the daughter's strength.[52] More traditional versions of the Demeter-Persephone myth center around Demeter's search for her daughter, who finally reappears only part of the year, thus creating the spring and summer months. The mother's seasonal sorrow is marked in the dormant earth when Persephone returns each fall to Hades where Pluto continues to hold her captive. Another contemporary reader interested in feminist revisions of this mother-daughter myth, Grace Stewart, has argued that, although not entirely successful, Demeter does in fact challenge the patriarchal order "on behalf of her daughter."[53]

Once again, Bersianik has been unable to resist the temptation to reclaim the rights to an ancient story in order to rework it for her own feminist purpose. And in this new version, it is the daughter who desperately pursues reunification with the mother and who in fact calls into being the long forgotten "statuefied" mother. Indeed, in her role as a daughter who writes, Avertine breathes life into this maternal giant from the past just as Bersianik herself has done with the female characters in her text, a creative *dédoublement* that should not go unnoticed. Exhausted from her extraordinary efforts to stir the caryatid, Avertine finally falls into the immense arms of the "Terrible Vivante" ("Terrible Living Woman") she has just set free. An emboldened mother figure who can now come to Avertine's aid, her giant gait carries her swiftly down from the Acropolis toward the female picnickers and the female reader who wait below. The text's final image can thus be read as a double engendering of mother and daughter, each one having been conceived and in a sense brought to life by the other:

Nous avons peur, nous reculons. Avertine n'a pas peur. Elle est épuisée. Elle pousse un grand soupir. La voilà qui s'endort dans les bras de la *Cariatide* qu'elle a mise au monde.   (228)

We are afraid, we step back. Avertine isn't afraid. She is exhausted. She heaves a great sigh. Now she is falling asleep in the arms of the *Caryatid* she has brought into the world.

Rewriting the Greek myth to advance and conclude her own feminist plot, Bersianik has thereby placed the woman writer at the

188   *Louky Bersianik*

center of the contemporary quest to unleash the engendering power of women's words. But as she also demonstrates in a final series of quotations from Plato that serve as an addendum to her own writing, a maternally coded discourse of "engendering," "giving birth," and "nurturing" has long been appropriated by men, and by Socrates in particular, at Plato's banquet. As I have suggested throughout this study, deconstructive textual maneuvers are not revolutionary in themselves. What matters, of course, is *what* is being dismantled and *how* it is being recast. In *Le Pique-nique sur l'Acropole*, Bersianik's subversive writing practice is aimed at an imperious male philosophical tradition that has systematically denied female autonomy and in which women have played no visible role—except as supplementary to the male reference point. In the end, Bersianik's literary quest is tied to what she continues to view as a crucial feminist project for our time: the contemporary woman writer's struggle to give life to words that refuse mastery over the other even as they affirm the power of her own female voice. With the final revisionary scene of an empowered caryatid on the move, a new mythos for writing in the feminine has indeed been born:

Ecrire c'est enjamber des murs, enjamber des morts, des mers, des siècles, c'est écraser le marbre statuaire, c'est faucher l'avenir, engendrer du futur archéologique.   (83)

Writing is leaping over walls, leaping over the dead, over seas, centuries, it's smashing the marble statuary, it's reaping the future, engendering an archaeological future.

Memory and Mythopoesis

American historian Linda Gordon has argued that "women's history is not just different, it is critical; it is against men's history."[54] Throughout her literary career, Bersianik has remained explicitly political in her call for a feminist re-viewing of the past and for a reexamination of the dominant patriarchal myths that have molded western European thought since the ancient Greeks. For Bersianik, writing against the status and treatment of women in male myths has thus become a viable form of political opposition to patriarchal thinking; it also provides her with a new vantage point from which to critique an entire tradition of consciously worked material that has preserved male authority by keeping women in their domesticated place. Like Gagnon, however, Bersianik has in recent years been increasingly drawn to a writing of the female unconscious as well. Yet even in her most expressively intimate texts, she continues to sound the depths of a herstory that is collectively inspired, mythically restaged, and strategically revalued.

In a brief but important theoretical essay, *Les Agénésies du vieux monde* (*Old World Agenesis*), which appeared in 1982, Bersianik directly addresses the issue of women's identification with the past. The marked insistence here on the linguistic, the historical, and the mythical, as well as on their various points of intersection and divergence, is an indication of the extent to which history, language, and myth are central to her understanding of what it means—and has meant—to be a woman in western culture. At the same time, the focus of Bersianik's feminist theorizing on language, history, and mythopoesis provides a conceptual framework for approaching her own particular writing practice. As her arguments demonstrate, Bersianik views language as an imaginative space where history and the contemporary age conjoin, where the past exerts its influence over the present, and where what she has termed our collective *mémoire mythologique* continues to surface in the modern consciousness.[55] This mythological memory presents us with a reservoir of images and symbols that must be explored and questioned if we are to locate and counter some of the more influential and telling examples of western misogyny.

However, the affirmative side of Bersianik's mythmaking project moves beyond the much-needed critique of earlier forms of misogynous representation to a concept of writing that encourages the surfacing of what she refers to as women's collective "archaeological memory"—or as she has playfully put it in English, "*My mory instead of his story.*"[56] Women need this feminine ancestral memory, Bersianik contends, in order to reassemble and sustain a collective gender identity that will reconnect them to the past, to their female ancestors, and to a viable notion of origins. Digging through the past thus becomes a way of struggling against women's collective amnesia. No longer simply an internal, private matter, the process of remembering in Bersianik's works has serious implications for women's sense of themselves as a group and as individuals. And as in the works of Mary Daly, the political call for "memoricity" over historicity has a somewhat spiritual, even utopian ring. Both Daly and Bersianik argue, in effect, for a poetic recasting of the past that can rescue women from their status as absent, disconnected figures, provide them with a sense of historical inheritance, and orient them toward the dawn of a new age.[57] Furthermore, this keen interest in women's memory—and in the act of remembering itself—also coincides with France Théoret's admittedly more restrained assertion that "in memory, we find women's plurality and their singularity."[58]

In the realm of Bersianik's literary explorations since *L'Euguélionne,* language does indeed appear to function as a mnemonic act, an attempt to uncover and reconstruct an archaeological memory too long neglected, for it is only by curing women's collective amnesia, Bersianik reasons, that today's women writers will be able to counter their historic sense of absence as women and begin to project themselves confidently and collectively into the future. On a more practical political level, she notes that our "mythological memory also teaches us that it is in groups or in couples that women have been the most effective," citing among her mythological examples the Muses, the Gorgons, the Camenae, the Erinyes, the Amazons, Charybdis and Scylla, Demeter and Persephone.[59] Thus, in addition to its function as social critique, remembering is an act of collective empowerment in her texts. To remember means to reconstruct what women have lost inasmuch as the seeds of women's identity lie buried in the past, in their forgotten hardships, in their unknown (because unspoken) pleasures, in their undocumented forms of resistance, and in the development of what Bersianik regards as a different sense of community.

Since the publication of *Le Pique-nique sur l'Acropole,* Louky Bersianik has contributed in her own unique way to the realization of women's mythological memory with a series of brief poetic meditations and dramatic pastiches. In *Maternative* (1980) and *Axes et eau* (1984), she expands upon key issues and further exploits literary techniques already recognized as central to her work. Both of these texts are, in a sense, supplementary writings that echo, elaborate, and build upon the cast of feminist characters and the network of feminist themes previously introduced in *L'Euguélionne* and *Le Pique-nique*. Bersianik's preoccupation with and intentional retracing of certain aspects of her earlier writings has not, however, pleased all of her readers. Indeed, as far as many critics have been concerned, *Maternative* and *Axes et eau* have passed relatively unnoticed, and when considered, they have frequently been criticized as more repetitious than innovative.

Less structurally unified and less thematically focused than either *L'Euguélionne* or *Le Pique-nique*, *Maternative* seems to suffer the common plight of texts whose contents have been written in bits and pieces rather than worked and reworked as a tightly constructed ensemble. Moreover, parts of *Maternative* have appeared to some as a duplication in poetic form of situations already addressed more effectively in the theoretical fiction of *Le Pique-nique*. In fact, Bersianik conceived of and wrote *Le Pique-nique* and most of the sections of *Maternative* during the same period (1977–79). On the other hand, Quebec critic André Brochu has acknowledged the structural complexity of *Axes et eau* (*Axes and Water*) and has also underscored the complicated system of intratextual and intertextual devices at work in this more recent collection. Yet he still concludes his brief review by lamenting the monotony of Bersianik's feminist project in the following way: "Such [feminine] landscapes and words are fascinating, they are also tiresome. *Batèche* [Holy baptism], they rewrite everything in the feminine."[60] While taking critic Pierre Nepveu to task publicly for what she views as his tradition-bound binary thinking when reviewing Gagnon's *La Lettre infinie*, Bersianik tackles the issue of the reader's "boredom" head on with a quotation from Barthes, whose influence on her has been substantial: "It can't be helped: boredom is not simple. We do not escape boredom (with a work, a text) with a gesture of impatience or rejection . . . there is no *sincere* boredom."[61] From Bersianik's vantage point, even boredom is not an *in*different matter.

Maternative combines a series of short poetic texts about characters already encountered in *Le Pique-nique* (Ancyl, Avertine, Aphélie, and Adizetu) with descriptions of several new lesbian couples and, in the concluding sections, with the emerging voice of the poet herself. Placing the intention of patriarchal discourse back at the site of its metaphysical beginnings, Bersianik opens *Maternative* with "Noli me tangere," an important reformulation of the myth of origins in which Bersianik gives her own feminist version of the agenesis of the patriarchal word. This ground-breaking text first appeared in a somewhat longer form in the special 1977 issue of *La Barre du jour,* an issue to which I refer in chapter 1. The power of this literary "tract" resides primarily in its ironic undermining of male authority and in its parodic use of biblical forms, as we note in the introductory stanza:

> La Chair est antécédente au Verbe
> Le Rêve est ascendant
> Le Verbe est subséquent
> . . . .
> Le Verbe est le projet de la Chair et non son commencement
> Le Verbe pseudo-initial est mâle et déconnecté
> de la Chair   (11)

> The Flesh is antecedent to the Verb
> The Dream is ascendent
> The Verb is subsequent
> . . . .
> The Verb is the project of the Flesh and not its point of origin
> The pseudo-original Verb is male and is disconnected to the Flesh

Bersianik thus begins her book with a short text on "La Genèse du verbe" ("The Genesis of the Verb") in which she ridicules the extent to which the body in patriarchal thinking has been separated from the *imaginary* (the realm of the presymbolic and prelinguistic)[62] and dominated through the *Verb* (i.e., the dominating action word of male-oriented discourse). This psychological severance has been effected in order to uphold the law of the fathers that sanctions patriarchal hegemony. Bersianik continues her irreverent attack by mocking the complete illogic with which the male verb has established its own legitimacy:

Quand le Verbe se fait Chair ressuscitée
on l'entend dire: ~~Noli~~ *me tangere*
Je suis intouchable, moi, le Verbe-Mâle
parce que je suis la loi

Et la loi c'est la loi/parce que la
loi c'est moi, dit le Verbe-Mâle
Le reste est Histoire sans Parole.   (12)

When the Verb becomes resuscitated Flesh
we hear it say: ~~Noli~~ *me tangere*
I am untouchable, me, the Male-Verb
because I am the law

And the law is the law/because the
law is me, says the Male-Verb
The rest is wordless History.

This issue of the law and of how modern women must learn
to speak against it in a way that reconnects the verb—no longer
capitalized—to the body, the touch, and the full range of our creative faculties is already an important theme in *Le Pique-nique.* Yet
even more so than in this preceding text, the selections in *Maternative* are poetic meditations on the harmful consequences for women
of the split subjectivity advanced by a western philosophical tradition disinterested in and, at times, visibly disturbed by the physicality of human experience. For despite the pretense of unity and
solidity and despite Freud's attempts to place the "drama" of male
sexual identity and desire (Oedipus) at the center of human development, notions of the self from the Greeks to the present time have
traditionally marginalized physical experience and denied the body's
crucial role in the signifying process. As Bersianik points out with
her usual sarcastic flair: "The *Penis-Verbum* isn't a hyphenated union
but a hyphenated distance" (17). Thus, while the patriarchal word
borrows its lawful authority from the presumed power of a male
organ turned symbol, sexuality and rationality, body and intellect,
never actually make contact. And despite their highly publicized
sexual status, women's bodies have, likewise, been kept at a distance—even from themselves.

The title of *Maternative* introduces what may well be the most
original and compelling network of poetic images in this text. For

as Bersianik has herself acknowledged, the sonorous plays with *Ma-ter[re]-native* (My native land), *Mater-native* (native Mother), and *Ma-[al]ternative* (My alternative) as well as other anagrammatic arrangements,[63] create a complex signifying chain that can never be entirely closed off. From the point of view of feminist mythmaking, the attempt to evoke notions of feminine geography, maternal origins, and an alternative vision simultaneously in the same title encourages a number of intriguing readings. My own view is that Bersianik's ability to locate a series of crisscrossing themes and images that can provide an appropriate landscape for the feminine imaginary is the most effective aspect of this work.

Through the image of the island Bersianik will explore both the positive and negative consequences of women's isolation in the world of men. On the one hand, she argues, women have often lived as solitary islands *à la dérive,* that is to say "aimlessly adrift," scattered between continents, and having no clear sense of integration or belonging. This feminist analogy was also explored in *L'Eu-guélionne* under the theme of exile. And in a series of brief remarks on the female imaginary, Bersianik does in fact link the image of the island to her own concept of feminist exile: "My imaginary is an island because I am still in exile. An island among thousands upon thousands of islands in an archipelago the size of a hemisphere."[64] But the island in *Maternative* is also the site of feminist mythopoesis in its most positive form, as it takes on the shape of a female embryo about to be reborn.

Bersianik develops her image of woman-as-island based on a feminist rereading of the Greek myth of Ortygie, the island later known as Delos. According to Greek legend, Ortygie was formed when a young woman, Asteria, transformed herself into a quail in order to flee the relentless amorous pursuit of Zeus. Equally adept at disguise, Zeus in turn adopted the form of an eagle in order to chase after his prey. In desperation and with no place to hide, Asteria transformed herself one final time into a rock and fell into the sea to become the island of Ortygie, which floated just beneath the water's surface. As Bersianik reimagines it, Ortygie is not only a place of refuge but also the site of a woman's awakening. Because she is finally out of danger and because solitude can be nurturing, this woman turned *île* will begin anew. In *Maternative*, the submerged presence of this embryonic female island promises the birth of women's sensual secrets and along with them, the proud awakening of a new women-centered sensibility:

Au fond de cette grotte insoupçonnée resplendissante d'eau et de sang et d'humeurs de splendeur vagabondes.
Mon désir croît de naître et crée la tempête sous globe
D'entre mes orteils—espaces d'île—elle me monte à la tête où trône ce croissant impérieux
Elle piaffe impatiente et se lève tout entière
Sans souci de mon être en naissance et de l'accueil de la température extérieure
Sans souci du sexe qui me fait conditionnelle déjà et me confère déjà le degré inférieur
Sans me laisser le temps de faire mon testament intemporel *in utero*
Imprudemment je suis le courant et *je tends* à naître
Courant vers l'instant où je ne serai plus l'océan
Où le toucher de l'immersion se sera retiré de moi pour toujours
A moins que je ne me saborde un jour et ne retourne séjourner en l'île
En L'I-I-I-LE   (138, 141)

In the depths of this unsuspecting dazzling grotto of water and blood and moods of vagabond splendor.
My desire to be born grows and creates a tempest in a glass ball
Between my toes—island spaces—it goes to my head where this imperious crescent reigns
It prances impatiently and stands completely upright
Without a care for my nascent self and for the reception the exterior temperature will give
Without a care for the sex that already limits me and already confers on me an inferior status
Without allowing me time to make my atemporal testament *in utero*
Imprudently I follow the current and *strain* to be born
Moving rapidly toward the moment when I will no longer be the ocean
Where the feel of immersion will be withdrawn from me forever
Unless I sink myself someday and come back to stay on the island
On THE I-I-I-S-LE

This emergence out of invisibility, which the island of Ortygie has in one sense clearly come to signify, is a central organizing theme in virtually all of Bersianik's work. Moreover, in the theoretical discussion forwarded in *Les Agénésies du vieux monde*, the power that results from women's newly acquired visibility becomes the primary focus of her final remarks. Like the caryatids in *Le Pique-*

nique, the island of Ortygie represents those aspects of women's experience that have been hidden from view and that are now beginning to surface. Ironically, their prior state of invisibility has given an awesome and terrible strength to women who have begun to love themselves and other women. Thus, asserts Bersianik, "our current power stems paradoxically from this gigantic *hole in our historical memory* which kept us invisible for so long and which makes us so *terribly alive* today. By this I mean that our very emergence out of invisibility is terrifying. *WHICH IS TO SAY THAT HAVING BEEN INVISIBLE FOR SO LONG HAS GIVEN US AN EX-TRAORDINARY SIZE.*"[65]

Bersianik's choice of the natural environment in *Maternative* as the setting in which to combat the masculinization of culture and with it, the general male dominance of space, should not be viewed as merely another form of pastoral reverie, although some have accused it of being just that. Clearly, Bersianik's metaphorical use of the ancient Mediterranean island of Ortygie is mythopoetic in its intent. Moreover, by reappropriating the misogynous overtones of the ancient myth and by affirming this geographical site of feminine flight, she has once again selected and reinterpreted a mythic space that remembers women's resistance to male dominance as a drama of mythic proportions. From the Greeks to the present day, the drama may be the same, but the frame of reference for reading the myth has certainly changed. At the same time, of course, this transposition of the ancient site of Asteria's furtive escape into a contemporary site of feminist rebirth is a marvelous example of poetic and political reversal. Finally, by locating the crisis of sexual awakening in nature, Bersianik has, in a sense, naturalized the ex-pression of women's physical desires and of her own nascent lesbian identity.

Yet the use of the island image also has a certain material appeal. Indeed, Bersianik's recourse to this particular myth appears to be grounded in the magnetism and the life-giving properties of the natural setting itself. In *Maternative,* the island whose rugged beauty lies floating just beneath the water's surface gives signs of an elemen-tal vitality all its own—combining the primary substances of water and earth to produce an almost primordial scene. By *elemental,* I mean not only a fundamental vitality but also the physical energy that resides in all organic matter.[66] Hence Bersianik's Ortygie does not appear to be a static, buried land mass, but rather a warm and nourishing maternal refuge for the gestation of a newly born woman:

> Même chair et perméable au sang
> Je suis portée apparue en l'inapparente
> Eau c'est mon berceau
> ORTYGIE
> De tant de merveilles et de monts
> Moi l'îlienne embryonnaire
> Suis tentée d'exister   (128)
>
> Same flesh and pervious to blood
> I am prone to appear in the unapparent
> Water is my cradle
> ORTYGIE
> With so many marvels and mountains
> Myself embryonic island-woman
> Am tempted to exist

This naturalizing of women's new coming-into-being takes place in a space that "knows" the particular feel and shape of feminine experience and desire. It is a space fashioned out of the raw materials of a nature unspoiled by the interests of those who would wish to control it. Thus, while the island takes on utopian dimensions in the texts of Brossard as a place where women can collectively assemble, love, and create—without interference and without being controlled by men—Bersianik's island is a site of maternal-native refuge and renascence.[67] The island of Ortygie is not the collective utopian result of radical feminist thinking, but the site of its embryonic beginnings. Politically speaking, Bersianik's mythic island is therefore the metaphorical point of departure for the development of a new concept of female subjectivity, one that is no longer defined in terms of a rigid enforcement of heterosexuality or a mandatory submission to male desire.

The elaborate rewriting of the myth of Ortygie in *Maternative* forces us to reconsider concepts of origin in male-oriented discourse and mythology. It also encourages us to contemplate some of the ways in which the disposition of space has been ordered, conquered, and colonized by men in order to promote their own authority and influence. Women, on the other hand, have possessed no such mastery over space—not even over their own space when they have it. It is for this reason that Ortygie remains submerged—hidden from male view. Lest we assume that Bersianik has inadvertently fallen into that age-old trap of mystifying Woman-as-Nature, however, it is important to emphasize that there is nothing one-sided, anti-intellectual, or submissive about this island birthing station. Indeed, Bersianik has strongly rejected the privileging of nature as the sole source of a feminine principle. "Not only are we supposed to be immersed in Nature," she points out, "but we are Nature with a capital 'N,' therefore we cannot transcend it; thus the sex linked to creation and civilization is justified in dominating us, in exploiting us and in appropriating Nature. An old, a very old idea, and it still works!"[68]

On the contrary, Bersianik's creative rereading and rewriting of the story of Ortygie, the place of last resort for the sexually harassed Asteria, is an empowering one. For mythopoesis, like reading itself, is an act of interpretation as well as a form of poetic invention. As such, it is, in the words of Tania Modleski, "crucially bound-up with power."[69] The politics underlying the creation of the female-island-embryo in *Maternative* are based on a struggle against separation, fragmentation, and exclusion. Bersianik has thus chosen to refashion and remember this myth in order to underscore what Modleski and others view as women's powerful ability as interpreters to disturb the authority and the privileged imaginary constructs of men. Clearly, she does not appear in any way intimidated by the power her island refuge or, for that matter, her awakened caryatids seem destined to unleash.

In an article entitled "Re-membering the Selves: Is the Repressed Gendered?," Jane Flax has questioned the contemporary fascination with postmodern discourse, particularly with its critique of subjectivity. Flax expresses a growing feminist concern about the political implications for women of a discourse that, while ostensibly valorizing the feminine, actually encourages women to accept their alienation, as well as their split or exploded sense of self. Moreover, Flax warns that "without participating in the retelling or reconstruction of collective memory, a sense of 'we' cannot emerge or be sustained. What history will our daughters have if we do not find ways to speak and to practice remembering? Without re-membered selves how can we act?"[70]

Although perhaps less "stylish" than others, the questions raised by Flax certainly speak to a number of the concerns Louky Bersianik has addressed in her own work. And while it is true that she has repeatedly explored the philosophical issues and embraced a number of the assumptions currently associated with the postmodern era (i.e., the death of Truth and the "master" narratives, antirationalism and radical negation, the interrogation of meaning and how it is constructed, the notion of a de-centered self, and women's unarticulated *jouissance*), Bersianik has done so from the point of view of women who are trying to combat repression and oppression on a daily basis and in real political terms. In the final analysis, the deconstructive moves that have served Bersianik so well in her rejection of patriarchal tradition have also prepared the way for a more decidedly integrative vision. For as she insists on imagining it, a *culture au féminin* will be a culture in which women "will belong to themselves completely, not only physically, but symbolically as well."[71]

5   *France Théoret*
Voicing the Agony of Discourse

Nothing exists that isn't the work of man, neither thought, nor speech, nor word. Nothing exists yet that isn't the work of man; not even me. Especially not me.

Annie Leclerc, *Parole de femme*

Women have often felt insane when cleaving to the truth of our experience.

Adrienne Rich, "Women and Honor: Some Notes on Lying"

Language in the feminine is not a new tongue in the sense of speaking a new idiom. Language in the feminine is a displacement of the symbolic. It is more than an affirmation of identity, it is another version of the real that is beginning to be elaborated.

France Théoret, *Entre raison et déraison*

If an important element of the modern literary topos is a mistrust of language and the desire to change it, as Alice Jardine and others have suggested,[1] the recent experimental efforts of Quebec women writers to write in the feminine appear to fit into Jardine's paradigm rather well. As far as the four writers discussed in this study are concerned, the general mood of radical interrogation with respect to language that has been so central in much of their work certainly seems to fall under Jardine's initial topology of modernity. As I have already pointed out, the hypersensitivity with regard to language and to the materiality of textual production, which has characterized examples of literary modernity in Quebec, has also influenced each of the writers examined here. Likewise, the theoretical reflections of *modernité* on the ways in which language works to legitimize or disrupt the prevailing symbolic and political orders have constituted important sites of literary inquiry for many women writers in Quebec since 1970.

In the works of Brossard, Gagnon, Bersianik, and Théoret, however, and as a result of their respective encounters with feminist thought, this hypersensitivity to language has become unavoidably gender-bound. For the texts they have produced have been marked not so much by particular forms of writing (fluid, broken, open-ended, nonlinear, litanylike, etc.)—although these forms are noticeable—nor have they all been characterized by certain theoretical perspectives and approaches to writing (psychoanalytic, semiotic, deconstructive). Despite numerous differences, the common ground appears to be an extreme insistence on the investigation of women's place in language and in the writing process itself. From the vantage point of feminist theorizing and contemporary women's writing, this heightened attention to language, power, and the linguistic production of signs has thus become an important way of assessing and challenging the social and political positions women occupy within the dominant culture. For Brossard, Théoret, and other women writing, as it were, under the sign of modernity, both the mistrust of and yearning for language outlined by Jardine have also been traversed by feminist appeals to associate language, ideas, and cultural production with material realities—especially the concrete realities of women's daily lives.

The works of Nicole Brossard and France Théoret in particular have underscored the political nature of the personal in intellectual activity and in everyday experience. And like Gagnon and Bersianik, both Brossard and Théoret have sought to uncover the various ways in which women have been and continue to be institutionally "silenced." In these respects and in others, the writings of France Théoret fully exemplify the considerations of Quebec's literary modernity and the political motivations of contemporary feminism. In them we find the intermingling of both currents—the modern mistrust of language resulting in the problematizing of representation itself and recent feminist critiques of the exclusion of women's discourse under patriarchy. The latter, Théoret believes, is not an indifferent omission, and it is one that more than accounts for the contemporary woman writer's pronounced longing for words of her own making.

Since the appearance of *Bloody Mary* in 1977, France Théoret has engaged in a series of experimental approaches to gender-marked writing that have been receiving increasing attention from feminist writers and critics both within and outside Quebec. As with Brossard, the writings of Théoret have embodied the call of *modernité* in Quebec to defy tradition, resist the dominant literary forms, and continually engender the "new." Théoret's work has clearly developed as a result of and in response to this (anti)tradition. At the same time, however, her texts have assumed the more political vantage point of feminist efforts to retrieve women's words from history, as well as the visionary, if at times paradoxical stance of contemporary French theories of the feminine which have invoked women's need to speak in a language outside the prescribed masculine order, to say it, as Irigaray would have it, in an*other* way.[2] Throughout her writing, Théoret offers a stinging critique of the totalizing trap of patriarchal language. The female voices in her writing often appear blocked, stifled, emprisoned in a language that is alien and that repeatedly "fails" them. They self-consciously position themselves in language as either submissive or rebellious daughters since the father's discourse provides them with no real access to power (should they want to share it), no possibility of articulating their historical oppression as women, and no linguistic space in which to explore sexuality in their own terms. To resist paternal authority and to seize the right to speak is not, however, an easy path. For as Jane Gallop has pointed out in her discussion of Irigaray (the daughter in revolt) and Freud (the authoritative father): "The law of the father gives her an identity, even if it is not her own, even if it blots out her feminine specificity. To give it up is not a 'simple' matter. It must be done over and over."[3]

In one of her initial contributions to the feminist newspaper, *Les Têtes de Pioche,* Théoret has in fact given us both the autobiographical and the theoretical contexts for reading the daughter's voice in her own texts:

Moi, la petite fille sage et modèle, j'ai été enfermée dans mon corps. La petite fille sage n'a que son corps pour domaine. C'est sa maison. Enfermée dans sa parole, enfermée pour tout rapport au savoir. Père ravageur du savoir des filles, seule une petite fille modèle pourra révéler ton nom.[+]

Me, the good and model little girl, I was locked up in my body. The good little girl has only her body as domain. It's her house. Locked up in her speech, locked up in all connections to knowledge. Father ravager of the knowledge of young girls, only a model little girl will be able to reveal your name.

One of Théoret's principal preoccupations since the mid-1970s has thus been the question of whether or not—and, if so, at what price—it is possible to insert the feminine into writing as a means of seizing cultural control over self-definition and to thereby pluralize the field of cultural meanings. She has also worked to expose the pivotal absence of women in a language they have inherited from men and to uncover the traces of women's voices in the margins of a discourse from which they remain alienated. To that end, her texts assume both the negative and positive functions of disruption, subversion, and feminine inscription as she alternates philosophical attempts at deconstruction with discursive gestures of self-affirmation and reconstruction.

As we shall see, the issues associated with literary modernity, feminism, and the politics of class in Quebec have left substantial marks on the work of Théoret as has the writing of Brossard. Théoret and Brossard met while they were both students at the Université de Montréal in 1965. Shortly thereafter, Théoret was invited to join Brossard and Soublière in their editorial work for *La Barre du jour*. Even though Théoret remained with the review a relatively short period of time (1966–69), Brossard's influence on her work would be far-reaching. To underscore this inspiration, Théoret dedicates *Bloody Mary* to her in 1977.

The common ground these two writers have shared is indeed rich and revelatory: their mutual attraction to Blanchot and the alluring "neutrality" of the insistently modern text, their founding in 1975 of the important Quebec feminist newspaper, *Les Têtes de Pioche,* their collaboration with other women writers to produce a series of monologues for the feminist play, *La Nef des sorcières* (1976), their increasing interest in French theories of *écriture féminine,* and their impulse to expose and strategically dispose of masculine representations of women in their respective works—the list could go on. What is remarkably dissimilar in their writings, however, is both the tone of the female voices encountered in their texts and, more generally speaking, the stance or positioning of the female writer with regard to the language she has inherited, the mental space of her oppression, and the surfacing or coming into being of a possible language of difference.

As I have already suggested, in the case of Brossard, writing is an act that inscribes itself in pleasure (*le plaisir*); it also provides women a strategic opportunity to affirm themselves as subjects.[5] Yet even though Brossard has held that the fundamental difference between men and women who write is the fact that women are afraid to write because they are afraid to take the initiative, to develop a personal vision,[6] this fear is rarely visible in Brossard's own writing—with the possible exception of *L'Amèr.* In fact, she gives little evidence in her texts of ever having had difficulty imagining herself as a writer (whether as a woman writer or, in her earlier texts, simply as a writer in general). While Brossard's shift to a more radically feminist approach to writing came after considerable reflection and political consciousness raising, her mature poetic voice—as we have already noted in chapter 2—is self-assured and utopian in its affirmative stance toward constructing a language and a culture of the future. Théoret, on the other hand, remains considerably more ambivalent about the project of writing.

For Théoret, language is formulated, if at all, with the greatest of pain. Her work thus far offers a convulsive mixture of pessimism and hope, anguish and exhilaration, at the prospect of linguistic revolt. And while clearly adding to the efforts of Brossard, Gagnon, and Bersianik when she writes to obliterate all ties with traditional bourgeois humanism, more often than not Théoret is locked in deadly battle with a language, a personal past, and the institutional forces that she holds responsible for the unnatural silencing of women who wish to create, responsible for what Tillie Olsen describes as "the unnatural thwarting of what struggles to come into being, but cannot."[7] The problems posed by language in her work are of such a magnitude as to become persuasive evidence in themselves of the woman writer's linguistic and cultural marginality within the dominant discourse.

Yet paradoxically, Théoret desperately hangs on to the notion that writing may offer women an exit out of the "prison-house of language" in which they are forever kept under wraps. As a result, the female voices that surface in her poetic narratives continually swing between the two poles of alienation and revolt, between an excessive sense of exclusion in language and an implacable hunger to "womanspeak" (Irigaray's *parler femme*), to derange the father's discourse, to take charge of their words and lives, and to effect change in the world around them. More so than the works of Brossard, Gagnon, or Bersianik, Théoret's texts point to the dialectical relationship that exists between the modern woman writer's anxiety over articulation—which verges at times on paralysis—and her passionate resolve in the pursuit of words. This seemingly contradictory response to language repeatedly marks Théoret's writings on the level of syntax, narrative construction, and sign system.

Words Written in Blood

Théoret's particular view of her own position in language is explicitly grounded in a difficult, working-class past to which she frequently refers in much of her work. In this regard, her writing is less "an arresting and denial of history," as Terry Eagleton has characterized the ahistorical, unpolitical perspectives of both modernism and postmodernism,[8] than a challenge to history that is steeped from its very inception in her own personal past and in the politics of oppression known in her family and social milieu for generations. Théoret's working-class background has also affected her taste for language. She herself admits to always having liked "a certain savagery in language, the capacity to enunciate one's emotions in a rough way."[9] And in fact, her most provocative writing operates as a kind of extended verbal assault, echoing the tough nature of her origins and the necessity of a forceful defiance to escape the traditional silence imposed on women who work to survive. Nowhere are the pain that results from women's alienation in language and the vehemency of Théoret's linguistic revolt more acute than in her first major text.

Bloody Mary is a short work comprised of three fragments each of which "voices" the mental and physical torments of women's silence in (male) myths, in everyday life, and in artistic creation. In each section, the focus is on an urgent search for words that might give the female speaker a physical presence (a face and a body in the mirror) and might somehow express the censored realities of women's lives. For Théoret, any successful move to articulate a woman's life involves penetrating the masks of social convention and thereby hastens the transgression of social codes. In Théoret's early writing in particular, this need to write translates as a crying out for recognition of women born in poverty, raised in self-depre- cation, and harshly conditioned in self-denial. The female voice in *Bloody Mary* imagines her pencil as a knife or a stake, as she sharpens her tongue and dreams of tearing through traditional phallocentric discourse with the force of an angry slash. The extreme physicality of this metaphorical gesture is a prime example of the convulsive manner in which the female body struggles to write itself in Théoret's text:

Trop proche du journal. Trop proche des réminiscences. J'ai toujours envie d'écrire. Toujours envie de hurler. Au lieu de tenir un crayon, je tiens un poignard un pieu, ça n'écrit pas.[10]

Too close to the diary. Too close to reminiscence. I always want to write. Always want to scream. Instead of holding a pencil, I hold a knife a stake, it doesn't write.

While the image of the pencil-knife-stake gives clear textual evi- dence of the woman writer's desire to inflict harm and bloody patriarchal discourse through an act of linguistic mutilation, the knife itself—as the preceding passage indicates—does not write. Or does it? In an earlier textual moment the female voice appears to contradict this implied powerlessness with the remark, "Avant toujours j'écris le couteau" (8) ("Before always I write the knife"). Indeed, in the hand of a woman, the knife as an instrument of writing suggests a subversive feminist appropriation of phallic imag- ery and male power. Further examples of women's sense of power and lack of power in language can be found throughout Théoret's text. This penchant for contradiction is, moreover, an important characteristic of her writing in general. In this initial yet remarkably mature work, the connection between women's writing and the physical destruction of patriarchal language is both metaphorical and real, resulting in rebellious fantasies about the potentially sweeping power of women's words and in the more visible textual "incisions" that slice through the smooth surfaces of the master's discourse. The publication of *Bloody Mary* in 1977 marked a crucial turning point in the literary direction of Montreal's important publishing house, Les Herbes Rouges, as well as in the general direction of feminist-inspired writing in Quebec.[11]

For French-speaking readers in Quebec, the title of *Bloody Mary* is itself a form of linguistic and cultural assault, evoking both the relatively harsh sounds of the English language and the unpopularity of an English queen (Mary I, 1553–58) whose troubled reign and strong ties to Catholicism resulted in religious persecution and much civil unrest. Théoret's title can also be read as a vulgarized evocation of the Virgin Mary whom the Catholic church has traditionally associated with purity and with the absolute absence of blood, that is to say, the absence of the physical, the sexual, the real.[12] More importantly for Théoret's positioning of women in language, however, is her shrewd linguistic use of the plurality of meanings attached to the adjective *bloody,* which can designate cruelty, murderousness, blood stains, or in British slang, being cursed or damned. The polysemic richness of the English word gives Théoret considerable room to explore the multiple and contradictory meanings it appears to evoke in her text. While the Mary of Catholic dogma has been purified to the point of transparency and muzzled into perennial silence, Théoret's female writer emerges as a new Mary whose words are "bloody" in every conceivable sense of the term.

As the polysemic play of "Bloody Mary" thus suggests, women's blood circulates on a variety levels in this text but always in connection with an awkward, untenable position in language as well. Indeed, for Théoret, the words women might speak were they free to do so would themselves be marked in blood, the blood of their menses that must not be mentioned, the blood of secret abortions, the blood issuing from the rape of young girls, all of which produce stains that society would prefer not to see. Unlike the numerous deconstructive attempts to cut up the language of the father in Théoret's text—causing paternal blood to flow—these bloody references to the female body are less abstract and much closer to the everyday reality of women's physical lives. They also point to the various ways in which women's language is, of necessity, concealed and "cleaned up" while it remains stubbornly stained in red:

> Les filles c'est fait pour laver des couches. —T'as pas besoin de ça pour laver les planchers.
> Kotex pourri dans la neige noire fin d'après-midi de mars.
> Ruelle.
> Le vent fou sur la peau de pas chance.   (16)

> Girls are made for washing diapers. —You don't need it for washing the floors.
> Rotten Kotex in the black snow late afternoon in March.
> Alley.
> Raging/insane wind on the skin of no luck.

Topographically speaking, the material appearance of Théoret's text is also "bloodied" since each of the three textual fragments is introduced by blank pages stained with a bloodlike ink, as is the text's cover.

As a characterization of women's historic marginalization, physical suffering, and silencing in patriarchal language and culture, the bloody Mary in Théoret's text provides the woman writer with a much more believable model for writing like a woman than either Mary I, who remained a religious pawn in the ideological debates of her time, or the viriginal Mary venerated by the Catholic Church. Théoret builds further on this attempt at revisionist mythmaking by substituting the coagulated blood of her own dead Mary for "the blood of Christ" in a painful gesture of communion with other women. The result of this ritualized female bonding in blood in no way resembles the presumed peace and salvation accorded the participants in the analogous Catholic communion. Instead, we are left with the reverberating cries of a woman who, like Mary, remains in captivity and whose words continue to be coated in blood:

Il était une fois dans la diarrhée du temps qui n'avance ni ne recule, une masse infâme nommée Bloody Mary qui à peine née fut livrée à un carrefour où jamais personne ne s'aventurait. Forêt, dédale, labyrinthe, trachée-artère. C'est un lieu mental: sans petit poucet, sans prince charmant. Pour Oedipe aux pieds enflés un berger royal. Pour Bloody Mary dehors dedans le rouge sur toutes surfaces. Les yeux rougis. Comme j'ai pleuré quand j'ai dit ma demande. On a sucé Bloody Mary. Paquet de sang coagulé peau: revêtement qu'on disait d'être d'âme. J'ai hurlé dans le noir des parois de mon ventre quand j'ai demandé après toi. L'enfermée le sang la tache.   (9)

Once upon a time in the diarrhea of time which neither advances nor retreats, there lived a filthy heap named Bloody Mary who scarcely born was sent off to a crossroads where no one ever ventured. Forest, maze, labyrinth, trachea. It's a mental space: without a Tom Thumb, without a Prince Charming. For Oedipus with his swollen feet a royal armchair. For Bloody Mary outside inside red on every surface. Red eyes. How I cried when I asked her. We sucked Bloody Mary. Bundle of coagulated blood skin: lining said to be of the soul. I screamed in the blackness of my abdomen walls when I asked you. The shut up woman the blood the stain.

Women's words and the blood from women's bodies leave subversive traces that Théoret wants to expose rather than mop up or erase. Thus, she observes that "les paroles malsaines des femmes le sont à un point tel qu'elles s'avortent avant le jour" (9) ("the words of women are so unclean as to abort themselves before morning"). The analogies created here between women's words and uncleanliness, between abortions and a repression that leads to silence, are doubly interactive since women's words are also likened to aborted material, bloody material that is thought unfit, unclean for others to receive. "In the beginning was an aborted word," says Lawrence Lipking.[13] Indeed, because of the effectiveness of institutional and societal pressures, Théoret suggests, it is women themselves who perform the necessary censorship of a language that is deemed impure.

As Marie Cardinal demonstrates in painful detail in *Les Mots pour le dire*,[14] which enjoyed much success in Quebec, when a woman bleeds in public, she is defying the social code of silence regarding the functioning of the female body. Her body becomes excessively and unacceptably visible; hence she is classified as a hysteric, as a woman who must be "cured." For Cardinal's female speaker, the act of articulating her pain as a daughter and as a woman within the psychoanalytic setting, of letting the censored words "stream out," eventually stops the flow of blood. In *Bloody Mary,* however, the words themselves are covered in blood—the appearance of one necessitates the appearance of the other. To speak as a woman— both in and from a female body, means to let the blood flow. Théoret will continue this analogy in a short section of *Une voix pour Odile* (1978) entitled "Le sang" ("Blood"). Fearing pregnancy, the female speaker in this textual fragment anxiously awaits the first signs of her menstrual blood and struggles to overcome the inevitable "interiorization of the law of the father" that fills women with a sense of disgrace about their own bodies, alienates them from their sexuality, and prohibits the invention of a language that refuses to hold anything back.

Returning to *Bloody Mary,* Théoret adds one final layer of signifi- cation to the image of blood—and one that may well be the most shocking of all—by suggesting that the language women have been schooled in, harnessed in, and have then unwittingly used at their own expense is itself a form of rape:

L'engorgée la possédée l'enfirouapée la plâtrée la trou d'cul l'odalisque la livrée la viarge succube fend la verge fend la langue serre les dents. Des passes je me fais la passe, je suis ma propre maison de passe."   (11)

The choked the possessed the bound in fur the painted up the ass hole the concubine the servant the virgin demon the penis penetrates the tongue penetrates grit your teeth. Passes I make a pass at myself, I am my own brothel.

The syntax and rhythm here appear to be chopped up like the inherited masculine language Théoret wants to "axe" and be done with. Moreover, the vulgarity inherent in the sexual stereotypes attributed to women is so insistent here that, ultimately, we are left numb. Her violation is our violation, the ravishing pace and intent of these mocking patriarchal words are both alien and uncomfort- ably familiar. In the end, the female speaker admits to her own complicity. The whole textual event leaves her (and the female reader) limp and speechless. The remainder of the page is blank. Théoret's female voice has silenced herself.

In her insightful discussion of female creativity and the blank page, Susan Gubar has argued that "because of the forms of self- expression available to women, artistic creation often feels like a

violation, a belated reaction to male penetration rather than a pos-
sessing or controlling," adding that women's ink is often "produced
through a painful wounding, a literal influence of male authority."[16]
This perspective on women in language is particularly applicable to
the early writing of France Théoret. For the female voice struggling
to speak in *Bloody Mary,* both body and language, outside and
inside, have come to resemble alien ground. A woman's boundaries
have indeed been violated here.

While the question of how, through what means, and from what
vantage point a violated woman "speaks" continues to occupy a
central place in Théoret's later writing as well, the texts themselves
are less strained, less sharp-edged than her earlier works. In *Bloody
Mary,* the woman writer's only recourse in her attempts at self-
articulation is to "unspeak" (*déparler*), to reverse the old syntax, to
stammer, repeat, contradict herself. Little by little, she will wear
down the structures of a forced discourse that, as Patricia Smart
has also suggested, sequesters women and divides them from one
another:[17]

L'obligation je suis obligée de parler pourquoi l'avoir cru les phrases s'in-
versent les mots viennent par derrière commencer par la fin défaire bout
pour bout le discours comme si c'était possible les phrases commencent par
la fin comme s'il y avait trou comme il y a un trou dans mon corps à partir
duquel je pourrais retourner bout pour bout ma peau par l'envers rouge
j'imagine rugueuse torture pour les yeux muette de terreur mon corps non
mes phrases oh! je déparle oh! j'ai déparlé comme je te vois comme je t'ai
vu   (23)

The obligation I am obliged to speak why have believed it the sentences
are inverted the words come from the end begin by the end undo bit for
bit the discourse as if it were possible the sentences begin at the end as if
there was a hole like a hole in my body from which I could turn over my
skin bit for bit with the red reverse side I imagine rough torture for the
eyes mute with terror my body no my sentences oh! I unspeak oh! I unspoke
as I see you as I saw you

Woman as Voice, Woman as Text

Théoret's project to turn conventional language "inside out" and
to expose the blood and wounds of an interior feminine discourse
continues in *Une voix pour Odile* (*A Voice for Odile*), the first text to

bring significant critical attention to her work. Published in 1978, *Une voix pour Odile* contains a series of twelve short sketches or fragments that pointedly dissolve the boundaries of theory, fiction, and autobiographical writing. In the initial and longest section, which bears the book's title, Théoret underscores the role of the woman writer-narrator and her threefold quest for "Je, langue, mère" ("I, language, mother"), a quest that echoes the one articulated by Brossard in *L'Amèr,* published one year earlier, but that now underscores a distinguishable social context as well. Théoret's probe for her own origins in language generates recollections of the gloomy religious repression and ideological conservatism of the Duplessis era of the 1950s, the era of her own childhood and adolescence:[18]

De Montréal à Montréal, durant cette décennie la plus morne du siècle, celle des années cinquante. Une presque enfant qui ne l'est presque plus. Une histoire de perdition du corps. A la lettre. Une langue à retrouver que je suis sûre de ne pas retrouver. J'ai changé de langue dans la même langue mais pas tout à fait changé dans une faille, une mémoire qu'on retrace. Je ne cherche pas mon identité, je cherche à faire bouger l'appris le corrigé le renié le désappris le perdu retrouvé ressassé qui fuit s'engage se retourne une poursuite un passage une passade. Je, langue, mère.[19]

From Montreal to Montreal, during that dreariest decade of the century, that decade of the 1950s. A near child who is barely one any longer. A story of a body wasted. Word for word. A language to recover that I'll surely not recover. I changed tongues in the same language but didn't completely change in a fissure, a memory we retrace. I'm not looking for my identity, I'm hoping to stir up the learned the corrected the repudiated the unlearned the lost retrieved scrutinized that flees becomes involved turns around a pursuit a passage a short stay. I, language, mother.

The triple focus of this personal search for self, tongue, and mother—the original site of all language—outlines the nature of the woman writer's relationship to writing throughout the text, a relationship Théoret will pursue in subsequent works as well. Through the act of writing, she embarks on a triple journey, an ontological, linguistic, and historical investigation of her own voice. Her struggle to speak—for many of these brief texts read very much like monologues—necessarily involves a process of reviewing and renaming the repressive conditions under which she and other women have been obliged to live.

Even before we begin *Une voix pour Odile,* however, the problem of language for women has already been raised on the book's cover and on the inside frontispiece, both of which display simulated photographs of handwritten manuscripts that have been crossed out, smudged, and corrected to the point of illegibility. These indecipherable and quintessentially modern tableaux offer us a visual reminder of Théoret's continued estrangement from language and along with it, her paradoxical refusal to be silenced. The narrative thread and underlying difficulty in the first selection, "Une voix pour Odile," is not the female narrator's inability to spin a lengthy story nor her disappointment with the incompleteness of her own descriptions and adolescent self-portrait, although she does feel the need to comment upon these deficiencies in her writing. The central issue here, and in the text as a whole, is her marginal position in language, in two languages in fact: the language of her working-class childhood and family ties, and the language learned in public institutions and perpetuated in the universities. Both languages have been imposed on her; neither conveys her personal and public experience as a woman. Always the outsider, Théoret's female speaker locates her own voice somewhere in the blank spaces, on the periphery of these two discourses. It emanates out of a body whose internal language is still virtually unknown to her:

La voix se fait circulaire périphérique vectorielle parfois. Le centre est vide. Il n'y a pas de centre. D'un délire féminin, c'est l'impensé. La marge me sert de cadre. Je me regarde dans les lignes, miroir, narcissisme. J'y force ce qui se cherche ce qui se court après ce qui se cache paraît disparaît un coin en oeil ma culotte se mouille lettre blanche. Mon corps écrit d'un souffle chaud une langue. Un silence, j'y suis. Je rattrappe mon corps. Substantif marqué à sa place la langue d'une femme sortie d'un pas encore pays pas encore langue pas encore voix qui s'échappe zigzague file le raidissement. La femme est encore enfermée au point d'un non-retour possible pour certaines manifestations dans le réel. Cet état de clôture dans le petit dedans n'est pas si personnel que ça. C'est connecté aux autres.   (11–12)

The voice makes itself circular peripheral vectorial at times. The center is empty. There is no center. Out of a feminine delirium, comes the unthinkable. The margin serves as my space. I see myself in the lines, mirror, narcissism. I force what is sought there what is pursued what is hidden appears disappears a corner of the eye my underwear is wet white letter. My body writes a language from a warm breath. A silence, I am there. I recover my body. Noun marked in its place the language of a woman coming out of a not yet country not yet language not yet voice which escapes zigzags tracks the stiffening. Woman is still enclosed to the point of a possible no-return for certain manifestations of the real. This state of closure inside the particular is not as personal as all that. It's connected to others.

As this passage indicates, Théoret's poetic efforts to explore the contradictory languages of the self engender a feverish, twisting search for words and an impatient desire to reconnnect words to the female body and the larger body politic. In regard to the latter, the allusion to the language of a country still waiting to be formed is an indication of the extent to which "the national question" in Quebec continues to surface in feminist-inspired texts such as this one, if only on a subliminal level. A sociological reading of *Une voix pour Odile* might well emphasize analogies between Théoret's efforts to assert an identity through a language of her own making and political attempts to establish an independent Quebec around the language issue. For Théoret, the frustration and near impossibility of articulation result in a chronic ontological angst. This feeling is one of acute uncertainty regarding her own subjectivity in language and her relationship with the collectivity.

In *Une voix pour Odile,* the ambiguous position of the female speaker in language finds its most emphatic expression in the following forms of linguistic and narrative sabotage: disrupted syntax, frequent repetitions, self-directed questions, circular movement, repeated interruptions in narrative flow, incomplete descriptions, memory fragments, inversions of meaning, self-contradiction, and a general de-centering of the female voice. "Les mots en loques" (37) ("Words in shreds"), says Théoret's narrator. In "Miroir, miroir, dis-moi qui est la plus belle" ("Mirror, mirror, tell me who's the most beautiful"), the narrator assumes for the most part a third-person stance and speaks of the adolescent whose silence and verbal confusion leave others perplexed. The young woman's loss of center and the dissolution of a fixed identity are conveyed in the repetitive phrases of the working-class bar where she works and in her professors' empty classroom nostalgia for the language of nineteenth-century French culture. With their exclusionary linguistic codes and male-oriented values, both of these discourses leave the young woman inarticulate, speechless, confused, isolated:

Elle est muette ou bégayante ou écrasée par le cri du dedans ou déparlante
ou disant l'exact contraire de ce qu'elle veut dire. Autant qu'elle se rappelle,
elle a toujours connu la difficulté de parole, la pensée difficultueuse, lui
a-t-on dit. Une jonction qui ne se fait pas: la terreur, à chaque fois, que ça
sorte tout de travers.   (30)

She is mute or stuttering or crushed by the cry inside or unspeaking or
saying the exact opposite of what she means. As far as she can remember,
she has always had difficulty with speech, overly complicated thought, they
tell her. A junction which is not met: the terror each time it comes out
cockeyed.

The mute daughter in this text is one in a long line of Quebec
daughters whose speech has been institutionally muzzled—a speech
Théoret clearly writes to unblock. But as the title indicates, *Une voix
pour Odile* is also a probe through writing in pursuit of a voice for
Odile, the hysterical, silenced, dead mother. Odile, we learn, was
the narrator's aunt who died in menopause after giving birth to
fifteen children—an all too common occurrence in Quebec history
given the pervasive power and influence of the Catholic Church in
family and social matters up until the post-World War II era.
Théoret has chosen Odile as the central enigma of her book because
of what the narrator does not know about her, because of her
disappearance, her absence, her erasure from the narrator's own life
and from history:[20]

Ma grand-mère, ma mère et moi. Je ne me rappelle plus d'Odile. Elle est
pourtant là sur la photo en longue robe noire assise sur la berceuse. C'est
un jour d'été ensoleillé un de ces jours d'envie de vivre. Je n'avais pas deux
ans lorsqu'Odile est morte. Elle disparue il y a la voix à inventer l'écho de
la voix le rappel de la voix qui se noie. Eaux de la naissance. J'y remonterai,
j'y viendrai au travers la mère hystérique, la tante ouvrière et mêmes les
vieilles filles religieuses.   (24–25)

My grandmother, my mother and me. I don't remember Odile anymore.
But she is there in the picture in a long black dress seated on the rocking
chair. It's a sunny summer day one of those days that make you want to be
alive. I was only two years old when Odile died. She disappeared there is
a voice to invent the echo of a voice the reminder of a voice that drowns.
Waters of a birth. I will go back through them, I will get there through the
hysterical mother, the working-class aunt and even the old nuns.

As the above passage suggests, the female voice in *Une voix pour
Odile* is a generational voice, one that seeks to unite families of
women and, ultimately, bond the personal and collective spheres of

women's experience. By linking her own battle with language to Odile's voiceless history, the woman writer in Théoret's text makes the collective leap and moves the personal into a new political sphere. So incompatible with her sunny surroundings and yet so characteristic of previous generations of Quebec "matrons," Odile's striking pose in black further underscores the political content behind this effort. The abstract quality and chantlike repetition of the word *voix* (voice) create an ingenious echoing effect as well, which is all the more enriched by the crucial rhyming in French of *voix* and *noie* (drowns). The sonorous play here is, of course, a deadly one since, for Théoret, maternal voices are in fact always drowned. Yet despite the apparent political nature of this quest for the words of a forgotten (and ignored) aunt, the attention placed on the quality of Odile's voice also personalizes these feminist attempts to remember. In searching for the territory of this ordinary voice in language, Théoret reminds us of the ordinariness of each woman's struggle to reconnect with her own past and with the daily life and death of women's words.

The attention Théoret brings to women's voices in this text is dramatic. We sense them, hear them, remark their absence, listen to the stammering, and witness the endless repetitions. This privileging of the voice, which continues throughout Théoret's later work as well, exemplifies what Cixous, Marini, Lamy, and others have noted as the crucial preoccupation with the female voice in feminine writing or *écriture au féminin*. Grounded in the body, woman's voice has been viewed as the material manifestation of her thought, emotion, and desire. Feminine writing and the voice, says Cixous, "are entwined and interwoven and writing's continuity/ voice's rhythm take each other's breath away through interchanging, make the text gasp or form it out of suspenses and silences, make it lose its voice or rend it with cries."[21] For Théoret, writing is the inscription of a voice that listens to itself and others, a voice that reclaims its instinctual rhythms, harnessing all its physical and psychic forces in the act of writing.[22]

Because Théoret incorporates largely autobiographical reflections on her childhood as well as on her own role as a writer of the text, the narrative in *Une voix pour Odile* moves back and forth between

present and past, between the languages of the barroom and classroom and the initial sounds—which are more like painful cries—of
a woman's language still in formulation. This continually oscillating
drama is further played out in the alternation of fiction and theory,
the intimately personal and the undeniably social. Théoret's search
for *je,* for the female speaking subject presumed to be at the center
of discourse, has yielded an *I* that is, itself, vacillating, a de-centered
other always in process, like the very language of the text. This *I* is
neither fixed, nor whole, neither logically nor harmoniously constituted. It is, moreover, continually assailed by the images and concepts of women that others seek to impose. When these repressive
voices of external authority invade her being, pass in judgment, and
suppress the woman writer's instinctive responses and independence
of thought, depression brutally marks Théoret's text. Eventually,
words cease:

Une chaise, une table, un appartement où je fuis en attendant. . . . Je marche
à côté de moi. Je suis dans la rue ou quelque part chez moi, encore dans
un endroit familier et je m'échappe incapable de retenir une parole, une
lecture, un projet que je n'ai pas noté dans un agenda. Je suis coupée et
dissolue dans un éclat de voix intérieures qui font gronder, gronder, trembler les parois invisibles qui me coupent du dehors. Il n'y a surtout pas
d'humour là-dedans. Il n'y a pas de mots. Le verbe est mort. Une tâche
urgente: circonscrire cet aveuglant mirage qui me coupe pendant de très
longs moments du langage.   (60–61)

A chair, a table, an apartment where I flee while waiting. . . . I walk next
to myself. I am on the street or somewhere at home, yet in a familiar place
and I escape unable to remember a word, a reading, a project that I haven't
noted in a weekly record. I am cut up and invalidated in a burst of interior
voices that rumble, rumble, tremble the invisible walls which cut me off
from the outside. There is certainly no humor inside there. There are no
words. The verb is dead. An urgent task: circumscribe this blinding mirage
that cuts me off from language for very long periods.

If Théoret's awakening to her own precarious subjectivity and
uncomfortable position in speech and in writing is a source of
terror—as it clearly is here—this new knowledge about her status
as a woman in the dominant culture also gives her unexpected
strength, the strength to resist a romantic, nostalgic, and stable
notion of self. In the final sections of *Une voix pour Odile,* the woman
writer makes it clear that she has come to view the very idea of a

unified identity as an oppressive and politically naive concept that she does not care to resurrect. "Je ne me suis pas vécue excentrée pour retourner vers je ne sais quelle source" (64) ("I have not lived myself ex-centered in order to return to some unknown source") affirms Théoret's female speaker. The narrative stance—if we may call it that—in *Une voix pour Odile* is a contradictory one in virtually every sense, fluctuating as it does between acute cynicism, interminable doubts, and nervous anticipation, between external and internal censure and release, between a feeling of linguistic emprisonment, a fascination with the sabotage of conventional language, and the need to explore a language that might somehow make a difference. As Hugues Corriveau correctly observes, "Théoret writes, is written, in the disorder of her position, writes a prose in which everything is possible, which unorganizes itself, represses and renders visible all at the same time."[23]

One of the final fragments in *Une voix pour Odile* takes its title, "Cochonnerie" ("Trash"), from Antonin Artaud's now infamous dictum, "Toute l'écriture est de la cochonnerie" ("All writing is trash/rubbish"). As Théoret explained in a recent interview, Artaud's influence on her has been considerable, particularly during her years as a university student.[24] This move toward the transgression, verbal anarchy, and obsessive *oralité* or oral character of Artaud's work coincides with Théoret's efforts to theorize about her own writing in the latter half of the text:

M'aboucher au réel insaisissable.
Le tombeau du verbe m'encercle. De prise aucune. En finir avec le jugement de dieu dit Artaud: le jugement des pères. Je dis à la lettre l'inexistence et le non-mouvement.   (66)

Get in touch with the unattainably real.
The tomb of the verb encircles me. No hold whatsoever. Let's be finished with the judgment of god says Artaud: the judgment of the fathers. I say literally inexistence and non-movement.

Théoret's brief evocation of Artaud is important if for no other reason than to underscore her own self-conscious link with one of the most tortured and yet visionary writers of the early twentieth-century avant-garde in France. The confusion, hysteria, and complete disaffection with the Logos, out of which Artaud's writings unfold, find a new and emphatically gender-marked expression in the groping female voice encountered in Théoret's text. In an effort to undo the rationality of reading, Théoret invites an entry into women's writing through hysteria, guilt, and fear:

L'hystérique est dangereuse. Des pulsions réactionnaires en perspectives, dit-on. Et le féminin masochiste? Et le féminin coupable? Sifflé et poussé au coeur du livre de la peur. Qui osera approcher cela verra l'envers du monde.   (67)

The hysteric is dangerous. Reactionary drives in prospect, they say. And the masochistic feminine? And the guilty feminine? Hissed and shoved to the heart of the book of fear. Whoever will dare to approach it will see the reverse side of the world.

Théoret does not, however, take refuge in the recent French theoretical efforts of Cixous and Irigaray (each, admittedly, very different in approach) to reclaim and valorize feminine hysteria, despite her familiarity with their work. With the exception of the quotation from Artaud, there is very little overt intertextual play in *Une voix pour Odile,* although the writing itself suggests a certain number of influences. Théoret is much less comfortable with the incorporation of theory per se in her writing than Brossard, Gagnon, or Bersianik. Indeed, the abstract nature of theory confounds the female speaker in *Une voix pour Odile,* and militant political theorizing in fiction is, she says, a contradiction in terms. She makes this observation despite the fact that Théoret herself has engaged increasingly in theorizing, if in a somewhat less academic fashion than Brossard, Gagnon, or Bersianik.

If the hysterical voice is the privileged voice in *Une voix pour Odile* and the female masochist is patriarchy's victim—as it appears they are, this then is not so much the result of Théoret's overt anti-Freudian theorizing or militant feminist politics so much as it is the consequence of the sheer weight of the real. For the female voice in Théoret's text speaks out of a pain and an intermittent "madness" that are known in the core of her being, although she herself acknowledges the echoes of her own violent savagery and displacement (ontological as well as linguistic) in the generations of women who have preceded her and in the writings of others. In its final pages, Théoret's text opens outward to the wanderings and contradictory impulses of an insurgent Alice who has entered the looking glass "folle de rage" ("mad with rage"), challenging the male specularization of woman (Irigaray) and smashing the images of phallocentric authority in a flow of words which resists direction or external control of any kind. While this final Cixousian "overflowing" suggests vulnerability as well as diffusion, it also characterizes a voice whose "power to be errant is strength":[25]

Je une phrase une perte une merde un creux un sanglot . . . rêve passion passivité ô sui ô cuit vivre sang luire dire univoque paresse délire freak freak gogo marde sens mot jus expérience l'alta gris glu gris glu entre
    unie vérité.   (73)

I a phrase a loss a piece of shit a chasm a sob . . . dream passion passivity oh followed oh cooked alive blood glisten say univocal idleness delirium freak freak gogo shit meaning word juice experience the alta grey glue grey glue between
    unified truth.

The voice in *Une voix pour Odile* is multiple (daughter, aunt, writer) and multidirectional. With its delirious breakneck speed, its nakedness and explosive exploration of the void, the female voice in Théoret's text demonstrates a force capable of the most dangerous kinds of linguistic disruption. At the same time, however, it emits an anguished cry that, as Cixous herself has described it, continually struggles to reclaim the right to speak: "Voice-cry. Agony—the spoken "word" exploded, blown to bits by suffering and anger, demolishing discourse: this is how she has always been heard before, ever since the time when masculine society began to push her offstage, expulsing her, plundering her. Ever since Medea, ever since Electra."[26]

The Writer and the Whore
or The Territory of Feminine Inscription

In *Une voix pour Odile* and the texts that follow, France Théoret probes the multiple sites of her physical, psychological, and social being in an effort to escape the oppressive sense of linguistic closure that hinders women's contiguity with the real. Throughout her writing we witness a discourse in disruption, dissolution, and gestation in which the agony of articulation and a secret love of words repeatedly interlace. This painfully modern recognition of women's problematic position in language has moved Théoret into the farthest boundaries of linguistic confusion, alienation, and silence. At the same time, however, it has also triggered her desire to explore a literary space where, as the female voice insists in *Nécessairement putain* (*Necessarily Whore*, 1980), "Les mots ne me sont plus donnés" ("Words are no longer given to me").[27]

The torment of articulation that so deeply marked *Bloody Mary* and *Une voix pour Odile* continues in *Nécessairement putain,* another relatively short text in which Théoret considers the cultural image and lived reality of the prostitute. "Générations mortes quel est votre nom?" ("Dead generations what is your name?"), asks the female narrator when thinking back through the generations of anonymous women victimized by male myths and by a materialist culture motivated by gain. Once again, Théoret attempts to locate a female voice, this time the voice of the prostitute who has been the most silenced woman of all. She is the woman about whom society does not speak, the woman with whom men sleep but do not speak, the woman who is forbidden to speak for "other" women, the woman who is not "respectable," and yet, according to the masculine myths to which she has been historically subjected, the woman who for many is the epitome of Woman. As Susanne Kappeler points out in her analysis of *The Pornography of Representation,* "The prostitute has no power: not only is she a woman (manumitted slave), but a woman 'outside society' as that society defines itself."[28]

Yet in an ironic twisting of perspective, Théoret builds not only on the thorough silencing and historic marginalization of the prostitute in patriarchal society, but also and more importantly perhaps for her own literary project, on the potential power of the "whore" to reverse the social codes and attack the relationships of abuse in which she is enchained: "Je ne suis pas humaine et je saccage vos tombes: je ne suis pas seule quand je parle où que je sois" (22) ("I am not human and I sack your graves: I am not alone when I speak wherever I am"). Paralleling the interest of American feminists in the political implications of the prostitute's cultural function and lived experience, Théoret's attempts to review and reenvision the prostitute through a woman's eye and in a woman's voice disturb the dominant mode of representing woman and raise questions about the network of signification that has resulted from the representation of woman as whore. This theoretical interrogation and feminist valorization of a previously denigrated female archetype is reminiscent of the work Cixous has done in her own writing on the image of the female hysteric who refuses to become "cured." Théoret's central positioning of the prostitute as one of the most marginalized of female figures has produced some of the most overtly political overtones in her writing yet.

In an article appearing in 1983 in the Quebec feminist magazine, *La Vie en rose,* Théoret comments on the interactive relationship of feminism and writing in her own work: "For me, feminism is what transformed my relationship to the real, what articulated it as well, it's what gives me the right to hope despite all the despair I see . . . I like to work on the commonplaces, the generally accepted ideas, the diverse ideologies, the stereotypes, in order to deconstruct them."[29] Given these interests, it is surely not surprising that Théoret should turn to the image of the prostitute, for who could be more commonplace, more stereotypically powerless, amoral, irredeemable, and preoccupied with sexual "success" in the male literary canon and in the dominant culture as well than the figure of the female prostitute? The originality and the power of Théoret's text lies in its ability to sabotage this tradition so thoroughly as to alter the literary premises on which this archetype has been constructed.

Like Denise Boucher, whose much attacked and much discussed *Les Fées ont soif* broke the prostitute's silence on the Quebec stage,[30] Théoret is fascinated by the seemingly infinite parallels between the hidden reality of the prostitute's life and the common experiences of women as a group. The historic object of male hatred, violence, and censorship, the whore functions as a mirror of recognition into which all women knowingly gaze. The virgin and the free spirit, the mother, the daughter, the working woman, the female voice struggling to free itself of male control, and of course, the woman writer herself are all drawn toward the disturbing magnetism of her form and toward the troubling resemblance on which Théoret relentlessly insists.

The tripartite structure of *Nécessairement putain* and the text's accompanying spatial movements provide the basis for the cultural deconstruction of "the whore." Divided into two parts, the first section of the text introduces both the space of confinement and the discursive void in which the prostitute and the dominated woman are placed—in reality and in the symbolic constructs of patriarchal thinking. Both the cultural and symbolic positioning of the whore are clearly the results of male fear. In the second section, the narrative carries us outside for a significant and contradictory walk in the body of a woman who is viewed and examined from the very moment she enters the street; thus, she exemplifies more fully than any other the object of the male look. But she is also a woman whose vital physical rhythms and engaging gait appear to create a new space of modulation and expansiveness, despite the constant and inescapable tracking of the male eye. Théoret's text concludes with a section that exposes the inherent brutality of familial relations based on the daughter's required submission to the father. In the final pages, the writer invokes the image of *la guerrière* or female warrior in order to displace the silent, "easy," and complicitous sex partner in the male master plot of prostitution—a plot that traditionally attributes to woman an uncontrollable sexuality, a propensity for immorality, and an unrelenting desire to submit and to be "mastered"—to reenact her state of feminine dependency through each new sexual act and with each man she meets. This patriarchal plot repeatedly tells us that for the prostitute, every encounter with a man is sexual and desired.

As in all of Théoret's works, the site from which a woman speaks is given special attention. The initial space in *Nécessairement putain* is confined entirely to the bedroom; the woman in this scene is either on the bed or at the window. In this most private of interior spaces, a woman recognizes that she is indeed enclosed, encircled in an unchanging and perpetual hall of male mirrors that continually reflect the same images, desires, gestures, and preconceived ideas. The contradictions generated in this space are many since the room is both her prison and her hiding place, and the woman described is alternately a self-conscious captive, a furtive child, or—reminiscent of Bersianik's female characters—a woman in exile:

Elle regarde au coin de la fenêtre un matin incertain et se dit qu'il vaut mieux se rendormir. La plage du lit offerte ne souffre pas de présence. Etrangère l'espace du refus des refus sur tous les modes. Il n'y a pas de langage possible pour un sismographe s'arrêtant sur des lèvres qui virent au bleu. . . . Une langue ne se parle pas qui n'arrive pas à s'énoncer. Etale le prisme. Souffrance d'une couleur si vive.   (5)

She looks in the corner of the window at an uncertain morning weather and decides that it's better to go back to sleep. The bed's outstretched beach suffers no other presence. Stranger the space of refusal all kinds of refusals. There is no language possible for a seismograph pausing on bluish lips. . . . A language isn't spoken that is unable to express itself. Display the prism. Suffering in such a vivid color.

A female body in a bed of silence, the reluctant captive, the sting from the inevitable slap, the disconnected actions of a sexuality that cannot express itself, "the impossible space"—all aspects of a woman's unspeakable scenario, fragments of a broken life narrated in *Nécessairement putain* with brutal candor and an ever-diminishing narrative distance until "she" and "I," the woman narrated and the narrator herself, become virtually interchangeable. Whether virgin or whore, mother or temptress, Mary or Eve, the ostensibly disparate roles accorded women in the patriarchal mythologies of our culture relegate them to the sidelines and all too often encase them in silence, in "le dit nié" ("the spoken negated"), says Théoret's narrator. This closing off of linguistic self-expression, which inevitably results in a further thwarting of self-exploration, builds the tension responsible for the eventual cry of the woman warrior's revolt in the final section of Théoret's text.

Already in the opening pages, we note the woman's alienation and sense the fiery implications of her impossible discursive space within the conventional social codes and within the unequal relationship of power and exchange that constitutes the system of prostitution itself. In the second short piece entitled "L'Honneur des pères" ("The Fathers' Honor"), we also witness a continuing *rapprochement* between the daughter and the whore, who are both caught in the perpetual cash nexus of sex for sale as well as in capitalism's incessant appraisal and marketing of female sexuality as a commodity. And as the text suggests, the value of exchange of the woman-commodity as well as its general pattern of circulation in the culture are always established among men, among those who stand to profit the most:

—Tu m'as donné ta parole. —Il n'y a pas de paroles parce qu'il y a mon cul. Et depuis que j'ai l'âge de penser par moi-même vous ne me parlez que de mon cul. A quoi bon la parole! —Où est ton honneur ma fille? —Dans mon cul papa. —Qu'as-tu fait de ton honneur ma fille? —J'ai voulu voir le monde papa.   (18)

—You gave me your word. —There's no word since there's my ass. And ever since I've been old enough to think for myself you only talk about my ass. So what's the use of words! —Where's your honor my girl? —In my ass daddy. —What did you do with your honor my girl? —I wanted to see the world daddy.

Visually set off from the rest of the text by its orange-colored pages and its central positioning, the second section of Théoret's textual triptych, entitled "La Marche" ("The Walk"), shifts the focus outward with a series of probing descriptions of a woman in movement and on city streets. As the privileged site of *modernité,* the urban landscape in Théoret's writing is the space toward which women appear most inescapably drawn and, at the same time, the site against which they resist the most. And whereas the anxious woman in the initial bedroom scene continually recedes from her surroundings—even to the point of hiding under the bedcovers, the woman encountered outside in "La Marche" appears to confront the assault of her immediate urban surroundings and the continuous gaze of men with a strange and disturbing ambivalence. She is, in effect, both resigned and resistant to her own objectification.

Théoret thus stages her own sense of oppression and feminist defiance as a writer in the body of the woman viewed as prostitute. On the surface of things, the female pedestrian in her text is the object of persistent scrutiny, seen in full detail and constantly followed. Yet somehow she escapes the deadening weight of the male look through her own light-footedness and continual movement as well as through her generosity, presumed superficiality, and lack of modesty. This woman walks for the sake of walking—a wandering linked to the thematics of *modernité,* no doubt, because of the indeterminate direction assigned her movement, but surely a feminist displacement as well since her woman's odyssey through city streets allows her to elude both the objectification of the male gaze and the fixed designations men assign to her as she walks. Reminiscent of Sarah Kofman's narcissistic woman, she is, in a word, radically, even criminally, "self-sufficient":[31]

Elle est là peut-être lorsqu'elle déploie vive toute sa richesse dehors. Elle est là comme, toujours comme, en tant que, voulant dire, s'arrêtant sur qui est là et s'ouvre extérieure d'un rêve retourné, elle se prête généreuse, elle s'offre globale, elle dépasse, elle émerge, elle signifie sans alourdir, elle présente, elle ne se raréfie d'aucune substance, elle éclaire, elle entraîne et réunit, elle voulant que ça soit et ça se fait, elle inclut, elle transparaît, elle par ce qu'elle allume sans contraindre, elle fardée ou non, elle au départ et à l'arrivée des choses, elle marche et ça se voit.   (24)

She is there perhaps when she displays live all her riches outside. She is there like, always like, as a, meaning, pausing with what is there and opens herself up outside a returning dream, she gives herself away generously, she offers herself globally, she exceeds, she emerges, she signifies without much weight, she presents, she doesn't rarefy herself with any substance, she enlightens, she carries away and reunites, she wanting it to be and take place, she includes, she appears through, she through what she incites without coercing, she made-up or not, she at the departure and arrival of things, she walks and that's obvious.

Throughout "La Marche," Théoret makes repeated use of the syntagma *elle est* (she is) to underscore the insistent need of the social eye to categorize and interpret *woman*. At the same time, however, this familiar mode of designation is continually undermined in the text by the narrator's inability to resolve the various and conflicting definitions that tend toward objectification and reductionism of the woman in question. Louise Dupré has also noted how the parallel formula, *je suis* (I am), is similarly subverted in Théoret's work since the female speaking subject can only be defined "in its negation, its alienation," while the negative form of this same pattern, *je ne suis pas* (I am not), "attempts to consolidate a subject that affirms itself positively."[32]

In the final analysis, while the woman in the streets appears to fit all of the descriptions attributed to her, she continually moves beyond them and, ultimately, transcends the fixity of all definitions.[33] Unsure of herself, the woman in "La Marche" has no desire to be assured of anything. Indeed for Théoret, assurance itself is a lie.

Thus, the woman-whore in her text advances without any clear sense of purpose, walking in her long gait with no particular destination or intention: "Elle n'a d'autre raison d'exister que sa propre existence" (29) ("She has no reason to exist other than her own existence").

The woman-as-whore in *Nécessairement putain* is she who lives and moves on the surface of things, carefully covering up her own pain. Yet even so, she remains vulnerable to every possible form of violence and superstition. In the end, she signifies everything and nothing simultaneously, "tout à fait superficielle. Poreuse et dangereusement opaque aussi. Inessentielle pour tout dire" (34) ("completely superficial. Porous and also dangerously opaque. Inessential in a word"). Théoret's streetwalker inverts the signs, disrupts expectations, and reminds us of what cannot be said about her, of what remains hidden from male view. Indeed, it appears that the dangerous impenetrability of the woman viewed as whore in Théoret's text constitutes her most subversive potential.

Despite this continual modulation between a woman defined and a woman in excess, however, the female voice in the final section of Théoret's text is still an object of the male gaze. For the woman-as-whore is forever positioned in the lens of the male camera eye to be looked at, unclothed, and displayed. Moreover, the logic of the male gaze insists on enclosing her in what Irigaray has called "a dominant scopic economy" that assigns her an essentially passive role.[34] In spite of all desire to the contrary, the woman-as-whore in *Nécessairement putain* submits to visual and erotic objectification through a process of "active" male viewing, through what Laura Mulvey has noted in the dominant cinema as woman's state of "to-be-looked-at-ness:"[35]

Et je suis nue, violemment nue, vue et nue d'être nue sans raison d'espérer sans borne de me justifier, de me confondre, vive, oeuvre vive.   (42)

And I am naked, violently naked, viewed and naked from being naked without reason for hope without a boundary to justify me, to identify with me, alive, live work.

Linking the appropriation of woman's body with that of her discourse, Théoret pursues the analogy between the woman writer and the whore, both caught in patriarchy's imposed trap of disguise, seduction, usage, and betrayal: "Je me suis laissée sculpter par vous, je me suis laissée dominer jusqu'à la lie et vous me suiviez où que je puisse être" (43) ("I let myself be sculpted by you, I let myself be dominated like scum and you followed me wherever I might be"). This unnamed "vous" is a generalized pronoun used to address the father, the pimp, the dominant male culture that has confiscated the speaker's body, voice, and writing. The daughter, the whore, the woman writer have obediently learned to please men too well, to turn men's "tricks," to play by their rules, and to mask the expression of feminine desire in a discourse that was never their own to begin with. Indeed, in *Nécessairement putain,* the necessity for makeup suggests the theatrical nature of the configuration of woman in patriarchal culture as well as the extent to which the women in this text are continually masked and separated from their own bodies by a discourse on beauty and femininity that has been constructed by and for men.

The speaking subject in the final section of this text is, in effect, an actress fatigued with her role, alienated from her lines, and unable to identify with the face and body she sees in the mirror. The role of the whore, like that of the actress, is a dramatic part sanctioned by the dominant culture, which exemplifies the position of women in language and in society at large. And as in the case of the actress, the prostitute's "charm" is certainly greatest when she is in the least control of her words and her body, when she imitates most perfectly the model men desire to see. As French critic Claudine Herrmann has also noted, the actress, the prostitute, and the silenced woman have much in common:

Woman however, always described as "chattering" has been mute for a long time. Not only because she has never been qualified to express her own views of society, but because it has always been indecent—prostitute sworn to the "law of silence" or woman of the world "used to" social conventions—for her to express herself about what constitutes her own particular circumstance. She has thus been limited to playing the role of an actress who repeats her lines, none of which have been invented by her. She triumphs at the moment when her alienation is the most complete, but whatever charm may be found in that moment, her words are always useless as discourse since before she has said them, they have already been written by someone else.[36]

Thus, the positions of Théoret and Herrmann converge around the issue of language and woman's place. The writer, the actress, the father's dutiful daughter are all "necessarily whores" because of their blind dependency on and subordination to the master, the pimp, the men who have institutionalized their silence and who benefit from their captivity, their theatrical masquerade, and their state of "being viewed." The better she imitates a culturally constructed image, the more she is applauded, appreciated, paid.

The spatial movement in *Nécessairement putain* moves progressively outward in what appear to be stages of an evolutionary process, from the bedroom, to the street, to the extreme boundary or *frontière* in the brief concluding section. Here a female speaker attempts to situate herself and her words in the uneasy space she claims as her own, on the boundary between confinement and freedom, between continual objectification and the formulation of a radically new notion of female subjectivity. It is an agonizing space filled with violent memories, inevitable concessions, extreme self-consciousness, and unrealized pleasure—a space at the limit of the possible bounded by the most rudimentary needs of survival and by a yearning for self-affirmation in an altogether different mode. In the end, Théoret acknowledges the death of "woman" in the male imagination and seems to invoke the work of Monique Wittig as the figures of writer and prostitute are finally subsumed into the nascent image of an army of watchful women warriors: "Il n'y a plus d'issue sinon peut-être à venir de la vigilante guerrière. Ah! Naître armée!" (52) ("There is no longer any exit except perhaps coming from the vigilant woman warrior. Oh! Army arise!").[37]

Refusing to close off and thereby contain the radical nature of this final image, Théoret concludes her narrative exploration with the promise of yet another text that will trace the evolution of a woman's consciousness from passivity to active defiance: "Un jour, je raconterai patiemment l'histoire de la jeune servante endormie devenue guerrière par la force des choses" (52) ("One day, I will patiently tell the story of a young sleeping servant who became a warrior by the force of circumstance"). If the text she envisions here does not yet exist, the theoretical bases for its development have already been established.

A Language for Electra: *Nous parlerons comme on écrit*

In 1982, France Théoret published *Nous parlerons comme on écrit* (*We will speak as we write*), an ambitious and original attempt to explore the complex interrelationships between writing and repression, discourse and desire. This "novel"—so termed on the title page despite its unconventional, wandering form—is in many ways the culmination of Théoret's experimental efforts up to that point. It is both a synthesis of her previous reflections on women in language and culture and a contextualizing of those positions in terms of her own life story. At the same time, *Nous parlerons comme on écrit* also marks an evolution in her work with its emphasis on the liberating potential of the act of writing and its affirmative view of women writing to and for other women.

As we have already noted in the later work of Madeleine Gagnon, Théoret's recent fiction takes enormous chances with the intimate mining of the woman writer's own private pain and creative needs. *Nous parlerons comme on écrit* is the story of a woman's voice in search of the links between writing and everyday language, between the realm of the imaginary and the realm of the real world. It is also a novel that appears to be in a continual process of auto-investigation, redirection, and redefinition as Théoret moves back and forth through the social and the personal dimensions of her own experience as a Quebec woman and as a child of the working class turned academic, then writer. The novel clearly contains numerous autobiographical elements, many of which have already appeared in fragmentary forms in earlier texts, but Théoret's fictional narration functions as a kind of mediator between her own painfully personal memories, political consciousness, and her more theoretical reflections on women's position in the writing process.

In *Nous parlerons comme on écrit,* Théoret once again translates her own exteriority to and in language through continued linguistic disruption and structures of opposition that contradict and ultimately negate many aspects of traditional narrative practice. At the heart of this literary experiment lies a destabilized female subject involved in a process of radical self-exploration and reassessment through the act of writing. Théoret's narrative journey engages us further in a private meditation on the nature of language in contemporary culture and on how language might, if transformed, begin to initiate much needed change in the essential patterns and character of women's lives.

As in earlier texts, language in *Nous parlerons comme on écrit* is born out of apprehension, uncertainty, and an unsettling intimacy with death itself. In the novel's opening line, a hesitant female speaker situates herself in death's arena: "Lorsque passe la mort, je dis présente"[38] ("When death passes, I say here"). Ugliness, illness, and death pervade much of the novel's first untitled section that focuses on scenes and emotions generated from the speaker's work-ing-class past. Her memories construct a vision of filth, nauseating odors, marital fights, and attempted suicides—her own and those of other women, while also painting a crushing portrait of external as well as internal desolation. Reconstituted in the present tense or through the use of infinitive constructions, the past infects the present, engulfs it, and a woman's voice relives the agonies, the loneliness of a life that literally made her ill, made her vomit. She protects herself from this pain through silence, through solitude. Thus, Théoret's narrative beginning presents the exposition of a voice that has broken its silence, the voice of a woman for whom writing becomes an act of unleashing (*le débouchage*), a curative form of spewing forth the grim reality of a world she once found un-speakable, un-narratable.

Almost immediately, the speech act itself becomes the focus of much attention in this novel. Such is the case on the first page when the writer shares a glimpse of her private anguish through a series of recollections of her trip to Mexico. These memory fragments prompt the surfacing of a disturbing and crucial image: a young girl's grueling efforts to "speak" her mind and to somehow change the course of her life. The young woman is described in the third person, as if somehow to effect a distancing with regard to her suffering, but this narrative distance quickly breaks down as the narrator herself becomes ever more close to the past she is reconsid-ering while still endeavoring to keep it in its place:

Les lendemains chanteront. Je signe des publicités dans la ville. Décor et il y a les intestins. Montréal n'est pas grand lorsqu'on revient de Mexico. Les bruits des nerfs de la nerveuse *avenida Insurgentes*. Une pièce de satin blanc une toute jeune fille recommence d'apprendre à vivre, exister vierge du droit au toucher. Elle se mange les lèvres, elle grince, griche des dents dans la nuit, elle se ronge les ongles jusqu'au sang, elle bégaie, hésite quand elle parle. Les lendemains chanteront.   (9)

The days to come will sing. I sign publicity in the city. Setting and there are the intestines. Montreal doesn't seem big when you return from Mexico. The noises of nerves of the nervous *avenida Insurgentes*. A piece of white satin a very young girl begins to learn to live again, live as virgin the right to touch. She chews her lips, she gnashes, grinds her teeth in the night, she bites her nails until bloody, she stutters, hesitates when she speaks. The days to come will sing.

   In this way, Théoret begins her novel with a series of contrasting images generated through a forceful blending of real and imaginary material, personal reflections, and excessive self-doubt. The juxtaposition of Montreal and Mexico City, which underscores the spatial, cultural, and personal dislocation of the female speaker, continues as a dominant leitmotiv throughout the narrative, since Mexico was the place where the narrator came to understand what it means to be locked out of discourse as Mexico itself is with respect to the capitalist discourse of the United States. Her linguistic dispossession as a woman and as a Québécoise whose roots are in the working class (her triple ghetto of sex, culture, class) is thus likened to the linguistic dispossession of Mexico itself, a country that constitutes little more than a silent presence in English-speaking North America. This rendering of Mexico as the space outside of and yet always dominated by its American neighbor becomes an attempt to feminize a geographic as well as a poetic region and, in so doing, to position women's alterity within discourse in a politically imaginative way.
   The Mexican cultural landscape "speaks" to Théoret's narrator through the silent medium of its vivid urban murals. As she reflects on those images, the woman writer compares her own contained discourse and alienated sensibility as a North American city dweller with the expansive newness of self-redefinition found in Mexico. There, the crowded arteries and noisy exchange of the Mexican

capital epitomize the vibrancy of a language capable of subsuming all conflicting social codes in an ever-expanding matrix of words in excess, an overflowing of signs. Théoret characterizes this language of urbanity and difference as a discourse of plenitude rather than authorized impoverishment, which is not unlike Brossard's poetic efforts in *French Kiss* and *Amantes*. Indeed, for both Théoret and Brossard, the city represents the supreme space of social and cultural interchange and, as a result, the most powerful territory of poetic inscription:

Les aztèques avaient appelé Mexico, la région la plus transparente. Une ville si énorme, étalée, conquise sur la terre marécageuse, architecture du sous-sol, aménagée pour survivre aux secousses sismiques. Il y a foule aux couleurs les plus hétéroclites, des klaxons, la fumée noire rejetée par les autobus bruyants. Les codes aparaissent noyés dans la circulation. En trop et de partout à la fois. Du mouvement, il en émerge plus que le nécessaire.
Densité des signes dans la ville. Foisonnement complice. S'il en était ainsi des mots? (115)

The Aztecs had called Mexico the most transparent region of all. A city so enormous, spread out, conquered on swampy land, basement architecture, laid out to survive seismic tremors. A crowd with the most unusual colors, horns, the black exhaust cast out by the noisy buses. The codes appear drowned in the traffic. In excess and everywhere at the same time. Out of the movement, there are more than enough.
Density of signs in the city. Complicitous expansion. If such were also the case with words?

The narrator's propensity for contrasting images leads to an initial series of associative pairings that evoke the contradictory nature of a feminine otherness in Théoret's text: the purity of adolescent innocence contrasts with the bloody passage into womanhood; the silence of repressed desire counters the anxious sexual urgency to articulate the female body; the apprehensiveness and stammering speech of a young girl stand in opposition to the presumed confidence of a mature woman writer. All this functions as a prelude to an ironic refrain of hope regarding the female writer's potential place in language and her future political impact, "Les lendemains chanteront" ("The days to come will sing"), which echoes the popular French Communist Party slogan of the late 1930s.[39] As Théoret's narrative progresses, however, the inferred distances between womanhood and innocence, discourse and silence, writer and adolescent, between "je" and "elle," the narrator and the narrated subject, are found to be illusory. In reality, Théoret's split and fragmented female speaker harbors each of these elements within her. She is alternately the thing named and its opposite. And like her discourse, she is in a continual process of internal vacillation and discord.

Thus the myth of the solid, unified subject is once again undermined as the narrative voice in *Nous parlerons* declares herself multiple, unclassifiable, off-center. The effects of this dislocation of the female subject are felt on virtually every page of Théoret's text. There can, in fact, be no authority for writing in this novel, only the ravaged remains of a woman's voice dispossessed. As a result, feminine discourse frequently becomes a series of interrupted attempts at self-disclosure during which we can almost sense the physical and mental frustration of articulation:

Les bruits de langue partout. Pas de centrement. Des croisements. C'est ralenti. C'est fulgurant. C'est déplacé. A perte de voix. L'avoir dans la bouche et passe si proche. Un souffle seulement, alangui. De ne pouvoir. Centrer. Offrir des trous sur toute surface.   (36)

The clamor of language everywhere. No centering. Crossings. It's slower. It's flashing. It's displaced. At a loss of voice. Have it in the mouth and come so close. Only a breath, languid. Not be able to. Center. Offer holes on every surface.

The rhythm and syntax in the preceding passage are clearly revelatory of Théoret's intent. The flow of words appears severed, abridged, while her speaking subject is grammatically eclipsed by the repeated use of the infinitive subject. Irigaray's theoretical notion of the effaced female subject, present in the margins and the blank spaces, is unquestionably at work in this text. Immersed in self-doubt and alienated from the very words she utters, Théoret's narrative voice continually teeters on the edge, between a costly yet persistent will to live and write and despair. She resists complete linguistic disintegration only through a desperate and ardent act of self-will.

The direct results of Théoret's inventive and anguished self-analysis, these disruptions in the processes of writing and reading intentionally mirror the diffuseness, oscillations, and holes in a feminine discourse that forms, deforms, and reforms itself as it proceeds or impulsively backtracks. Phrases become fragments; images are introduced only to be contradicted and perhaps reinvisaged at some later fictional moment. Poetic rhythms and sonorous repetitions interweave with the narrative elements of autobiograpical fiction. Structurally speaking, *Nous parlerons comme on écrit* appears to start on all sides, engaging us in a continual process of redirection and disorderly multiplicity as a female voice wanders back and forth through the personal and social content of buried memories and present-tense reflections on language, art, and solitude. As in prior works, a problematic gap exists here as well between articulation and the object of feminine desire. The reasons for Théoret's own fascination with the writings of Virginia Woolf, Antonin Artaud, and Marguerite Duras become clear when reading this novel, since they too have insisted upon exposing the obscure and voiceless space that exists between words and matter, between poetic expression and lived experience.

With *Nous parlerons comme on écrit*, France Théoret creates a fissured narrative landscape where the established codes and the power of eternalizing images are continually assailed. As Suzanne Lamy also remarked in her own discussion of this novel,[40] Théoret's use of antithetical terms pushes the text toward the realm of nonsense, where words, images, and states of being are affirmed, then negated, to such an extent that at times the entire narrative process appears to falter, verging on chaos:

Rester monstrueusement encagée. Non-sens. Elle dérive emportée elle ne sait où car elle n'affirme rien. . . . Lorsque s'effondre ce qui n'a pas encore eu lieu, la dernière énigme demeure liée à la parole. D'où peut-elle parler? Le chaos la précède, elle est terre mêlée de boue, elle ne connaît pas la solidité. J'ai une peur infinie de mes manques de jugement, mes émotions sont marquées depuis le plus petit sursaut se dit-elle.   (91)

Remain monstrously encaged. Non-sense. She drifts carried away she doesn't know where since she affirms nothing. . . . When what has not yet taken place collapses, the final enigma remains linked to speech. From where can she speak? Chaos precedes her, she is earth mixed with mud, she knows no solidity. I have a tremendous fear of my lack of judgment, my emotions have been branded from the very beginning she says to herself.

The subtle slippage from "elle" to "je" (from "she" to "I") in the preceding passage is yet another instance of shifting narrative identification, a moment in which the psychological and scriptorial boundaries separating the writer of the text, the narrative voice, and the fictionalized character begin to blur. In an oppressive atmosphere of emotional and ontological self-doubt, Théoret transforms her own chronic frustrations with and in language into images of women's collective isolation and discursive dissolution. Clearly, the kind of invalidation and literal pulverizing of language in this text through assertion and negation is more gender-specific and decidedly Québécois than it is, strictly speaking, modern. There is, in fact, a discernibly positive aspect to Théoret's own irresolution in language since it is this very state of fluctuation and radical self-doubt that forces her to resist the lure and the lie of (authorial) certainty.

If *Nous parlerons comme on écrit* portrays a seemingly endless minefield of linguistic dangers for its female speaker-writer and her characters, it does not demolish the practice of writing altogether. Indeed, in an ironic move from destruction to rebirth, Théoret's disruptive discourse becomes a barren, but nevertheless neutralized ground on which we begin to discern the faint contours of a new language in germination. Out of the ashes, a phoenix emerges with the face of a woman's pain: "A l'état de décomposition, le langage. Fermentation" (136) ("At the state of decomposition, language. Fermentation"). A massive rupture with linguistic conformity, self-censure, and the constraints of conventional literary forms must occur in this text before any kind of authentic experience in language can be established or sustained. This undoing of the master's language has a purgative function and eventually allows repressed material—words, thoughts, feelings—to resurface.

The novel's second section, entitled "La Boule verte" ("The Green Ball"), introduces a counterpoint to the squalid world of working-class reality through the act of writing. In response to the incessant obstruction of her own words and the general trivializing of verbal communication while growing up, the woman writer in Théoret's text admits to having created a second secret life for herself. As an adolescent, she countered the false order of commercial, institutional, and familial discourse with the more honest chaos of words inscribed in the dead of night. Bearing a remarkable resemblance to the *écriture de nuit* in Madeleine Gagnon's *Lueur* and to what the mature writer in Théoret's text later likens to an endless chorus of indistinct murmurs, this adolescent "night writing" allowed her to articulate the unthinkable, to acquaint herself with the pleasure of anticipation, and to become a captive explorer of her own awakening passions. The attention she apparently gave to her nocturnal voices is an indication of the young woman's extreme eagerness, whatever the cost, for a language separate from the reality around her.

By constructing another identity outside society's rigid laws and immutable structures, Théoret's young writer, who ironically renames herself Ninon, "ni oui, ni non" ("neither yes, nor no"), attempts to sweep away all imposed social codes and frequents the cavernous shadows of her most intimate fears and yearnings. In the nudity of darkness, she seeks to animate the pure chemistry of her own body-text: "Je vais brûler pendant la nuit sur la nécessité de faire corps avec la langue" (66) ("I'm going to burn up at night over the need to become corporeal with language"). Is this an ironic critique of the early modernist texts of Brossard and company? The image certainly suggests their youthful exuberance for the body as text and their extreme disinterest in the real.[41] In any event, Théoret's aspiring writer in hiding tells us that writing "is in her veins," a comment that stresses the physical grounding of her nocturnal rites of passage through a world of forbidden words and nascent feminine desires.

In the novel's third section, "Une histoire dans la boule verte" ("A Story in the Green Ball"), a *mise en abyme* or mirroring effect occurs as the story about a writer and her past becomes the backdrop for yet another story, presumably written by the narrator herself, about a young girl, Louise Valois, and her exchange of letters with a friend, Lise-Anne, whose departure from Montreal first provoked their epistolary pact. Even after Lise-Anne returns to the city, the two friends continue to write each other letters without communicating in any other fashion. Although we never see more than brief fragments of their letters, it is through this epistolary dialogue that Louise begins to uncover the pleasures and anguish of a language yet to be born. Her solitary attempts to share herself through words, which seem to have a distinct life of their own, force Louise to confront the resistant nature of language itself:

Une fois rangée sur le comptoir près de l'évier la vaisselle qu'elle lavera, elle pense commencer la lettre. Répondre à l'amie. Parler et nouer, tracer des perspectives. D'où viennent les mots? Elle n'est pas là où elle est dépassée indéfiniment. Qui creuse sans fin, elle irait appelée vers ce qui travaille bruyamment dans la faille qui ouvre au moment où elle s'y attend le moins. La quête solitaire, l'indomptable demande inavouée.   (87)

Once the dishes she will wash have been laid out on the counter near the sink, she thinks about beginning the letter. Answer her friend. Speak and knot, outline perspectives. Where do words come from? She's not there where she is overtaken indefinitely. Endless digging, she would summon up what ferments noisily in the chasm that opens the moment she least expects it. The solitary quest, the indomitable unavowed request.

In an essay on Madame de Sévigné and women's correspondence in the seventeenth century, Elizabeth Goldsmith has argued that the epistolary discourse of the period strove to "cultivate a conversational style akin to the discourse of the salons."[42] The desire to imitate the "naturalness" of daily conversation in letter writing would, in turn, influence the development of the epistolary novel itself. In short, Goldsmith contends that for women, the epistolary tradition has often sought to approach writing under the spell, as it were, of spoken language. What Théoret has achieved in *Nous parlerons comme on écrit* is the evocation and complete reversal of that epistolary tradition. She does so by demonstrating that spoken language has become impoverished as well as hopelessly male-centered and must therefore be reinvented altogether through feminine letters. Such is the case, for example, with the monosyllabic discourse of the male bar customers in the narrator's adolescent memories. For Louise and Lise-Anne, who together pledged an oath of continued correspondence, writing creates a new feminine space of articulation and self-discovery. At the same time, it unites them in a common hope: to share the secret force of words that one day will effect a transformation of the way we speak and live. Thus, the language of their epistolary exchange must not imitate ordinary speech but, on the contrary, replace it:

Elle va répondre à la lettre. Les mots heureux. Heureuse de penser aux mots. Ils viennent s'arranger un peu d'eux-mêmes sur les pages. Etablie

discrètement l'entente de l'une à l'autre. Laisser émerger sur la seule lon-
gueur d'onde, des mots et participer ainsi du tissue des échanges comme à
livre ouvert.   (79)

She is going to answer the letter. Happy words. Happy to think about
words. They seem to arrange themselves independently on the pages. The
understanding of one for the other discreetly established. Let words emerge
on the only wave length, and thereby participate in the fabric of exchanges
like an open book.

    With the story of Louise and Lise-Anne, Théoret veils women's
problematic coming to language in the apparent innocence of the
epistolary act. But this gentle masking of intent does not deceive her
reader nor the father of Louise Valois who, like the unsympathetic
patriarch in Marie-Claire Blais' *Manuscrits de Pauline Archange,*
dismisses his daughter's letter writing as a waste of time and an
irksome thwarting of his own eroding authority. The correspondence between the two young girls is a form of female bonding
through writing that parallels the important bonding through reading that occurs in the novel's first section when the narrator and her
English-speaking friend exchange the texts of Virginia Woolf and
Colette.[43] At the same time, however, the gesture of letter writing
in Théoret's text is a metaphor for writing in the feminine itself
insofar as the letter constitutes a transgressive act of linguistic address to another woman, which in turn invites yet another woman-
centered address. "It is in writing," Cixous reminds us, "from
woman and toward woman, and in accepting the challenge of the
discourse controlled by the phallus, that woman will affirm woman
somewhere other than in silence, the place reserved for her in and
through the Symbolic."[44]
    In the face of the pervasive negativity and self-doubt that filled
her youth and haunt her adult life, the narrator's resilient and
implacable desire for the written word is all the more remarkable.
Among the fleeting memories of schoolgirl exchanges and conversations with her mother, she conjures up a female world in which
spoken words are pleasurable but often inconsequential. In the
world of her youth, maternal discourse repeatedly lost its direction
and meaning in the shadow of the patriarch. Within the confines of
her parents' bar, however, language was a form of commercial

transaction, conforming tightly to the economic laws of customer-centered discourse:

Annulation depuis longtemps derrière le signe de piastre. On a rien vu, rien entendu. On sait rien. On sait vivre, trop parler nuit et pourtant, parole coupée car parler c'est grossier, c'est répliquer. . . . La parole reste nouée, faire que vive et advienne la demande insensée. Coupée.   (108)

Cancellation for a long time behind the dollar sign. We saw nothing, heard nothing. We know nothing. We know living, speaking too much at night and yet, speech cut off since talking is vulgar, it's talking back. . . . Speech tied in knots, make sure the senseless request takes place. Cut off.

The penultimate chapter of the novel, "Lamento d'Arianna" ("Arianna's Lament"), is an orchestrated and mournful cry of living death, which underscores the attention paid throughout the text to the musical quality of the female voice. In this song of emptiness, the narrator remembers her eighteenth year, the young girls she taught—their poverty, poor eyesight, psychological blocks—the school administrators and their need to maintain "control," the friends who were all getting married around her. Her own roles as teacher, wage earner, and adult anchor her in the real at the expense of her inner voices and of her own writing. She no longer reads, no longer writes letters. In recognizably Sartrian terms, she ironically discloses her avoidance of self-examination, her shrinking creativity, and increasing "solidification."

This period of tacit acceptance, of psychological hardening and creative impoverishment, reads as an essential prelude to the conscious rediscovery of language that occurs in the novel's final section. Here, Théoret's narrator acknowledges the paradoxical nature of her own relationship to words, which is simultaneously one of dispossession and intense longing. Her walk through city streets in search of a female friend is a lyrical attempt at self-inscription in the heart of the urban sphere, which is unplanned much like *la marche* in *Nécessairement putain*. But if Théoret's North American city exudes some of the color and noise of life that have rendered Brossard's early urban landscapes so vibrant and so full of desire, Théoret's city is also an unharmonious conglomerate of styles and ill-planned reconstruction projects, where winter leaves its harshest traces on the very stones that defy it.

The narrator's accelerated pace on the street in the final pages of the novel accompanies her futile search for an unnamed woman, until she eventually empties herself of disappointment and wanders alone. In the end, however, her resistance is keen even in the face of deception and solitude: "Même si je suis seule, on n'aura pas ma peau. J'ai les mains tendues et vides" (174) ("Even if I am alone, they won't get rid of me. My hands are outstretched and empty"). By no means a conclusion, this final image bears the insistent mark of Théoret's greatest fear, a fear that has plagued the writer since her earliest texts: that no one is there to receive her words and respond in turn. And what if we were the woman in question? And what if we dared to embrace her pain and write our own?

Perhaps we can now understand how Théoret's title, *Nous parlerons comme on écrit,* invites a wishful and collective affirmation of the future, despite the agony of articulation and the isolation women live everyday. As the narrator reminds herself when reflecting on the act of writing to a female friend, writing to another woman means inventing a language that stirs rather than restricts creativity. In Théoret's title, we find words that mirror those previously uttered in a pact of friendship, when two young girls struggled to create a written bond. In this imaginative move from correspondence to speech that *Nous parlerons comme on écrit* affirms so dramatically, feminine discourse seeks a genuine emotional exchange rather than a fetishizing of the act of writing or of speech itself:[45]

Il y a un an ou deux déjà, au moment d'écrire une première lettre à une correspondante, l'angoisse unique, formulée: si elle ne comprenait pas. De quelle langue s'agit-il? Apprendre des mots, avoir une langue. L'insensé rappel de ce qui ne va pas de soi. Et la promesse, tel un pacte scellé dans la cour de l'école plus tôt. Elles avaient décidé, nous parlerons comme on écrit.   (92)

A year or two ago, while writing an initial letter to a correspondent, the unique anguish, formulated: what if she didn't understand. Which language to use? Learn words, have a language. The insane reminder of what is not self-evident. And the promise, like a pact sealed earlier on the school playground. They had decided, we will speak as we write.

Thus, the act of writing, like the epistolary exchange at the novel's center, is viewed as an act of love, a solitary yet generous attempt of the present to reshape both syntax and meaning even while risking incoherence and rejection: "J'écris pour qu'on s'aime dans la mobilité les uns des autres en dehors de toute surveillance et de toute punition" (74–75) ("I write so that we can love one another each in our own movement beyond all surveillance and all punishment").

In *Nous parlerons comme on écrit,* language emerges out of contradiction and negation, after obliterating virtually all the surrounding edifices of power. For Théoret, to write means, in effect, to challenge the old order, to break with the repressive schemes of the past, and to rebuild language and hence culture in the larger sense, with the woman writer's own sense of justice and visionary ideals. *Nous parlerons comme on écrit* addresses the issue of women's entry into language on a personal as well as a collective level and, as the title indicates, raises one of the more probing questions of women's experimental writing today: Is it possible to speak and live as one writes? Despite the extreme precariousness of Théoret's own position in language, she would doubtless respond that women today cannot afford to assume otherwise:

Les mots sont les mots, les mots ne sont que les mots, ils volent, les mots font d'autres mots, les mots perversement glissés à la racine, les mots endeuillés comme couteaux coupants, et pourtant, les mots mis en acte, font l'acte.   (118)

Words are words, words are only words, they fly/steal, words make other words, words sliding perversely to the root, words in mourning like knives cutting, and yet, words put into action, create the act.

Through a shrewd bit of revisionist mythmaking towards the end of the novel, Théoret reclaims the inestimable power of women's words just as she reclaims the ancient figure of Electra, the sister who no longer waits for a brother's return to speak her peace and to act in the full knowledge of her own courageous and effective justice. Indeed, in *Nous parlerons comme on écrit,* it is the inherently modern force of this mythical spectre from the past that tames the woman writer's fears of solitude and enables her to imagine dismantling the barriers to a discourse that will assert itself, in the name of women's muted history, as a self-consciously and radically inventive female act.

Many parallels and direct lines of influence can be traced between the works of France Théoret and the distinctive contributions of Nicole Brossard, Madeleine Gagnon, and Louky Bersianik. Yet Théoret's extreme problematizing of her own search for words, coupled with what she depicts as the precariousness of female identity in language and in culture generally, also point to some of the important differences of perspective in her writing. "I repeat over and over again," says Théoret in 1986, "words, I need all of them. I have never had enough words. My language has been continually reworked, invaded, cut off, diverted; my relationship to language has never been stable."[46] Far less utopian in her vision than either Brossard or Bersianik and less comfortable, it seems, with the private withdrawal that appears to characterize Gagnon's later works, Théoret has confronted the pain of women's socially imposed silence and battled identification with the law-giving father without giving up hope for an inner space of poetic renewal and without relinquishing her dream of a female collectivity in the making.

6 *Afterword*

How can we read these texts without revisiting our own lives? Our long forgotten past, each of us reconstructs it with multiple interpretations, reinvents it and continually rewrites it over the course of time. And when some aspect of the unexplored confronts us in the mirror where the self is reflected plural, physical, phantasmic, social, political, the image trembles with surprise and sometimes with fright.

> Suzanne Lamy, *Quand je lis, je m'invente*

The text is neither discrete nor self-contained, but is constructed in the discourses that articulate it, in an interactive context of reader and text. Every text is a pre-text. The author, as reader, is rewriting precursor texts: the reader, as author, rewrites the author's text, investing it with meaning in the context of her own life and experience.

> Barbara Godard, "Becoming My Hero, Becoming Myself: Notes Towards a Feminist Theory of Reading"

Feminist critics of literature and film produced by men have obliged us to confront many of the blatant as well as more subtle ways in which women readers and film viewers have been lured into identifying against themselves.[1] Theorizing on the need to resist this uncomfortable phenomenon, Teresa de Lauretis and others have encouraged us to examine how, as with writing, strategies of reading can also become forms of cultural resistance in which a woman reader's power is established in direct proportion to her ability to undercut, outmaneuver, and contradict the sexual politics engendered in a conventionally male-oriented text or film.[2] On the other hand and in addition to its focus on the difference of women's writing, "gynocritics" as proposed by Showalter and others, has frequently stressed the rereading, reviewing, and reassessment of women's texts with respect to the already established literary canon.[3] The importance of this activity for feminist critics and, more generally speaking, for future readers of women writers is already well established.

But what happens when a feminist reader begins to read and identify with the works of feminist writers who are, themselves, self-consciously and overtly writing against a male literary tradition and toward the construction of some new vision of themselves in language and in the world? What processes of reading are privileged when a feminist critic sets out to explore both the creative dynamics at work in a woman writer's text and the feminist vision that has given shape to many of the collective aspirations it appears to express? Although I cannot begin to theorize on this process in a general way within the limits of the present study, I would like to offer a few brief personal comments about it with regard to the writers I have already discussed.

In the case of my own position as a feminist reader of feminist-inspired texts, several observations seem relevant. The first involves a developing awareness during the preparation of this study that my frequent role as a resisting reader of the traditional French male canon was finally being mirrored in the works I had set out to explore. The posture I had previously adopted as a resisting reader could now find its reflection in the role of the feminist writer confronting the literary and political inheritance passed on to her by men. It is also true, of course, that among Quebec women writers, the grounds for this canonical resistance have been established in part by the clearly marginal status of the Quebec writer with respect to the literary tradition of France. The question of national identity aside, however, the effect of this *dédoublement* of feminist reader and writer has been reassuring, to say the least. Both the site and the act of resistant reading have seemed less lonely and less alienating to me as a result. At the same time, the dynamics of the reading process have become considerably more complicated.

As I have noted throughout this study, the sense of a collective plot of resistance to male texts and to a male canonical economy is especially strong in the works of Brossard, Gagnon, Bersianik, and Théoret. Like the feminist critic at work, each of these writers has, in her own way, challenged the male canonical tradition head-on as she writes. Each has done so, moreover, with the presence of an allied female reader clearly in mind.

In form and in content, the poetic and political alignments of female reader and writer are, in fact, consciously and passionately intertwined in many of the texts I have discussed. The consequences of these emerging literary relations have been both satisfying and empowering. As a feminist, I suppose there is always a certain pleasure to be taken in the knowledge that our own cultural resistance in the act of reading occurs through the words of another woman. In the particular kind of radical complicity feminist readers can share with writers such as those studied in this book, it is not the text or pre-text we resist, but the entire tradition against which the experimental woman writer has boldly positioned herself and her work. Throughout this study, I have therefore critiqued and reread tradition (whether French, European, or Québécois) as an accomplice, always with another woman at my side.

Another significant and welcome change for me has been the realization that the kind of identification required in many of these feminist texts from Quebec does not occur at the expense of abandoning my own experience as a woman. I am no longer unnoticed, disbelieved, unimagined. In this regard and despite the rather different forms of feminist politics practiced by Brossard, Gagnon, Bersianik, and Théoret, I have been able to enter their women-centered worlds and return to myself without having been reduced to silence. Indeed, through the act of reading I have been encouraged to initiate my own forms of remembering and reinventing—a project about which their writings have so often theorized.

Suzanne Lamy first introduced many readers, including myself, to issues of language and gender identity in the works of contemporary Quebec women writers. Her inventive approach to feminist criticism attempted to establish "a loving relationship" with these experimental women's texts. In Quebec, Lamy's critical posture legitimized the poetic intimacy of the relationship between feminist reader and writer as few had dared to do before her. "They spoke to me, I loved their intonations, their engravings," she remarked. "Accomplice, an interior space was opening within me. Very quickly, I knew they were part of me and that I needed them, that without them a self slipped away, no longer existed."[4]

If the act of writing has become a feminist gesture of intense concentration in most of the works discussed in this study, so too has the act of reading. For reading, like writing, constructs political parameters that extend far beyond the boundaries of the text and far beyond the realm of fiction. At the same time, however, the politics of reading must not overlook concerns for the personal and for the differences among women and among women writers, a point repeatedly emphasized by recent feminist discussions of contemporary reading practices. My own view is that a somewhat fluid movement from the personal to the political and back again is a necessity in a reader-conscious criticism that seeks to understand the interconnections of text, culture, and female writer.

Finally, a number of the more powerful feminist readings of women's writing today continue to remind us that interpretation need not be ideologically "pure" or all encompassing to be compelling. Some readings may, in fact, contradict others. Like the discourse contemporary women writers have themselves inherited and in which many of them have located the site of their feminist revolt, we are never entirely sure of our position in many of these experimental texts, nor must we be. Yet this recognition does not mean that we give up trying to map the contours of our experience as readers or abandon altogether the power of critical analysis.

More than an act of resistance or "re-vision,"[5] I have come to view the project of reading in this book as one similar to the act of translation. As noted in chapter 2, Brossard has actively promoted this notion of reading as translation in *Le Désert mauve*. Like Brossard's evolving triptych, my own readings have involved a process of identification, extended contemplation, selective resistance, and continuing self-discovery, resulting each time in the reworking and rewording of another woman's text. From the standpoint of reading as a feminist strategy to help move us beyond male canonical authority toward a reconstruction of the female (reading) subject, this shift in emphasis from critiquing and reviewing to rewriting may at times be a subtle one, but it is probably not inconsequential. Thus conceived, reading demands that we assume responsibility for the words we transmit and for the future they might create. "Truly," affirms Brossard, "the sensational effect of reading is a feeling we cannot express, unless we underline. *With each reading, the intimacy of eternity is an intrigue we invent.* All reading, every reading, is a desire for an image, an intention to re/present, which gives us hope."[6]

Notes
Bibliography
Index

Notes

Introduction

1. Elizabeth A. Meese, *Crossing the Double-Cross* (Chapel Hill: University of North Carolina Press, 1986), 119.

2. For an overview of contemporary feminist theatre in Quebec, see Jane Moss, "Women's Theater in Quebec," in *Traditionalism, Nationalism, and Feminism: Women Writers of Quebec*, ed. Paula Gilbert Lewis (Westport, Conn.: Greenwood Press, 1985), 241–54.

3. Caroline Bayard, "Qu'en est-il au fait de la théorie depuis que les dieux sont morts?," in *Féminité, Subversion, Ecriture*, ed. Suzanne Lamy and Irène Pagès (Ville Saint-Laurent: Remue-ménage, 1983), 188.

4. Tania Modleski, "Feminism and the Power of Interpretation: Some Critical Readings," in *Feminist Studies/Critical Studies*, ed. Teresa de Lauretis (Bloomington: Indiana University Press, 1986), 136.

1. *Writing in the Feminine: Social and Theoretical Contexts*

1. This phrase is borrowed from the book by Hélène Cixous and Catherine Clément, *La Jeune Née* (Paris: Union Générale d'Editions, 1976), which has been translated by Betsy Wing as *The Newly Born Woman* (Minneapolis: University of Minnesota Press, 1986).

2. I use these "labels" somewhat cautiously to suggest rather than to categorize some of the various currents in Quebec feminism that have had the most impact on the writers in this study. For the purposes of general discussion, I will use the term socialist feminist to designate an orientation shared by differing groups of feminists in Quebec who have been inspired by Marxist and socialist theories of economic exploitation, alienation, and class struggle under capitalism, as well as by Marxist-socialist analyses of the relationships between the material conditions of people's lives, political power, and the cultural construction of ideology. Socialist feminists in Quebec have usually considered women's membership in a particular social class to be at least as "significant" in determining the nature or degree of

their oppression as gender itself. Feminist groups whose general perspective and political projects have often been subsumed under the term *radical feminism* represent another strain of Quebec feminism, initially influenced by American feminists such as Kate Millett, Shulamith Firestone, and Adrienne Rich, among others. Radical feminists in Quebec commonly view the dominant sociopolitical and familial structures of modern society as key elements in a patriarchal system that functions at the expense of women and for the benefit of men. Although not necessarily disinterested in the issue of class exploitation, radical feminists in Quebec have tended to concern themselves with the relations of power between the two sexes. Lesbian separatists have taken radical feminist analyses of patriarchy and the pervasiveness of phallocentrism further yet by arguing that the only way to counter the forces of patriarchal institutions and patriarchal thought successfully is to separate themselves entirely from men (sexually, emotionally, psychologically, intellectually, artistically, and politically). Lastly, although their impact on the four women writers discussed in this study has been far less crucial, "liberal" or "reformist" feminists have been primarily associated with a current of Quebec feminism that views women's position in society as unsatisfactory to the extent that women are not treated as the equals of men. The focus of this strain of feminism—by far the most popular—is on changing certain laws, providing additional professional opportunities, and creating social services so that women can function in society as the equals of men. Additional contexts for the use of these terms will be given in the course of this chapter.

3. See Gagnon's comments in my interview, "Ecrire au féminin: Interview avec Denise Boucher, Madeleine Gagnon et Louky Bersianik," *Québec Studies* 2 (1984): 125–42.

4. I borrow the expression from Alicia Ostriker's *Writing Like a Woman* (Ann Arbor: University of Michigan Press, 1983).

5. Caroline Pestieau, "Women in Quebec," in *Women in the Canadian Mosaic*, ed. Gwen Matheson (Toronto: Peter Martin, 1976), 66.

6. Nicole Brossard, *The Aerial Letter*, trans. Marlene Wildeman (Toronto: Women's Press, 1988), 46. Originally published as *La Lettre aérienne* (Montreal: Remue-ménage, 1985). "The revenge of the cradle" refers to the openly pronatalist stance of the Catholic Church in Quebec during the nineteenth and twentieth centuries as a method of ensuring the growth of the francophone population and the continuation of French Catholic culture in Quebec, despite anglophone economic and political dominance over the province from the mid-1800s until the 1960s.

7. Nadia Fahmy-Eid and Nicole Laurin-Frenette, "Theories of the Family and Family/Authority Relationships in the Educational Sector in Québec and France, 1850–1960," in *The Politics of Diversity: Feminism, Marxism and Nationalism*, ed. Roberta Hamilton and Michèle Barrett (London: Verso Press, 1986), 295.

8. As I have noted elsewhere, both the precocious young writer in Marie-Claire Blais' fictional trilogy (*Manuscrits de Pauline Archange*, 1968; *Vivre! Vivre!*, 1969; *Les Apparences*, 1970) and the autobiographical narrator in Claire Martin's *Dans un gant de fer* (vol. 1, 1965; vol. 2, 1966) discover the monstrousness of growing up female within the confines of convent schools, where they are taught that puberty is a punishment from God and where the mounting sexual frustrations of the nuns invariably lead to increased cruelty and the physical abuse of female students. See Karen Gould, "The Censored Word and the Body Politic: Reconsidering the Fiction of Marie-Claire Blais," *Journal of Popular Culture* 15.3 (1981): 14–27.

9. See Nicole Brossard, "L'Avenir de la littérature québécoise," *Etudes françaises* 13.3–4 (1977): 285.

10. Ironically, however, as Micheline Dumont, Michèle Jean, Marie Lavigne, and Jennifer Stoddart have pointed out in their important history of Quebec women over four centuries, many women in the religious orders had benefited from the prominent position of the Catholic Church in the administration of social services in Quebec (in hospitals, preschools, schools, clinics, etc.) and had obtained some measure of independence with regard to men as a result. For these women of the Church, the secularization and bureaucratization of the Quebec state during the 1960s undermined their gains as women and effectively diluted and eventually replaced women's prior authority in the predominantly female environment of Quebec's social services with a new cadre of male bureaucrats. Thus for women as a group, the trends toward secularization and bureaucratization in the early 1960s gave rise to some of the important contradictions in both the discourse on modernization articulated by the Liberal Party of Jean Lesage and in the structural changes in Quebec society that were beginning to take place. See Micheline Dumont et al., *L'Histoire des femmes au Québec depuis quatre siècles* (Montreal: Quinze, 1982), 433–36.

11. In 1980, the Parti Québécois led by René Lévesque held a provincial referendum that asked for public support to negotiate on the question of "sovereignty-association" with the federal government. The Parti Québécois proposal was defeated, and in 1986, Parti Québécois officials removed the independence project from the party platform—a decision that led to a bitter split and the eventual resignation of a number of Parti Québécois party members devoted to the independence project.

12. See Andrée Yanacopoulo's preface to her edited collection, *Au nom du père, du fils et de Duplessis* (Montreal: Remue-ménage, 1984), 7.

13. During the "reign" of Duplessis, the Liberal Party was the leading opposition party in Quebec. See Dominique Clift, *Quebec Nationalism in Crisis* (Montreal: McGill-Queen's University Press, 1982), 7.

14. Marcelle Maugin, "Le Régime Duplessis," in *Au nom du père, du fils et de Duplessis*, ed. Andrée Yanacopoulo (Montreal: Remue-ménage, 1984), 24.

15. Anne Légaré, "Cet hier dans aujourd'hui," in *Au nom du père, du fils et de Duplessis*, ed. Andrée Yanacopoulo (Montreal: Remue-ménage, 1984), 49.

16. Paul-André Linteau et al., *Histoire du Québec contemporain: Le Québec depuis 1930* (Montreal: Boréal Express, 1986), 557.

17. For American readers, it may be interesting to note that from 1960 to 1970 foreign investment in Quebec rose from 22 billion to 44 billion Canadian dollars and that throughout the decade, American investment constituted "the lion's share" with 75 percent to 80 percent of the total. Figures quoted and metaphor borrowed from Linteau et al., 416.

18. Dumont et al., 437–43.

19. Robert Schwartzwald, "Literature and Intellectual Realignments in Quebec," *Québec Studies* 3 (1985): 46.

20. While my focus here is on the feminist movement of the 1970s in Quebec and on those events and perspectives—both cultural and political—that have influenced its outlook and general direction, I do not mean to suggest that the women's movement in Quebec was nonexistent before this time. Women activists had played significant roles in the political debates and proposed social reforms in Quebec during the nineteenth and early twentieth centuries as well. For further discussion of their contributions, see the excellent collection of essays edited by Marie Lavigne and Yolande Pinard in *Les Femmes dans la société québécoise* (Montreal: Boréal Express, 1977).

21. See Véronique O'Leary and Louise Toupin, eds., *Québécoises Deboutte!*, vol. 1 (Montreal: Remue-ménage, 1982), 27. This is a volume of republished issues from the leftist feminist newspaper of the same name that the *Centre des femmes* published from 1972 to 1975. *Québécoises deboutte* translates as "Quebec women arise" (literally, "Up on your feet!"), but there is also a linguistic play here with the word *debout*, an adverb that has only one neutral form in French, but which the authors of the slogan chose to mark in the feminine with a typical feminine ending, *tte*. This change at the end of the word also forces the French speaker to pronounce the final consonant *t*, which in standard French is normally silent, giving the word considerably more linguistic force. Moreover, in Quebec an *e* is sometimes added to the word in colloquial speech (*deboute*). Thus, the *tte* ending in *Québécoises Deboutte!* valorizes not only the feminine linguistic form, but also the Québécois language as opposed to more standardized French. In her own writing, Nicole Brossard makes frequent feminist use of the mute *e* at the end of words in the feminine to draw our attention to either the erasure or the self-conscious affirmation of the feminine as well as to the sexual politics at work in French grammar.

22. Madeleine Gagnon, "Mon Corps dans l'écriture" in *La Venue à l'écriture* (Paris: Union Générale d'Editions, 1977), 64. Subsequent references to this edition will appear parenthetically in the text.

23. See O'Leary and Toupin, 76–77.

24. Diane Lamoureux, *Fragments et collages: essai sur le féminisme québécois des années 70* (Montreal: Remue-ménage, 1986), 106–9.

25. In one of the first important feminist novels to emerge in Quebec in the early 1970s, Hélène Ouvrard develops this analogy of women's spatial "territory" and her sexual difference. See Hélène Ouvrard, *Le Corps étranger* (Montreal: Jour, 1973).

26. Lamoureux, 121. A telling example of the contradictions in the feminist politics of a number of women's groups inspired by the nationalist project at this time was a situation reported by Janet Kask concerning the FLF's change of attitude about counseling English-speaking women on abortion: "The situation deteriorated last fall when a political split at the Women's Centre on Ste. Famille St., where counseling was done by French-speaking and English-speaking women's liberation groups, resulted in a French-only policy. A woman from the Front de Libération de la Femme which runs the relocated service downtown, assured me that any woman will get counseling if she speaks French or brings along a translator." See Janet Kask, "Abortion in Quebec," in *MOTHER Was Not a Person*, ed. Margaret Andersen (Montreal: Black Rose Books, 1972), 157.

27. Francine Fournier, "Quebec Women and the Parti Québécois," in *Quebec and the Parti Québécois,* ed. Marlene Dixon and Susanne Jonas (San Francisco: Synthesis, 1978), 60.

28. In the case of the actual proposed legislation on maternity leaves, however, the Parti Québécois reduced the original amount of financial support it sought to make available. See the discussion of "Les Femmes et le P.Q." ("Women and the P.Q.") presented by Michèle Jean and Nicole Brossard in the December 1976 issue of *Les Têtes de Pioche,* reprinted in 1980 (Montreal: Remue-ménage, 1980), 73.

29. Dumont et al., 494.

30. For an overview of recent developments in language law legislation in Quebec, see Marc V. Levine, "Language Policy and Quebec's *visage français:* New Directions in *la question linguistique,*" *Québec Studies* 8 (1989): 1–16. For a general overview of Quebec's language policies since 1977, see Michel Plourde, *La Politique linguistique du Québec (1977–1987)* (Quebec: Institut québécois de recherche sur la culture, 1988).

31. See Sylvain Massé, "Le Déclin de l'empire démographique québécois," *Québec Studies* 8 (1989): 111–18.

32. During its twelve years in print, *La Barre du jour* published fifty-seven issues. For an informative discussion of the history and evolution of *La Barre du jour* and its sequel, *La Nouvelle Barre du jour,* see the special issue devoted to it in *Voix et images* 10.2 (1985).

33. See "Politiques éditoriales publiées hors BJ/NBJ et inédites," *Voix et images* 10.2 (1985): 44.

34. *Parti pris* enjoyed considerable political and literary influence during the mid-1960s and brought together the writings of left-wing intellectuals (poets, novelists, political activists) around the themes of nationalism, socialism, and revolution.

35. As Louise Forsyth notes, "Brossard shared the immediate socio-political goals of the *Parti pris* generation and was also in agreement with many of its views and priorities: nationalism must confront the problems of the present and make an absolute break with past traditions; analysis is essential to any effective form of political action; a people alienated from its language is without the means to envisage and affirm its freedom and autonomy; the real problem is interiorized fear and defeat." See Forsyth, "Beyond the Myths and Fictions of Traditionalism and Nationalism: The Political in the Work of Nicole Brossard," in *Traditionalism, Nationalism, and Feminism: Women Writers of Quebec,* ed. Paula Gilbert Lewis (Westport, Conn.: Greenwood Press, 1985), 159.

36. Nicole Brossard in an interview, "Ce que pouvait être, ici, une avant-garde," *Voix et images* 10.2 (1985): 71.

37. Jean-François Lyotard, *The Postmodern Condition: A Report on Knowledge,* trans. Geoff Bennington and Brian Massumi (Minneapolis: University of Minnesota Press, 1984).

38. Alice Jardine, *Gynesis: Configurations of Woman and Modernity* (Ithaca, N.Y.: Cornell University Press, 1985), 24.

39. Nicole Brossard, *Double Impression* (Montreal: L'Hexagone, 1984), 34–36.

40. Nicole Brossard, in an excerpt from a political editorial published outside *La Barre du jour.* See *Voix et images* 10.2 (1985): 45.

41. Mary Jacobus, *Reading Woman: Essays in Feminist Criticism* (New York: Columbia University Press, 1986), 290.

42. Haeck traces the origins of the independent stance of *modernité* back to the expression of nationalist sentiment in the early part of the century: "Modernity begins here [in Quebec] in 1925 with the text of Marie-Victorin, 'The Province of Quebec, Country to Discover and to Conquer,' in which Marie-Victorin criticizes the Québécois for their lack of interest in the 'contemporary scientific movement': 'We will only be a true nation when we cease being at the mercy of foreign capital, of foreign experts, of foreign intellectuals: only at the moment when we will be masters first by our knowledge, then by the physical possession of the resources of our land, our fauna, our flora.' " See Philippe Haeck, *La Table d'écriture: Poéthique et modernité* (Montreal: VLB Editeur, 1984), 345.

43. See Frederic Jameson's foreword to Lyotard, *Postmodern Condition,* xvi–xvii.

44. Toril Moi, *French Feminist Thought* (New York: Basil Blackwell, 1987), 12.

45. Several recent critical studies have suggested, however, that in Que-

bec the taste for the modern has had its roots in the important cultural space a number of surrealists occupied in the francophone province during the 1940s and 1950s. See, in this regard, André-G. Bourassa's *Surréalisme et littérature québécoise: Histoire d'une révolution culturelle* (Montreal: Les Herbes Rouges, 1986) and Paul-Emile Borduas' surrealist manifesto, *Refus global* (Montreal: Parti pris, 1977).

46. These characteristics of the postmodern perspective along with others are discussed by Ihab Hassan in *The Postmodern Turn: Essays in Postmodern Theory and Culture* (Columbus: Ohio State University Press, 1987).

47. Yvan Lamonde appears to agree with this somewhat loose distinction between *modernité* and *postmodernité* in Quebec. See Lamonde's brief article, "La Modernité au Québec: pour une histoire des brèches," in *Modernité/ Postmodernité du roman contemporain,* Cahiers du département d'études littéraires, no. 11, ed. Madeleine Frédéric and Jacques Allard (Montreal: Univérsité du Québec à Montréal, 1987), 188.

48. Linda Hutcheon, *A Poetics of Postmodernism: History, Theory, Fiction* (New York: Routledge, 1988), 209.

49. See Janet Paterson, "A Poetics of Transformation: Yolande Villemaire's *La Vie en prose,*" in *A Mazing Space: Writing Canadian Women Writing,* ed. Shirley Neuman and Smaro Kamboureli (Edmonton, Alberta: Longspoon/NeWest, 1986), 322–23.

50. For an inside and somewhat caustic view of the *modernité/postmodernité* debate and the institutionalization of modernity as a cultural concept in Quebec, see Pierre Milot's *Camera obscura du postmodernisme* (Montreal: L'Hexagone, 1988).

51. Terry Eagleton, *Against the Grain* (London: Verso Press, 1986), 140.

52. France Théoret, "Writing in the Feminine: Voicing Consensus, Practicing Difference," in *A Mazing Space: Writing Canadian Women Writing,* ed. Shirley Neuman and Smaro Kamboureli, trans. A. J. Holden Verburg, (Edmonton, Alberta: Longspoon/NeWest, 1986), 362.

53. See, for example, Pierre Nepveu, "BJ/NBJ: difficile modernité," *Voix et images* 10.2 (1985): 164.

54. France Théoret, "Le Fantasme de la BJ, c'est la théorie," *Voix et images* 10.2 (1985): 89.

55. Susan Suleiman raises a similar question in a provocative article dealing with the father-son drama in Georges Bataille's pornographic writing: "Is there a model of textuality possible," she asks, "that would not necessarily play out, in discourse, the eternal Oedipal drama of transgression and the Law—a drama which always, ultimately, ends up maintaining the latter?" See Susan Rubin Suleiman, "Pornography, Transgression, and the Avant-Garde: Bataille's *Story of the Eye,*" in *The Poetics of Gender,* ed. Nancy K. Miller (New York: Columbia University Press, 1986), 132.

56. This particular question continues to perplex feminist writers like France Théoret, whose comments in 1982 suggest that modernity's inclination to reverse

the system of logocentrism and reclaim the mother as the site of civilization's origin still flounders in the midst of the same dualism it has repeatedly vowed to overturn. Feminist writers who have privileged the mother have at times been the subject of similar criticisms. See France Théoret, "La Mère peut-elle être moderne?" *La Nouvelle Barre du jour* 116 (1982): 47–50.

57. Louise Dupré, "From Experimentation to Experience: Québécois Modernity in the Feminine," in *A Mazing Space: Writing Canadian Women Writing*, ed. Shirley Neuman and Smaro Kamboureli (Edmonton, Alberta: Longspoon/NeWest, 1986), 357–8.

58. Théoret, "Writing in the feminine," 363.

59. Lamoureux, 125.

60. Jean Royer, "Notre Corps d'écriture" (interview with Louky Bersianik), in *Ecrivains contemporains: Entretiens I: 1976–1979* (Montreal: L'Hexagone, 1982), 73.

61. Michèle Jean, "La Gauche et le féminisme au Québec," in *Les Têtes de Pioche* (Montreal: Remue-ménage, 1980), 162.

62. Armande Saint-Jean, "Préface," in *Les Têtes de Pioche* (Montreal: Remue-ménage, 1980), 8.

63. Nicole Brossard, "La Vie privée est politique," in *Les Têtes de Pioche* (Montreal: Remue-ménage, 1980), 21.

64. Monique Roy, "Madeleine Gagnon," *Les Cahiers de la femme/Women's Studies* 1.1 (1978): 5.

65. Mary Daly, *Gyn/Ecology: The Metaethics of Radical Feminism* (Boston: Beacon Press, 1978), 380.

66. Audre Lorde, *Sister Outsider* (Trumansburg, N.Y.: Crossing Press, 1984), 37.

67. France Théoret, *Entre raison et déraison* (Montreal: Les Herbes Rouges, 1987), 149.

68. Hélène Cixous, "The Laugh of the Medusa," trans. Keith Cohen and Paula Cohen, *Signs* 1.4 (1976): 879. Originally published as "Le Rire de la Méduse," *L'Arc* 61 (1975): 39–54.

69. Cixous, "Medusa," 875.

70. Luce Irigaray, *Speculum of the Other Woman*, trans. Gillian C. Gill (Ithaca, N.Y.: Cornell University Press, 1985), 142.

71. Luce Irigaray, *This Sex Which Is Not One*, trans. Catherine Porter (Ithaca, N.Y.: Cornell University Press, 1985). Origininally published as *Ce Sexe qui n'en est pas un* (Paris: Minuit, 1977).

72. Cixous, "Medusa."

73. Verena Andermatt Conley explains Cixous' adapted use of Lacan's notion of the imaginary in the following terms: "Writing takes place at the level of the imaginary, a Lacanian term Cixous borrows without further elaboration. Making use of Lacan's distinctions between the imaginary and the symbolic, she privileges the former, the realm of identification and doubling. Any relation between two things is necessarily imaginary. Fiction

is linked to the imaginary and the Ego as a location of the subject's primary and secondary identifications. As an imaginary nature, the Ego is a function of unawareness that makes ideology and knowledge possible. Hence the importance for those in power to control the production of images, the imaginaries of others. Characterization in fiction is always based on restriction of the imaginary. . . . Against literary production that sustains the status quo, Cixous argues for a new kind of production, a writing from the imaginary, with its infinite multiplicity of identifications precluding a stable subject. She urges for figuration, not characterization, with possibilities of reading in different directions." See Verena Andermatt Conley, *Hélène Cixous: Writing the Feminine* (Lincoln: University of Nebraska Press, 1984), 25–26.

74. Brossard, *The Aerial Letter*, 76.

75. As Cixous envisions it, this writing would be "the inscription of something that carries in everyday language the determination of the provisional name of femininity, and which refers precisely to something that I would like to define in the way of an economy, of production, of bodily effects of which one can see a great number of traits." See Conley, 131.

76. Brossard, *The Aerial Letter*, 67.

77. Louky Bersianik, "Aristotle's Lantern: An Essay on Criticism," in *A Mazing Space: Writing Canadian Women Writing,* ed. Shirley Neuman and Smaro Kamboureli, trans. A. J. Holden Verburg (Edmonton, Alberta: Longspoon/NeWest, 1986), 46.

78. Louky Bersianik, "Comment naître femme sans le devenir," in *La Nouvelle Barre du jour* 172 (1986): 64.

79. Brossard, *The Aerial Letter*, 42.

80. Madeleine Gagnon, Préface, *Cyprine,* by Denise Boucher (Montreal: L'Aurore, 1978), 9–10.

81. Louky Bersianik, *Maternative: Les Pré-Ancyl* (Montreal: VLB Editeur, 1980), 13. Subsequent references to this edition will appear parenthetically in the text.

82. Marcelle Brisson, "Femme et écriture," *Arcade* 11 (1986): 27.

83. Brossard, *The Aerial Letter*, 78. This phrase originally appeared in *Amantes* (Montreal: Quinze, 1980), 49.

84. Louky Bersianik, *Axes et eau: Poèmes de 'La bonne chanson'* (Montreal: VLB Editeur, 1984), 205.

85. Shirley Neuman, "Importing Difference," in *A Mazing Space: Writing Canadian Women Writing,* ed. Shirley Newman and Smaro Kamboureli (Edmonton, Alberta: Longspoon/NeWest, 1986), 400.

86. Irigaray, *This Sex Which Is Not One,* 23, 28.

87. Christiane Makward, "To Be or Not to Be . . . A Feminist Speaker," trans. Marlène Barsoum, Alice Jardine, and Hester Eisenstein, in *The Future of Difference,* ed. Hester Eisenstein and Alice Jardine (New Brunswick, N.J.: Rutgers University Press), 100.

88. This move toward privileging the biological as the creative source of

écriture féminine (particularly the centrality of the maternal body in Cixous' early work) has been hotly debated by a number of American critics, including Ann Rosalind Jones and Domna Stanton, who have pointed out some of the philosophical as well as political pitfalls of valorizing difference by means of what appears to be an essentialist argument. See Ann Rosalind Jones, "Writing the Body: Toward an Understanding of *l'écriture féminine,*" in *Feminist Criticism and Social Change,* ed. Judith Newton and Deborah Rosenfelt (New York: Methuen, 1985), 86–101. See also Domna C. Stanton, "Language and Revolution: The Franco-American Dis-Connection" in *The Future of Difference,* ed. Hester Eisenstein and Alice Jardine (New Brunswick, N.J.: Rutgers University Press, 1985), 73–87 and "Difference on Trial: A Critique of the Maternal Metaphor in Cixous, Irigaray, and Kristeva," in *The Poetics of Gender,* ed. Nancy K. Miller (New York: Columbia University Press, 1986), 157–82. For some probing questions on the distinctions between masculine and feminine writing in the Canadian context, see Donna Bennet, "Naming the Way Home," in *A Mazing Space: Writing Canadian Women Writing,* ed. Shirley Neuman and Smaro Kamboureli (Edmonton, Alberta: Longspoon/NeWest, 1986), 228–45.

89. Adrienne Rich, *Of Woman Born: Motherhood as Experience and Institution* (New York: Norton, 1976), 21.

90. Théoret, *Entre raison et déraison,* 152.

91. Brossard, *The Aerial Letter,* 98.

92. Théoret, "Writing in the feminine," 364.

2. Nicole Brossard: Beyond Modernity or Writing in the Third Dimension

1. I borrow the term from Paul de Man, *Blindness and Insight* (Minneapolis: University of Minnesota Press, 1971), 147.

2. For her thoughts on the innovations and traps of *modernité,* see Nicole Brossard, "L'Epreuve de la modernité ou/et les preuves de modernité," *La Nouvelle Barre du jour* 90–91 (1980): 57–63.

3. Haeck, *La Table d'écriture,* 165.

4. See Claude Beausoleil's "Présentation critique," *Un livre,* by Nicole Brossard (Montreal: Quinze, 1980).

5. See Nathalie Sarraute, *L'Ere du soupçon* (Paris: Gallimard, 1956).

6. Nicole Brossard, *Picture Theory* (Montreal: Nouvelle Optique, 1985), 51. Subsequent references to this edition will appear parenthetically in the text.

7. See "La NBJ: le lieu du risque" (interview with Hugues Corriveau, Louise Cotnoir, Lise Guèvremont), *Voix et images* 10.2 (1985): 104.

8. Maurice Blanchot, *Le Livre à venir* (Paris: Gallimard, 1959), 303.

Blanchot's influence was extensive among Quebec's literary avant-garde during the 1960s.

   9. Brossard, "Ce que pouvait être, ici, une avant-garde," 80.

   10. Nicole Brossard, *Le Centre blanc* (Montreal: L'Hexagone, 1978), 89. This edition includes Brossard's major volumes of poetry published from 1965 to 1975. All further references to poems originally published in separate editions of *L'Echo bouge beau, Suite logique,* and *Le Centre blanc* will be to this edition and will be included in the text.

   11. Nepveu, "BJ/NBJ: difficile modernité," 163. This essay indicates the extent to which Nepveu is ill at ease with the amount of critical attention already devoted to Brossard and others affiliated with the literature of *la modernité* and *la nouvelle écriture*. He characterizes most readings of Brossard's work as "euphoric and romantic" (161).

   12. Brossard, *Double Impression,* 32.

   13. André Roy, "La Fiction vive: entretien avec Nicole Brossard sur sa prose," *Journal of Canadian Fiction* 25–26 (1979): 31.

   14. Suzanne Lamy, *d'elles* (Montreal: L'Hexagone, 1979), 56.

   15. Nicole Brossard, *Amantes* (Montreal: Quinze, 1980), 29. Subsequent references to this edition will appear parenthetically in the text.

   16. Louise Dupré, "Les Utopies du réel," *La Nouvelle Barre du jour* 118–19 (1980): 86.

   17. Nicole Brossard, *Un livre* (Montreal: Quinze, 1980), 21. *Un livre* was first published in Montreal in 1970 by Editions du Jour. Subsequent references to the 1980 edition will appear parenthetically in the text.

   18. Nicole Brossard, *A Book,* trans. Larry Shouldice (Toronto: Coach House Press, 1976), 21. Subsequent references to this edition will appear parenthetically in the text.

   19. Roland Barthes, *The Pleasure of the Text,* trans. Richard Miller (New York: Hill and Wang, 1975), 17. Brossard herself cites this passage from Barthes: "Le plaisir du texte, c'est ce moment où mon corps va suivre ses propres idées—car mon corps n'a pas les mêmes idées que moi," in *Le Plaisir du texte* (Paris: Seuil, 1973), 30. See Brossard, "L'Avenir de la littérature québécoise," 391.

   20. Louise Forsyth, "Regards, Reflets, Reflux, Réflections: exploration de l'oeuvre de Nicole Brossard," *La Nouvelle Barre du jour* 118–19 (1982): 221. Forsyth observes: "In order to celebrate her solidarity with other women more effectively, she watches herself write" (22).

   21. "Un livre à venir: Rencontre avec Nicole Brossard," *Voix et images* 3.1 (1977): 9.

   22. Although the desiring body is central to the kind of writing that interests Cixous—*l'écriture féminine* or feminine writing—the biological sex of the writer is not particularly significant as Toril Moi points out in her brief overview of Cixous' theoretical work. See Moi's chapter on Cixous in *Sexual/Textual Politics: Feminist Literary Theory* (New York: Methuen, 1985).

Yet Cixous does privilege the female body, and the maternal body in particular, in her own writing, arguing that woman's body is "more body" and is therefore capable of producing more writing (*écriture*): "More so than men who are coaxed toward social success, toward sublimation, women are body. More body, hence more writing" ("Medusa," 886).

23. Nicole Brossard, *French Kiss* (Montreal: Jour, 1974), 7. Subsequent references to this edition will appear parenthetically in the text.

24. Nicole Brossard, *French Kiss or A Pang's Progress,* trans. Patricia Claxton (Toronto: Coach House Press, 1986), 11. Subsequent references to this edition will appear parenthetically in the text.

25. For a comparative discussion of contemporary Quebec women writers on the city, see my article, "Spatial Poetics, Spatial Politics: Quebec Feminists on the City and the Countryside," *American Review of Canadian Studies* 12.1 (1982): 1–9.

26. Brossard, "La Femme et l'écriture," *Liberté* 18.4–5 (1976): 13. This passage was referred to and translated by Louise H. Forsyth in her introductory essay, "Errant and Air-born in the City," *The Aerial Letter,* by Brossard, trans. Marlene Wildeman (Toronto: Coach House Press, 1978), 12.

27. *L'Amèr* is another example of Brossard's continual play with words; it suggests *la mer* (the sea), *la mère* (the mother), and the adjective *amer* (bitter, sour, harsh); *ou le chapitre effrité* translates less problematically as "or the disintegrating chapter." As Barbara Godard points out in the preface to her own translation, the silent (unpronounced or mute) *e* at the end of *mère* has been removed in Brossard's text "to underline the process of articulating this silence" (*These Our Mothers or: The Disintegrating Chapter* [Toronto: Coach House Quebec Translations, 1983], vii).

28. Irigaray, *Speculum,* 143.

29. Louise Forsyth is correct to point to the ways in which the word *la mère* is linked through its sound and meanings to other words such as: *la mer, l'amour, la larme, la matière, la matrice, l'imaginaire, l'amer.* See Louise Forsyth, "L'Ecriture au féminin: *L'Euguélionne* de Louky Bersianik, *L'Absent aigu* de Geneviève Amyot, *L'Amèr* de Nicole Brossard," *Journal of Canadian Fiction* 25–26 (1979): 210.

30. Nicole Brossard, *L'Amèr ou le chapitre effrité* (Montreal: Quinze, 1977), 32. Subsequent references to this edition will appear parenthetically in the text.

31. Brossard, *These Our Mothers or: The Disintegrating Chapter,* trans. Barbara Godard (Toronto: Coach House Quebec Translations, 1983), 34. Barbara Godard has attempted to do justice to Brossard's frequent plays with double meanings by including them in her translation. Such word plays and multiple meanings are indicated by the /. Subsequent references to this edition will appear parenthetically in the text.

32. The absent vowels in Brossard's *m're* and in Godard's translation, "m ther," are intentional; they serve to underscore the mute *e*, the absent

(missing) sound that is frequently found at the end of feminine adjectives in French. This linguistic strategy on the level of the phoneme forces the reader to consider the sound that has been left out (repressed).

33. Nicole Brossard, *Lovhers,* trans. Barbara Godard (Montreal: Guernica, 1986), 17. Subsequent references to this edition will appear parenthetically in the text.

34. Nicole Brossard, *Le Sens apparent* (Paris: Flammarion, 1980), 14.

35. Daly, *Gyn/Ecology,* 391–92.

36. Lorde, 55.

37. Quoted from the 1983 English translation, *These Our Mothers,* 45.

38. Brossard, "Entretien avec Nicole Brossard sur *Picture Theory,*" *La Nouvelle Barre du jour* 118–19 (1982): 191.

39. Jane Gallop, *The Daughter's Seduction: Feminism and Psychoanalysis* (Ithaca, N.Y.: Cornell University Press, 1982), 61.

40. Brossard, *The Aerial Letter,* 75–76.

41. Jardine, *Gynesis,* 25.

42. Nicole Brossard, "L'Angle tramé du désir," in *La Théorie, un dimanche* (Montreal: Remue-ménage, 1988), 23.

43. In an interview shortly after the publication of *Picture Theory,* Brossard explains how the notion of "picture theory" already fascinated her in *Amantes* because of its double emphasis on image and theory. After reading Wittgenstein, she was further drawn to the term to describe her writing at the time. Brossard translates Wittgenstein's use of the term as *tableau de réalité* or as *peinture de la réalité* (a painting or portrait of reality). See "Entretien avec Nicole Brossard sur *Picture Theory,*" 177–78.

44. Brossard, *The Aerial Letter,* 100.

45. Louise Forsyth has also written an important article on the concepts of space and motion in Brossard's work. See Louise Forsyth, "Destructuring Formal Space/Accelerating Motion in the Work of Nicole Brossard," in *A Mazing Space: Writing Canadian Women Writing,* ed. Shirley Neuman and Smaro Kamboureli (Edmonton, Alberta: Longspoon/NeWest, 1986), 334–44.

46. Nicole Brossard, *Le Désert mauve* (Montreal: L'Hexagone, 1987), 11, 181. Subsequent references to this edition will appear parenthetically in the text.

47. The term is borrowed from Guy Scarpetta in his study of the postmodern era, which he characterizes as a heterogeneous spectacle of competing values, proliferating codes, and erratic movements. See Guy Scarpetta, *L'Impureté* (Paris: Grasset & Fasquelle, 1985).

48. See Richard Rhodes, *The Making of the Atomic Bomb* (New York: Simon and Schuster, 1987), 675–76.

49. Mélanie is linguistically linked to the night on several occasions, in the English phrase, "Of course Mélanie is night teen" (50), and in her mother's alliterative explanation, "Mélanie, mais la nuit" (31).

50. Patrocinio P. Schweickart, "Reading Ourselves: Toward a Feminist Theory of Reading," in *Gender and Reading: Essays on Readers, Texts, and Contexts,* ed. Elizabeth A. Flynn and Patrocinio P. Schweickart (Baltimore: Johns Hopkins University Press, 1986), 31–62.

51. In *"Le Desért Mauve* de Nicole Brossard, on l'indicible référent," an unpublished paper delivered at the American Council for Québec Studies in Quebec City, 23 Oct. 1988, Henri Servan also noted the extent to which the sound of *or* (gold), which he links to light, circulates in words like *Lorna, Laure,* etc.

52. Suzanne Lamy, *Quand je lis, je m'invente* (Montreal: L'Hexagone, 1984), 14.

53. Brossard, "L'Angle tramé du désir," 25.

54. Brossard, *Amantes,* 96.

3. *Madeleine Gagnon: The Solidarity and Solitude of Women's Words*

1. See, for example, Jovette Marchessault's less than friendly review of *Retailles,* " 'Retraite' par Soeur Madeleine Gagnon et Soeur Denise Boucher," *Les Têtes de Pioche* (Montreal: Remue-ménage, 1980), 130; André Vanasse's lukewarm review of *Lueur* entitled "Nouveaux romans?" in *Lettres québécoises* 15 (1979): 14–16; Lucie Lequin's recognition of Gagnon's contribution to *l'écriture féminine* in "Les Femmes québécoises ont inventé leurs paroles," *American Review of Canadian Studies* 9.2 (1979): 113–24; and Jean Royer's appreciation of *Lueur* in "Regards sur la littérature québécoise des années 70," *Le Devoir,* 21 Nov. 1981.

2. Gabrielle Frémont, "Madeleine Gagnon: Du politique à l'intime," *Voix et images* 8.1 (1982): 31.

3. Gagnon, "Mon Corps dans l'écriture." In addition to its appearance in *La Venue à l'écriture* in 1977, this essay along with *Pour les femmes et tous les autres, Poélitique, Antre,* and several other texts have been republished in *Autographie: 1. Fictions* (Montreal, VLB Editeur, 1982).

4. Denise Boucher became a household name in Quebec in 1976 when her play *Les Fées ont soif* was momentarily banned from a reputable Montreal theatre for its "disrespectful" representation of the Virgin Mary on stage— a clear indication in the minds of many Quebec feminists that the clergy's influence in the province was still substantial, despite the move toward secularization initiated in the early years of The Quiet Revolution. See Denise Boucher, *Les Fées ont soif* (Montreal: Intermède, 1978).

5. Isabelle de Courtivron and Elaine Marks, eds., *New French Feminisms* (Amherst: University of Massachusetts Press, 1980).

6. Michèle Barrett, "Ideology and the Cultural Production of Gender," in *Feminist Criticism and Social Change,* ed. Judith Newton and Deborah Rosenfelt (New York: Methuen, 1985), 83.

7. The editor, Yvon Boucher, published two issues of *Le Québec littéraire,* one in 1974 and one in 1976.

8. Madeleine Gagnon, *Poélitique* (Montreal: Les Herbes Rouges, 1975). No pagination in this text.

9. Madeleine Gagnon, *Pour les femmes et tous les autres* (Montreal: L'Aurore, 1974), 18. Subsequent references to this edition will appear parenthetically in the text.

10. Philippe Haeck, Review of *Pour les femmes et tous les autres, Le Devoir,* 22 March 1975.

11. Madeleine Gagnon, "La Femme et l'écriture," *Liberté* 18.4–5 (1976): 250.

12. Denise Boucher and Madeleine Gagnon, *Retailles: complaintes politiques* (Montreal: L'Etincelle, 1977), 24. Subsequent references to this edition will appear parenthetically in the text.

13. Madeleine Gagnon, "Ce que je veux s'écrire ne peut pas m'écrire autrement," *Les Nouvelles littéraires,* 26 May 1976, 19.

14. Lamy, *d'elles,* 48.

15. Conley, 64.

16. It should be noted, however, that while the most internationally well-known women writers from Quebec today remain Anne Hébert and Marie-Claire Blais, their literary projects are not linked in any fundamental way to the experimental project of *écriture au féminin,* despite important feminist themes in their work and an interest in narrative experimentation.

17. Lacan reasons as follows: "The phallus is the privileged signifier of that mark [of man's relation as a subject to the signifier] in which the role of the logos is joined with the advent of desire. It can be said that this signifier is chosen because it is the most tangible element in the real of sexual copulation, and also the most symbolic in the literal (typographical) sense of the term, since it is equivalent there to the (logical) copula. It might also be said that, by virtue of its turgidity, it is the image of the vital flow as it is transmitted in generation." See Jacques Lacan, *Ecrits: A Selection,* trans. Alan Sheridan (New York: Norton, 1977), 287.

18. I borrow this delightful double entendre from Jane Gallop's witty and shrewd discussion of the disproportionate signifying function of the phallus both in Lacan's discourse and in his public appearances. See Jane Gallop, *The Daughter's Seduction,* 15–42 in particular.

19. "Language is a skin: I rub my language against the other. It is as if I had words instead of fingers, or fingers at the tip of my words. My language trembles with desire." See Roland Barthes, *A Lover's Discourse,* trans. Richard Howard (New York: Hill and Wang, 1978), 73.

20. Susan Rubin Suleiman, "Writing and Motherhood," in *The (M)other Tongue: Essays in Feminist Psychoanalytic Interpretation,* ed. Shirley Nelson Garner, Claire Kahane, Madelon Sprengnether (Ithaca, N.Y.: Cornell University Press, 1985), 358.

21. Makward, "To Be or Not to Be," 96.

22. Jean Royer, "Dans l'eau des mots," in his republished interviews, *Ecrivains contemporains: Entretiens I: 1976–1979* (Montreal: L'Hexagone, 1982), 80.

23. Madeleine Gagnon, *Lueur: roman archéologique* (Montreal: VLB Editeur, 1979), 15. Subsequent references to this edition will appear parenthetically in the text.

24. Madeleine Gagnon, *Antre* (Montreal: Les Herbes Rouges, 1978), 46. In the process of recalling her own liquid memories, Gagnon remembers the many Ophelias who have drowned in silence for the sake of male mythology. It is no longer Noah, she suggests, who can save women from the *déluge,* but women themselves. We are reminded here of another important Quebec writer, Hélène Ouvrard, whose novel *La Noyante* also exposes the duplicity of the Ophelia archetype, which lures women into silence and suicide. See Hélène Ouvrard, *La Noyante* (Montreal: Québec/ Amérique, 1980).

25. I borrow the term from French writer Chantal Chawaf in "La Chair linguistique," *Les Nouvelles littéraires,* 26 May 1976.

26. Louky Bersianik, *Les Agénésies du vieux monde* (Montreal: L'Intégrale, 1982), 19.

27. See Susan Gubar, " 'The Blank Page' and the Issues of Female Creativity," *Critical Inquiry* 8.2 (1981): 248.

28. Jovette Marchessault, *La Mère des herbes* (Montreal: Quinze, 1980). For a discussion of the grandmother figure as exemplary of feminine power in Marchessault's novel, see the first part of my contribution to "Inscriptions of the Feminine: A Century of Women Writing in Quebec," *American Review of Canadian Studies* 15.4 (1985): 363–88 (written in collaboration with Mary Jean Green and Paula Gilbert Lewis).

29. See Cécile Cloutier, "UTINAM!," *La Barre du jour* 56–57 (1977): 107.

30. In an interview with the Quebec feminist magazine *La Vie en rose,* Gagnon comments on the length of *Lueur,* emphasizing once again the relationship between the demands of motherhood in her own life and the time allowed for writing, a relationship she says directly influenced the nature of her writing practice: "The only year I wrote a real novel [*Lueur*] was because I had a sabbatical leave. Otherwise, fragments because of the children. The duration of a poem had the duration of the interim between two feeding-times." See "De la chair à la langue," *La Vie en rose,* May 1983, 55.

31. See Madeleine Gagnon's interview with Jean Royer, "Dans l'eau des mots," 81.

32. Madeleine Gagnon, *Au coeur de la lettre* (Montreal: VLB Editeur, 1982), 20. Subsequent references to this edition will appear parenthetically in the text.

33. Lucie Robert and Ruth Major, "Percer le mur du son du sens, une entrevue avec Madeleine Gagnon," *Voix et images* 8.1 (1982): 19.

34. This comment was made with respect to the diaries of Anaïs Nin, but it is equally applicable to the genre of women's letters as well. See Rachel Blau DuPlessis et al., "For the Etruscans: Sexual Difference and Artistic Production—The Debate over a Female Aesthetic," in *The Future of Difference,* ed. Hester Eisenstein and Alice Jardine (New Brunswick, N.J.: Rutgers University Press, 1985), 141.

35. Jane Gallop, "Annie Leclerc Writing A Letter with Vermeer," in *The Poetics of Gender,* ed. Nancy K. Miller (New York: Columbia University Press, 1986), 139.

36. Annie Leclerc, "La Lettre d'amour" in *La Venue à l'écriture* (Paris: Union Générale d'Editions, 1977), 119.

37. Madeleine Gagnon, *La Lettre infinie* (Montreal: VLB Editeur, 1984), 48. Subsequent references to this edition will appear parenthetically in the text.

38. In an address given in 1983 on the relationship between writing and love, Gagnon describes writing as a "transitional, transactional object between the presence of love and its absence. . . . Writing is a conjuration of the fate of lost love and the repetitive promise of its eternal return." See Gagnon, "Ecrire l'amour," in *Ecrire l'amour: communications de la onzième rencontre québécoise internationale des écrivains* (Montreal: L'Hexagone, 1984), 68.

39. See the discussion of Bersianik's *L'Euguélionne* in chapter 4.

40. Suleiman has noted a similar positioning of Irigaray's female speaker addressing the male philosopher and male lover in *Amante marine* (1980) and in *Passions élémentaires* (1982). Despite the accusatory tone in Irigaray's texts, Suleiman argues that the use of the familiar *tu* form of address "suggests a recognition of the other as a possible interlocutor." See Susan Rubin Suleiman, "(Re)writing the Body: The Politics and Poetics of Female Eroticism," in *The Female Body in Western Culture,* ed. Susan Rubin Suleiman (Cambridge: Harvard University Press, 1986), 15.

4. *Louky Bersianik: Language, Myth, and the Remapping of Herstory*

1. Meese, 5.

2. This term derives from the title of a recent essay collection whose contributors include, among others, Nicole Brossard, Louky Bersianik, and Mary Daly. See *L'Emergence d'une culture au féminin,* ed. Marisa Zavalloni (Montreal: Saint-Martin, 1987).

3. Bersianik, *Les Agénésies,* 20.

4. I borrow this expression from Cheris Kramarae's article, "Proprietors of Language," in *Women and Language in Literature and Society*, ed. Sally McConnell-Ginet, Ruth Borker, and Nelly Furman (New York: Praeger, 1980), 58–68.

5. See Jardine, *Gynesis*.

6. Hutcheon defines "ex-centrism" in postmodern art as the displacement known to "those who are marginalized by a dominant ideology," 35.

7. Martha Noel Evans, *Masks of Tradition: Women and the Politics of Writing in Twentieth-Century France* (Ithaca, N.Y.: Cornell University Press, 1987), 224.

8. Irigaray's notion in *Speculum*.

9. Lillian Smith initially developed the notion of women's lack of loyalty to civilization in her article, "Autobiography as a Dialogue between King and Corpse" (1962), republished in *The Winner Names the Age: A Collection of Writings by Lillian Smith*, ed. Michelle Cliff (New York: Norton, 1978); Adrienne Rich has elaborated on Smith's notion in her essay, "Disloyal to Civilization: Feminism, Racism, Gynephobia," in *On Lies, Secrets, and Silence: Selected Prose 1966–1978* (New York: Norton, 1979), 275–310.

10. In an interview, Bersianik commented on the mixed reception her book received in feminist circles throughout Quebec: "When *L'Euguélionne* appeared in 1976, certain women writers who called themselves feminists and who had access to the media and literary criticism complained about this book on all sorts of grounds: it wasn't Marxist, it wasn't stylishly 'unreadable,' it was too simple, it was too complicated, it was elitist, it was too popular in its appeal, it rejected men, it didn't reject them strongly enough, it was too humorous and therefore not serious enough, etc., etc." See Gould, "Ecrire au féminin," 126.

11. Luce Guilbeault et al., *La Nef des sorcières* (Montreal: Quinze, 1976). A play that includes theatrical monologues written by Luce Guilbeault, Marthe Blackburn, France Théoret, Odette Gagnon, Marie-Claire Blais, Pol Pelletier, and Nicole Brossard, this collaborative effort has enjoyed considerable success and reflects not only the keen interest at the time in collectively designed feminist projects and texts, but also the effective blending of theoretical, theatrical, and everyday concerns.

12. Bersianik, "Louky Bersianik et la mythologie du futur: De la théorie-fiction à l'émergence de la femme positive," *Lettres québécoises* 27 (1982): 64–65.

13. Bersianik, *Axes et Eau*, 147–49.

14. Jennifer Waelti-Walters, "When Caryatids Move: Bersianik's View of Culture," in *A Mazing Space: Writing Canadian Women Writing*, ed. Shirley Neuman and Smaro Kamboureli (Edmonton, Alberta: Longspoon/ NeWest, 1986), 299.

15. Mary Daly, *Beyond God the Father: Toward a Philosophy of Women's Liberation* (Boston: Beacon Press, 1973), especially 100–102.

16. Louky Bersianik, *L'Euguélionne* (Montreal: La Presse, 1976), 390. Subsequent references to this edition will appear parenthetically in the text.

17. Louky Bersianik, *The Euguélionne*, trans. Gerry Denis, Alison Hewitt, Donna Murray, and Martha O'Brien (Victoria: Press Porcépic, 1981), 338. Subsequent references to this edition will appear parenthetically in the text.

18. See Bersianik's discussion of the oppressive authority of male critics in Quebec in "Aristotle's Lantern," especially 40–43.

19. "Louky is the surname my husband gave me at the beginning of our relationship. Even my family calls me Louky which they prefer over Lucile. As for my family name, Durand, it was associated with my books written for children, and then it was my father's name, not mine. In *L'Euguélionne*, there is a very intense search for identity in one of my characters who looks for the name she bore before her marriage. I had thought of taking the name of my mother: Bissonnet, but there again it was a man's name since it was the name of her father. I asked myself: 'Does the name of a woman exist somewhere?' There aren't any, not in a single genealogy. It's always the name of the father (the 'fundamental signifier'!). So I decided to give myself a name so that it would be my very own, to invent it myself. In this way, I alone have it." See her interview, "Louky Bersianik et la mythologie du futur," 62.

20. Raymond Queneau, *Zazie dans le métro* (Paris: Gallimard, 1959).

21. Irigaray, *Speculum*, 47.

22. Irigaray, *Speculum*, 48.

23. Jane Gallop emphasizes the importance of this assertion in *The Daughter's Seduction*, 65.

24. Neuman, "Importing Difference," 394.

25. Louky Bersianik, "Noli mi tangere," *La Barre du jour* 56–57 (1977): 151. Reprinted in *Maternative*.

26. Bersianik, "Aristotle's Lantern," 44.

27. See Monique Wittig and Sande Zeig, *Lesbian Peoples: Material for a Dictionary* (New York: Avon, 1979), originally published in French as *Brouillon pour un dictionnaire des amantes* (Paris: Grasset et Fasquelle, 1976), and Cheris Kramarae and Paula A. Treichler, *A Feminist Dictionary* (Boston: Pandora Press, 1985).

28. Daly, *Gyn/Ecology*.

29. Nancy K. Miller, "Arachnologies: The Woman, The Text, and the Critic," in *The Poetics of Gender*, ed. Nancy K. Miller (New York: Columbia University Press, 1986), 287.

30. Froula uses this phrase to characterize the resisting readings of Beauvoir, Millett, Fetterley, Showalter, and others. See Christine Froula, "When Eve Reads Milton: Undoing the Canonical Economy," in *Canons*, ed. Robert von Hallberg (Chicago: University of Chicago Press, 1983), 151.

31. While French translators have tended to translate the title as *Le Banquet*, a number of American scholars clearly prefer *The Symposium* as a

more accurate rendering of the Greek word. Whatever the merits of either translation, Bersianik has clearly worked in the French tradition with French translations and her use of the image of the banquet and the word play it generates stems from this experience.

32. Bersianik, herself, has acknowledged her intention here in an interview. See "Louky Bersianik et la mythologie du futur," 68.

33. See Luce Irigaray, *Ethique de la différence sexuelle* (Paris: Minuit, 1984), 27.

34. Louky Bersianik, *Le Pique-nique sur l'Acropole* (Montreal: VLB Editeur, 1979), v. Subsequent references to this edition will appear parenthetically in the text.

35. Juliet Mitchell and Jacqueline Rose, eds., *Feminine Sexuality: Jacques Lacan and the école freudienne* (New York: Norton, 1985), especially chapter 6 on "God and the *Jouissance* of The Woman."

36. Bersianik has defended her right to speak out against clitoridectomy, which is still observed in Africa, arguing that female mutilation is unjustifiable in any culture. Simone de Beauvoir took a similar stand on clitoridectomy, despite criticisms from some black women in Europe and North America that white western women have no business speaking for either Third World women or for their cultural practices. Beauvoir countered their criticism with the following argument: "There's a kind of racism, on the contrary, in not wanting to look at these sorts of conditions. . . . Because that means that deep down one doesn't care what happens to little black girls, and there are about thirty thousand a year who undergo excision, and to find that trivial, finally, not to deal with that, that proves that we think that it's fine for them, naturally, we don't want any of it. And it's much more feminist, logical and universal, and not racist, to be involved in these sorts of questions." See Hélène V. Wenzel, "Interview with Simone de Beauvoir," *Yale French Studies* 72 (1987): 15.

37. See Rich, *Of Woman Born* and Daly, *Gyn/Ecology*.

38. Suzanne Lamy made this point in relation to feminist intertextuality in Brossard's *Amantes* and Massé's *Dieu*. See Lamy, *Quand je lis, je m'invente*, 40.

39. Carole Massé, *Dieu* (Montreal: Les Herbes Rouges, 1979).

40. In an overview of postmodern theories, Matei Calinescu notes how "the aesthetics of postmodernism has been described as essentially 'quotationist' or 'citationist,' in clear-cut opposition to the 'minimalist' avant-gardes, which . . . banned reference as 'impure.' " See Matei Calinescu, *Fives Faces of Modernity* (Durham, N.C.: Duke University Press, 1987), 285.

41. Suleiman makes a similar observation about the dynamics of intertextuality as practiced in the works of Cixous and Wittig. See Suleiman, "(Re)Writing the Body," 20.

42. Judith Fetterley, *The Resisting Reader: A Feminist Approach to American Fiction* (Bloomington: Indiana University Press, 1978), xx.

43. Catherine MacKinnon, "Feminism, Marxism, Method, and the State," *Signs* 7.3 (1982): 537.

44. By "transgressive," I mean to suggest the way in which the women's dialogue violates male law and the poetics it has inspired, rather than seeking to replace it with another form of authority.

45. It is worth noting that while mythologists may argue that the Erechtheum was built to celebrate a female deity, Athena, Bersianik contends that Athena, who never recognized her mother, has always been on the side of men and the powers wielded by the male gods. This explains, Bersianik believes, why Athena was so popular in patriarchal Athens.

46. Irigaray, *This Sex Which Is Not One,* 214.

47. Irigaray, *This Sex Which Is Not One,* 141.

48. Ironically, in his introduction to Plato's *Symposium,* Benjamin Jowett argues that "more than any other Platonic work the *Symposium* is Greek both in style and subject, having a beauty 'as of a statue.' " See Benjamin Jowett, "Introduction to *The Symposium*" in *Plato's Dialogues on Love and Friendship* (New York: Heritage Press, 1968), 39.

49. From an interview given to Jean Royer in *Le Devoir,* 24 Nov. 1979. Republished as "Notre Corps d'écriture," in *Ecrivains contemporains: Entretiens I: 1976–1979,* ed. Jean Royer (Montreal, L'Hexagone, 1982), 74.

50. Hélène Cixous, *Souffles* (Paris: Des femmes, 1975).

51. See Cixous' discussion of the "feminine voice," *The Newly Born Woman,* 92–95.

52. This notion of "the gift" is crucial to Cixous' concept of the "feminine" in writing as well and allows her to distinguish between masculine and feminine approaches to writing in terms of the intention of the giver, the implied values affirmed in the act of giving, and the "type of profit the giver draws from the gift" (*The Newly Born Woman,* 87).

53. Grace Stewart, *A New Mythos: The Novel of the Artist as Heroine, 1877–1977* (Montreal: Eden Press Women's Publications, 1981), 46.

54. Linda Gordon, "What's New in Women's History," in *Feminist Studies/Critical Studies,* ed. Teresa de Lauretis (Bloomington: Indiana University Press, 1986), 28.

55. Bersianik, *Les Agénésies,* 21.

56. Bersianik, *Les Agénésies,* 18.

57. Aside from her general interest in Bersianik's work, Mary Daly has been especially influenced by Bersianik's theorizing on women's amnesia and collective need for a sense of themselves in the past. See the numerous references to Bersianik in Daly's *Pure Lust: Elemental Feminist Philosophy* (Boston: Beacon Press, 1984), especially 36, 94.

58. France Théoret, "Eloge de la mémoire des femmes," in *La Théorie, un dimanche* (Montreal: Remue-ménage, 1988), 190.

59. Bersianik, *Les Agénésies,* 22.

60. André Brochu, "Autour d'Alain Grandbois indélébile," *Voix et images* 11.2 (1986): 342.

61. Barthes, *The Pleasure of the Text,* 25. Bersianik also criticizes Nepveu for his use of rigid clerical vocabulary to dismiss *Axes et eau* as a "childish" text. Moreover, the very fact that Bersianik sees the critical response to her work as part of an institutionalizing of culture that feminist writers must publicly question in their own theoretical work is a fascinating phenomenon. There is more going on here, it seems, than merely a "sour grapes" response. See Bersianik, "Aristotle's Lantern," 45–46. See also Pierre Nepveu, "L'Essentiel et le frivole," *Spirale,* May 1985, 6.

62. This notion of the imaginary is, in part, a borrowing from Lacan's concept of the *Imaginary,* which is characterized as the realm of perception, hallucination, and ego-identification as distinguished from his concept of the *Symbolic,* which is the realm of discourse and symbolic action. But it should be emphasized that Bersianik, like Théoret, uses this term rather loosely and with a committed feminist intent to denote those areas of experience that exist *outside of* or *prior to* symbolic formation and discursive activity—both of which have been traditionally controlled by men and by patriarchal law. For discussions of the Lacanian Imaginary and Symbolic in relation to feminist theory, see Jane Gallop, *Reading Lacan* (Ithaca, N.Y.: Cornell University Press, 1985) and Jacqueline Rose, *Sexuality in the Field of Vision* (London: Verso Press, 1986), especially chapter 7.

63. In addition to the fairly straightforward syllabic play at work here, Bersianik has suggested a number of anagrams in this title, including the words *rêvant* (dreaming), *matin* (morning), *Marie-Eve,* and *ta main verte* (your green hand). See her interview, "Louky Bersianik et la mythologie du futur," 68.

64. Louky Bersianik, "La Dérive du continent noir," *Le Devoir,* 24 Nov. 1979, 6.

65. Bersianik, *Les Agénésies,* 24.

66. Mary Daly has attached these definitions and others to the word *elemental* so as to endow it with a broad range of feminist meanings. See Daly, *Pure Lust,* 7–8.

67. Renée-Berthe Drapeau has also commented on the utopian function of the island in Brossard's *Le Sens apparent.* See Renée-Berthe Drapeau, *Féminins singuliers: Pratiques d'écriture: Brossard, Théoret* (Montreal: Triptyque, 1986), 89–90.

68. Bersianik, "Arbre de pertinence et utopie," in *L'Emergence d'une culture au féminin,* ed. Marisa Zavalloni (Montreal: Saint-Martin, 1987), 121.

69. Modleski, "Feminism and the Power of Interpretation," 136.

70. Jane Flax, "Re-membering the Selves: Is the Repressed Gendered?," *Michigan Quarterly Review* 26.1 (1987): 106–7. (Special issue on "Women and Memory.")

71. Bersianik, "Arbre de pertinence et utopie," 122.

5. France Théoret: Voicing the Agony of Discourse

1. Alice Jardine, "Pre-texts for the Transatlantic Feminist," *Yale French Studies* 62 (1981): 232. (Special issue on "Feminist Readings: French Texts/American Contexts.")

2. See Irigaray, *This Sex Which Is Not One,* especially chapter 4.

3. Gallop, *The Daughter's Seduction,* 78.

4. See France Théoret's article, "LA PETITE FILLE SAGE," *Les Têtes de Pioche* (Montreal: Remue-ménage, 1980), 39.

5. "Un livre à venir: Rencontre avec Nicole Brossard," 6.

6. "Un livre à venir: Rencontre avec Nicole Brossard," 12.

7. Tillie Olsen, *Silences* (New York: Delta/Seymour Lawrence, 1979), 6.

8. Eagleton, 139.

9. See Théoret's responses to questions raised at the first National Festival of Poetry, Trois-Rivières, 1985 in *Choisir la poésie* (Trois-Rivières, Ecrits des Forges, 1986), 106–7.

10. France Théoret, *Bloody Mary* (Montreal: Les Herbes Rouges, 1977), 18. In the text, this passage is presented in large characters and in bold face on a separate page to underscore the importance of the thought and the subversive context of the imagery. Subsequent references to this edition will appear parenthetically in the text.

11. For an informative, inside look at the development of Les Herbes Rouges, see the interview with its editors, the Hébert brothers, conducted by Richard Giguère and André Marquis, "Les Herbes Rouges, 1968–88: Persister et se maintenir," *Lettres québécoises* 52 (1988–89): 14–21.

12. "A woman who doesn't know pleasure [*qui ne jouit pas*] is a virgin," says Denise Boucher in her introductory remarks to her play, *Les Fées ont soif,* 9.

13. Lawrence Lipking, "Aristotle's Sister: A Poetics of Abondonment," in *Canons,* ed. Robert von Hallberg (Chicago: University of Chicago Press, 1983), 88.

14. Marie Cardinal, *Les Mots pour le dire* (Paris: Grasset and Fasquelle, 1975).

15. Here again, it should be noted that this passage is a crucial one for Théoret and is therefore printed in large script and positioned separately at the end of the text's first section.

16. Gubar, 256.

17. Patricia Smart, "Quand la fille du bar se met à parler: la poésie de France Théoret," *Dalhousie French Studies* (1985): 153. (Special issue on "La Poésie québécoise depuis 1975.")

18. Quebec clinical psychologist Marcelle Maugin argues that "what most succinctly characterizes the reign of Duplessis [1936–39; 1944–59], is once again the quasi perfect agreement between the government and the clergy, and the total mystification which resulted for women. It is difficult today to imagine the harmony which existed at that time between the two

institutions." Maugin also notes the dualistic thinking inherent in Duplessis' discourse: "Duplessis always presents pairs of opposites to his listeners (countryside/city, natural/intellectual, familial/political, motherhood/working women, etc.) which reflect and repeat the fundamental antagonism good/bad, pure/impure, etc." See Maugin, 31, 36.

19. France Théoret, *Une voix pour Odile* (Montreal: Les Herbes Rouges, 1978), 13. Subsequent references to this edition will appear parenthetically in the text.

20. It is almost impossible not to see the affinities here between Théoret's monologue of the daughter in search of the aunt and Irigaray's monologue of the daughter addressed to her mother in *Et l'une ne bouge pas sans l'autre* (*And One Doesn't Stir without the Other*), published in 1979. Irigaray ends her short text with the contradictory sense of life given and life lost: "And the one doesn't stir without the other. But we do not move together. When the one of us comes into the world, the other goes underground. When the one carries life, the other dies. And what I wanted from you, Mother, was this: that in giving me life, you still remain alive" (Luce Irigaray, "And One Doesn't Stir without the Other," trans. Hélène Vivienne Wenzel, *Signs* 7.1 [1981]: 67).

21. Cixous and Clément, 92. Marcelle Marini develops a similar appreciation of the feminine voice in the writing of Marguerite Duras. See Marcelle Marini, *Territoires du féminin: avec Marguerite Duras* (Paris: Minuit, 1977). When discussing women's writing in France and Quebec, Suzanne Lamy also argued that writing in the feminine appears to "save the trace of what passes in the voice, as if from the body to the letter, a tone or palpable fluidity remained" (Lamy, *Quand je lis je m'invente*, 14).

22. France Théoret, "Ce grand vide qu'on dit intérieur," *Etudes littéraires* 16.1 (1983): 163.

23. Hugues Corriveau, "Des yeux qui écrivent," *Estuaire* 38 (1985): 16.

24. Théoret also comments on her admiration for Claude Gauvreau (1925–71), a major poet and dramatist of Quebec's *automatisme* movement during the late 1940s and 1950s. Gauvreau was another resolute supporter of "the modern" and has also been an important influence on Brossard and Gagnon. See Théoret, "Le Fantasme de la BJ, c'est la théorie," 87–88.

25. Cixous and Clément, 91.

26. Cixous and Clément, 94.

27. France Théoret, *Nécessairement putain* (Montreal: Les Herbes Rouges, 1980), 52. Subsequent references to this edition will appear parenthetically in the text.

28. Susanne Kappeler, *The Pornography of Representation* (Minneapolis: University of Minnesota Press, 1986), 157.

29. See Théoret, "De la chair à la langue," 54.

30. "It's by namin' what I don't have that I find out what I want," says the prostitute Madeleine in Boucher's feminist play, *Les Fées ont soif*, 81.

31. Through her constant movement and indifference to the male gaze, Théoret's woman in the streets echoes some of the narcissistic self-sufficiency in Sarah Kofman's reflections on the affirmative narcissistic woman. See Sarah Kofman, *The Enigma of Woman*, trans. Catherine Porter (Ithaca, N.Y.: Cornell University Press, 1985), 50–68.

32. Louise Dupré, "Qui parle?," *Estuaire* 38 (1985): 45–46.

33. This resistance to fixed definitions and general strategy of affirmation through negation is also found in *Vertiges*, another short text by Théoret that appeared in 1979: "Ne suis ni vierge, ni putain, ni grande dame, ni servante. Ne suis pas la pythie aimée ou maudite. Si près de la loi, la folie et j'ai mille visages pour les convenances. Toutes frontières ouvertes du dedans au dehors. Le caviardage au centre de la parole" (France Théoret, *Vertiges* [Montreal: Les Herbes Rouges, 1979], 15). ("Am neither virgin, nor whore, nor great lady, nor servant. Am not the beloved or accursed priestess. So close to the law, madness and I have a thousand faces for propriety's sake. All frontiers opened from the inside outward. Block-out at the center of speech.")

34. Irigaray, *This Sex Which is not One*, 26.

35. Laura Mulvey, "Visual Pleasure and Narrative Cinema," *Screen* 16.3 (1975): 11.

36. Claudine Herrmann, *Les Voleuses de langue* (Paris: Des femmes, 1976), 18.

37. I am referring here to Monique Wittig's modern "feminist" classic, *Les Guérillières* (Paris: Minuit, 1969).

38. France Théoret, *Nous parlerons comme on écrit* (Montreal: Les Herbes Rouges, 1982), 9. Subsequent references to this edition will appear parenthetically in the text.

39. Théoret's only slightly veiled allusion to the slogan of the French Communist Party, "Le communisme est la jeunesse du monde et il prépare des lendemains qui chantent" ("Communism is the youth of the world and it is preparing days that will sing"), bears the mark of her own socialist leanings. But it also underscores a more generalized call for a different kind of future, while at the same time offering a somewhat cynical view of the Communist Party's revolutionary gains thus far.

40. Suzanne Lamy, "Des résonances de la petite phrase: 'Je suis un noeud' de France Théoret," in *Féminité, Subversion, Ecriture*, ed. Suzanne Lamy and Irène Pagès (Montreal: Remue-ménage, 1983), 145.

41. Théoret has admitted that her own eventual disaffection with the group at *La Barre du jour* was due primarily to their increasing efforts "to evacuate meaning from the text" at a time when she herself was beginning to move in the other direction (Théoret, "Le Fantasme de la BJ, c'est la théorie," 90).

42. Elizabeth C. Goldsmith, "Madame de Sévigné's Epistolary Retreat," *L'Esprit créateur* 23.2 (1983): 70.

43. In a fascinating discussion of her meeting with France Théoret and

the bases of their ensuing friendship, the anglophone Quebec writer Gail Scott admits to being the "amie anglaise" in *Nous parlerons comme on écrit* and acknowledges the importance of biographical elements in their respective texts. "As we grew closer," says Scott, "I playfully projected on her the qualities of Colette, a giant woman writer from French culture whom I in fact admired more than she did. And, sometimes, too, I took on for her what she called the 'reassuring asceticism' of Virginia Woolf. We knew these projections were absurd, but they were a way of getting behind the masks, I think, of the ethnic reticences that are an old story in Quebec and that were particularly virulent during the 70s." Gail Scott, "Virginia and Colette on the Outside Looking In," in *A Mazing Space: Writing Canadian Women Writing*, ed. Shirley Neuman and Smaro Kamboureli (Edmonton, Alberta: Longspoon/NeWest, 1986), 367.

44. Cixous and Clément, 93.

45. Marcelle Marini (73) characterizes "le discours du féminin" in precisely these terms.

46. Théoret, "Writing in the feminine," 365.

6. *Afterword*

1. In the American male tradition of fiction considered in *The Resisting Reader*, Judith Fetterley repeatedly makes the point that "the female reader is co-opted into participation in an experience from which she is explicitly excluded; she is asked to identify with a selfhood that defines itself in opposition to her; she is required to identify against herself" (xii).

2. Teresa de Lauretis, *Alice Doesn't: Feminism, Semiotics, Cinema* (Bloomington: Indiana University Press, 1984), 7.

3. Elaine Showalter first proposed the concept of *gynocritics* in "Feminist Criticism in the Wilderness," *Critical Inquiry* 8.2 (1981): 179–205.

4. Lamy, *d'elles*, 12.

5. Adrienne Rich's oft cited call for "re-vision" signaled the need for an "act of looking back, of seeing with fresh eyes, of entering an old text from a new critical direction" (Rich, *On Lies, Secrets, and Silence*, 35).

6. Brossard, *The Aerial Letter*, 157.

Bibliography

Louky Bersianik

Major Works and Selected Essays

Les Agénésies du vieux monde. Montreal: L'Intégrale, 1982.
"Arbre de pertinence et utopie." In *L'Emergence d'une culture au féminin,* edited by Marisa Zavalloni, 117–32. Montreal: Saint-Martin, 1987.
Axes et eau: Poèmes de 'La bonne chanson.' Montreal: VLB Editeur, 1984.
Au beau milieu de moi. Photography by Kèro. Montreal: Nouvelle Optique, 1983.
"Comment naître femme sans le devenir." *La Nouvelle Barre du jour* 172 (1986): 57–66. (Special issue: "Le Forum des femmes.")
"La Dérive du continent noir." *Le Devoir,* 24 Nov. 1979, 6.
"L'Espace encombré de la signature." *La Nouvelle Barre du jour* 157 (1985): 91–97. (Special issue: "L'Ecriture comme lecture.")
L'Euguélionne. Montreal: La Presse, 1976. Reprint. Montreal: Stanké, Collection 10/10, 1985.
Kerameikos. With Graham Cantieni. Saint-Lambert: Noroît, 1987.
"La Lanterne d'Aristote." In *La Théorie, un dimanche,* 81–106. Montreal: Remue-ménage, 1988.
Maternative: Les Pré-Ancyl. Montreal: VLB Editeur, 1980.
"Noli mi tangere." *La Barre du jour* 56–57 (1977): 148–64.
Le Pique-nique sur l'Acropole: Cahiers d'Ancyl. Montreal: VLB Editeur, 1979.

Works Translated into English

"Aristotle's Lantern: An Essay on Criticism." Translated by A. J. Holden Verburg. In *A Mazing Space: Writing Canadian Women Writing,* edited by Shirley Neuman and Smaro Kamboureli, 39–48. Edmonton, Alberta: Longspoon/NeWest, 1986.
The Euguélionne. Translated by Gerry Denis et al. Victoria: Porcépic Press, 1981.

"Noli me tangere." Translated by Barbara Godard. *Room of One's Own* 4.1 (1978): 98–110.

"Women's Work." Translated by Erika Grundmann. In *In the Feminine: Women and Words/Les Femmes et les mots. Conference Proceedings, 1983*, edited by Ann Dybikowski et al., 155–65. Edmonton, Alberta: Longspoon NeWest, 1985.

Interviews

"Entrevue: Louky Bersianik: Entre la dictée de l'inconscient et le tremblement de la conscience." *Arcade* 11 (1986): 63–74.

"Louky Bersianik et la mythologie du futur: De la théorie-fiction à l'émergence de la femme positive." (Interview with Donald Smith.) *Lettres québécoises* 27 (1982): 64–65.

"Lucile Durand interviewe Louky Bersianik." *Lettres québécoises* 26 (1982): 53–55.

"Notre Corps d'écriture." (Interview with Jean Royer.) In *Ecrivains contemporains: Entretiens I: 1976–1979*, edited by Jean Royer, 72–78. Montreal: L'Hexagone, 1982.

Nicole Brossard

Major Works and Selected Essays

Amantes. Montreal: Quinze, 1980.

L'Amèr ou le chapitre effrité. Montreal: Quinze, 1977. Reprint. Montreal: L'Hexagone, 1988.

"L'Angle tramé du désir." In *La Théorie, un dimanche*, 11–26. Montreal: Remue-ménage, 1988.

Aube à la saison. In *Trois*. Montreal: A.G.E.U.M., 1965. Reprint. *Le Centre blanc*, 7–37. Montreal: L'Hexagone, 1978.

"L'Avenir de la littérature québécoise." *Etudes françaises* 13.3–4 (1977): 283–93.

L'Aviva. Montreal: NBJ, 1985.

"Ça fait jaser." *Sorcières* 14 (1978): 23–24. (Special issue: "La Jasette.")

"Ce que pouvait être, ici, une avant-garde." *Voix et images* 10.2 (1985): 68–85.

Le Centre blanc. Montreal: Orphée, 1970. Reprint. Montreal: L'Hexagone, 1978.

Character/Jeu de lettres. With Daphne Marlatt. Montreal: NBJ, 1986.

"Le Cortext exubérant," *La Barre du jour* 44 (1974): 2–22. Reprint. *Le Centre blanc*, 385–408. Montreal: L'Hexagone, 1978.

Le Désert mauve. Montreal: L'Hexagone, 1987.

"Djuna Barnes: de profil moderne." In *Mon Héroine,* proceedings from *Les lundi de l'histoire des femmes: an 1. Conférences du théâtre expérimental des femmes, Montréal 1980–81,* 189–214. Montreal: Remue-ménage, 1981.

Domaine d'écriture. Montreal: NBJ, 1985.

Dont j'oublie le titre. Marseille: Ryôan-ji, 1985.

Double Impression. Montreal: L'Hexagone, 1984.

L'Echo bouge beau. Montreal: L'Estérel, 1968. Reprint. *Le Centre blanc,* 35–129. Montreal: L'Hexagone, 1978.

"L'Ecrivain." In *La Nef des sorcières,* 73–80. Montreal: Quinze, 1976.

"L'Epreuve de la modernité ou/et les preuves de modernité." *La Nouvelle Barre du jour* 90–91 (1980): 57–63.

"La Femme et l'écriture." *Liberté* 18.4–5 (1976): 10–13. (Special issue: "La Femme et l'écriture. Actes de la rencontre québécoise internationale des écrivains.")

French Kiss. Montreal: Jour, 1974.

Journal intime. Montreal: Les Herbes Rouges, 1984.

La Lettre aérienne. Montreal: Remue-ménage, 1985.

Un livre. Montreal: Jour, 1970. Reprint. Montreal: Quinze, 1980.

Mauve. With Daphne Marlatt. Montreal: NBJ, 1985.

Mécanique jongleuse suivi de Masculin grammaticale. Montreal: L'Hexagone, 1974. Reprint. *Le Centre blanc,* 239–88. Montreal: L'Hexagone, 1978.

Mordre en sa chair. Montreal: L'Estérel, 1966. Reprint. *Le Centre blanc,* 39–84. Montreal: L'Hexagone, 1978.

La Partie pour le tout. Montreal: L'Aurore, 1975. Reprint. *Le Centre blanc,* 289–355. Montreal: L'Hexagone, 1978.

Picture Theory. Montreal: Nouvelle Optique, 1985.

Le Sens apparent. Paris: Flammarion, 1980.

Sold-out. Montreal: Jour, 1973. Reprint. Montreal: Quinze, 1980.

Sous la langue/Under Tongue. Bilingual edition. Translated by Susanne de Lotbinière-Harwood. Montreal: L'Essentielle and Ragweed Press, 1987.

Suite logique. Montreal: L'Hexagone, 1970. Reprint. *Le Centre blanc,* 131–80. Montreal: L'Hexagone, 1978.

"La Tête qu'elle fait," *La Barre du jour* 56–57 (1977): 83–92. (Special issue: "Le Corps/Les Mots/L'Imaginaire.")

"La Vie privée est politique." In *Les Têtes de Pioche,* 21–22. Montreal: Remue-ménage, 1980.

Works Translated into English

The Aerial Letter. Translated by Marlene Wildeman. Toronto: Women's Press, 1988.

A Book. Translated by Larry Shouldice. Toronto: Coach House Press, 1976.

Daydream Mechanics. Translated by Larry Shouldice. Toronto: Coach House Press, 1980.

"The Face She Makes." Translated by Josée LeBlond. *Room of One's Own* 4.1 (1978): 39–43.

French Kiss or A Pang's Progress. Translated by Patricia Claxton. Toronto: Coach House Press, 1986. (Originally published as *Turn of a Pang.* Translated by Patricia Clayton. Toronto: Coach House Press, 1976.)

Lovhers. Translated by Barbara Godard. Montreal: Guernica, 1986.

"On Our Protest Writing." Translated by H. J. Lanthier. *Ellipse* 4.2 3 (1979): 20–27.

"Picture Theory." Translated by Luise von Flotow. In *Ink and Strawberries: An Anthology of Quebec Women's Fiction,* edited by Beverley Daurio and Luise von Flotow, 75–89. Toronto: Aya Press, 1988.

The Story So Far: 6/Les Stratégies du réel. Translated by Patricia Claxton et al. Toronto: Coach House Press, 1979.

These Our Mothers or: The Disintegrating Chapter. Translated by Barbara Godard. Toronto: Coach House Quebec Translations, 1983.

"Traversing Fiction." Translated by Barbara Godard. *Fireweed* 1 (1978): 20–21.

"The Writer." Translated by Linda Gaboriau. *Fireweed* 5–6 (1979–80): 106, 108, 110, 112, 114, 116. (Special issue: "Women and Language.")

Interviews

"Entretien avec Nicole Brossard sur *Picture Theory.*" *La Nouvelle Barre du jour* 118–19 (1982): 177–201.

"La Fiction vive: entretien avec Nicole Brossard sur sa prose." (Interview with André Roy.) *Journal of Canadian Fiction* 25–26 (1979): 31–40.

"Un livre à venir: Rencontre avec Nicole Brossard." (Interview with Michel van Schendel and Jean Fisette.) *Voix et images* 3.1 (1977): 3–18.

"Nicole Brossard: Entrevue." (Interview with Caroline Bayard and Jack David.) *Lettres québécoises* 4 (1976): 34–37.

Madeleine Gagnon

Major Works and Selected Essays

Antre. Montreal: Les Herbes Rouges, 1978. Reprint. *Autographie I: Fictions.* Montreal: VLB Editeur, 1982.

Au coeur de la lettre. Montreal: VLB Editeur, 1982.

Autographie I: Fictions. Montreal: VLB Editeur, 1982.

"Ce que je veux s'écrire ne peut pas m'écrire autrement," *Les Nouvelles littéraires,* 26 May 1976, 19.

"Ecrire l'amour." In *Ecrire l'amour: communications de la onzième rencontre québécoise internationale des écrivains*, 67–72. Montreal: L'Hexagone, 1984.

"Ecriture, sorcellerie, féminité." *Etudes littéraires* 12 (1979): 357–61. (Special issue: "Féminaire.")

"La Femme et l'écriture." *Liberté* 18.4–5 (1976): 249–56. (Special issue: "La Femme et l'écriture. Actes de la rencontre québécoise internationale des écrivains.")

"Femmes du Québec, un mouvement et des écritures." With Mireille Lanctôt. *Le Magazine littéraire* March 1978, 97–99.

Les Fleurs du Catalpa. Montreal: VLB Editeur, 1986.

L'Infante immémoriale. Trois-Rivières: Ecrits des Forges, 1986.

La Lettre infinie. Montreal: VLB Editeur, 1984.

Lueur: roman archéologique. Montreal: VLB Editeur, 1979.

"Mon Corps dans l'écriture." With Hélène Cixous and Annie Leclerc. In *La Venue à l'écriture*, 63–116. Paris: Union Générale d'Editions, 1977. Reprint. *Autographie I: Fictions*. Montreal: VLB Editeur, 1982.

Les Morts-vivants. Montreal: HMH, 1969. Reprint. Montreal: VLB Editeur, 1982.

"Parler l'écriture ou écrire la parole." In *Modernité/Postmodernité du roman contemporain*. Cahiers du département d'études littéraires, no. 11, edited by Madeleine Frédéric and Jacques Allard, 15–22. Montreal: Université du Québec à Montréal, 1987.

Pensées du poème. Montreal: VLB Editeur, 1983.

Poélitique. Montreal: Les Herbes Rouges, 1975. Reprint. *Autographie I: Fictions*. Montreal: VLB Editeur, 1982.

Portraits du voyage. With Jean-Marc Piotte and Patrick Straram le Bison ravi. Montreal: L'Aurore, 1974.

Pour les femmes et tous les autres. Montreal: L'Aurore, 1974. Reprint. *Autographie I: Fictions*. Montreal: VLB Editeur, 1982.

"Pourquoi, pour qui, comment écrire?" *Chroniques* 1.6–7 (1975): 122–26.

Préface. In *Cyprine: essai-collage pour être une femme*, by Denise Boucher. Montreal: L'Aurore, 1978.

Retailles: complaintes politiques. With Denise Boucher. Montreal: L'Etincelle, 1977.

Works Translated into English

"Body I." Translated by Isabelle de Courtivron. In *New French Feminisms*, edited by Isabelle de Courtivron and Elaine Marks, 179–80. Amherst: University of Massachusetts Press, 1980.

"My Body in Writing." Translated and introduced by Wendy Johnston. In *Feminism in Canada: From Pressure to Politics*, edited by Geraldine Finn and Angela Miles, 269–82. Montreal: Black Rose Books, 1982.

Interviews

"Dans l'eau des mots." (Interview with Jean Royer.) In *Ecrivains contempo-rains: Entretiens I: 1976–1979,* edited by Jean Royer, 79–85. Montreal: L'Hexagone, 1982.
"De la chair à la langue." (Interview with Louise Dupré.) *La Vie en rose,* May 1983, 53–56.
"Entrevue de Madeleine Gagnon." (Interview with Michèle Pontbriand.) *Moebius* 26 (1985): 1–16.
"Madeleine Gagnon." (Interview with Suzy Turcotte.) *Nuit Blanche* 25 (1986): 52–53.
"Madeleine Gagnon, écrivain: 'Je ne suis pas un oracle.' " (Interview with Monique Roy.) *La Gazette des femmes* 1.3 (1980): 17–18.
"Percer le mur du son du sens, une entrevue avec Madeleine Gagnon." (Interview with Lucie Robert and Ruth Major.) *Voix et images* 8.1 (1982): 5–21.
"Vivre de sa plume au Québec." (Interview with Gérald Gaudet.) *Lettres québécoises* 49 (1988): 16–18.

France Théoret

Major Texts and Selected Essays

Bloody Mary. Montreal: Les Herbes Rouges, 1977.
"Ce grand vide qu'on dit intérieur." *Etudes littéraires* 16.1 (1983): 163–66. Reprint. *Entre raison et déraison*. Montreal: Les Herbes Rouges, 1987.
"L'Echantillon." In *La Nef des sorcières*, 31–38. Montreal: Quinze, 1976.
"Ecrire — l'amour, dit-elle — Ah! Harlequin, dit-il." *Ecrire l'amour: communications de la onzième rencontre québécoise internationale des écrivains,* 44–47. Montreal: L'Hexagone, 1984. Reprint. *Entre raison et déraison*. Montreal: Les Herbes Rouges, 1987.
"Ecriture au féminin et institutions." *Dialogues et culture* 27 (1985): 223–25.
"Eloge de la mémoire des femmes." In *La Théorie, un dimanche*, 175–91. Montreal: Remue-ménage, 1988.
Entre raison et déraison. Montreal: Les Herbes Rouges, 1987.
"La Femme et l'écriture." *Liberté* 18.4–5 (1976): 122–25. (Special issue: "La Femme et l'écriture. Actes de la rencontre québécoise internationale des écrivains.")
"L'homme qui peignait Staline." *La Nouvelle Barre du jour* 181 (1986): 85–95. (Special issue: "Géographies.")
Intérieurs. Montreal: Les Herbes Rouges, 1984.
"La Mère peut-elle être moderne?" *La Nouvelle Barre du jour* 116 (1982): 47–50.

Nécessairement putain. Montreal: Les Herbes Rouges, 1980.
Nous parlerons comme on écrit. Montreal: Les Herbes Rouges, 1982.
"LA PETITE FILLE SAGE." In *Les Têtes de Pioche,* 39. Montreal: Remue-ménage, 1980.
"Quand la mémoire dérive trop." *Estuaire* 18 (1981): 121–30.
"Situation actuelle de la poésie." In *Choisir la poésie,* 37–39. Trois-Rivières: Ecrits des Forges, 1986.
Transit. Montreal: Les Herbes Rouges, 1984.
"La Turbulence intérieure." *La Nouvelle Barre du jour* 172 (1986): 73–79. (Special issue: "Le Forum des femmes.") Reprint. *Entre raison et déraison.* Montreal: Les Herbes Rouges, 1987.
Vertiges. Montreal: Les Herbes Rouges, 1979.
Une voix pour Odile. Montreal: Les Herbes Rouges, 1978.

Works Translated into English

"Territories of Criticism." Translated by Patricia Kealy. In *In the Feminine: Women and Words/Les Femmes et les mots. Conférence Proceedings, 1983,* edited by Ann Dybikowski et al., 95–98. Edmonton, Alberta: Longspoon, 1985.
"Walking." Translated by Luise von Flotow. In *Ink and Strawberries: An Anthology of Quebec Women's Fiction,* edited by Beverley Daurio and Luise von Flotow, 68–70. Toronto: Aya Press, 1988.
"Writing in the Feminine: Voicing Consensus, Practicing Difference." Translated by A. J. Holden Verburg. In *A Mazing Space: Writing Canadian Women Writing,* edited by Shirley Neuman and Smaro Kamboureli, 361–73. Edmonton, Alberta: Longspoon/NeWest, 1986.

Interviews

"De la chair à la langue." (Interview with Louise Dupré.) *La Vie en rose,* May 1983, 53–56.
"Une écriture responsable." (Interview with Gérald Gaudet.) *Estuaire* 38 (1986): 103–17. (Special issue: "France Théoret: L'Imaginaire du réel.")
"Entretien avec France Théoret." (Interview with Danielle Fournier.) *Moebius* 23 (1984): 71–77.
"Entrevue avec France Théoret." (Interview with Patricia Smart.) *Voix et images* 14.1 (1988): 11–23.
"Le Fantasme de la BJ, c'est la théorie," *Voix et images* 10.2 (1985): 87–92.
"France Théoret: Les Sciences exactes de l'être." (Interview with Jean Royer.) *Le Devoir,* 15 May 1982: 19, 36. Reprint. *Ecrivains contemporains: Entretiens I 1976–1979,* edited by Jean Royer 308–13. Montreal: L'Hexagone, 1982.

Secondary Sources

Barrett, Michèle. "Ideology and the Cultural Production of Gender." In *Feminist Criticism and Social Change,* edited by Judith Newton and Deborah Rosenfelt, 65–85. New York: Methuen, 1985.

Barthes, Roland. *A Lover's Discourse.* Translated by Richard Howard. New York: Hill and Wang, 1978. Originally published as *Fragments d'un discours amoureux.* Paris: Seuil, 1977.

———. *The Pleasure of the Text.* Translated by Richard Miller. New York: Hill and Wang, 1975. Originally published as *Le Plaisir du texte.* Paris: Seuil, 1973.

Bayard, Caroline. "Qu'en est-il au fait de la théorie depuis que les dieux sont morts?" In *Féminité, Subversion, Ecriture,* edited by Suzanne Lamy and Irène Pagès, 185–93. Ville Saint-Laurent: Remue-ménage, 1983.

Beausoleil, Claude. *Les Livres parlent.* Trois-Rivières: Ecrits des Forges, 1984.

———. "Présentation critique." In *Un livre,* by Nicole Brossard, v-viii. Montreal: Quinze, 1980.

Bennet, Donna. "Naming the Way Home." In *A Mazing Space: Writing Canadian Women Writing,* edited by Shirley Neuman and Smaro Kamboureli, 228–45. Edmonton, Alberta: Longspoon/NeWest, 1986.

Blanchot, Maurice. *Le Livre à venir.* Paris: Gallimard, 1959.

Borduas, Paul-Emile. *Refus global.* Montreal: Parti pris, 1977.

Boucher, Denise. *Cyprine: essai-collage pour être une femme.* Montreal: L'Aurore, 1978.

———. *Les Fées ont soif.* Montreal: Intermède, 1979.

Bourassa, André-G. *Surréalisme et littérature québécoise: Histoire d'une révolution culturelle.* Montreal: Les Herbes Rouges, 1986.

Brisson, Marcelle. "Femme et écriture." *Arcade* 11 (1986): 26–32.

Brochu, André. "Autour d'Alain Grandbois indélébile." *Voix et images* 11.2 (1986): 341–49.

Calinescu, Matei. *Five Faces of Modernity.* Durham, N.C.: Duke University Press, 1987.

Cardinal, Marie. *Les Mots pour le dire.* Paris: Grasset and Fasquelle, 1975.

Chawaf, Chantal. "La Chair linguistique." *Les Nouvelles littéraires,* 26 May 1976.

Cixous, Hélène. "The Laugh of the Medusa." Translated by Keith Cohen and Paula Cohen. *Signs* 1.4 (1976): 875–99. Originally published as "Le Rire de la Méduse." *L'Arc* 61 (1975): 39–54.

———. *Portrait de Dora.* Paris: Des femmes, 1976.

———. *Souffles.* Paris: Des femmes, 1975.

———. "La Venue à l'écriture." With Madeleine Gagnon and Annie Leclerc. In *La Venue à l'écriture,* 9–62. Paris: Union Générale d'Editions, 1977.

Cixous, Hélène, and Catherine Clément. *The Newly Born Woman.* Translated by Betsy Wing. Minneapolis: University of Minnesota Press, 1986. Originally published as *La Jeune Née.* Paris: Union Générale d'Editions, Collection 10/18, 1975.

Clift, Dominique. *Quebec Nationalism in Crisis.* Montreal: McGill-Queen's University Press, 1982.

Cloutier, Cécile. "Utinam!" *La Barre du jour* 56–57 (1977): 93–115. (Special issue: "Le Corps/Les Mots/L'Imaginaire.")

Cohen, Yolande. "Thoughts on Women and Power." Translated by Francine Sylvestre-Wallace. In *Feminism in Canada: From Pressure to Politics,* edited by Geraldine Finn and Angela Miles, 229–50. Montreal: Black Rose Books, 1982.

Conley, Verena Andermatt. *Hélène Cixous: Writing the Feminine.* Lincoln: University of Nebraska Press, 1984.

Corriveau, Hugues. "Des yeux qui écrivent." *Estuaire* 38 (1985): 13–22.

Courtivron, Isabelle de, and Elaine Marks, eds. *New French Feminisms.* Amherst: University of Massachusetts Press, 1980.

Daly, Mary. *Beyond God the Father: Toward a Philosophy of Women's Liberation.* Boston: Beacon Press, 1973.

———. *Gyn/Ecology: The Metaethics of Radical Feminism.* Boston: Beacon Press, 1978.

———. *Pure Lust: Elemental Feminist Philosophy.* Boston: Beacon Press, 1984.

Derrida, Jacques. *L'Ecriture et la différence.* Paris: Seuil, 1967.

Drapeau, Renée-Berthe. *Féminins singuliers: Pratiques d'écriture: Brossard, Théoret.* Montreal: Triptyque, 1986.

Dumont, Micheline, Michèle Jean, Marie Lavigne, and Jennifer Stoddart. *L'Histoire des femmes au Québec depuis quatre siècles.* Montreal: Quinze, 1982.

Duplessis, Rachel Blau, and Members of Workshop 9. "For the Etruscans: Sexual Difference and Artistic Production—The Debate over a Female Aesthetic." In *The Future of Difference,* edited by Hester Eisenstein and Alice Jardine, 128–56. New Brunswick, N.J.: Rutgers University Press, 1985.

Dupré, Louise. "From Experimentation to Experience: Québécois Modernity in the Feminine." In *A Mazing Space: Writing Canadian Women Writing,* edited by Shirley Neuman and Smaro Kamboureli, 355–60. Edmonton, Alberta: Longspoon/NeWest, 1986.

———. "Qui parle?" *Estuaire* 38 (1985): 41–47. (Special issue: "France Théoret: L'Imaginaire du réel.")

———. "Les Utopies du réel." *La Nouvelle Barre du jour* 118–19 (1980): 83–89. (Special issue: "Traces: écriture de Nicole Brossard.")

Duras, Marguerite, and Xavière Gauthier. *Les Parleuses.* Paris: Minuit, 1974.

Eagleton, Terry. *Against the Grain.* London: Verso Press, 1986.

Evans, Martha Noel. *Masks of Tradition: Women and the Politics of Writing in Twentieth-Century France*. Ithaca, N.Y.: Cornell University Press, 1987.

Fahmy-Eid, Nadia, and Nicole Laurin-Frenette. "Theories of the Family and Family/Authority Relationships in the Educational Sector in Québec and France, 1850–1960." In *The Politics of Diversity: Feminism, Marxism and Nationalism*, edited by Roberta Hamilton and Michèle Barrett, 287–302. London: Verso Press, 1986.

Fetterley, Judith. *The Resisting Reader: A Feminist Approach to American Fiction*. Bloomington: Indiana University Press, 1978.

Flax, Jane. "Postmodernism and Gender Relations in Feminist Theory." *Signs* 12.4 (1987): 621–43.

———. "Re-membering the Selves: Is the Repressed Gendered?" *Michigan Quarterly Review* 26.1 (1987): 92–110. (Special issue: "Women and Memory.")

Forsyth, Louise. "Beyond the Myths and Fictions of Traditionalism and Nationalism: The Political in the Work of Nicole Brossard." In *Traditionalism, Nationalism, and Feminism: Women Writers of Quebec*, edited by Paula Gilbert Lewis, 157–72. Westport, Conn.: Greenwood Press, 1985.

———. "Destructuring Formal Space/Accelerating Motion in the Work of Nicole Brossard." In *A Mazing Space: Writing Canadian Women Writing*, edited by Shirley Neuman and Smaro Kamboureli, 334–44. Edmonton, Alberta: Longspoon/NeWest, 1986.

———. "L'écriture au féminin: *L'Euguélionne* de Louky Bersianik, *L'Absent aigu* de Geneviève Amyot, *L'Amèr* de Nicole Brossard." *Journal of Canadian Fiction* 25–26 (1979): 199–211.

———. "Errant and Air-born in the City." In *The Aerial Letter*, by Nicole Brossard, translated by Marlene Wildeman, 9–26. Toronto: Coach House Press, 1978.

———. "Nicole Brossard and the Emergence of Feminist Literary Theory in Quebec since 1970." In *Gynocritics/La Gynocritique*, edited by Barbara Godard, 211–21. Toronto: ECW Press, 1987.

———. "Regards, Reflets, Reflux, Réflections: exploration de l'oeuvre de Nicole Brossard." *La Nouvelle Barre du jour* 118–19 (1982): 11–25. (Special issue: "Traces: écriture de Nicole Brossard.")

Fournier, Francine. "Quebec Women and the Parti Québécois." In *Quebec and the Parti Québécois*, edited by Marlene Dixon and Susanne Jonas, 60–63. San Francisco: Synthesis, 1978.

Frémont, Gabrielle. "Casse-texte." *Etudes littéraires* 12 (1979): 315–30. (Special issue: "Féminaire.")

———. "Madeleine Gagnon: Du politique à l'intime." *Voix et images* 8.1 (1982): 23–34.

———. "Petite Histoire d'un grand mouvement." In *Questions de culture*

9: *Identités féminines: mémoire et création,* 173–82. Quebec: Institut québécois de recherche sur la culture, 1986.

Froula, Christine. "When Eve Reads Milton: Undoing the Canonical Economy." In *Canons,* edited by Robert von Hallberg, 149–75. Chicago: University of Chicago Press, 1983.

Gallop, Jane. "Annie Leclerc Writing a Letter with Vermeer." In *The Poetics of Gender,* edited by Nancy K. Miller, 137–56. New York: Columbia University Press, 1986.

———. *The Daughter's Seduction: Feminism and Psychoanalysis.* Ithaca, N.Y.: Cornell University Press, 1982.

———. *Reading Lacan.* Ithaca, N.Y.: Cornell University Press, 1985.

Giguère, Richard, and André Marquis. "Les Herbes Rouges, 1968–88: Persister et se maintenir." *Lettres québécoises* 52 (1988–89): 14–21.

Godard, Barbara. "Becoming My Hero, Becoming Myself: Notes Toward a Feminist Theory of Reading," *Canadian Fiction Magazine* 57 (1986): 142–49. (Special issue: Tessera: "Feminist Fiction/Theory.")

———. "Mapmaking: A Survey of Feminist Criticism." In *Gynocritics/La Gynocritique,* edited by Barbara Godard, 1–30. Toronto: ECW Press, 1987.

———. "Nicole Brossard: *Amantes* and *L'Amèr.*" *Broadside* 2.7 (1981): 14–15.

———. Preface. In *These Our Mothers or: The Disintegrating Chapter,* by Nicole Brossard, translated by Barbara Godard. Toronto: Coach House Quebec Translations, 1983.

Goldsmith, Elizabeth C. "Madame de Sévigné's Epistolary Retreat." *L'Esprit créateur* 23.2 (1983): 70–79.

Gordon, Linda. "What's New in Women's History." In *Feminist Studies/ Critical Studies,* edited by Teresa de Lauretis, 20–30. Bloomington: Indiana University Press, 1986.

Gould, Karen. "The Censored Word and the Body Politic: Reconsidering the Fiction of Marie-Claire Blais." *Journal of Popular Culture* 15.3 (1981): 14–27.

———. "Ecrire au féminin: Interview avec Denise Boucher, Madeleine Gagnon et Louky Bersianik." *Québec Studies* 2 (1984): 125–42.

———. "Female Tracings: Writing as Re-vision in the Recent Works of Louky Bersianik, Madeleine Gagnon, and Nicole Brossard." *American Review of Canadian Studies* 13.3 (1983): 74–89.

———. "Setting Words Free: Feminist Writing in Quebec." *Signs* 6.4 (1981): 617–42.

———. "Spatial Poetics, Spatial Politics: Quebec Feminists on the City and the Countryside." *American Review of Canadian Studies* 12.1 (1982): 1–9.

Gould, Karen, Mary Jean Green, and Paula Gilbert Lewis. "Inscriptions of the Feminine: A Century of Women Writing in Quebec." *American*

Review of Canadian Studies 15.4 (1985): 363–88. (Special issue: "Women in Canada.")

Griffin, Susan. *Woman and Nature: The Roaring Inside Her.* New York: Harper and Row, 1978.

Gubar, Susan. " 'The Blank Page' and the Issues of Female Creativity." *Critical Inquiry* 8.2 (1981): 243–63.

Guilbeault, Luce, et al. *La Nef des sorcières.* Montreal: Quinze, 1976.

Haeck, Philippe. *La Table d'écriture: Poéthique et modernité.* Montreal: VLB Editeur, 1984.

———. Review of *Pour les femmes et tous les autres,* by Madeleine Gagnon. *Le Devoir,* 22 Mar. 1975.

Hassan, Ihab. *The Postmodern Turn.* Columbus: Ohio State University Press, 1987.

Herrmann, Claudine. *Les Voleuses de langue.* Paris: Des femmes, 1976.

Hutcheon, Linda. *A Poetics of Postmodernism: History, Theory, Fiction.* New York: Routledge, 1988.

Irigaray, Luce. "And One Doesn't Stir Without the Other." Translated by Hélène Vivienne Wenzel. *Signs* 7.1 (1981): 60–67.

———. *Ethique de la différence sexuelle.* Paris: Minuit, 1984.

———. *Passions élémentaires.* Paris, Minuit, 1982.

———. *Speculum of the Other Woman.* Translated by Gillian C. Gill. Ithaca, N.Y.: Cornell University Press, 1985. Originally published as *Speculum de l'autre femme.* Paris: Minuit, 1974.

———. *This Sex Which Is Not One.* Translated by Catherine Porter. Ithaca, N.Y.: Cornell University Press, 1985. Originally published as *Ce sexe qui n'en est pas un.* Paris: Minuit, 1977.

Jacobus, Mary. *Reading Woman: Essays in Feminist Criticism.* New York: Columbia University Press, 1986.

Jameson, Frederic. Foreword. In *The Postmodern Condition: A Report on Knowledge,* by Jean-François Lyotard, translated by Geoff Bennington and Brian Massumi. Minneapolis: University of Minnesota Press, 1984.

Jardine, Alice A. *Gynesis: Configurations of Woman and Modernity.* Ithaca, N.Y.: Cornell University Press, 1985.

———. "Pre-texts for the Transatlantic Feminist." *Yale French Studies* 62 (1981): 220–36. (Special issue: "Feminist Readings: French Texts/American Contexts.")

Jean, Michèle. "La Gauche et le féminisme au Québec." In *Les Têtes de Pioche,* 162. Montreal: Remue-ménage, 1980.

Jean, Michèle, and Nicole Brossard. "Dossier: Les Femmes et le P.Q." In *Les Têtes de Pioche,* 73–74. Montreal: Remue-ménage, 1980.

Jones, Ann Rosalind. "Writing the Body: Toward an Understanding of *l'écriture féminine.*" In *Feminist Criticism and Social Change,* edited by Judith Newton and Deborah Rosenfelt, 86–101. New York: Methuen, 1985.

Jowett, Benjamin. "Introduction to *The Symposium.*" In *Plato's Dialogues on Love and Friendship,* edited by Benjamin Jowett. New York: Heritage Press, 1968.

Kappeler, Susanne. *The Pornography of Representation.* Minneapolis: University of Minnesota Press, 1986.

Kask, Janet. "Abortion in Quebec." In *MOTHER Was Not a Person,* edited by Margaret Andersen, 154–57. Montreal: Black Rose Books, 1972.

Kofman, Sarah. *The Enigma of Woman.* Translated by Catherine Porter. Ithaca, N.Y.: Cornell University Press, 1985.

Kramarae, Cheris. "Proprietors of Language." In *Women and Language in Literature and Society,* edited by Sally McConnell-Ginet, Ruth Borker, and Nelly Furman, 58–68. New York: Praeger, 1980.

Kramarae, Cheris, and Paula A. Treichler. *A Feminist Dictionary.* Boston: Pandora Press, 1985.

Kristeva, Julia. *Desire in Language: A Semiotic Approach to Literature and Art.* Edited by Leon S. Roudiez. Translated by Thomas Gora, Alice Jardine, and Leon S. Roudiez. New York: Columbia University Press, 1980.

Kuhn, Annette. *Women's Pictures: Feminism and Cinema.* Boston: Routledge and Kegan Paul, 1982.

Lacan, Jacques. *Ecrits: A Selection.* Translated by Alan Sheridan. New York: Norton, 1977. (Originally published as *Ecrits.* Paris: Seuil, 1966.)

Lamonde, Yvan. "La Modernité au Québec: pour une histoire des brèches." In *Modernité/Postmodernité du roman contemporain.* Cahiers du département d'études littéraires, no. 11, edited by Madeleine Frédéric and Jacques Allard, 185–89. Montreal: Université du Québec à Montréal, 1987.

Lamoureux, Diane. *Fragments et collages: essai sur le féminisme québécois des années 70.* Montreal: Remue-ménage, 1986.

Lamy, Suzanne. *d'elles.* Montreal: L'Hexagone, 1979.

———. "Des résonances de la petite phrase: 'Je suis un noeud' de France Théoret." In *Féminité, Subversion, Ecriture,* edited by Suzanne Lamy and Irène Pagès, 139–49. Montreal: Remue-ménage, 1983.

———. *Quand je lis, je m'invente.* Montreal: L'Hexagone, 1984.

Lauretis, Teresa de. *Alice Doesn't: Feminism, Semiotics, Cinema.* Bloomington: Indiana University Press, 1984.

Lavigne, Marie, and Yolande Pinard, eds. *Les Femmes dans la société québécoise.* Montreal: Boréal Express, 1977.

Leclerc, Annie. "La Lettre d'amour." In *La Venue à l'écriture,* 117–52. Paris: Union Générale d'Editions, 1977.

———. *Parole de femme.* Paris: Grasset and Fasquelle, 1974.

Légaré, Anne. "Cet hier dans aujourd'hui." In *Au nom du père, du fils et de Duplessis,* edited by Andrée Yanacopoulo, 41–61. Montreal: Remue-ménage, 1984.

Lequin, Lucie. "Les Femmes québécoises ont inventé leurs paroles." *American Review of Canadian Studies* 9.2 (1979): 113–24.

Levine, Marc V. "Language Policy and Quebec's *visage français:* New Directions in *la question linguistique.*" *Québec Studies* 8 (1989): 1–16.

Linteau, Paul-André, René Durocher, Jean-Claude Robert, and François Ricard *Histoire du Québec contemporain: Le Québec depuis 1930.* Montreal: Boréal Express, 1986.

Lipking, Lawrence. "Aristotle's Sister: A Poetics of Abandonment." In *Canons,* edited by Robert von Hallberg, 85–105. Chicago: University of Chicago Press, 1983.

Lorde, Audre. *Sister Outsider.* Trumansburg, N.Y.: Crossing Press, 1984.

Lyotard, Jean-François. *The Postmodern Condition: A Report on Knowledge.* Translated by Geoff Bennington and Brian Massumi. Minneapolis: University of Minnesota Press, 1984. (Originally published as *La Condition postmoderne: rapport sur le savoir.* Paris: Minuit, 1979.)

MacKinnon, Catherine. "Feminism, Marxism, Method, and the State." *Signs* 7.3 (1982): 515–44.

Makward, Christiane. "To Be or Not to Be . . . A Feminist Speaker," translated by Marlène Barsoum, Alice Jardine, and Hester Eisenstein. In *The Future of Difference,* edited by Hester Eisenstein and Alice Jardine, 95–105. New Brunswick, N.J.: Rutgers University Press, 1985.

Man, Paul de. *Blindness and Insight.* Minneapolis: University of Minnesota Press, 1971.

Marchessault, Jovette. *La Mère des herbes.* Montreal: Quinze, 1980.

———. "'Retraite' par Soeur Madeleine Gagnon et Soeur Denise Boucher." In *Les Têtes de Pioche,* 130. Montreal: Remue-ménage, 1980.

Marini, Marcelle. *Territoires du féminin: avec Marguerite Duras.* Paris: Minuit, 1977.

Massé, Carole. *Dieu.* Montreal: Les Herbes Rouges, 1979.

Massé, Sylvain. "Le Déclin de l'empire démographique québécois," *Québec Studies* 8 (1989): 111–18.

Maugin, Marcelle. "Le Régime Duplessis." In *Au nom du père, du fils et de Duplessis,* edited by Andrée Yanacopoulo, 13–40. Montreal: Remue-ménage, 1984.

Meese, Elizabeth A. *Crossing the Double-Cross: The Practice of Feminist Criticism.* Chapel Hill: University of North Carolina Press, 1986.

Miller, Nancy K., "Arachnologies: The Woman, The Text, and the Critic." In *The Poetics of Gender,* edited by Nancy K. Miller, 270–95. New York: Columbia University Press, 1986.

Milot, Louise. "Nicole Brossard: Une influence coûteuse." In *Modernité/ Postmodernité du roman contemporain.* Cahiers du département d'études littéraires, no. 11, edited by Madeleine Frédéric and Jacques Allard, 77–86. Montreal: Université du Québec à Montréal, 1987.

Milot, Pierre. *La Camera obscura du postmodernisme.* Montreal: L'Hexagone, 1988.

Mitchell, Juliet, and Jacqueline Rose, eds. *Feminine Sexuality: Jacques Lacan and the école freudienne.* New York: Norton, 1982.

Modleski, Tania. "Feminism and the Power of Interpretation: Some Critical Readings." In *Feminist Studies/Critical Studies,* edited by Teresa de Lauretis, 121–38. Bloomington: Indiana University Press, 1986.

Moi, Toril. *French Feminist Thought.* New York: Basil Blackwell, 1987.

———. *Sexual/Textual Politics: Feminist Literary Theory.* New York: Methuen, 1985.

Moss, Jane. "Women's Theatre in Quebec." In *Traditionalism, Nationalism, and Feminism,* edited by Paula Gilbert Lewis, 241–54. Westport, Conn.: Greenwood Press, 1985.

Mulvey, Laura. "Visual Pleasure and Narrative Cinema." *Screen* 16.3 (1975): 6–18.

Nepveu, Pierre. "BJ/NBJ: difficile modernité." *Voix et images* 10.2 (1985): 159–65.

———. "L'Essentiel et le frivole." *Spirale,* May 1985, 6.

———. "Nicole Brossard et France Théoret: la pensée/l'impensable." *Lettres québécoises* 20 (1980–81): 24–27.

Neuman, Shirley. "Importing Differences." In *A Mazing Space: Writing Canadian Women Writing,* edited by Shirley Neuman and Smaro Kamboureli, 392–405. Edmonton, Alberta: Longspoon/NeWest, 1986.

O'Leary, Véronique, and Louise Toupin, eds. *Québécoises Deboutte!* Vols. 1–2. Montreal: Remue-ménage, 1982–83.

Olsen, Tillie. *Silences.* New York: Delta/Seymour Lawrence, 1979.

Ostriker, Alicia. *Writing Like a Woman.* Ann Arbor: University of Michigan Press, 1983.

Ouvrard, Hélène. *Le Corps étranger.* Montreal: Jour, 1973.

———. *La Noyante.* Montreal: Québec/Amérique, 1980.

Paterson, Janet. "A Poetics of Transformation: Yolande Villemaire's *La Vie en prose.*" In *A Mazing Space: Writing Canadian Women Writing,* edited by Shirley Neuman and Smaro Kamboureli, 315–23. Edmonton, Alberta: Longspoon/NeWest, 1986.

Pestieau, Caroline. "Women in Quebec." In *Women in the Canadian Mosaic,* edited by Gwen Matheson, 57–69. Toronto: Peter Martin, 1976.

Plourde, Michel. *La Politique linguistique du Québec (1977–1987).* Quebec: Institut québécois de recherche sur la culture, 1988.

Queneau, Raymond. *Zazie dans le métro.* Paris: Gallimard, 1959.

Rich, Adrienne. *Of Woman Born: Motherhood as Experience and Institution.* New York: Norton, 1976.

———. *On Lies, Secrets, and Silence: Selected Prose 1966–1978.* New York: Norton, 1979.

Rhodes, Richard. *The Making of the Atomic Bomb.* New York: Simon and Schuster, 1987.

Rose, Jacqueline. *Sexuality in the Field of Vision.* London: Verso Press, 1986.

Roy, Monique. "Madeleine Gagnon." *Les Cahiers de la femme/Women's Studies* 1.1 (1978): 5.

Royer, Jean. "Regards sur la littérature québécoise des années 70." *Le Devoir,* 21 Nov. 1981.

Saint-Jean, Armande. "Préface." In *Les Têtes de Pioche,* 5–10. Montreal: Remue-ménage, 1980.

Saint-Martin, Lori. "Suzanne Lamy, pour une morale de la critique." *Voix et images* 13.1 (1987): 29–40. (Special issue: "Suzanne Lamy.")

Sarraute, Nathalie. *L'Ere du soupçon.* Paris: Gallimard, 1956.

Scarpetta, Guy. *L'Impureté.* Paris: Grasset & Fasquelle, 1985.

Schwartzwald, Robert. "Literature and Intellectual Realignments in Quebec." *Québec Studies* 3 (1985): 32–56.

Schweickart, Patrocinio P. "Reading Ourselves: Toward a Feminist Theory of Reading." In *Gender and Reading: Essays on Readers, Texts, and Contexts,* edited by Elizabeth A. Flynn and Patrocinio P. Schweickart, 31–62. Baltimore: Johns Hopkins University Press, 1986.

Scott, Gail. "Virginia and Colette on the Outside Looking In." In *A Mazing Space: Writing Canadian Women Writing,* edited by Shirley Neuman and Smaro Kamboureli, 367–73. Edmonton, Alberta: Longspoon/NeWest, 1986.

Servan, Henri. *"Le Désert mauve* de Nicole Brossard, ou l'indicible référent." Unpublished paper presented in Quebec at American Council for Québec Studies conference, 23 Oct. 1988.

Sherzer, Dina. *Representation in Contemporary French Fiction.* Lincoln: University of Nebraska Press, 1986.

Showalter, Elaine. "Feminist Criticism in the Wilderness." *Critical Inquiry* 8.2 (1981): 179–205.

Smart, Patricia. "Quand la fille du bar se met à parler: la poésie de France Théoret." *Dalhousie French Studies* (1985): 153–62. (Special issue: "La Poésie québécoise depuis 1975.")

Smith, Lillian. *The Winner Names the Age: A Collection of Writings by Lillian Smith,* edited by Michelle Cliff. New York: Norton, 1978.

Stanton, Domna C. "Difference on Trial: A Critique of the Maternal Metaphor in Cixous, Irigaray, and Kristeva." In *The Poetics of Gender,* edited by Nancy K. Miller, 157–82. New York: Columbia University Press, 1986.

———. "Language and Revolution: The Franco-American Dis-Connection." In *The Future of Difference,* edited by Hester Eisenstein and Alice Jardine, 73–87. New Brunswick, N.J.: Rutgers University Press, 1985.

Stewart, Grace. *A New Mythos: The Novel of the Artist as Heroine, 1877–1977.* Montreal: Eden Press Women's Publications, 1981.

Suleiman, Susan Rubin. "Pornography, Transgression, and the Avant-

Garde: Bataille's *Story of the Eye.*" In *The Poetics of Gender,* edited by Nancy K. Miller, 117–36. New York: Columbia University Press, 1986.

———. "(Re)Writing the Body: The Politics and Poetics of Female Eroticism." In *The Female Body in Western Culture,* edited by Susan Rubin Suleiman, 7–29. Cambridge: Harvard University Press, 1986.

———. "Writing and Motherhood." In *The (M)other Tongue: Essays in Feminist Psychoanalytic Interpretation,* edited by Shirley Nelson Garner, Claire Kahane, and Madelon Sprengnether, 352–77. Ithaca, N.Y.: Cornell University Press, 1985.

Vanasse, André. "Nouveaux romans?" *Lettres québécoises* 15 (1979): 14–16.

Waelti-Walters, Jennifer. *Fairytales and the Female Imagination.* Montreal: Eden, 1982.

———. "When Caryatids Move: Bersianik's View of Culture." In *A Mazing Space: Writing Canadian Women Writing,* edited by Shirley Neuman and Smaro Kamboureli, 298–306. Edmonton, Alberta: Longspoon/NeWest, 1986.

Wenzel, Hélène V. "Interview with Simone de Beauvoir." *Yale French Studies* 72 (1987): 5–32. (Special issue: "Simone de Beauvoir: Witness to a Century.")

Wittig, Monique. *Les Guérillères.* Paris: Minuit, 1969.

Wittig, Monique, and Sande Zeig. *Brouillon pour un dictionnaire des amantes.* Paris: Grasset & Fasquelle, 1976. (Published in English as *Lesbian Peoples: Material for a Dictionary.* New York: Avon, 1979.)

Yaguello, Marina. *Les Mots et les femmes.* Paris: Payot, 1978.

Zavalloni, Marisa, ed. *L'Emergence d'une culture au féminin.* Montreal: Saint-Martin, 1987.

Index

Abortion, 15; and linguistic repression, 211
Abraham, 147
Acropolis, 46, 173, 176, 179, 183, 185, 187, temple of Erechtheum, 180, 271n.45
Alienation: in city, 232; dialectics of, 109; female subjectivity and, 226; in language, 170, 203, 205, 211, 213–14, 221, 230, 232, 234, 240; poverty and, 231; of woman writer, 205; women's exile, 158, 171; of working-class women, 117–18
Amyot, Geneviève, xviii
Anti-war movement, 32
Aquin, Hubert, xiii, 10, 55
Archaeological writing, 131–41, 144, 149; accessibility of, 138
Aristophanes, 175
Aristotle, 173, 177, 181
Artaud, Antonin, 47, 218, 219, 235
Asteria, legend of, 194, 196, 198
Athena, 271n.45
Atkinson, Ti-Grace, 41
Atomic bomb, 96, 99–100
Authority: of male author, 41, 172, 236; of male critic, 269n.18; phallocentric, 220; through wounding, 212; writing as denial of, 192, 198, 234
Autobiographical in writing, 110, 131–32, 143, 146, 202, 205, 216, 230, 235

Barnes, Djuna, 41, 83
Barrett, Michèle, 111
Barthes, Roland, 20, 21, 22, 55, 70, 128, 191; *A Lover's Discourse,* 265n.19; *The Pleasure of the Text,* 70, 261n.19
Bataille, Georges, 47, 70, 257n.55
Bayard, Caroline, xxi–xxii
Beausoleil, Claude, 54

Beauvoir, Simone de, 170, 270n.36
Beckett, Samuel, 3, 56
Bersianik, Louky, 1–51, 55, 60–61, 63, 64, 67, 71, 128, 135, 136, 142, 147, 149, 150–199, 201, 204, 205, 219, 223, 243, 245–46; *Les Agénésies du vieux monde,* 135, 153, 189–90, 195; *Axes et eau,* 68, 158, 190, 191; *L'Euguélionne,* 156–72, 173, 176, 182, 190, 191, 194, 268n.10, 269n.19; *Maternative,* 190–98; "Noli me tangere," 192; *Le Pique-nique sur l'Acropole,* 68, 156, 167, 173–88, 190, 191, 193, 195–96
Bhagavad-Gita, 99
Bible, 157, 159, 174; Christ figure, 161; feminist anti-Bible, 165; parody of biblical forms, 159, 192
Birth rate in Quebec, 6, 16
Blais, Marie-Claire, 6, 41, 43, 265n.16; *Les Manuscrits de Pauline Archange,* 239, 253n.8
Blanchot, Maurice, 20, 21, 22, 56–57, 142, 203, 260–61n.8
Body, in signifying process, 193; in writing, 70, 139. *See also* Female body
Bouchard, Louise, xviii
Boucher, Denise, xviii, 120, 121, 124, 125; *Cyprine,* 47; *Les Fées ont soif,* 222, 264n.4, 273n.12; 274n.30; *Retailles,* 110
Bourassa, Robert, 14, 16
Brecht, Bertold, 111
Breton, André, 47
Brisson, Marcelle, 44
Brochu, André, 191
Brossard, Nicole, 1–51, 52–107, 110, 119, 124, 126, 128, 139, 142, 146, 151, 154, 156–57, 169, 172, 177, 182, 183, 197, 201, 202, 203–4, 205, 219, 233, 237, 240, 243, 245–46, 247–48; *The Aerial Letter,* 88,

302   *Index*

69, 79–81, 182–84; feminism and, 66, 77, 107, 145; feminist poetics of, xvi, 40; as inscription of pleasure, 70, 204; letter writing in, 239; male critic on, 191; mistrust of language in, 200; mythopoesis in, 188; as *ouverture*, 60, 83; physicality of, xx, 42, 74, 185, 237, 274n.21; as restorative act, 181; textuality and, 36; thematics of, 30; women's history and, 153; women's voices and, 41–42; "writing like a woman," 4, 57, 208. *See also Ecriture féminine*

Xanthippe (Socrates' wife), 176, 183

Zeig, Sande, 171
Zeus, 194

Karen Gould is Director of Women's Studies and Associate Professor of French at Bowling Green State University in Ohio. She is the author of *Claude Simon's Mythic Muse* and coeditor of *Orion Blinded: Essays on Claude Simon*. She has published widely on Quebec women writers and feminist theory in journals such as *Voix et images*, *L'Esprit créateur*, *Signs*, *French Review*, *Modern Language Studies*, and *American Review of Canadian Studies*, as well as in edited collections. She is also the editor of *Québec Studies*, an interdisciplinary journal devoted to the study of Quebec society and French Canadian culture. She received a Senior Research Fellowship from the Canadian government to complete this book.